All Ten
The Ultimate Bowling Feat

Chris Overson

First published in Great Britain by
Association of Cricket Statisticians and Historians
Bedford MK40 4FG.
© ACS, 2017

Chris Overson has asserted his right under the Copyright, Designs
and Patents Act 1988 to be identified as the author of this work.

British Library Cataloguing-in-Publication Data.
A catalogue record for this book is available from the British Library.

ISBN: 978 1 908165 89 3
Typeset and printed by The City Press Leeds Ltd

Contents

Foreword

Richard Johnson: Middlesex, Somerset and England

Ten for 45: Middlesex v Derbyshire, 1994

Strangely enough, as a 19-year-old, when I took all ten against Derbyshire I didn't really appreciate then the significance of what I had achieved. It was only my eleventh first-class match, I hadn't yet even taken a five-for and I was still trying to establish myself in the Middlesex side. I was just pleased to get among the wickets. My parents who were being updated with developments were I think quite excited however! 'He's got another one'.

I don't even think I bowled particularly well, and I'm sure that many bowlers who took an all-ten would say that they bowled much better on other occasions with less reward. My first over, to Kim Barnett, included two rank long hops. One went for four, one was caught at gully. At the end of the over I said to umpire Peter Willey that my bowling didn't feel quite right. 'Don't worry' he said. 'You'll probably get a five-for'. I settled down after that and by tea I had taken seven wickets. By now I was struggling a bit though. I was to have a knee operation later in the season and wondered if I could carry on. However, my opening partner Kevin Shine encouraged me to keep going, and I'm glad he did as a few overs later, having taken nine wickets, I was watching Devon Malcolm walk to the crease. Unfortunately I only had one ball left in the over. What should I bowl? I managed the perfect yorker but Devon dug it out and got down to the other end. With plenty of time left Mike Gatting then did his best to help me get my all-ten by bringing on Desmond Haynes to trundle for a couple of overs and, despite some scares, I eventually picked up Matthew Taylor, probably to the best ball I bowled in the innings.

After that my career was a combination of success and injury. Although I was injured quite often I don't look back on my career with regret. I am very pleased to have achieved what I did.

All-tens have become very uncommon. The only one in England since mine has been Ottis Gibson's in 2007, and the last one abroad was by Zulfiqar Babar in December 2009. As a bowler I would quite like to see another one achieved, although ideally not against Middlesex or England!

Introduction

For a bowler, taking all ten wickets in an innings is the ultimate statistical feat. It has been achieved only 81 times in nearly 60,000 first-class matches, although it is perhaps surprising that it has been achieved even that often. Assuming that in many cases the conditions were helpful to bowlers or the opposition weak you might expect that the bowlers at the other end would take at least one wicket – Jim Laker taking all-ten twice in 1956 whilst the prolific Tony Lock went wicketless is an obvious example. Sometimes chance plays a part, a batsman playing and missing or a fielder dropping a catch, whether on purpose or not.

Until the 1960s all-tens had been relatively common in England and Wales, but they have since become rare with only two in the last fifty years. We could speculate on the reasons. Pitches are covered, wickets are generally less helpful to spinners (although many all-tens have been taken by quicker bowlers), the number of leg-side fielders has been restricted. Over the same period overseas bowlers have begun to catch up, taking 12 all-tens and bringing the total taken overseas to 21. Although all-tens have been reasonably well spread chronologically there were five in 1921 and four in 1956. Why? It was probably just chance. The weather was bad in 1956 and unfriendly to batsmen, but 1954 and 1958 were also spectacularly poor summers and nobody managed an all-ten.

The figures below show the change in the frequency of all-tens over time. The 10,000th first-class match was played in July 1921, by which time the feat had been performed 32 times. The rate held up reasonably well over the next 10,000 matches played, but has clearly fallen sharply since.

Number of first-class matches played		Number of all-tens
1 - 5,000	(August 1898)	18
5,001 - 10,000	(July 1921)	14
10,001 - 20,000	(May 1953)	24
20,001 - 30,000	(February 1974)	13
30,001 - 40,000	(June 1992)	5
40,001 - 50,000	(March 2007)	4
50,001 - 58,000	(September 2017)	3
		81

In the first 19 years after the Second World War there were 12 all-tens in England, of which nine occurred on outgrounds, a disparity not apparent between the Wars. There is certainly evidence that at some of these grounds conditions were particularly favourable to bowlers, presumably because of the limited pitch preparation compared with that at headquarters, but whether this was true at other grounds would need further investigation.

The bowlers taking all-tens cover a wide range, from the great to the journeymen, from those with long prolific careers to those with short careers, from the fast to the slow, from those bowling under or round arm to those with more conventional actions. No particular type has dominated. There are 76 names on the list (some bowlers being greedy and performing the feat more than once) but many greats are missing: no Barnes, Bedser, O'Reilly, Lillee, Murali or Warne for example. In fact Bedser, Lillee and Warne never once got past eight wickets. Spare a thought also for the 50-odd bowlers who either took the first nine wickets to fall in an innings, but not the tenth, or the only nine to fall. There are many sad stories here. For example J.T.Hearne took nine wickets in an innings no fewer than eight times without managing an all-ten. In 1896, playing for MCC against the Australians, he nearly got there, but the absence of George Giffen, who had withdrawn through illness, denied him the chance of converting nine for 73 into a full house. And playing for Sri Lanka against Zimbabwe in 2002 Murali had overnight figures of nine for 51. Next morning a simple bat-pad catch was put down off his bowling first ball, and with Henry Olonga falling next over Jim Laker's Test record analysis of ten for 53 was safe.

Given cricket's vast literature it is surprising that nobody has written a book about the game's most famous bowling feat, hence this attempt to chronicle each occurrence. I have concentrated mainly on the match (and particularly the innings) in which the all-ten was taken - and added something on some of the more noteworthy of the bowlers' victims. I have also briefly summarised each bowler's career. The lives of the more famous bowlers will already be familiar to aficionados, but some bowlers are less well known, and I think it is important to include brief career information both for completeness and to give context.

A few bowlers have taken ten wickets in an innings in first-class matches which were not eleven-a-side. I have excluded these, both to save some space and also because I don't think they really count as 'all-ten'. Apologies therefore in particular to William (F.W.) Lillywhite who took ten second-innings wickets for Players against Gentlemen at Lord's in 1837 and would have been the first entry in this book if all instances of ten wickets in an innings had been included. As the Gentlemen had 16 men (albeit one was absent hurt) I don't think he should feel too aggrieved. You will however read about nephew James later in the book.

Unless otherwise stated all figures refer to first-class cricket.

All matches described involved six-ball overs with the following exceptions:

England and Wales: matches before 1894 (four balls), between 1894 and 1899 (five balls) and in 1939 (eight balls). Australia: eight balls except 1883/84 (four balls).

The match scores have been taken from the excellent CricketArchive website. A few scores contain minor discrepancies that it has not been possible to resolve. Also in a few cases full information is not available about bowling analyses, fall of wickets, the names of umpires or captains, or who won the toss. Captains are indicated by * and wicketkeepers by +.

Edmund Hinkly

Kent v England, 1848

Lord's Cricket Ground, St John's Wood on 10, 11 July 1848 (3-day match)
Toss won by England
England won by 55 runs
England 120 (E Hinkly 6-?) and 74 (E Hinkly 10-?); Kent 90 (J Wisden 7-?) and 49 (J Wisden 5-?)

England second innings

R Kynaston	b Hinkly	0
J Dean	b Hinkly	2
W Clarke	st Dorrinton b Hinkly	10
+T Box	c Hillyer b Hinkly	18
J Guy	not out	28
G Parr	b Hinkly	4
T Sewell	b Hinkly	6
J Wisden	c Adams b Hinkly	0
OC Pell	c Hillyer b Hinkly	2
FW Lillywhite	st Dorrinton b Hinkly	0
FH Hervey-Bathurst	b Hinkly	0
Extras	(b 4)	4
Total	all out)	74

Fall of wickets 1-1, 2-2, 3-31, 4-32, 5-38, 6-56, 7-?, 8-70, 9-70, 10-74

Kent bowling: WR Hillyer ?-?-?-0, E Hinkly ?-?-?-10, W.Martingell ?-?-?-0

Kent: W Martingell, W Pilch, TM Adams, F Pilch, A Mynn, N Felix, WR Hillyer, W Dorrinton (wk), CJ Harenc, HE Knatchbull, E Hinkly

Edmund Hinkly, the first bowler to take all-ten in a first-class match, was a Man of Kent, born in 1817 in the Wealden village of Benenden, west of Tenterden. The village sign depicts two other contemporary Benenden cricketers - wicketkeeper Ned Wenman, who kept to Hinkly a number of times, and Wenman's Kent colleague Richard Mills. Neither however played in the game in which Hinkly bowled himself into the record-books. Cricketers of their day needed other means of earning money when not playing, and by trade Hinkly was a shoemaker.

He was a left-arm fastish bowler, 5ft 7in tall and of wiry build. Like most of his time he bowled round arm and was one of the first swervers. He is also described as breaking the ball from leg, a combination which suggests that he could be a difficult customer to face. However, because of poor health his career was fairly short. Most of his first-class cricket was played for Kent, but as he lived for many years near The Oval he also played some games for Surrey. County cricket had not yet fully evolved, many of the present first-class counties had not yet been formed, and like many cricketers of his time Hinkly found employment as a professional for a number of teams throughout the country, including Watford, his first professional engagement in 1844.

Hinkly's first-class career began in 1846 with three matches for the great Kent side which included Alfred Mynn, Fuller Pilch, William Hillyer and Nicholas Felix. He had relatively little success, bowling in only two innings and taking just three wickets. As allrounder Mynn, arguably the first great cricket personality, and medium pacer Hillyer, one of the best bowlers of his day, bowled unchanged in two innings and took most of the wickets, Hinkly's initial lack of opportunity is not surprising.

His all-ten came in his fourth first-class match and his first at Lord's. England fielded a strong side that included, among many of the best cricketers of the day, John Wisden, who would himself take a famous all-ten two years later, and George Parr of Nottinghamshire ('The Lion of the North') who was to become England's leading batsman. Hinkly himself often played for the All-England Eleven during the late 1840s.

Lord's was not the impressive arena it would later become. Leading cricket writer and reporter Frederick Gale described it as 'practically a country ground, as it was almost open country northwards and westwards'. Apart from the small one-roomed pavilion which could hold about 40 or 50 members, the only seating for spectators was provided by low backless benches circling the ground. Gentlemen could of course watch the Eton v Harrow match from their carriages, or until it was banned in 1869, from horseback. Improvements were slow. A rudimentary telegraph board had been introduced in 1846, and scorecards were first issued in 1848. The grass was cropped by sheep held in special pens situated at the ground. The ground boys had the pleasure of clearing up after them. The pitch itself was rolled constantly but the use of a scythe was not permitted and mowers weren't used until 1868. The pitch was rough and dangerous. Batsmen had to contend with frequent shooters, alternating with what W.G. Grace called 'bumping balls'. Which delivery you received sometimes depended on which side of the small pieces of gravel dotting the wicket the ball pitched. Lord's was not alone among major grounds in providing dangerous playing conditions, but it was certainly one of the worst offenders. It is not therefore surprising that Hinkly's match, like many of the period, was low scoring and although scheduled for three days was over in two.

The Kent v England match was then one of the most attractive of the season. At least 5,000 attended on each day. *The Times* report for the first day says little about the cricket but does more importantly list the male members of the aristocracy who were there. England's first innings 120 was the highest total in a match in which scores got progressively lower. Hinkly took six wickets including that of 49-year-old William Clarke (founder of the All-England Eleven, the most famous of a number of mid-Victorian touring teams), who opened and made just three, and Sussex wicketkeeper Tom Box who made 36, the highest individual score in the match. Hinkly wasn't much of a batsman but when Kent went in he at least helped William Dorrinton put on 21 for the last wicket and, with an undefeated seven, was the only batsman who was not bowled. He then quickly got to work in England's second innings, bowling MCC Secretary Roger Kynaston without scoring and James Dean of Sussex soon afterwards. After that the only batsman who withstood him with any success was Nottinghamshire's Joseph Guy who went in at 31 for three and remained undefeated with 28. 'All ease and elegance', for a number of years Guy was a regular for the All-England Eleven and for the Players against the Gentlemen. He was also an occasional wicketkeeper, and became a very reliable long stop. However he found little support as Hinkly swept away the England batting, including, for the second time in the match Parr, the season's leading run-scorer. Another Hinkly victim was Wisden, one of four ducks. 1848 wasn't a good year for batsmen: there was just one century and 13 fifties in 28 first-class matches, but after John Lee's century (for Cambridge University against Gentlemen of Kent) Wisden later made the second highest score with 92 for Sussex against Nottinghamshire.

Hinkly's penultimate victim was William Lillywhite (who as mentioned in the Introduction had taken ten wickets in an innings against 16 Gentlemen in 1837). He then finished off the England second innings, as he had the first, by bowling Frederick Hervey-Bathurst for a duck, a score that in a 30-year career the 41-year-old fast bowler would eventually equal in over a third of his 138 completed innings. The unsuccessful bowlers at the other end during Hinkly's historic feat were Hillyer, with 85 wickets the season's leading wicket-taker, and medium pacer William Martingell, a decidedly useful bowler who would finish his career with 529 wickets.

Although Hinkly was probably not 'fast' by present standards, he must have been fairly pacy. Despite this, wicketkeeper Dorrinton was able to stump two batsmen in the England second innings because, at the time, despite wearing only rudimentary protection, wicketkeepers usually stood up to the stumps whoever the bowler. Long stop was therefore a key fielding position to stop those balls that the keeper chose to leave or failed to collect. Sadly, Dorrinton died aged 39 only a few months later from a chill contracted while playing for the All-England Eleven on damp northern grounds.

Kent needed 105 to win. As this total had only been reached in six out of 19 completed innings at Lord's so far in 1848 their chance of success was slight. And with Wisden adding five wickets to his first innings seven, so it proved.

Hinkly had further successes in 1848 and 1849, but after that his first-class appearances were relatively limited. As late as 1856 however, aged 39, he had one last great performance left, taking 13 wickets in the match for All-England against Nottinghamshire at Newark. He played his last first-class match two years later, finishing a 46-match career with 189 wickets.

During the 1850s Hinkly often appeared as a 'given man' brought in to strengthen local teams (which might sometimes field as many as 22 players) in their matches against one of the professional touring sides. He spent his later years in south London and was recorded in the 1871 Census as a cricket ball maker. He died in 1880.

John Wisden

North v South, 1850

Lord's Cricket Ground, St John's Wood on 15 July 1850 (3-day match)
North won by an innings and 19 runs
Umpires: S Dakin, AJD Diver
South 36 (W Clarke 6-?) and 76 (J Wisden 10-?); North 131 (T Sherman 6-?)

South second innings

J Dean	b Wisden	0
JM Lee	b Wisden	6
W Caffyn	b Wisden	24
+T Box	b Wisden	1
N Felix	b Wisden	0
J Chester	b Wisden	17
R Kynaston	b Wisden	0
A Mynn	not out	17
J Lillywhite	b Wisden	0
T Sherman	b Wisden	2
FH Hervey-Bathurst	b Wisden	4
Extras	(b 3, lb 1, nb 1)	5
Total	(all out)	76

Fall of wickets 1-?, 2-?, 3-?, 4-?,5-?, 6-?, 7-?, 8-?,9-?,10-76

North bowling: J Wisden ?-?-?-10, W Clarke ?-?-?-0, RF Skelton ?-?-?-0

North: T Hunt, RB Smythies, J Guy, G Parr, RT King, Lord Burghley, G Chatterton (wk), RF Skelton, J Wisden, Lord Guernsey, W Clarke

Even if 'The Little Wonder' had never played cricket John Wisden's name will always be synonymous with the game as founder of the famous Almanack. He was however a considerable cricketer: in modern parlance probably a 'bowling allrounder'. Born in Brighton in 1826 Wisden had originally been apprenticed to his father Thomas, a builder. His potential was soon spotted, and when his first-class career ended in 1863 he had taken 1,109 wickets, a total only then exceeded by Kent's William Hillyer, and Sussex team-mate, James Dean. In all matches his record was phenomenal, averaging 225 wickets a season between 1848 and 1859. He also scored 4,140 first-class runs at 14.12, including two centuries, a modest record by modern standards but scores were low when he played and it compares very favourably with contemporary major batsmen.

'A remarkably good-tempered little fellow with a most comical expression of face', surprisingly for a 'fast' bowler Wisden was under 5ft 6 in tall. At the start of his career he weighed only seven stone although by the end he had reached eleven stone. He bowled very accurately with a very smooth round-arm action, bringing the ball back from outside the off stump. Towards the end of his career, as his fitness declined, he often bowled under arm, but as one of sport's early entrepreneurs his burgeoning business interests no doubt compensated for his failing cricketing powers. In 1855 Wisden set up a cricketing and cigar business with Fred Lillywhite;

in 1859, with George Parr, he took the first England touring team abroad; he was also Secretary of the Cricketers' Fund Friendly Society for over 20 years. And of course the first Almanack appeared in 1864.

Wisden's famous all-ten was achieved in a match scheduled to last three days, but which finished in one. Obviously Lord's pitches hadn't improved yet. It may seem strange that he appeared for the North. However, in 1849, even at the age of 23, he was looking for business opportunities and with Parr had become joint proprietor of a cricket ground at Leamington, Warwickshire. By the relaxed rules of the time he was thereby qualified to play for the North! Having made his first-class debut in 1845 Wisden was approaching the height of his powers. The previous season he had taken 129 wickets and his fine form continued in 1850. At the end of June, playing for Sussex, he took eight wickets in an innings for the fourth time in his career, against an MCC side two of whom, Alfred Diver and Samuel Dakin, would later be umpiring while he took his all-ten.

Despite the presence at Lord's of some of the greatest cricketers of the day, including William Caffyn, Nicholas Felix and Alfred Mynn, South's batting failed completely twice. Wisden took three wickets in their meagre first innings and William Clarke six. Mynn, caught by Lord Burghley off Wisden's bowling, would be the only batsman dismissed in this manner in the match. North then collapsed against the pace of Surrey's Thomas Sherman and at 53 for eight a decent lead looked unlikely. However the later batsmen brought about a recovery, Wisden scoring 22, Clarke 13, and top-scorer Lord Guernsey 27 not out. His Lordship was a surprising saviour. In a 21-match first-class career, played mainly for MCC, he averaged only 7.14 and if Clarke hadn't got out first he might even have beaten what would remain his highest first-class score, 28 not out!

South went in again a daunting 95 behind. Dean, Box, Kynaston and Hervey-Bathurst had all been victims of Hinkly's all-ten two years before. They were now to suffer the same fate again as Wisden ripped through South's batting, uniquely hitting the stumps ten times. As well as Dean and Box, Wisden's victims included another Sussex colleague, John Lillywhite, cousin of James. Surrey's Caffyn top scored in each South innings with 9 and 24. Allrounder Caffyn was just beginning a first-class career that lasted until 1873. After touring with Parr's 1863/64 team he stayed behind to coach in Australia, making an important contribution to the development of the game there. Some might say he did too good a job! He easily outlived all other participants in Wisden's match, dying in 1919 aged 91.

Not surprisingly a number of South batsmen failed to score. However the only batsman in the match who registered a pair was Roger Kynaston. With an eventual career average of 9.15 from 166 matches he wasn't one of the most prolific batsmen of the period. His only stroke apparently was a slash between cover point and mid off, which is probably why he reportedly took his stance with his legs as far from the wicket as possible. One of the other batsmen who 'failed to trouble the scorers' was the rather more eminent Felix, whom Wisden eventually dismissed no fewer than 31 times in first-class cricket. Having been Hinkly's final victim two years before, Hervey-Bathurst now became Wisden's final victim. After a perhaps not unsurprising first-innings duck, this time he had at least reached the dizzy heights of four; batting nine times it was a score he managed to reach just twice during the season.

One of the bowlers at the other end to Wisden was 51-year-old Clarke. In ten matches in 1850 it was the only innings in which he bowled without taking a wicket. Throughout most of the 1850s Wisden remained one of the best bowlers in England. In his fascinating book *Number One* Simon Wilde argues that during the mid-1850s he was the best, taking over the accolade from the wily Clarke before handing it to Nottinghamshire's fast bowler John Jackson. Wisden had played for Clarke's All-England Eleven. However in 1852 he left and, with Dean, set up the rival United All-England Eleven. Clarke probably wasn't best pleased that his young business rival was also now the better bowler. Wisden was clearly a busy man: in 1852 he also began coaching at Harrow School, a post he held for four years. V.E.Walker, the next bowler after Wisden to take an all-ten, was a pupil at the time.

Wisden seems to have liked Lord's. Playing 68 first-class matches there it was easily his most frequently visited ground. Conditions obviously suited him. He had a better strike rate (probably a term unfamiliar to Victorians!) than at other grounds and not surprisingly also took significantly more wickets there: 400 in all, including 56 in five games in 1850.

Wisden's good form continued during the rest of 1850. At Lord's a fortnight later, playing for Under 36, he missed another all-ten by one wicket, Nottinghamshire's James Grundy, making his first-class debut, spoiling things by bowling Box midway through the Over 36 innings. Finishing with 103 wickets and 374 runs Wisden was the season's leading wicket-taker and run-scorer, as well as being the only century-maker (and only Surrey's wicketkeeper Thomas Lockyer exceeded his 14 catches).

Wisden died of cancer in 1884 a successful businessman. Not all of his colleagues fared so well. Box had tried many forms of employment with little success before becoming attendant and ground-keeper at Prince's Cricket Ground, Middlesex's then home ground, where he collapsed at a match in 1876 whilst putting up the score, dying three hours later. Dean put on weight, suffered from asthma and bronchitis and was found dead in bed on Christmas Day 1881. His old friend John Wisden had seen him the previous evening. Perhaps they spent their last hours together reminiscing about old times over a final drink?

Edward Walker

Vyell Edward (Teddy) Walker is one of only four bowlers to have taken all-ten in a first-class match more than once. He was born in Southgate, then a village north of London and now part of the London Borough of Enfield, in 1837, the fifth of seven brothers all of whom played for Middlesex. None of the brothers married, although all of their five sisters did. V.E. began his cricket at preparatory school in Stanmore, learning the game on The Common (where Angus Fraser and Mark Ramprakash would later play). Later at Harrow he changed from bowling round arm to under arm. The Walkers were a wealthy family because of their famous brewery. They were great benefactors and the eldest son, John, relaid the bumpy Chapel Fields pitch at Southgate to produce what is now the famous Walker Cricket Ground. In 1855 he founded the Southgate Cricket Club which has played there ever since.

At first Southgate played local teams, but at the end of 1858 they became more ambitious and arranged a match against the United England Eleven. Southgate won (albeit they had 16 players), V.E.Walker top scoring in both Southgate innings. Annual matches against one of the great itinerant teams of the day continued into the 1860s, giving the people of Southgate and further afield the chance to see many contemporary leading players. These matches were festive occasions, in some ways the forerunners of later county cricket festivals. Entrance was free, crowds were estimated at around 10,000, the Great Northern Railway ran special trains to the local station, and the ground was ringed with marquees and tents. Middlesex also played one match there in June 1859, against Kent. The county team had not yet been organised on a formal basis and John Walker arranged the match at his own expense, together with a return at Canterbury. Middlesex won both matches, each time including five Walkers, John Wisden and Thomas Hearne (another famous Middlesex surname). Middlesex returned to the ground again for a few seasons in the 1990s. Surrounded by trees and with the spire of Christ Church as a backdrop it still has a pleasant rural feel.

England v Surrey, 1859

Kennington Oval, Kennington on 21, 22, 23 July 1859 (3-day match)
Toss won by England
England won by 392 runs
Umpires: T Barker, T Sewell
England 172 (W Caffyn 5-84) and 390 (VE Walker 108); Surrey 131
(VE Walker 10-74) and 39 (J Jackson 6-21)

Surrey first innings

W Mortlock	b Walker	5
*FP Miller	c Grundy b Walker	1
F Burbidge	st Stephenson b Walker	25
FB Caesar	c Grundy b Walker	23
W Caffyn	st Stephenson b Walker	0
HH Stephenson	c Daft b Walker	0

+T Lockyer	c Daft b Walker	8
CG Lane	c Jackson b Walker	9
J Caesar	not out	16
G Griffith	c Carpenter b Walker	37
W Martingell	c Wisden b Walker	2
Extras	(b 4, lb 1)	5
Total	(all out, 85 overs)	131

Fall of wickets 1-5, 2-6, 3-39, 4-39, 5-39, 6-56, 7-72, 8-77, 9-126, 10-131

England bowling: J Jackson 36-15-46-0, VE Walker 43-17-74-10, J Bickley 6-3-6-0

England: T Hayward, R Daft, RP Carpenter, J Grundy, AJD Diver, J Lillywhite, J Wisden, E Stephenson (wk), VE Walker (capt), J Jackson, J Bickley

Walker's first all-ten came in his twenty-first first-class match. He had already had considerable success, taking five or more wickets in an innings 11 times. However, his performance for England against Surrey at The Oval in July 1859, both with bat and ball, surpassed anything he, or anybody else, had achieved before. Considered probably the best allround cricketer in the world at the time, he was about to show why.

By the end of the 1850s Surrey were the best team in the land. In 1858 they had beaten England by an innings and 28 runs, mainly due to six wickets in each innings by Heathfield Stephenson and a century by William Caffyn. In 1861/62 Stephenson was to lead the first England side to tour Australia. It included six Surrey colleagues. However the following year saw a complete reversal, England winning by 392 runs in a match in which Walker took 14 wickets and scored 128 runs, a total not far off the combined Surrey total of 170.

The match was played before a 'numerous assemblage of spectators'. The Oval was still a fairly new ground and facilities were rudimentary. There was a pavilion, but no facilities for the general public; with no seating yet or even built-up embankments, they just stood in a ring around the ground. After heavy overnight rain England, captained by Walker, made 172. Cambridgeshire's Thomas Hayward top scored with 67. Sadly, dying in 1876 aged 41, he did not live long enough to see the great success enjoyed by his nephew Tom for Surrey and England. William Caffyn bowled unchanged taking five for 84.

Walker opened the England bowling with John 'Foghorn' Jackson (who had twice taken nine wickets in an innings the previous season). It was an interesting pairing. Walker had impressive side whiskers and a centre parting, Jackson was over six foot tall and 14 stone; Walker would die in the family home, Jackson in the Liverpool workhouse; and Walker bowled slow under arm, Jackson fast round arm. Following a short slightly stooped run Walker usually bowled round the wicket (to prevent his knuckles hitting the stumps). His hand was usually higher than his hip, suggesting that he was borderline round arm, with the result that the ball came at the batsman from a considerable angle. He spun the ball both ways, just enough, and varied his pace considerably, including a ball tossed very high with a parabolic flight. A tug of his cap warned slip and wicketkeeper that a faster ball was on the way. These skills he supplemented with athletic fielding, particularly to his own bowling.

The openers, including Surrey captain Frederick Miller, the season's second highest run-scorer, who was caught at point, went quickly. Two more Fredericks, Burbidge and Caesar (older brother of the more famous Julius), then took the score to 39, at which point Walker took three wickets in an over. Burbidge and Caffyn were both stumped by Yorkshireman Edwin Stephenson who was not related to Walker's next victim Heathfield Stephenson. Seventy for six at the close, Surrey quickly lost two more wickets next morning. The more famous Caesar, one of the best batsmen of his day, having come in surprisingly late at number nine, was then joined by renowned hitter George Griffith and they put on 49 before Griffith joined Stephenson and Lockyer in being caught at long on. Both Caesar and Griffith would die before the age of fifty. Walker having taken nine wickets, Caesar was missed off his bowling, but fortunately no harm was done as John Wisden caught William Martingell at mid on soon after to end the innings at half past two. Walker had bowled unchanged for 43 overs. Jackson toiled unsuccessfully for 36 overs at the other end. As he was the season's leading wicket-taker with 83 wickets it was a rare failure. Wisden who took 39 inexpensive wickets during the season was still a useful bowler and it is therefore perhaps surprising that he wasn't given a few overs at least to provide some rest to the main bowlers. (Although of course as he was getting wickets steadily Walker probably wasn't likely to take himself off!) Having stood for Wisden's all-ten Alfred Diver, a member of the England team, had now played in a match in which an all-ten had been taken.

England wasted no time in building on their small lead. By close of play they were 281 for six with Walker, who had made an undefeated 20 in his first innings, 57 not out. The Laws at the time made no provision for declaring and so next day England kept going, Walker eventually being stumped by Lockyer off the medium-pace bowling of William Martingell for 108, comfortably passing his previous highest score of 51. It was the only century of Walker's career, and one of only three made in the season. England's 390 was easily the highest score of the season: in 30 first-class matches 300 was reached just three times, The Oval being the venue on each occasion. Set 432 to win (and starting their innings at 4.30 on the last day!) Surrey capitulated completely in bad light and were dismissed for 39 in 80 minutes. After his first-innings failure Jackson redeemed himself by taking six for 21, whilst at the other end Walker took four for 17 in 15 overs, finishing the match by catching Martingell off his own bowling. Surrey were perhaps unlucky not to be saved by the weather on the final day since, because of rain, no play was possible at all at nearby Lord's (Eleven Gentlemen of I Zingari v 22 Gentlemen of the Houses of Lord's and Commons!). Strangely, although Walker made two more fifties in 1859, after that he went another six seasons and 53 matches before scoring another, but then made up for this by scoring six in 1866.

Middlesex v Lancashire, 1865

Old Trafford, Manchester on 20, 21, 22 July 1865 (3-day match)
Toss won by Lancashire
Lancashire won by 62 runs
Lancashire 243 and 178 (VE Walker 10-104); Middlesex 243 and 116
(R Iddison 5-45)

Lancashire second innings

SH Swire	b VE Walker	16
FJ Crooke	st Morley b VE Walker	20
JF Leese	c Haines b VE Walker	0
R Iddison	c and b VE Walker	6
J Makison	st Morley b VE Walker	0
EJ Bousfield	c Wilkinson b VE Walker	15
E Whittaker	c RD Walker b VE Walker	39
AB Rowley	c RD Walker b VE Walker	60
R Blackstock	b VE Walker	5
+W Perry	c and b VE Walker	0
FR Reynolds	not out	13
Extras	(lb 3, w 1)	4
Total	(all out, 102.2 overs)	178

Fall of wickets 1-31, 2-33, 3-43, 4-43, 5-50, 6-67, 7-135, 8-145, 9-145, 10-178

Middlesex bowling: T Hearne 8-6-6-0, AJA Wilkinson 7-4-6-0, RD Walker 2-1-3-0, G Howitt 36-14-49-0, W Catling 5-2-6-0, VE Walker 44.2-5-104-10

Middlesex: AJA Wilkinson, J Haines, B Robertson, RD Walker, T Hearne, VE Walker, G Hearne, W Catling, TA Mantle, G Howitt, JH Morley (wk)

Walker nearly achieved his second all-ten in Middlesex's initial first-class match, played at the Cattle Market Ground, Islington in 1864. Sussex were dismissed in their first innings for 111 and as he left the field Walker was congratulated on apparently taking all ten wickets (for 63 runs). However confusion was caused by the dismissal of Charles Payne who had top scored with 28. He had (it was thought) been stumped by a ball which had rebounded from wicketkeeper Ted Pooley's pads while he was out of his ground. Unfortunately for Walker however Payne had touched the ball on its way through and was deemed to be run out. (Under current laws the decision would of course be stumped.) Apparently it was Charles Payne himself, later to become a first-class umpire, who was instrumental in getting his dismissal re-classified.

Walker's second all-ten therefore had to wait until July 1865, for Middlesex against Lancashire at Old Trafford. The county club had been formed in 1864, in no small part due to Walker's efforts. He captained the county team from its inception until 1872, before handing over to his brother Isaac who carried on until 1884. V.E. was by all accounts an astute and considerate captain, encouraging to younger players. Lancashire's county club had also been formed in 1864 and Walker's feat came in their inaugural first-class match. As inter-county cricket was still in its early days it is not easy to assess the comparative strengths of the counties.

Lancashire played just two matches in 1865, both against Middlesex. Although they won the first, fielding a weakened side they lost the return at the Cattle Market Ground, Islington. Middlesex had a decent record in 1865, losing just once as against three victories, one of which was against the strong Surrey team.

Eight of the Lancashire side at Old Trafford were amateurs, three of whom were making their first-class debuts. This reliance on amateurs could cause selection problems during the early years because they were keen to play at Old Trafford but less willing to travel away. The three professionals were the prominent Yorkshire allrounder Roger Iddison who had been in dispute with his county and was making his debut for their red rose rivals; wicketkeeper William Perry, playing in the last first-class match of a two-match career; and Frederick Reynolds who later became assistant secretary and then general manager of the Old Trafford ground, a position he held until 1908 when he retired aged 74. Reynolds also produced a three-volume work recording the scores of all Lancashire matches from 1864 to 1883.

As it was still in the country and therefore fairly inaccessible, Old Trafford initially had problems attracting good crowds. Amateurs had the use of a spacious dressing-room in the pavilion while the professionals changed in a small shed on the opposite side of the ground. Oddly, although Lancashire scored 243 in the first innings at Old Trafford, a score that Middlesex exactly equalled, Walker did not bowl (although he took a catch). Brother Russell had top scored for Middlesex with 84 whilst V.E. had been caught and bowled by Reynolds without scoring.

First-class debutants Samuel Swire and Frederick Crooke gave Lancashire's second innings a useful start, but after Walker bowled Swire and James Morley made the first, and penultimate, stumping of a one-match first-class career, the middle order collapsed. From 67 for six however they were revived by a seventh wicket partnership of 68 between Edwin Whittaker and Alexander Rowley (later to be stepfather of Lancashire great Archie MacLaren). Rowley would eventually make three fifties in a 31-match career. In 14 matches Whittaker would never improve on his 39 but he did however do a great service to Lancashire cricket by paying to have Old Trafford properly fenced and enclosed.

Walker had had to sweat again for his last wicket. Having caught and bowled wicketkeeper Perry for a duck for his ninth wicket, he must have been pleased to see a man coming in last who in a 65-match career would never get near fifty. However Reynolds stuck around long enough to see Rowley to his fifty and the score increase by 33 before brother Russell's brilliant one-handed catch over his head gave Walker his second all-ten. Two of Walker's victims were caught and bowled; a very proactive fielder to his own bowling, over his career one in seven of his wickets fell this way. This is, for example, double the rate achieved in another era by another fine fielder to his own bowling, Tony Lock (an imperfect comparison in many ways but still of value in putting Walker's fielding in some perspective). Walker had completed his second all-ten exactly five years to the day since his first. Most of the bowling at the other end during Lancashire's innings had been done by fast left-arm bowler George Howitt who was from Nottinghamshire and a cousin of future England player William Scotton. On his first-class debut he had provided an ideal economic foil to Walker's more tempting fare. Walker had also been well supported by wicketkeeper Morley who, as well as his two stumpings, had conceded just one bye in two innings lasting 209 overs.

Anthony Wilkinson, who had made a first-innings 59, was absent for the Middlesex second innings and they never looked like getting close to their target of 179. V.E. (29) and Russell Walker (28) were the only real contributors as Iddison and Reynolds worked their way through their batting.

Walker only took 12 other wickets in 1865, mainly because he bowled relatively little, and when he did generally met with very limited success. This pattern seemed to continue for the rest of his career. However, he finished on a high: in his penultimate match, aged 40, he took five for 62 in the Nottinghamshire first innings at Lord's in July 1877 before signing off at Trent Bridge the following month with a career total of 334 wickets at 16 runs apiece and 3,384 runs at an average of 17. Walker was later president of MCC and of Middlesex County Cricket Club. A regular attender at Lord's till the end, he died in 1906 aged 69 leaving Russell the only surviving brother.

George Wootton

All-England Eleven v Yorkshire, 1865

Bramall Lane, Sheffield on 17, 18, 19 July 1865 (3-day match)
Toss won by All-England Eleven
All-England Eleven won by an innings and 255 runs
Umpires: W Slinn, GH Wright
All-England Eleven 524 (T Hayward 112, RP Carpenter 134; I Hodgson 5-127); Yorkshire 125 and 144 (G Wootton 10-54)

Yorkshire second innings

A Walker	b Wootton	6
C Appleton	c Hayward b Wootton	18
T Darnton	not out	81
W Smith	b Wootton	0
L Greenwood	c and b Wootton	3
+G Holgate	b Wootton	5
J Thewlis	b Wootton	21
J Berry	c Carpenter b Wootton	4
W Cuttell	b Wootton	0
J Dawes	b Wootton	2
I Hodgson	c Oscroft b Wootton	0
Extras	(b 4)	4
Total	(all out, 63.3 overs)	144

Fall of wickets 1-9, 2-50, 3-50, 4-56, 5-86, 6-116, 7-142, 8-142, 9-144, 10-144

All-England Eleven bowling: RC Tinley 25-3-76-0, G Wootton 31.3-9-54-10, J Jackson 7-4-10-0

All-England Eleven: W Oscroft, J Smith, T Bignall, T Hayward, RP Carpenter, E Whittaker, G Parr (capt), J Jackson, G Wootton, S Biddulph (wk), RC Tinley

Three days before V.E.Walker's second all-ten George Wootton performed the feat on the other side of the Pennines. Wootton was one of England's leading bowlers of the 1860s, taking over 100 wickets in four successive seasons. He wasn't very tall and bowled left-arm medium-fast with a round-arm action. He was a rustic left-hand bat who usually batted down the order, averaging just over 10 in 301 first-class innings. However, he had his moments. In 1869 he and William McIntyre put on 165 against Kent, a Notts' ninth wicket partnership record that stood until 1994.

Born at Clifton, Nottinghamshire in 1834, before becoming a professional cricketer Wootton had been a butcher. He was nearly 27 when he made his first-class debut. It was suggested that his rather shy disposition might have dissuaded him from pushing himself forward earlier. In 1862 he secured a post on the Lord's staff, a much sought after placement because it provided regular work during the summer and was reasonably well paid. As a consequence Wootton actually played more matches in his career for MCC (83) than he did for his county (52). The disparity in terms of wickets taken was even greater with 564 for MCC compared with only

180 for Nottinghamshire. Most MCC matches were played at Lord's where conditions for batsmen still left much to be desired. It was suggested that nobody ever bowled so many shooters there. However, Wootton still needed to bowl accurately to take advantage of the conditions; wide shooters don't get many wickets, and a high proportion of his victims were bowled.

Wootton's all-ten was however not taken at Lord's but at Bramall Lane, Sheffield for the All-England Eleven against a Yorkshire side not yet the power it later became, and weakened by the absence of five leading players because of a dispute. The exact nature of the dispute is a little unclear, but it seems to be related to their earlier refusal to play against Surrey. It clearly affected Yorkshire's season. Using 25 cricketers they played nine matches, losing seven and drawing two. The All-England Eleven had a full programme of fixtures, almost exclusively all non-first-class. They had just come from playing Longsight (Manchester) and after Sheffield would move on to play Burton-on-Trent, in each case defeating teams of 22. Wootton had got close to an all-ten earlier in the season, taking nine for 37 for MCC against Oxford University, but Nottinghamshire team-mate James Grundy had nipped in and spoiled the party. And three years later Grundy's only wicket of the innings (admittedly the first) again prevented a Wootton full house, this time for MCC against England. (Grundy himself took nine wickets in an innings once. Who took the tenth? George Wootton!)

This was Bramall Lane's tenth first-class match; having been laid out in 1854 the first match (Yorkshire versus Sussex) had taken place the following year. The ground was also used for other sporting purposes, notably for football beginning in December 1862 when the first match was played there (Hallam versus Sheffield FC). Six years later the ground staged the world's first floodlit football match.

Going in first against Yorkshire a strong All-England side, captained by George Parr, made 524, the then first-class record score. Progress was slow: the innings lasted 320 four-ball overs. The crowd was small, but those present were no doubt pleased to see as much as possible of the stars who, despite batting well into the second day, had still left themselves just enough time to dismiss the home side twice. Everybody got double figures, with chief contributors the Cambridgeshire pair Thomas Hayward and Robert Carpenter (according to *Wisden* for some seasons 'by general consent the two best bats in England') who both scored centuries. As already mentioned, Hayward would be the uncle of Surrey great Tom Hayward, whilst Carpenter's son Herbert would be a future Essex stalwart.

In reply Yorkshire failed twice, losing 19 wickets on the third day. Wootton wasn't really needed in the first innings, the Nottinghamshire pair under-arm bowler Cris Tinley and paceman John Jackson, who took nearly 1,000 first-class wickets between them, doing most of the work. The last wicket to fall was Ike Hodgson. Batting eleven for good reason, he was run out for two. Having already bowled 98 overs in taking five for 127 he was probably a bit tired. Bowling round arm, he was first in the line of successful Yorkshire left-arm spinners. He died from consumption two years later aged 39.

By mid-afternoon Yorkshire were following on. This time Wootton got more of a chance, bowling unchanged for 31 overs. Charles Appleton, not out in the first innings, consequently opened in the second (apparently an ancient custom which hadn't yet quite died out). Yorkshire made a decent start but then two wickets fell at 50, including first-class debutant William Smith. Smith had taken four catches in England's innings, but unfortunately he then supplemented this promising start with a pair. He had a curious career. Two years later he made 60 and 90 in successive innings, both against Lancashire, but in his other 17 first-class innings made just 110 runs. After Smith's departure wickets fell steadily until the score reached 142 for six, at which point the tail capitulated rapidly, the last wicket, Hodgson again, falling at ten to seven. It had been an exciting finish, with the visitors' hopes nearly frustrated by a 20-minute break for rain at 6 o'clock. After two innings in the match in which the stumps had been hit just twice Wootton had disturbed them a further six times. The only batsman that Wootton had failed to dismiss in the match was Thomas Darnton, who did his best to hold the Yorkshire innings together, making over half his side's runs. (Bowling medium pace he had also taken three wickets in the England innings.) Surprisingly this was his only score of over 30 in a 20-match first-class career. County Durham-born like Smith, Darnton was another cricketer who did not survive to see his 40th birthday. As at The Oval in 1859 John Jackson again bowled unsuccessfully while a colleague took an all-ten, albeit that this time he only bowled seven overs.

Wootton played in three more first-class matches in 1865, bowling 59 overs. Surprisingly he took no more wickets, but still finished with 84 in the season, a total only exceeded by James Lillywhite's 87.

Most of those playing at Bramall Lane would be past their best when the opportunity to play Test cricket arose, but two of the Yorkshire side had an indirect connection: Luke Greenwood was the uncle of Andrew Greenwood who played in the first Australia-England Test in March 1877, and William Cuttell's son Willis made his name with Lancashire and appeared twice for England in South Africa in 1898/99.

Wootton retired from county cricket in 1871 having decided that he was no longer good enough, although neither his captain nor the Nottinghamshire committee agreed. He remained on the MCC groundstaff for two more years, finishing his career with 983 wickets at 13 apiece. Wootton was clearly a well-respected figure. To mark his retirement MCC granted him as benefit the Whit Monday match between North and South. Over 10,000 paid at the turnstiles over the two days. He was not totally lost to the first-class game as he did some umpiring, standing in 30 matches between 1871 and 1883. Apparently he didn't enjoy it very much, his quiet personality not suited to the kind of criticism directed at umpires when they make a mistake.

Unlike some of his contemporaries George Wootton lived to a ripe old age, dying in 1924 in his 90th year. His *Wisden* obituary commented that he maintained an interest in the game and attended the 1921 Trent Bridge Test match, watching the play without wearing glasses!

William Hickton

Lancashire v Hampshire, 1870

Old Trafford, Manchester on 21, 22, 23 July 1870 (3-day match)
Lancashire won by ten wickets
Umpires: C Coward, W Kay
Lancashire 262 (AN Hornby 132, F Tate 6-63) and 6-0; Hampshire 138 and
129 (W Hickton 10-46)

Hampshire second innings

EL Ede	c Birley b Hickton	25
G Carter	b Hickton	14
J May	not out	14
A Seymour	b Hickton	0
H Holmes	c Reynolds b Hickton	14
CV Eccles	c AB Rowley b Hickton	23
AH Wood	c AB Rowley b Hickton	3
G Ubsdell	b Hickton	9
C Martin	b Hickton	1
TH Wilson	b Hickton	2
F Tate	b Hickton	12
Extras	(b 7, lb 4, w 1)	12
Total	(all out, 83.2 overs)	129

Fall of wickets 1-3, 2-5, 3-29, 4-69, 5-86, 6-87, 7-102, 8-113, 9-117, 10-129

Lancashire bowling: FH Birley 7-3-12-0, W Hickton 36.2-19-46-10,
AB Rowley 40-21-59-0

Lancashire: AN Hornby, J Ricketts, EB Rowley (capt), JF Leese, DW
MacKinnon, AB Rowley, TH Rushton, W Hickton, WJ Marchbank (wk), FH
Birley, FR Reynolds

Bill Hickton was born in Hardstoft, Derbyshire in 1842. Most of his first-
class cricket was played for the county of his birth, but initially he turned
out for Lancashire. He bowled round arm at a pace categorised at the time
as fast. He was an archetypal Victorian professional cricketer, playing for
more than one county (sometime in the same season when the opportunity
arose), as well as for other clubs playing non-first-class cricket. It could be
a hard life, not well paid, and not paid at all in the winter, but preferable
to the other alternatives which were usually working in a factory, down a
mine, or as a farm labourer. Some might receive benefits, but many eminent
players still ended their lives in poverty. Some of the hardness of this life
can be detected in contemporary photographs of Hickton which show a
fairly tall well-built man, moustached, short-haired and with side whiskers
meeting under the chin. Like some other colleagues his cricketing wear
resembled that of a working man of the period: a non-white collarless
shirt, knotted neckerchief, and flannel trousers supported by a wide belt.

Hickton had made his first-class debut in 1867, for Lancashire against
Surrey at The Oval. By the start of the 1870 season he had played 17
matches and taken 98 wickets, including five or more wickets in an innings

11 times. Lancashire started the season well, beating Surrey by eight wickets at the end of May, with Hickton taking six for 17 in the Surrey second innings. The team that met Hampshire included three players, Joseph Leese, Alexander Rowley and Frederick Reynolds, who had been in the Lancashire side at the same venue five years before when V.E.Walker had taken all-ten against them. They were captained by Edmund Rowley, Alexander's younger brother. The Hampshire team of the early 1870s wasn't terribly strong. It played just two first-class matches in 1870, both against Lancashire, both lost, and then played no more first-class cricket until 1875. Only two of the team that Hickton skittled ever scored a first-class fifty (none scored a hundred), and only two ever took five or more wickets in an innings. Three were making their first-class debuts: Charles Eccles, captain Arthur Wood, and Frederick Tate who made a very good start to a very short career. Both umpires were standing for the first time. For umpire Kay it would be his sole first-class match. However Cornelius Coward would eventually officiate in 98 matches, although not on a regular basis until the 1880s as he was still a Lancashire player; having made his debut for them in 1865 he would play for them until 1876.

Lancashire batted first and were all out for 262 just before close of play, an innings dominated by Albert (A.N.) Hornby's 132, the first of 16 centuries in a 437-match career. Future England captain 'Monkey' Hornby would lead Lancashire through most of the 1880s and '90s, as would his son, also Albert, in the period up to the Great War. For Hampshire, fast bowlers Tate (six for 63) and John May (four for 80), each of whom would only play four first-class matches, shared the wickets. Hampshire's first innings lasted 80 four-ball overs but yielded only 138 runs, Hickton taking four for 27 and Francis Birley three for 76 on debut with his right-arm slows. Birley only played five first-class matches but was later to achieve greater success on the football field, playing in four FA cup finals (for Oxford University and Wanderers) and twice for England.

Hampshire went in again. The follow-on was then compulsory if a team was 80 runs behind, although no doubt Lancashire were in any case happy to have another go at the Hampshire batting. The score at the close was 52 for three with Edward Ede, who had made 37 in the first innings, still there on 23. Although Hampshire again batted for some time next day they failed to set Lancashire a decent target and the match finished just after two o'clock. There is little to be said about the Hampshire batting, except perhaps to commend Eccles, Ede and May for providing some resistance to Hickton. Eccles played in three first-class matches and his 23 was his highest score. Ede opened the batting and top scored in each innings - a praiseworthy performance given that his final career average was 9.46. His twin brother George, who had captained the county during the 1860s and been its secretary, was also a fine horseman. He had ridden the Grand National winner in 1868 but tragically had been killed steeplechasing at Aintree two years later. May made 28 in the first innings and remained undefeated with 14 whilst Hickton created havoc in the second. Alfred Seymour was less successful, scoring 2 and 0 in this, his only match for Hampshire. An amateur, he played just one other first-class match in his career. Interestingly this had been for Lancashire the previous season, when he had performed with some success, scoring 20 and 25 against a good Sussex attack. Despite the many fine bowlers who have performed for the county since, Hickton's ten for 46 is still a Lancashire record. No other county innings bowling record has stood so long. It is still also (just) the best against Hampshire, although if Ottis Gibson (ten for 47) had been slightly more frugal at Chester-le-Street in 2007 that record would have gone. The *Hampshire Advertiser* reported that Hickton 'received the usual reward', which according to the *Manchester Guardian* was the 'Queen's portrait'. A sovereign, perhaps?

Most of the bowling at the other end had been done by the captain's brother who sent down 40 overs of economical but unsuccessful slow left-arm spin. Hickton, who had hit the stumps six times, would finish his career with 284 first-class wickets, of which over half (153) would be bowled. And he was capable of piercing better defences than those presented by the feeble Hampshire batting. The first time he encountered W.G.Grace (for Lancashire against M.C.C. in 1869) he had bowled the great man for six, as well as having him caught for a duck in the second innings. According to *The Chronicle of W.G.* by J.R.Webber (quoting *The Daily Telegraph* as his source), shortly before dismissing WG in the second innings, Hickton had an appeal turned down and his 'prolonged open display of dissatisfaction with the umpire's decision on the lbw was out of place and evinced bad taste'. Clearly, like many bowlers, Hickton could be roused to anger when things weren't going well!

The following season Hickton played for both Derbyshire and Lancashire. The newly formed Derbyshire County Cricket Club played two matches, both against Lancashire. Hickton played for them in both matches. In the first, at Old Trafford, Derbyshire won by an innings and 11 runs, largely due to the bowling partnership of Hickton, seven for 74, and Dove Gregory, nine for 55. Lancashire's first innings score of 25 is still their lowest ever in first-class cricket. The pairing perhaps paved the way for other more famous Derbyshire pace bowling partnerships to follow. Sadly they had little chance to further this success because Gregory (confusingly also known as Gregory Dove) died two years later having taken 25 wickets in a four-match career. After 1871 Hickton played solely for Derbyshire, and was a regular member of the team until 1878. Involved with the Manchester Broughton Club for over thirty years, two years later he was still good enough to take eight wickets for them in their match against the Australian tourists.

His cricketing days over, Bill Hickton became a butcher. He died in February 1900 in Lower Broughton, Manchester. His son, also William, played briefly for Worcestershire in 1909.

Samuel Butler

Oxford University v Cambridge University, 1871

Lord's Cricket Ground, St John's Wood on 26, 27 June 1871 (3-day match)
Toss won by Oxford University
Oxford University won by eight wickets
Umpires: T Hearne, G Wootton
Oxford University 170 (E Bray 5-38) and 25-2; Cambridge University 65
(SE Butler 10-38) and 129 (SE Butler 5-57)

Cambridge University first innings

WB Money	b Butler	23
F Tobin	c Hadow b Butler	5
FER Fryer	b Butler	1
AT Scott	b Butler	1
*+W Yardley	c Pelham b Butler	25
CI Thornton	b Butler	4
HCP Stedman	not out	1
FC Cobden	b Butler	0
E Bray	b Butler	0
WN Powys	b Butler	0
EE Ward	b Butler	0
Extras	(lb 5)	5
Total	(all out, 48.1 overs)	65

Fall of wickets 1-22, 2-24, 3-28, 4-35, 5-62, 6-64, 7-64, 8-64, 9-65, 10-65

Oxford University bowling: SE Butler 24.1-11-38-10, S Pelham 14-10-5-0,
CK Francis 10-5-17-0

Oxford University: W Townshend, W Law, CJ Ottaway, WH Hadow, EFS
Tylecote (capt, wk), B Pauncefote, GRC Harris, C Marriott, CK Francis, SE
Butler, S Pelham

Samuel Butler played in four University matches at a time when this was
one of the major matches of the season. His first was the famous 'Cobden's
match' in 1870, in which he played a key, if unwanted, part. Converting
from a slow to fast round-arm bowler at Eton, he made an immediate
impression at Oxford and his place in the team to play Cambridge
University at Lord's on 27 June 1870 was assured. The drama came in the
final hour. Chasing 179 to win in a little under three hours Oxford had
reached 153 with three wickets down and the second day crowd of 10,000
must have thought that they were certain to win. However, wickets began
to fall and when Butler went in the score was 175 for seven. He had had a
quiet match so far, bowling only a few overs, but now had a chance to make
his mark. Squeezing out four more runs should have been easy. However,
Oxford had made it harder for themselves by agreeing to play until 7.30 if
necessary in order to finish the match that day and when Butler went in it
was past seven o'clock and the light poor. His partner Frederick Hill was
well set but took a single off the first ball of what proved to be the last
over of the match bowled by fast bowler Frank Cobden. Hill apparently
regretted this decision for the rest of his life. The next ball was a half-

volley. Butler hit it hard, only to be brilliantly caught at mid off by Alfred Bourne, the only catch of his four-match first-class career. Cobden's next two balls bowled batsmen numbers ten and eleven. Cambridge had won a famous match by two runs, their fourth successive victory against Oxford, and Cobden's hat-trick had made history. Butler would redeem himself and make his own little bit of history next year.

He began the 1871 season in good form, including taking ten wickets against MCC at Oxford, and eight for 25 in the only MCC innings of the return. Wisden estimated that 'at least 21,000 of the upper crust of English society' were present over the two days of the University match, including 'an unprecedentedly large number of ladies'. Many of those attending would have passed through the newly installed turnstiles (or 'tell-tale' machines according to *Wisden*). Both teams were reasonably experienced: the Oxford side included seven former Blues, Cambridge eight. Both were captained by their wicketkeepers. Oxford's captain was Edward Tylecote who would go on to play for Kent and England. Three years previously he had scored 404 not out for Classical against Modern at Clifton, a then world record individual score. William Yardley, the Cambridge captain, also played for Kent. In 1870 he made the first century in a University match. He was an interesting character. One of the best batsman of his day, he got a racquets Blue, became a barrister, and was a successful playwright.

After recent heavy rain the outfield was slow and Oxford, batting first in pleasant sunshine, made 170. Their previous year's captain Bernard Pauncefote top scored with 50, while freshman George Harris, who later became the rather influential Lord Harris, made one of his side's three ducks. Cambridge went in at 3.45, Butler opening the Oxford attack opposite the slow spin of Sidney Pelham. Cambridge started well enough, Walter Money, playing in his fourth University match, and Frederic Tobin putting on 22, the best opening partnership of a low-scoring match, before Tobin was caught at point. Three more wickets then went quickly, bringing in Charles 'Buns' Thornton, a famed hitter of the ball, to partner Yardley. The score having risen to 62 and with two good batsmen at the wicket Cambridge would have had hopes of emulating Oxford's score. However at this point Butler swept away the middle and lower order, taking the last six wickets in just 16 balls. Yardley was caught at short leg but after that Butler needed no help from the field. Eight of his victims were bowled, including Thornton who 19 years later, batting for his own Eleven, would be on the receiving end of a Sammy Woods' all-ten, and Cobden whose first-ball duck Butler no doubt found particularly satisfying.

The 6ft 2in well-built Butler, with luxuriant side whiskers in the fashion of the time, must have been a frightening proposition at Lord's. The infamous pitches were gradually improving: two weeks before the Oxford number four Walter Hadow had scored 217 there as Middlesex made 485 in reply to MCC's 338. However, they could still be dangerous, as sadly evidenced in 1870 during the match between MCC & Ground and Nottinghamshire when George Summers, batting for the visitors, was hit on the head by a ball from Derbyshire fast bowler John Platts; a blow from which he later died. Of the game *Wisden* said that 'the wickets were excellent', but it also said that Summers was bowled by a shooter in the first innings, and as there is a suggestion that the fatal ball in his second pitched on a stone, this sounds unlikely.

Following on Cambridge soon lost Money. In the last of his 29 first-class matches Butler had bowled him twice in the same day. Cambridge finished the first day on 64 for two but didn't last too long next morning, Butler finishing with another five wickets, for 57 runs. He again dismissed Yardley, sending his off stump six yards out of the ground. Left 25 to win before a crowd of some 7,000 that would surge onto the ground at the end, Oxford knocked off the runs before lunch for the loss of two wickets. Ironically the winning run came from Cobden's bowling. One of the umpires was another all-ten man, George Wootton.

Butler is still the only man to take all-ten in the University match. His match figures of fifteen for 95 are also a record for the match and the second best ever for an Oxford bowler in first-class cricket, bettered only by Bernard Bosanquet's fifteen for 65 against Sussex in 1900.

The match having finished early and the weather good it was decided to entertain the large crowd by playing a match in the afternoon between MCC & Ground and a combined Oxbridge team. Umpire Wootton reverted to playing and bowled the unfortunate Walter Money for one.

Butler played his last University match in 1873 taking six more wickets. Oxford had been left 174 to win and Butler went in with the scores level and seven wickets down. As Geoffrey Bolton pointed out in his *History of the OUCC*, it was a fine example of poetic justice that Butler again had a chance to score the winning run. We can only guess his thoughts as he walked to the wicket at the end of the second day. Fortunately there was a happier outcome for him this time as he edged his first ball past slip for four. The ghost of Cobden was, at least partly, laid to rest.

Butler took 94 first-class wickets in his four-year Oxford career. This may seem a modest total, but not until 1897 did anybody achieve 100 wickets for them, left-arm medium pacer Foster Cunliffe eventually extending his tally to 181. Butler's first-class career ended the following year with two matches for the Gentlemen. He moved to Somerset where he became a barrister and JP, playing for the county in their pre-first-class days. Samuel Butler died in 1903 aged 53.

James Lillywhite

South v North, 1872

St Lawrence Ground, Canterbury on 5, 6, 7 August 1872 (3-day match)
Toss won by South
North won by an innings and 46 runs
Umpires: WH Fryer, W Goodhew
South 131 and 142 (F Morley 5-50): North 319 (J Lillywhite 10-129)

North first innings

T Bignall	b Lillywhite	18
E Lockwood	c Pooley b Lillywhite	68
A Greenwood	c Thornton b Lillywhite	52
R Daft	c Pooley b Lillywhite	64
RP Carpenter	c Thornton b Lillywhite	57
HN Tennent	b Lillywhite	1
T Emmett	not out	27
M McIntyre	c Humphrey b Lillywhite	1
+G Pinder	c Fryer b Lillywhite	18
F Morley	b Lillywhite	0
JC Shaw	c Walker b Lillywhite	3
Extras	(b 7, lb 3)	10
Total	all out, 173.2 overs)	319

Fall of wickets 1-34, 2-113, 3-149, 4-262, 5-264, 6-275, 7-278, 8-311, 9-311, 10-319

South bowling: J Lillywhite 60.2-22-129-10, E Willsher 37-21-40-0, FER Fryer 29-7-59-0, WG Grace 15-4-28-0, T Hearne 12-5-13-0, ID Walker 13-4-25-0, CI Thornton 7-3-15-0

South: H Jupp, R Humphrey, FER Fryer, ID Walker, CI Thornton, HRJ Charlwood, WG Grace, EW Pooley (wk), T Hearne, J Lillywhite, E Willsher

Sussex county cricket has an unequalled family tradition. The first bowler to take all-ten for Sussex was Cyril Bland against Kent in 1899 in an innings in which Fred Tate, father of the great Maurice, went wicketless. The next was Ian Thomson against Warwickshire in 1964. In that side were Richard Langridge (son of James, nephew of John; pillars of the side from the 1920s to the 1950s), Les Lenham (father of Neil; both scored over 10,000 runs for Sussex), and Tony Buss (who with brother Mike took 1,419 wickets for the county). Many other families have contributed fully to Sussex cricket, and it began with the Lillywhites. James' father worked on the Duke of Richmond's Goodwood estate and it was here that young James became a tile-maker whilst also playing locally. By the time he made his first-class debut in 1862 aged 20 the name Lillywhite was already famous in the cricketing world. His uncle was the famous slow bowler William, two of whose sons, John and James, played for Sussex. A third, Fred, was an entrepreneur with many cricketing interests.

England's captain in the very first Test match, Lillywhite's place in cricket history is assured. He toured Australia six times as player or manager/

umpire. He acquitted himself well in his two-match Test career, taking eight wickets. There were some reservations however about his captaincy: it was said that he didn't bowl himself enough, and could be unduly influenced by stronger personalities in the side. Late 19th-century touring involved lengthy, arduous travel and, although his motivation was usually financial, Lillywhite was clearly a man of fortitude and determination. He bowled slow-medium left-arm, varying flight and pace skilfully whilst maintaining exceptional accuracy over long spells. When he had played his last match in 1885 he had taken 1,210 wickets, a total then exceeded by only six other bowlers. A useful bat, he made two first-class centuries.

Lillywhite's all-ten came in his most prolific season since his debut. In all first-class matches he took 94 wickets, a total he exceeded just once when he dismissed 110 batsmen in 1873. The South v North match had been a feature of the famous Canterbury Week for several years. The Week had begun in 1842. It was a colourful and popular occasion with a ball and theatricals in the evenings. In the early 1870s however, apart from tents, there was little other accommodation at the St Lawrence Ground. There were few seats for spectators and the amateurs had to change in a small tent, whilst the professionals had to make their own arrangements (often at a nearby inn).

North fielded a strong side comprising ten players from Nottinghamshire, Yorkshire and Lancashire along with, perhaps surprisingly geographically, Cambridgeshire's Robert Carpenter. I suppose this was balanced by the South including Cambridge University's Frederick Fryer. It rained most of the first day, the Bank Holiday, and play was impossible. Next day was fine, a strong westerly wind helping to dry the pitch. The large crowd present 'comprised many of the leading families, both of the city and the neighbourhood' and again 'an unusually large number of ladies' were present, adding colour to the occasion. The Laws of Cricket did not yet mention boundaries and it had been agreed that 'all hits to the seated visitors' should count four and not be run out.

South's innings began badly: Surrey's Richard Humphrey run out off the third ball, county colleague Harry Jupp bowled next over. After that, despite the presence of a late-arriving W.G.Grace, the innings never really recovered. Fryer, the only member of the side apart from Edgar Willsher who never made a first-class century, top scored with 55.

North began their innings at 1.40. Nottinghamshire's Thomas Bignall was missed by Grace at mid off with his score eight but was bowled soon after by Lillywhite. Ephraim Lockwood and Andrew Greenwood ('two clipping little Yorkshire batsmen': *Wisden*) then took the score to 113 before the hard-hitting Greenwood, who had also been dropped by Grace, fell to a well-judged catch at long on by Charles Thornton. Nottinghamshire's Daft was cheered to the wicket and, after Lockwood had been caught by Ted Pooley ('a catch at wicket that few keepers would have secured'), he and Carpenter took the score to 262. Lillywhite had been rested, but on return he dismissed Daft, followed quickly by Hector Tennent. Tennent, born in Tasmania, educated in Scotland, and the least eminent of the North team, had a modest but varied cricket career, including matches for MCC,

Lancashire, the 1878 Australian tourists, and Scotland (non-first-class). Thornton then held another good catch in the deep to dispose of Carpenter who had hit well on the leg side, and after that apart from Tom Emmett nobody contributed significantly as Lillywhite gained further reward for his persistence. When stumps were drawn at 7 o'clock the score was 313 for nine. Having made 444 runs for the loss of 19 wickets the teams had certainly made up for the lost first day.

Lillywhite would have had to wonder overnight whether he would get all ten. He had previously taken nine wickets in an innings twice. On the second occasion, against Kent in 1863, the other wicket had fallen to a run-out. He would have been heartened by the fact that one of the not out batsmen was Nottinghamshire's J.C. (Jemmy) Shaw, one of the finest bowlers of the period, but also one of the very worst batsmen. He had to wait a little longer next morning as rain prevented play until quarter to twelve, but Shaw didn't disappoint, soon hitting a catch to Isaac Walker at mid off from the second ball of Lillywhite's 61st over. Six bowlers, including Willsher and Grace (4,138 first class wickets between them), had sent down 113 wicketless (4-ball) overs at the other end. As Grace had turned up late, made a 'badly played' 15, bowled without success and dropped two catches *Wisden* wasn't impressed: [he was] 'quite out of form in bowling, batting, and fielding'.

The South batted little better in their second innings, the left-arm fast pair Shaw and Morley sharing eight wickets. Lillywhite top scored for the South with 29 not out - although perhaps he might not have done if WG had batted, but the great man had left early to travel with the team that the MCC secretary R.A.Fitzgerald was taking to North America.

South's innings, and the match, ended at 3.40 pm. Fortunately for the sizeable crowd a fresh wicket was soon prepared, and by 4.20 another contest was under way: a 12-a-side, but first-class, match between Gentlemen of MCC and Kent. Five players appeared in both games (not including Lillywhite), with Thornton and Willsher managing to be dismissed twice on the same day playing in different matches.

As well as playing, Lillywhite was always looking for other professional opportunities. He coached, became secretary of the United South of England XI, umpired in 247 first-class matches, was agent for the 1878 and 1880 Australian tourists, and with the Nottinghamshire pair Alfred Shaw and Arthur Shrewsbury jointly promoted four tours to Australia in the 1880s, not always to his financial benefit. And of course the name Lillywhite lived on because of the famous sports goods business, James taking on the London business started by his cousin John. He was also a licensee in Chichester. He had his financial ups and downs but around the turn of the century things improved, and until his death he was receiving a comfortable investment income. James Lillywhite continued to live in Sussex until his death in 1929. Aged 87, he outlived all the members of that first English Test team, most of whom had not even survived into the 20th century.

Alfred Shaw

Marylebone Cricket Club v North, 1874

Lord's Cricket Ground, St John's Wood on 1, 2 June 1874 (3-day match)
Toss won by North
North won by 45 runs
Umpires: T Hearne, W Price
North 175 (A Shaw 10-73) and 106 (F Morley 5-48); MCC 154 and 82 (JC Shaw 5-44)

North first innings

E Lockwood	c Grace b Shaw	38
A Greenwood	b Shaw	4
*AN Hornby	c Buller b Shaw	53
W Oscroft	b Shaw	24
HS Reynolds	b Shaw	13
T Emmett	c Grace b Shaw	13
WB Clarke	c Coote b Shaw	4
A Hil	st Biddulph b Shaw	1
+T Plumb	not out	7
M McIntyre	c Biddulph b Shaw	11
JC Shaw	b Shaw	0
Extras	(b 6, lb 1)	7
Total	all out, 89.2 overs)	175

Fall of wickets 1-19, 2-99, 3-108, 4-129, 5-147, 6-151, 7-154, 8-159, 9-175, 10-175

MCC bowling: A Shaw 36.2-8-73-10, F Morley 24-8-49-0, WG Grace 22-7-35-0, RO Clayton 7-3-11-0

MCC: WG Grace, CP Coote, C Marriott, CF Buller, FJ Crooke, G Bird, W Penn, A Shaw, RO Clayton, S Biddulph (wk), F Morley

W.G.Grace thought Alfred Shaw 'perhaps the best bowler in England' during the 1870s. And he should know: Shaw dismissed him 49 times, a total unsurpassed by any other bowler. Of medium height, Shaw bowled with an easy action following a brisk six-pace run up. He could bowl a sharp off break, but largely relied on turning the ball just enough, together with subtle variations of pace. Above all he was famed for his remarkable accuracy: over half of his (mainly 4-ball) overs were maidens, and he bowled more overs than he conceded runs. In terms of stamina, persistence and economy, many of his analyses are astonishing, albeit on pitches often helpful to bowlers.

Born in Burton Joyce, Nottinghamshire in 1842, the youngest of 13 children, Shaw left school at the age of ten following his mother's death, initially working as a farm hand. He first appeared at Lord's in the Colts match against MCC in May 1864. With 13 wickets he made quite an impact, and his first-class debut followed next month. He played regularly for Nottinghamshire until 1886 and was also on the MCC groundstaff. In a first-class career that lasted until 1897 he took just over 2,000 wickets, the second bowler after Grace to reach this total. He bowled the first ball in Test cricket; appropriately it was a 'dot'. In all he played seven Tests, taking 12 wickets. Born a little later, he might have made a significant impact on the international stage.

Thirty-two-year-old Shaw had been playing first-class cricket for nearly ten years when he took all-ten against a strong North of England side in June 1874. He had taken 100 wickets in a season for the first time in 1871 and was embarking on a period of increasing returns that would culminate in 201 wickets in 1878, a total only then surpassed by James Southerton's 210 in 1870. The North had of course been on the receiving end of James Lillywhite's all-ten just two years before, and five of that side were playing at Lord's. And, together with Shaw, three of the side (Yorkshiremen Andrew Greenwood, Tom Emmett and Allen Hill) would play in the very first Test match at Melbourne nearly three years later.

Having purchased the freehold of the ground MCC had started to develop Lord's, and the first Grand Stand (demolished in the 1920s) now stood on the north side opposite a new Tavern. North began their innings just after midday in bright, hot weather against the bowling of Shaw from the pavilion end and Nottinghamshire colleague Fred Morley. Shaw bowled Greenwood at 19 and 'Monkey' Hornby, the North captain, joined Ephraim Lockwood. A sizeable partnership quickly developed and with the score 58 Grace put himself on. The change was unsuccessful and the next wicket did not fall until Shaw came back, off his fourth ball having Hornby caught by Middlesex's Charles Buller at long on for 53, after a partnership of 80 that was easily the highest of the match. Buller's *Wisden* obituary suggests that his contemporaries will remember the former Harrow captain as 'one of the greatest batsmen of his day' but also says that 'Into the scandals that marked Mr Buller's private life and caused his social eclipse, this is obviously not the place to enter' (apparently referring to his discharge from the Army because of bankruptcy, and later involvement in a high-profile society divorce scandal).

Lockwood went soon afterwards for 38, well caught by Grace at point, and Shaw began to work his way through the North's batting. The quiet and unassuming Yorkshireman Lockwood made exactly 1,000 runs in 1874, a total exceeded only by Grace and Surrey's Harry Jupp. He was perhaps unlucky not to play Test cricket. His last chance probably went when rheumatism prevented him travelling to Australia in 1881/82.

Lunch was taken at 159 for seven, and with the first ball after the interval Shaw had Emmett caught low down at point by Grace, redeeming himself for previously dropping the Yorkshireman in the same position. The innings ended soon afterwards at 3.30, Shaw completing his all-ten by bowling J.C. Shaw, one of five Nottinghamshire colleagues playing for the North, for a (not unusual) duck. Jemmy Shaw had been Lillywhite's tenth victim and he now bestowed the same honour upon his unrelated namesake. Nobody exceeded the 139 wickets that Grace took in 1874 (he also made most runs and was the leading fielder!), but this time he had bowled without reward. Morley, one of six bowlers who took 100 wickets during the season, was similarly unsuccessful.

As well as Grace, Shaw had received particular help from wicketkeeper Sam Biddulph, who caught Martin McIntyre, a dismissal involving three Nottinghamshire colleagues, and stumped Hill, who three years later would take Test cricket's first wicket and hold its first catch (off Shaw's bowling). Biddulph had been the All-England Eleven keeper when George Wootton took all-ten against Yorkshire in 1865. Sadly he died of kidney disease less than two years later aged only 35. Umpire Thomas Hearne was probably getting a bit blasé about all-tens. He had played when Walker and Lillywhite had taken theirs, umpired when Butler took his, and had now officiated during another.

MCC's innings finished just before the close, Grace top scoring with 43. The hot weather continued the following day. The match was scheduled for three days but according to *The Chronicle of WG* 'It had been planned to start at 11.00 to finish the match in two days because tomorrow was Derby Day, but play did not begin until 11.30'. North's second innings total might have been worse. They had been 63 for eight, but McIntyre (21) and Hornby, who batted bravely for an undefeated 21 after going in down the order because of a bruised hand, ensured that MCC were set a tricky target. This time the damage was done by the pace of Morley (five for 48) who hit the stumps four times whilst Shaw (three for 43) bowled almost unchanged at the other end. Chasing 128 MCC, all out at 4.15, never looked like getting close and those who wanted could go to The Derby. The ball with which Shaw had taken all-ten was mounted by MCC and later presented to him.

Like Lillywhite, Shaw impacted on cricket in many ways. He was involved in several tours to North America and Australia as player, captain, manager or promoter. With Arthur Shrewsbury he set up a sports goods business in 1880. Surviving the deaths of both partners it finally closed soon after the start of the Second World War. Shaw was also an early champion of the rights of fellow professionals: he was one of a number of players who refused the terms initially offered by Notts to play against the 1880 Australians, and a year later was involved in a more protracted dispute mainly centred on the terms offered to the players by autocratic county secretary Captain Holden.

With the exception of one game in 1897 Shaw's Nottinghamshire career ended in 1887, at which time he was the county's highest ever wicket-taker. Remarkably for a professional he was County captain from 1883 until 1886. Nottinghamshire won the Championship in all four seasons and then replaced him, the Committee believing that younger blood was needed. The Committee at least showed its gratitude by giving him a benefit match – five years later, and only 28 years after his county debut! Shaw's first-class career did not end there. He had been managing Lord Sheffield's famous ground near Uckfield and in 1894 he turned out for Sussex, remarkably topping the county averages.

After his playing career was over Shaw became a full-time umpire, continuing until the end of 1905. He had also been a pub landlord. He died in 1907 in Gedling, Nottinghamshire.

Edward Barratt

Players v Australians, 1878

Kennington Oval, Kennington on 2, 3 September 1878 (3-day match)
Toss won by Players
Australians won by 8 runs
Umpires: W Caffyn, J Potter
Australians 77 (ED Barratt 10-43) and 89 (W McIntyre 6-24); Players 82 (FR Spofforth 7-37) and 76 (FR Spofforth 5-38)

Australians first innings

AC Bannerman	c McIntyre b Barratt	4
C Bannerman	c Barlow b Barratt	51
TP Horan	c Watson b Barratt	0
WL Murdoch	st H Phillips b Barratt	0
FR Spofforth	st H Phillips b Barratt	14
GH Bailey	c Lillywhite b Barratt	0
*DW Gregory	c J Phillips b Barratt	0
+JM Blackham	st H Phillips b Barratt	0
HF Boyle	c J Phillips b Barratt	8
TW Garrett	c Watson b Barratt	0
FE Allan	not out	0
Extras		0
Total	(all out, 57 overs)	77

Fall of wickets 1-12, 2-14, 3-16, 4-50, 5-50, 6-50, 7-50, 8-64, 9-64, 10-77

Players bowling: ED Barratt 29-11-43-10, A Watson 14-4-23-0, J Lillywhite 8-4-9-0, GG Hearne 6-4-2-0

Players: W Rigley, RG Barlow, J Phillips, GG Hearne, HRJ Charlwood, J Wheeler, A Watson, H Phillips (wk), James Lillywhite (capt), ED Barratt, W McIntyre

The only bowler apart from Jim Laker to take an all-ten against the Australians Ted Barratt took 790 first class wickets, most of them for Surrey. He bowled (very) slow left-arm, turning the ball considerably, pitching it around off stump with the intention of getting his victims caught in the packed off side or else stumped. Born in Stockton-on-Tees, County Durham in 1844, by trade a plumber, he learned his cricket with the local club and had a variety of professional appointments, including employment at Lord's as a groundstaff bowler. He made his first-class debut in 1872 at the newly opened Prince's ground (in Knightsbridge, just south of Harrods), taking eight for 60 for North against a strong South team and then, having qualified by residence, his Surrey debut four years later. Curiously his first six wickets for the county were all Ted Pooley stumpings.

The 1878 Australian tourists were captained by Dave Gregory. It was the second Australian team to tour Britain, following the 1868 Aboriginals. Although Australian cricket was not yet considered ready to meet the full might of an English team, the party included Charles Bannerman, who had already made a Test century, two more who would do so (Billy Murdoch and the County Cork-born Tom Horan), plus a powerful hand of bowlers. Playing 15 first-class matches and 22 others (mainly against odds) the Australians were a great attraction, especially after famously beating a strong MCC side (Grace and all) early in the tour. Their team at The Oval was a strong one, which is more than could be said for the Players XI, which was unrepresentative of English professional cricket, as most of the top players refused to play because they were not being paid enough. In the circumstances the Players did well to lose by only eight runs.

Barratt had come late to first-class cricket. Aged 34, having taken 92 wickets in 1877, this was only his second full season. The Australians already knew him well. Earlier in the year, for Surrey at The Oval, he had taken 11 wickets against them.

The Players match involved a number of spectacular collapses. Play began at half past 12 in pleasant early autumn weather before a crowd of some 10,000, most of whom would have paid one shilling (5p) admission. Facilities at The Oval were still limited and it is doubtful whether all of those ringing the ground in a compact circle had a decent view of play when the Bannerman brothers went out to bat, James Lillywhite the Players' captain having decided to field first. Alick, born in Australia, unlike older brother Charles who was from south-east London, went quickly, caught at mid on by William McIntyre, brother of Shaw's penultimate all-ten victim four years before. He was soon followed by Horan, caught at slip by Scot Alec Watson who would play successfully for Lancashire for over 20 years, and Murdoch who was stumped. They both made ducks. They would not be alone in their failure in the innings, or the match. Fred Spofforth, the first great Australian bowler, came in next. Born in Australia but dying in England Spofforth would reverse the journey made by a number of his contemporaries. He put on 34 with Bannerman before Barratt had him stumped. At 50 for three on a slow pitch the tourists were well placed; but once Spofforth went and Barratt took three more wickets in his next over, at 50 for seven they weren't. *Wisden* quaintly described this as 'an awful smash up of Australian wickets'. There was no recovery, although Harry Boyle resisted for a while before being caught at cover point just before lunch with the score 64 for eight. Opener Charles Bannerman was last out, caught at point by Lancashire's Dick Barlow for 51, a fine effort and more than double any other score in the match. He was easily the Australians' most successful batsman, making four of the tourists' eight first-class fifties (no centuries).

For the first time in an all-ten nobody had been bowled or leg-before. Barratt had had particular help from the Sussex Hastings-born brothers Phillips, wicketkeeper Henry stumping three batsmen and younger brother James holding two catches at cover point. Whilst he had bowled unchanged from the Vauxhall End, three bowlers who would eventually garner well over 3,000 wickets between them went empty-handed at the Pavilion End: Watson, Lillywhite, who of course had already claimed an all-ten, and Kent's George Hearne, a member of the famous clan which included his uncle, the much-aforementioned Thomas.

The Players' innings followed a similar pattern to that of the Australians: a reasonable start and then a massive collapse, 59 for two becoming, thanks to six successive ducks, 82 all out. Spofforth did the damage taking seven for 37 including a hat-trick. It had been an exciting first day. Curiously the Australians' second innings also started well and then disintegrated: 45 without loss becoming 70 for nine (and another duck for Murdoch and famous wicketkeeper Jack Blackham). The second day crowd, expecting an exciting finish, had risen to 15,000. In a crucial partnership Gregory and Tom Garrett took the score to 89 before Barratt had Garrett caught at cover point, strangely his only wicket in an innings in which the Lancashire pair McIntyre and Dick Barlow, who hadn't been needed first time around, did most of the bowling.

Going in just before four o'clock chasing 85, the Players made only 76. Barratt was the last wicket to fall, bowled by a Spofforth 'sparkler' for a duck, equalling his first-innings score. The spectators had had their excitement and crowded the front of the pavilion until the Australians emerged to acknowledge their cheers. The match had been such a financial success that the originally agreed payment of £10 to the English players was increased to £20, an amount which if known beforehand would almost certainly have ensured that a much stronger team could have been assembled. Barratt also received a £5 bonus (and the match ball). He might have received more. A collection in recognition of his great performance was carried out among the spectators by two gentlemen claiming to be acting on behalf of the ground authorities. They weren't, and the money went into their pockets, not Barratt's.

Within two hours of the final wicket falling the importance of a mere game of cricket was put into perspective. Not far from The Oval some 650 passengers died on the Thames when the paddle steamer *Princess Alice* was struck by the collier *Bywell Castle*. A disaster fund was set up, the Australians subscribing £100. In addition a further match between North and South was played at The Oval in aid of the fund. Barratt played for the South in a well-attended match that raised £258.

Barratt was at his best in the early 1880s, taking 445 wickets in four seasons, peaking in 1883 with 148 victims. There was no Australian tour that year otherwise Barratt might have gained England selection, but in any case Yorkshire's Ted Peate who had a short but brilliant career usually got the important slow left-arm place. Surrey certainly got their money's worth out of Barratt: often their only reliable bowler, over the four years he bowled more than twice as many overs and took more than twice as many wickets as any other bowler. And then by the middle of the 1885 season his Surrey career was over. Perhaps because of his exertions his performance declined, and he was no longer needed.

Barratt's next few years were busy: he remained a member of the Surrey groundstaff, he coached, he umpired, and he became landlord of *The Duchy Inn* close to The Oval. Surrey granted him the Yorkshire match in 1887 as a benefit. Although it only lasted two days, it attracted a decent crowd of over 10,000. Sadly he died of consumption in 1891 aged only 46.

George Giffen

Australian XI v Combined XI, 1883/84

Association Ground, Sydney on 15, 16, 18 February 1884 (4-day match)
Toss won by Australian XI
Australian XI won by nine wickets
Umpires: JW Fletcher, J Swift
Australian XI 318 and 20-1; Combined XI 222 (GE Palmer 6-75) and 113 (G Giffen 10-66)

Combined XI second innings

*HH Massie	c McDonnell b Giffen	29
TW Garrett	c Scott b Giffen	3
SP Jones	c and b Giffen	10
H Moses	c sub (G Alexander) b Giffen	14
RC Allen	c Palmer b Giffen	0
E Evans	lbw b Giffen	2
+PM Lewis	not out	19
AP Marr	b Giffen	5
FR Spofforth	c Bannerman b Giffen	14
T Powell	b Giffen	3
T Nunn	c Blackham b Giffen	0
Extras	(b 9, nb 3, w 2)	14
Total	(all out, 50 overs)	113

Fall of wickets 1-42, 2-42, 3-52, 4-52, 5-59, 6-80, 7-93, 8-107, 9-113, 10-113

Australian XI bowling: GE Palmer 16-8-27-0, G Giffen 26-16-66-10, HF Boyle 8-3-6-0

Australian XI: PS McDonnell, AC Bannerman, WL Murdoch (capt), G Giffen, GJ Bonnor, WE Midwinter, HJH Scott, JM Blackham (wk), GE Palmer, HF Boyle, WH Cooper

George Giffen was well named Australia's W.G.Grace. In a career lasting 25 years some of his performances outdid even those of the great Doctor. It is impossible to adequately describe his many achievements in a short chapter; however he is one of only five Australians to have scored 10,000 runs and taken 1,000 wickets (the other four had substantial county careers), and the only bowler to take 17 wickets in a match in Australia, to take 16 or more wickets in a match as many as five times, and to take 40 wickets over the course of five successive innings (for the Australians in 1886).

Born in Adelaide in 1859 Giffen showed early promise and at 15 was allowed to bowl in the nets at W.G.Grace's visiting England team. He played for Norwood, the strongest of the Adelaide premiership clubs. A muscular 5ft 11in he made his debut in South Australia's inaugural first-class match against Tasmania in November 1877 bowling slow to medium off breaks from an eight-pace run-up, a style of bowling largely to fade from Test cricket by the beginning of the First World War. Cleverly varying flight and pace, he had a well disguised slower ball which probably accounted for the fact that ten of his 103 Test wickets were caught and bowled. As a batsman Giffen had a solid defence and a full range of scoring shots.

With as yet no Sheffield Shield, relatively few first-class matches were played in Australia each season. By the start of 1884 Giffen was an established Test cricketer, South Australia's first, and had been picked for the forthcoming Australian tour of England. As preparation a programme of practice matches had been arranged. Most were against odds but two, against sides styled 'Combined XI', were first-class. Facilities at what was to become the Sydney Cricket Ground were still basic. Nevertheless, when the ground had staged its first Test (although not recognised as such at the time) two years before, a crowd of 16,000 had been attracted to the second day.

Ten of the Combined XI played for New South Wales, with Victoria providing wicketkeeper Percy Lewis. With eight past or future internationals, including 1884 tourists Fred Spofforth and Sammy Jones, the Combined XI had a more than decent side. The Australian XI led off with 318, captain Billy Murdoch top scoring with 83. In the first match against the Combined XI in January he had made 279 not out and a few months later at The Oval he would make Test cricket's first double-century. The Combined XI began their reply on the second day before a crowd of 5,000. The fielding side had to contend with a wind that blew almost a gale throughout the day. On the other hand the batsmen had to contend with a pitch that had been cut up by the previous day's activities. In the circumstances Jones' 88 against a strong attack (Giffen three for 62) was a masterly performance. Second top-scorer Spofforth, going in with eight wickets down in worsening conditions, had hit out at everything and made 29 in 12 minutes.

Following on (still compulsorily) the Combined XI started well reaching 42 without loss. However Giffen, who was to bowl unchanged, then got into his stride and by the close the score had subsided to 52 for four. The fourth wicket to fall had been Reginald Allen who failed to emulate the one he scored in the first innings. Allen, who played a solitary Test three years later, died in 1952 which gave him plenty of time to follow the successful England career of his nephew Gubby Allen (who would take his own all-ten in 1929). It was clear that the match didn't have much longer to run and next day the crowd was a meagre 1,000. Harry Moses was not out overnight. Four years later he would run out of partners against Victoria three runs short of becoming Australia's second triple-centurion. He stayed for a while before being caught by the tourists' manager George Alexander who was acting as a substitute, but after that the end came soon. 'Joey' Palmer and Harry Boyle were still major Test bowlers but would remain wicketless at the other end while Giffen ran through the opposition. He must have been very keen to finish the job quickly because after bowling the last over on the second day he bowled the first on the third. This was permitted then, as long as the bowler did not change ends more than twice in the innings or bowl more than two overs in succession. Captain Hugh Massie had top scored before Giffen had him caught by Percy McDonnell, like Massie a future captain of his country. A magnificent forcing batsman and banker by profession Massie played in nine Tests.

Only one was in England, but it was the celebrated Oval Test of 1882 and without his second innings contribution in a low-scoring match Australia would never have won a famous victory. Sammy Jones made only ten this time caught and bowled by Giffen, perhaps a victim of that wicked slower ball. Last man out, Kent-born Thomas Nunn, was a bit of a makeweight. Batting eleven and not bowling he had an undistinguished five-match career. Two of Giffen's victims, Garrett and Spofforth, had also been part of Ted Barrett's full house in 1878.

The Australian XI duly reached their simple target. Perhaps in order to give him the honour of scoring the winning run Giffen was sent in to open. If so the plan failed because he was bowled by Spofforth for just 2, which was at least an improvement on his first innings one.

Given the conditions *Cricket: A Weekly Record of the Game* regretted that each side did not have a fresh wicket to bat on. At the time the Laws allowed for this after rain (both sides agreeing) and they were about to be amended to allow a change if the pitch became unfit. Captains have rarely availed themselves of this opportunity.

Giffen would go on to take nine wickets in an innings four times. The closest he came to turning nine into another ten was two years later at the County Ground, Derby, when he dismissed the first eight Derbyshire batsmen before the penultimate wicket fell to a run-out.

Giffen eventually toured England five times, achieving the 1,000 run/100 wicket double three times. Signing off his Test career in 1896 having become the first to complete the corresponding Test double, he was then the current highest wicket-taker in England – Australia Tests and Australia's highest run-scorer. At State level, South Australia relied heavily on Giffen, and he didn't let them down. By the time he had played his last match for them he was their leading run-scorer and their leading wicket-taker, his allround performances continuing to attest to his great skill and stamina. He played first-class cricket until his mid-40s and even in 1903, aged 44, scored 81 and 97 not out and took 15 wickets against Victoria at Adelaide.

Did this Superman have any faults? Well, he wasn't a very good captain, mainly because he kept himself on too long. Two of the six instances of Australians bowling over 500 balls in an innings involve Giffen as both bowler and captain. However he was often the best bowler in the side, and when he set the then record for the most balls bowled in a Test match (708 in 1894/95) he wasn't captain.

When he finally gave up playing he still contributed to the game by coaching local boys. In 1925, after 43 years service, he retired from the GPO. Apparently he used to fret about promotion opportunities lost because of time spent away playing cricket. Sadly he did not live long to enjoy his pension, dying in November 1927. A grandstand at the Adelaide Oval was named after him. Most of it has disappeared following redevelopments, but a life-size bronze statue of him now stands at the ground.

W.G.Grace

Marylebone Cricket Club v Oxford University, 1886

The University Parks, Oxford on 21, 22 June 1886 (2-day match)
Toss won by Oxford University
Marylebone Cricket Club won by an innings and 28 runs
Oxford University 142 and 90 (WG Grace 10-49); MCC 260 (WG Grace 104)

Oxford University second innings

EHF Bradby	b Grace	0
P Coles	c Attewell b Grace	1
AK Watson	b Grace	0
*HV Page	st Kemp b Grace	26
JH Brain	c Hine-Haycock b Grace	15
W Rashleigh	b Grace	19
C Wreford-Brown	c Attewell b Grace	13
EH Buckland	b Grace	4
+AR Cobb	c de Paravicini b Grace	0
HW Forster	not out	0
JH Ware	lbw b Grace	10
Extras	(lb 2)	2
Total	(all out, 72.2 overs	90

Fall of wickets 1-0, 2-0, 3-11, 4-41, 5-51, 6-74, 7-80, 8-80, 9-80, 10-90

MCC bowling: WG Grace 36.2-17-49-10, W Wright 25-12-28-0, W Attewell 11-7-11-0

MCC: WG Grace (capt), EJC Studd, C Booth, TR Hine-Haycock, PJ de Paravicini, MC Kemp (wk), W Wright, W Attewell, Lord GW Scott, EA Nepean, VA Titchmarsh

On figures alone W.G.Grace is one of the greatest cricketers ever, but when his contribution to the development of the game is added in, a good case can be made that he is, despite two obvious stellar overseas contenders, the greatest ever. He played first-class cricket from 1865 until 1908, scored 54,211 runs, took 2,809 wickets and held 876 catches (and made five stumpings!). To select just two of many impressive achievements: he made a century and took ten wickets in a match 14 times (only George Giffen and Frank Woolley did it even six times), and in eight days in 1876 in three successive innings he scored 344, 177 and 318 (in which three matches he also bowled 181 four-ball overs). In addition, according to J.R Webber, Grace also garnered some 45,000 runs and 4,600 wickets in minor cricket. All that is perhaps missing is a major Test career. Having said that, given that he didn't get the chance to play for England until he was thirty-two, 1,098 runs at an average of 32 and with two 'big' centuries is pretty impressive. Remember also that he qualified, eventually, and practised as a doctor, and in his younger, slimmer days was a considerable athlete.

By the mid-1880s Grace's girth had increased considerably. Having initially bowled quickish round arm he had slowed down to become an artful bowler of rolled leg breaks (or did the batsman just think they turned?). Although he was an impressive, tall, bearded figure his leisurely amble up to the wicket (probably wearing his MCC cap), ungainly action and seemingly innocuous delivery added to his ability to deceive. Flighting the ball cleverly and maintaining strict control over length and direction, he often bowled round the wicket which accounts for the 197 batsmen caught in his famous square-leg trap. A fine fielder he caught and bowled as many as 222 of his victims. He didn't bowl much in Tests and his figures against Australia (nine wickets for 236 runs) might suggest that better class batsmen were less susceptible to his wiles. However, he still numbered three Test centurions among his victims.

Because of examinations Oxford were forced to field a weakened team for their home match against MCC; only five of the side subsequently appeared against Cambridge. It was their last home game before the University match (which, despite Oxford having beaten Surrey and given the Australians a good game, the Light Blues were expected to win, but didn't). *The Times* thought that MCC had sent down a strong side; *Cricket* considered it only moderate. The truth was somewhere in between. Most of the team were fairly average amateurs, but any eleven with Grace in it (1,846 runs and 122 wickets in 1886) could not be described as moderate. And his skills were supplemented by those of two outstanding professional bowlers: Kent and Nottinghamshire's Walter Wright and Nottinghamshire's William Attewell. Together they would eventually take nearly 3,000 wickets in their respective careers.

Dull with a bitterly cold north wind, the weather on the first day wasn't very much like midsummer. The Parks is a beautiful ground, but with only a pavilion for shelter spectators needed to be well wrapped up. Going in first at 12.15 Oxford made a one-run-an-over 142, Grace who opened the bowling picking up two wickets in 32 overs and taking two catches. The only batsman who made a significant contribution was Oxford captain Herbert Page who was bowled by Attewell one short of his fifty. Page had a decent career with Gloucestershire, as did his son Dallas who sadly, aged 25, was killed in a motor accident returning home after the last match of the 1936 season, his second as county captain. Herbert Page was also a useful medium-pace bowler: the previous month he had taken all-ten in a minor match for M.C.Kemp's XI against Hertford College.

Opening the batting for MCC Grace reached his fifty just before the close. The north wind continued to blow next day, but at least the sun came out. Grace had been well entertained the previous evening at a banquet given by Vincent's Club. He had started the morning with some shaky net practice, but after that showed no sign of any hangover as he continued to dominate the batting, and the weak Oxford bowling. He was finally dismissed leg-before for 104 by Page having hit 15 fours and a straight driven six.

Over 100 runs behind and facing a very good attack Oxford probably didn't start their second innings with any great feelings of optimism as Grace opened the bowling again. And they would not have been heartened by losing two wickets without a run on the board, including Edward Bradby playing the only match of a first-class career whose only runs were the boundary he hit in the first innings. Percival Coles, who was also playing his last first-class match, went soon afterwards but then Page and Joseph Brain put on 30, the highest partnership of the innings, before Brain was brilliantly caught on the square-leg boundary. Brain was a gifted batsman who had hit a century for Gloucestershire against the 1884 Australian tourists. He became a major figure in Glamorgan cricket, although dying in 1914 he did not live long enough to see his adopted county achieve first-class status. Page, top scoring again, went soon after, stumped by Manley Kemp. A week before, Kemp, aged 25, had made 175 for Gentlemen of England against Cambridge University, taking his side from 21 for six to 298 all out. *Wisden* said that his batting would not readily be forgotten by those who had the good fortune to witness it. In 134 matches however, played mainly for Oxford University and Kent, it would be his only century.

William Rashleigh went next. A fortnight later he would become the first freshman to make a century in the University match, when he and Kingsmill Key (143) put on 243 for the first wicket. Declarations not allowed, the remaining batsmen then attacked so recklessly that nobody else reached double figures.

With three Oxford wickets falling at 80, including Arthur Cobb who would die suddenly of typhoid fever later in the year, the end was nigh. Last man in was John Ware. He was a leg-spinner, although he didn't take any wickets in MCC's innings. Like Bradby he was playing his only first-class match. He celebrated by hitting a four and a six before Grace pinned him in front. For someone who had a certain reputation for being a bit intimidating in the field it is perhaps surprising that this was the only wicket that fell to him this way in the match. On the other hand, over his career about one in 11 of his victims were leg-before, so one out of 12 in the match is about par.

Grace had previously taken ten wickets in an innings in a 12-a-side match (Gentlemen of MCC against Kent in 1873), a feat also performed by his brother E.M. in 1862. He had also taken nine wickets three times, although the only other time he got close to all-ten was for South against North in 1875 when he took the first eight before James Lillywhite took the ninth (thanks to a brilliant catch at mid on by Grace!).

Later in 1886 Grace became the first bowler to reach 2,000 first-class wickets. He would remain the leading wicket-taker of all-time until 1919 when Wilfred Rhodes overtook him. 1886 was the ninth and last season in which he took 100 wickets although, despite approaching middle age, he would still have the energy to take another 800 first-class wickets (as well as score 25,000 runs!) before he finally retired.

George Burton

Kennington Oval, Kennington on 19, 20, 21 July 1888 (3-day match)
Toss won by Middlesex
Surrey won by three wickets
Umpires: C Payne, CK Pullin
Middlesex 161 and 53 (GA Lohmann 7-32); Surrey 163 (G Burton 10-59) and 52-7

Surrey first innings

R Abel	c Vernon b Burton	0
*J Shuter	b Burton	17
JM Read	c Robertson b Burton	29
WW Read	c Robertson b Burton	3
KJ Key	c Hadow b Burton	51
+H Wood	c Robertson b Burton	0
MP Bowden	c Robertson b Burton	21
GA Lohmann	c O'Brien b Burton	5
CA Trouncer	c Hadow b Burton	26
J Beaumont	not out	7
GG Jones	c Walker b Burton	0
Extras	(b 3, lb 1)	4
Total	(all out, 111.3 overs)	163

Fall of wickets 1-9, 2-32, 3-46, 4-53, 5-53, 6-89, 7-105, 8-156, 9-162, 10-163

Middlesex bowling: G Burton 52.3-25-59-10, FGJ Ford 15-9-27-0, J Robertson 23-13-34-0, FM Hadow 6-3-9-0, AJ Webbe 12-6-16-0, SW Scott 3-0-14-0

Middlesex: JG Walker, AJ Webbe (capt), SW Scott, TC O'Brien, EM Hadow, GF Vernon, PJ de Paravicini, FGJ Ford, J Robertson, G Burton, HW Bryant (wk)

George Burton is not perhaps one of the most famous names in cricket history. However, he took 529 wickets for Middlesex, a total which at the time he played his last match for them at the end of 1893 was easily a county record. A hardworking and accurate right-arm slow bowler with a round-arm action, Burton was the mainstay of the Middlesex attack during the 1880s, and was their leading wicket-taker in every season bar one from 1881 to 1890.

Burton was born in Hampstead, Middlesex in 1851. By trade a coachsmith, even when he became a Middlesex regular he often worked for several hours before taking the field. Unusually he did not make his first-class debut until he was 30, having played club cricket in north London. A photograph taken in 1878 shows that he sported a beard of which W.G. Grace would have been proud. His first match was at the end of May 1881 against Surrey at Lord's. Opening the bowling, with his second ball he had Harry Jupp caught. It was a considerable scalp. Jupp scored England's first Test fifty and was coming to the end of a career that left him Surrey's top run-scorer.

Burton's successful debut was followed by a decade of steady wicket-taking, punctuated by a number of highlights. Although he never played Test cricket he appeared in five matches for Middlesex against the Australians with some success, notably in 1886 when he had match figures of fourteen for 192 in a match that the visitors won by just one wicket.

Burton's all-ten was the high point of the most successful season of his career. His county's reliance on him was particularly marked and is illustrated by the fact that he took 87 wickets for them in 13 matches, whilst the next most successful bowler, pace man James Robertson, took just 28. In his first match of the season for Middlesex, at Lord's, he had second-innings figures of seven for 18 in 17.2 overs as Yorkshire were skittled for 43 to lose by nine wickets in two days. Two months later Burton took his all-ten against Surrey.

Since Edward Barratt's all-ten there in 1878 facilities at The Oval had improved, with concrete embankments around the ground making viewing easier. The Championship was not formally organised until 1890. Before then champions were 'proclaimed by the press'. *Wisden* lists Surrey as unofficial champions in 1888, and with 12 wins out of 14 there really were no other contenders, and so Burton's feat was especially meritorious. *Wisden*'s reports of Surrey matches at The Oval in 1888 were curiously variable in length: some reports ran to over a page of detailed text, others were much shorter. Unfortunately for Burton, the report of the Middlesex match fell into the latter category and he got little more mention than the fact that his taking of all ten wickets was 'a great feat'. He was the only professional in a Middlesex team that batted first and scored 161. Although the Middlesex captain, Alexander Webbe, went quickly, steady scoring by James Walker (43), Stanley Scott (60) and Tim O'Brien (37) had left them well placed at one point at 149 for three. Walker wasn't one of the famous Southgate Walkers, but a Scot from Glasgow.

Surrey batted for a few overs at the end of the first day and Burton quickly dismissed the prolific Bobby Abel to leave them 12 for one at the close. Abel's previous match had been his Test debut at Lord's, and earlier in the season at the same venue Burton had dismissed him six short of his century, in a match that followed Abel's 160 against a Cambridge University attack which included Sammy Woods, the next bowler to take an all-ten in England.

Rain prevented play on Friday, the scheduled second day, and left the pitch in a 'treacherous' state for what proved to be an exciting last day. Surrey captain John Shuter, who would play his one and only Test later in the summer at The Oval, resisted for a while before becoming the only one of Burton's victims not to be caught. Seven of the first eight Surrey batsman were, or would be, Test cricketers, but it was the eighth, Kingsmill Key, going in at number five and scoring 51 before being caught at long off by Edward Hadow, who was the only one to pass 30. Middlesex (and Burton) would have been glad to see him go. The previous season, in the second of two first-class matches played at Chiswick Park, he had made 281 for

Oxford University against them. Together with Hylton Philipson (150) he had posted 340 for the seventh wicket, a then-world record partnership for any wicket. Walter Read topped the season's averages and had made 338 against Oxford University the previous month, but he didn't last long against Burton, going to one of four catches at slip by James Robertson (another Scot). The stars having departed Surrey would have been bowled out for a lot less if it hadn't been for Charles Trouncer who went in at 105 for seven and put on 51 with Key. The least accomplished member of the side, in a nine-match career he would never get past 30 or take a wicket. Burton completed his all-ten by inflicting a duck upon fast bowler George Jones who was playing the last of his 162 first-class innings. The Surrey innings closed at 2 o'clock with a lead of just two runs. Burton had bowled virtually unchanged for 52.3 overs. His figures were a county record which stood until 1900 when it was broken by Albert Trott. The county amateurs later commemorated Burton's feat by presenting him with an inkstand and candlesticks.

Conditions remained difficult and second time around Middlesex could make nothing of George Lohmann (seven for 32). They were not alone: the great bowler was to take 209 wickets in the season at a cost of 10.90 each, and go on to take over 200 in each of the following two years. Surrey needed only 52 to win, not a straightforward task given the conditions, but with Abel and Shuter taking the score to 16 without loss it was starting to look easy. However once they were separated the middle order collapsed against Burton and fast round-armer Robertson who bowled unchanged for forty overs, taking three wickets each (Key was run out), before the home side just made it.

Burton was in a purple patch. Having set the Middlesex innings bowling record, in his next game he took sixteen for 114 against Yorkshire at Bramall Lane, Sheffield, to set the match bowling record (which he jointly holds with J.T. Hearne). This is one of the longest-standing county records; only the Derbyshire record, set in 1876, goes back further. *Wisden* again went overboard in reporting Burton's great feat: 'Middlesex won by six wickets, thanks chiefly to Burton and Mr O'Brien'. (In a low scoring match T.C. O'Brien scored 27 and 79 not out.)

After his 1888 zenith, Burton's returns diminished and he lost his place in the Middlesex team at the beginning of 1891 as Yorkshireman John Rawlin and the great J.T. Hearne came to the fore. He remained a member of the MCC groundstaff until 1906, and was awarded two benefit matches. He also stood as a first-class umpire in a number of matches, was scorer for the county (and in the 1921 Test at Lord's), coached at Mill Hill School, and was honorary secretary to the Cricketers' Fund Friendly Society until his death at Covent Garden, London aged 79 in 1930.

Albert Moss

Canterbury v Wellington, 1889/90

Hagley Oval, Christchurch on 27, 28 December 1889 (3-day match)
Toss won by Canterbury
Canterbury won by 39 runs
Canterbury 138 (CH Dryden 7-58) and 111 (CH Dryden 5-35); Wellington 71 (AE Moss 10-28) and 139 (AFG Harman 5-35)

Wellington first innings

A Blacklock	b Moss	9
*WJ Salmon	c Marshall b Moss	1
RV Blacklock	c Garrard b Moss	0
M Moorhouse	c Marshall b Moss	2
CH Dryden	c Marshall b Moss	4
EW Brooke	c EJ Cotterill b Moss	8
WP McGirr	c Barnes b Moss	20
AI Littlejohn	not out	13
S Nicholls	c and b Moss	0
+PHW Ogier	b Moss	5
HW Lawson	b Moss	4
Extras	(b 4, lb 1)	5
Total	(all out, 42.3 overs)	71

Fall of wickets 1-3, 2-3, 3-9, 4-18, 5-25, 6-28, 7-57, 8-57, 9-65, 10-71

Canterbury bowling: AE Moss 21.3-10-28-10, CW Garrard 14-6-22-0, ABM Labatt 7-3-16-0

Canterbury: G Marshall (wk), HS de Maus, ABM Labatt, AFG Harman, CW Garrard, WJ Cotterill, TW Reese, GL Rayner, EJ Cotterill (capt), WEP Barmes, AE Moss

Of all the bowlers who have taken an all-ten none had a shorter career than Albert Moss, or arguably a more remarkable life. He is still the only bowler to have taken all-ten on first-class debut, or to have performed the feat in New Zealand.

Born in Hugglescote, Leicestershire in 1863, his father a maker of high-quality shoes, Moss became a pupil-teacher, suggesting that he was well educated, and also that his father could afford for him to stay on at school to be trained (pupil-teachers were paid a small wage). He married Mary Hall from Loughborough and the couple sailed to New Zealand to escape the tuberculosis which was ravaging his family. He began teaching, joined Lancaster Park Cricket Club in Christchurch, and gained a place in the Canterbury team. Canterbury had played the inaugural first-class match in New Zealand against Otago in January 1864.

Five feet 8 inches tall and well-built, Moss bowled at a sharp pace with a low, slinging action. His Canterbury debut has of course gone into history. The match lasted for only two of its three scheduled days. It was one of ten first-class matches played in New Zealand that season, five of which were matches involving a touring (second string) New South Wales side that drew one match and won the others easily. A domestic championship, the Plunket Shield, was still nearly twenty years away. The match was played at Hagley Oval, in the beautiful Hagley Park, named in honour of the Lyttelton family seat in Worcestershire. The other two home matches that Moss played for Canterbury took place at Lancaster Park, the main first-class ground in Christchurch until it was damaged irreparably by the 2011 earthquake. Having been played there spasmodically until 1921, first-class cricket has returned to the Oval on a more regular basis in recent years.

Twenty-six wickets fell on a first day played in bright sunshine before a small crowd. English-born Moss would not have felt alone: three players on each side had been born 'back home', and in fact only seven had been born in New Zealand, the remainder coming from Australia (6), Scotland (2) and Fiji (1). Canterbury batted first, 20-year-old Andrew Labatt top scoring with 47. Moss, going in last, began his brief first-class career with a duck to give Charles Dryden his seventh wicket, to which he would add another five in Canterbury's second innings. (Some sources describe Dryden as a leg-spinner, others as bowling medium pace). As Moss would only score 13 runs in eight first-class innings, nought wasn't a bad score.

Getting considerable lift from a pitch still affected by overnight rain, Moss then began to demolish the Wellington innings. The Wellington team wasn't used to making big scores. Between them the eleven played 144 first-class matches, accumulating fewer than 3,000 runs, with no centuries. Also there was a suggestion that the journey to the match had left some of the team still suffering from the effects of seasickness. First to go was their Australian-born captain William Salmon, caught by Scottish-born wicketkeeper George Marshall. (Marshall only kept occasionally and, according to Mike Batty's article about Moss's feat in *The Cricket Statistician 143*, the contemporary press referred to him as short-stop). Robert Blacklock joined younger brother Arthur, but not for long, and after that a steady procession of single figure dismissals left the visitors 28 for six. It might have been worse. The younger Blacklock was missed by George Rayner at long leg off Charles Garrard with only two wickets down (and so of course an all-ten might only have been a nine-for), and Moss dropped Edgar Brooke, an easy chance, off his own bowling. Brooke eventually misjudged a Moss slower ball and was caught at mid on by Canterbury captain Edward Cotterill before an aggressive seventh wicket partnership of 29 between William McGirr and Alexander Littlejohn at least provided some resistance. In the circumstances McGirr's 20 was a considerable achievement given that he had had to bat with a runner (Robert Blacklock), having strained a ligament while bowling. He lived long enough to see his son Herb play two Test matches against Harold Gilligan's 1929/30 MCC tourists. At 38 years 101 days Herb still remains New Zealand's oldest Test debutant.

Once McGirr left, well caught at slip by Edward Barnes, Moss quickly polished off the tail, Sydney Nicholls falling to another well disguised slower ball, William Ogier and Henry Wallace to yorkers. Moss's figures were the cheapest all-ten to date, and might have been even better had he not had three catches dropped.

Canterbury, 94 for six overnight, quickly lost their last four wickets next morning to leave Wellington 179 to win. In a 24-match first-class career lasting 30 years Canterbury number seven Thomas (T.W.) Reese scored only 374 runs and took no wickets. He was however a very good fielder (he probably had to be) and did a great service to cricket by compiling two substantial histories covering New Zealand cricket between 1841 and 1933. The pitch had improved but although McGirr (31) again provided late order resistance the visitors were beaten by 39 runs. This time Frederick Harman (five for 43), another first-class debutant, did the damage but it was Moss (three for 44) who set the ball rolling by taking three of the first four wickets to fall, all bowled.

Moss played three more matches that season and then (apart from one appearance as an umpire a year later, coincidentally in a Wellington-Canterbury match) never appeared on a first-class cricket field again. He had taken 26 wickets at 11 apiece, 25 of which were taken before he eventually scored his maiden first-class run! The reasons for the brevity of Moss's career seem to be related to personal rather than cricketing issues. The main problem seemed to be gambling, although drink was apparently also involved.

His life went downhill. In 1891 he was tried for wounding his wife with intent to murder. He was found not guilty on the grounds of insanity and remanded for nearly five years before being deported to South America. He later went to South Africa where, although he found work, he was still troubled and unable to settle. Divorced from Mary, he had decided to end his life in the waters of Cape Town docks. Fortunately, he remembered seeing a Salvation Army premises in the city and sought their help. He joined the Army and eventually became a probationary-lieutenant.

Meanwhile Mary was teaching in New Zealand. When Moss had taken his all-ten the ball had been mounted and presented to him. It was a treasured possession and Mary now had it. In the context of the sadness of a broken marriage the ball was to be of major significance again in Moss's life. Mary was on a walking holiday at the beginning of the First World War, when a piece of paper blew against her leg. It was from the Salvation Army magazine *War Cry* and picking it up she noticed that, remarkably, it included a reference to the work of a Captain Albert Moss. Could this be her ex-husband? Mary made enquiries and found out that it was. In autumn 1915 Moss was working at a Salvation Army farm when a parcel arrived for him containing the ball and a note from Mary. This led to reconciliation and remarriage. Three years later the couple moved back to England where sadly Mary predeceased him, dying in 1928. Moss passed away in 1945 in Essex, a well-respected member of the Salvation Army.

Sammy Woods

Cambridge University v CI Thornton's XI, 1890

FP Fenner's Ground, Cambridge on 12, 13 May 1890 (3-day match)
Toss won by CI Thornton's XI
Cambridge University won by four wickets
Umpires: RP Carpenter, A Millward
CI Thornton's XI 68 (EC Streatfeild 5-41, SMJ Woods 5-19) and 133 (SMJ Woods 10-69); Cambridge University 130 (J Briggs 5-63) and 73-6

CI Thornton's XI second innings

*CI Thornton	b Woods	0
J Briggs	c Woods	19
TC O'Brien	c MacGregor b Woods	7
CJM Fox	b Woods	0
HW Forster	c Woods	0
W Wright	c Woods	0
AJ Webbe	b Woods	35
GF Vernon	c Gosling b Woods	8
PJ de Paravicini	c and b Woods	44
+J Carlin	not out	10
AW Mold	b Woods	2
Extras	(b 6, lb 1, nb 1)	8
Total	(all out, 69 overs)	133

Fall of wickets 1-0, 2-16, 3-16, 4-20, 5-20, 6-29, 7-39, 8-102, 9-131, 10-133

Cambridge University bowling : EC Streatfeild 20-7-32-0, SMJ Woods 31-6-69-10, DLA Jephson 18-8-24-0

Cambridge University: GH Cotterill, RN Douglas, RC Gosling, RAA Beresford, FS Jackson, G MacGregor (wk), H Hale, EC Streatfeild, SMJ Woods (capt), AJL Hill, DLA Jephson

Len Braund, Arthur Wellard, Ian Botham, Viv Richards and others, Somerset cricket has taken many non-natives to its heart, but probably none more so than fast-bowling allrounder Sammy Woods. Taunton was said to be in mourning when he died in 1931, crowds lining the route to his last resting place near the County Ground.

Born in Sydney in 1867 and sent to England to complete his education, his cricketing performances at Brighton College earned him a first-class debut for G.N. Wyatt's XI against the 1886 Australians. It was a career that would last until 1910. Soon afterwards he moved to Somerset which, apart from a spell at Cambridge and Army service during the First World War, was to be home for the rest of his life.

Woods entered Cambridge University in 1888, his qualifications being social and sporting rather than academic. Two seasons later he was captain of cricket. The first match of the season was against C.I. Thornton's XI. Thornton was one of Victorian cricket's great personalities: a mighty hitter, he originated the Scarborough Cricket Festival, was a Blue in all his four years at Cambridge, and was twice bowled by Samuel Butler in the match in which Butler took his famous all-ten. His eleven played an annual match against Cambridge until the turn of the century. He had assembled a reasonably strong team with seven amateurs to do the batting, a professional to keep wicket and three more to bowl. (At the end of the season Johnny Briggs, Arthur Mold and Walter Wright would be among the season's top ten wicket-takers.) *Wisden* commented that some of the batsmen were likely out of practice; unsurprising given that the season had only just started. *Wisden* thought that the 1890 Cambridge eleven was the best for at least a decade. Five of the side at Fenner's were making their first-class debuts, including the redoubtable F.S.Jackson, Ledger Hill who would go on to score a Test century, and Digby Jephson who would take six for 21 bowling lobs for the Gentlemen against a strong Players' side at Lord's in 1899.

On a damp pitch 26 wickets fell on the first day. The visitors' first innings lasted for just an hour and a half, Woods taking five for 19 and the medium pace first-class debutant Edward Streatfeild five for 41. The tall Charterhouse-educated Streatfeild would play in all four University matches between 1890 and 1893 (and also obtain two soccer Blues). Cambridge replied with 130. Woods hadn't yet shown much indication that he would go on to be a useful batsman and was stumped for a duck by Nottinghamshire's John Carlin off Briggs. Carlin had a curious career. For most of it he played a handful of matches each season, sometimes keeping wicket, and then finished with two fairly full seasons at the start of the 20th century. Wicketkeeper Gregor MacGregor top scored with 36. Not yet 21 he was already a Scottish rugby international and would make his England cricket debut later in the season.

Thornton's XI began their second innings disastrously, Woods quickly bowling Thornton for a duck. Briggs though showed some resistance. An outstanding slow left-arm spinner, the first bowler to take 100 Test wickets, he could bat a bit and had a Test hundred to his name. However, he left just before the close, which came with the score 29 for six. By the early 1890s Woods was at his peak as the most successful amateur bowler of the time. He was a fearsome proposition: over six feet tall, well-built, bowling fast with a deadly yorker and a deceptive slower ball, and apart from a catch by MacGregor, fearlessly standing up, he hadn't so far needed any other help in disposing of the opposing batsmen.

It was traditional at Cambridge for the captain to entertain the opposition, and on the second morning Thornton and the other amateurs sat down to the perhaps dubious pleasure of a lobster and beer breakfast (although more traditional fare was also available). Perhaps not surprisingly after such a start to the day, the visitors quickly lost George Vernon when play began. Vernon was also a rugby international as well as having played one Test. A Cambridge victory seemed imminent. However a partnership of 63 between Middlesex captain Alexander Webbe and county colleague Percy de Paravicini, who compensated for a first-innings duck by making the highest score of the match, meant that Cambridge would be left a tricky target. De Paravicini (Old Etonians) would later gain three England soccer caps, some consolation for a centuryless 121-match first-class career. Last man in Arthur Mold was a fine bowler, albeit with a suspect action, who twice took nine wickets in an innings during the season. However he was no batsman, and Woods soon had his all-ten. Cambridge struggled to get the 72 they needed to win before a cool 19 not out by debutant Jackson, foreshadowing greater things to come, saw them home by four wickets.

Woods' innings and match figures (fifteen for 88) are still Cambridge records and he is still the only bowler who has taken an all-ten at Fenner's. One or two have got close since, notably Fred Titmus who took the University's first nine second innings wickets in 1962 before (very) occasional leg-spinner Bob Gale caught and bowled the last man.

For both Thornton and de Paravicini it was the third match involving an all-ten in which they had participated. For umpire Robert Carpenter, having played in the matches in which Lillywhite, Wootton and Walker achieved a full house, it was a fourth.

In all matches for Cambridge between 1888 and 1891 Woods took 190 wickets, a total exceeded by only three other bowlers. He had been an immediate success there, and such was his impact that in his first season he was selected for the Gentlemen against the Players and for the touring Australians, including in all three Tests. Eight years later in South Africa he would play another three Tests, this time for England.

Woods' last University Match in 1891 was appropriately dramatic. Cambridge were left just 90 to win, but struggled in poor light and when he went in the score was 89 for eight. Not expecting to bat, he was without pads or gloves. He ran from the Lord's pavilion to the Nursery End, ran out to the first ball, and drove it to the long on boundary. It was a fitting end to a glittering career which also included three rugby Blues (but no degree!).

Woods' qualification to play for Somerset was perhaps a little tenuous, although this was also to be true of a number of future Somerset heroes. He became one of the pillars of the side, scoring over 12,000 runs and taking nearly 600 wickets. As his powers as a bowler declined his batting prospered. His natural game was aggressive, his reach enabling him to drive the ball hard on both sides of the pitch. Appointed captain in 1894 many rated his leadership of a constantly changing side over a 12-year period very highly. For most of his tenure he was also a paid joint-secretary, a not uncommon arrangement. For Woods, it was really just a way of ensuring that he stayed with Somerset; it is unlikely he did much secretarial work.

Woods was naturally gifted at many sports, achieving particular success at rugby playing 13 times for England as a wing forward. He never married, had a proper job, or his own home (usually staying with one of many friends or taking a room in a pub or hotel). His death in 1931 came a few days after his 64th birthday.

Tom Richardson

Surrey v Essex, 1894

Kennington Oval, Kennington on 18, 19, 20 June 1894 (3-day match)
Toss won by Essex
Surrey won by an innings and 261 runs
Umpires: J Lillywhite, RA Thoms
Essex 72 (T Richardson 10-45) and 105 (T Richardson 5-50); Surrey 438 (W Brockwell 108)

Essex first innings

J Burns	c Marshall b Richardson	9
HA Carpenter	b Richardson	0
HGP Owen	b Richardson	5
H Hailey	b Richardson	3
RJ Burrell	b Richardson	31
+TM Russell	b Richardson	0
CP McGahey	b Richardson	1
*AP Lucas	b Richardson	5
CJ Kortright	c Hayward b Richardson	5
W Mead	b Richardson	11
H Pickett	not out	1
Extras	(lb 1)	1
Total	(all out, 30.3 overs)	72

Fall of wickets 1-0, 2-13, 3-14, 4-27, 5-33, 6-47, 7-54, 8-55, 9-67, 10-72

Surrey bowling : T Richardson 15.3-3-45-10, FE Smith 13-4-22-0, AE Street 2-0-4-0

Surrey: R Abel, JM Read, TW Hayward, W Brockwell, DLA Jephson, R Henderson, AE Street, GW Ayres, FE Smith, C Marshall (wk), T Richardson

Born in Byfleet, Surrey in 1870 of Romany stock, and learning his cricket on Mitcham's famous Common, Tom Richardson was England's first great fast bowler. He took 2,104 first-class wickets, many of them on shirtfront Oval pitches, and with only one ball available per innings. Over six feet tall, with a good physique, his strengths were great stamina, relentless accuracy and the ability to bring the ball back sharply from the off. He kept the ball up, never trying to intimidate. Early in his career there had been concerns about the fairness of his action. Fortunately, if he did throw, the problem seems to have been remedied quickly. How fast was he? Contemporaries Clem Hill, the great Australian batsman, and Richardson's Surrey bowling partner Bill Lockwood both saw Harold Larwood bowl and thought the Surrey man quicker. Maybe they were being unduly loyal to the past, but Richardson was clearly fairly swift.

Surrey were the team of the 1890s, winning the Championship six times, whilst Essex had only been granted first-class status for the first time in 1894 and their matches did not count for the Championship until the following year. They were captained by ex-Surrey batsman Alfred 'Bunny' Lucas who played five Tests including the first one in England at The Oval in 1880 and the famous Oval Ashes Test two years later. Surrey were in the midst of a good run that was to see them regain the Championship from Yorkshire. Essex on the other hand, in the words of *Wisden*, 'had a most disastrous season' and their only win was against a weakened Oxford University side.

Richardson was a relative newcomer to the Surrey side. 1893 had been his first full season. It had been an impressive start with 174 first-class wickets, and he maintained this form in 1894 taking 91 wickets in just nine matches before the Essex match. With nine for 47 the previous season against Yorkshire he had already been close to an all-ten, but unfortunately the ninth wicket (George Hirst) fell to Bill Brockwell. By 1894 The Oval had become a major sporting venue, hosting many other sports outside summer, including rugby, hockey, lacrosse and particularly football. With one exception, every FA Cup Final until 1892 was played there by which time the attendance had reached 33,000. The match was clearly outgrowing the venue, but in any case the Committee decided that given the damage football caused to the turf it should be discontinued. *Wisden* commended groundsman Sam Apted for the condition of the ground which was now better than it had been for several years. 'Upwards of £1,300' had been spent on levelling and returfing the ground towards the Vauxhall End, one benefit of which had been an improvement in Surrey's outfielding.

It had rained overnight and the weather was still poor on a severely curtailed first day of the Essex match. One of the umpires was James Lillywhite who had taken all-ten at Canterbury 22 years before. Six of the Essex side were amateurs, whereas Surrey's captain Digby Jephson was their only amateur. Some of the Essex side had their better days ahead of them. A much loved character, in 400 matches Charles McGahey would make some 19,000 runs for the county, and finish his days as Essex scorer. Opener Herbert Carpenter would eventually make 22 centuries for the county, the first of which would come against Surrey, Richardson et al, the following season. He came from good cricketing stock: his father Robert Carpenter had been one of umpire Lillywhite's ten victims and his nephew Jack O'Connor would make nearly 28,000 runs for Essex. Wicketkeeper Thomas Russell also had cricket in his blood, relatives including son Jack (C.A.G.), the first Englishman to score two hundreds in a Test, and cousin Tich (Freeman), who would take three all-tens for Kent between the Wars, including one against Essex.

Lucas won the toss and chose to bat. When rain stopped play at 1.15 with the score 55 for eight he might have wondered if he had made the right decision. Having taken eight for 32 from his 13 overs Richardson probably lunched happily. Although the wet conditions would have made the run up difficult for him, the soft pitch had probably given his off cutter more purchase and helped him hit the stumps six times so far, and induce Russell to play on. Play resumed at 3.25 and the 15 minutes that the weather allowed was just enough for Richardson to take the last two wickets, the final one being fellow fast bowler Charles Kortright who was well caught by Tom Hayward running in from third man. The Essex innings had been a procession lasting just an hour and a quarter,

Richardson bowling unchanged for his ten for 45, a county record which stood until 1921.

The only batsman who provided any resistance was John Burrell who scored 31 in three quarters of an hour before losing his middle stump with the score 54 for seven. This was 23-year-old Burrell's second first-class match and his performance hinted at a promising career. However, it was not to be: ten matches would produce just 200 runs.

Surrey, starting their innings in better conditions the next day, passed the Essex total before losing a wicket and, led by Bill Brockwell with 108, rattled up 438. This was a good performance against a decent Essex attack: Charles Kortright was thought to be the fastest bowler of his day, and by some as the fastest ever; only four bowlers have beaten Walter Mead's 1,472 wickets for the county; and Harry Pickett was to take his own all-ten the following season (although perhaps surprisingly he only bowled 14 out of 164 overs in the Surrey innings). Essex didn't do much better second time around, Richardson taking another five wickets to finish with match figures of 15 for 95. This was the first of five times that Richardson took fifteen wickets in a match, a number unequalled by any fast bowler, and exceeded by few of any pace. Top-scorer this time was Kortright whose 34 included a few lusty hits against the lobs of Digby Jephson, before Richardson had him caught in the deep by Maurice Read.

1894 was the start of an astonishing run that saw Richardson take 1,005 wickets in four successive home seasons. He also had a short, but brilliant, Test career: in only 14 matches, all against Australia, he took 88 wickets at 25.22 apiece. He averaged a wicket every 51 balls. To put this into perspective, playing in the next decade, the great Sidney Barnes' strike rate against Australia was 54.

Unfortunately because of overwork some of Richardson's fire and stamina had left him by the end of the decade. He was a very good bowler for a few years, but no longer a great one, and after a few matches at the beginning of 1904 he slipped quietly out of the side. His 1,775 wickets for Surrey has never been exceeded. He became a publican in Kingston, and then in Bath. He had been offered the chance of qualifying for Somerset but played for them just once, unsuccessfully, against the 1905 Australians and the West Country venture fell through. Returning to Surrey in 1907 he became a publican on Richmond Green. At the end of June 1912 he travelled to France for a short holiday. He collapsed and died there suddenly on 2 July while climbing a rocky path. Earlier suggestions that he committed suicide have been proved unfounded. The Gentlemen v Players match at The Oval was suspended for 20 minutes on the afternoon of his funeral.

Harry Pickett

Essex v Leicestershire, 1895
County Championship

County Ground, Leyton on 3, 4, 5 June 1895 (3-day match)
Leicestershire won by 75 runs
Umpires: W Clements, H Draper
Leicestershire 111 (H Pickett 10-32) and 190 (CJ Kortright 8-63); Essex 103
(AD Pougher 5-29, A Woodcock 5-53) and 123 (A Woodcock 7-62)

Leicestershire first innings

M Chapman	b Pickett	14
J Holland	c Russell b Pickett	1
W Tomlin	b Pickett	9
AD Pougher	c Russell b Pickett	10
CC Stone	b Pickett	0
*CE de Trafford	c Kortright b Pickett	29
F Geeson	c Mead b Pickett	4
D Lorimer	b Pickett	0
A Woodcock	b Pickett	20
JH King	not out	12
+JP Whiteside	b Pickett	7
Extras	(lb 5)	5
Total	(all out, 54 overs)	111

Fall of wickets 1-2, 2-16, 3-18, 4-35, 5-67, 6-71, 7-71, 8-76, 9-99, 10-111

Essex bowling : W Mead 21-4-50-0, H Pickett 27-11-32-10, CJ Kortright
6-2-24-0

Essex: HGP Owen (capt), HA Carpenter, GF Higgins, CP McGahey, H Hailey,
AP Lucas, J Burns, TM Russell (wk), CJ Kortright, W Mead, H Pickett

Henry (Harry) Pickett took 114 wickets for Essex in 52 first-class
appearances, a modest haul. However, in a career which lasted from
1881 until 1897, in all matches for Essex (which only became a first-class
county in 1894) he took over 700 wickets. Stocky and of average height he
bowled fast-medium off a short 12-step run-up. He was a significant figure
in the formative years of the county club. The official history says that
'he symbolises all that became good in Essex cricket. He was the honest
workman, the bread-and-butter cricketer upon whom success is founded'.
And a major county record that is going to be very difficult to beat still
stands to his name.

Pickett was born in Stratford, Essex (now part of Greater London) in 1862.
His performances for local clubs soon brought him to the attention of
the county and he made his debut for them in 1881. He quickly became
established, and his success also led to his engagement by MCC, for whom
he made his first-class debut at Lord's against Sussex in 1884.

Just a word about Pickett's batting. In 94 first-class innings he averaged
just over eight (an average inflated by a high number of not outs). However,

on a remarkable first day at Southampton in June 1891 in which over 500 runs were scored, he partnered Charles Kortright (158) in an eighth wicket stand of 244, making 114 in only 90 minutes. Pickett's success was unexpected, albeit it was in a non-first-class match. Unfortunately, after this innings, double figures generally continued to be a good score for him.

Pickett's all-ten might never have happened. He seemed to be coming towards the end of his county career and in 1894 he was 'an utter failure', taking just 11 wickets. But he was still in the team the following season, and started in slightly better form. Even so his performance in the match at the county headquarters, Leyton in East London, against Leicestershire must have caused some surprise. Leicestershire, like Essex, were appearing in the Championship for the first time in 1895 and had started the season well, including a win over eventual Champions Surrey at The Oval.

Leyton was never a lovely ground, but it was an interesting one with, eventually, an impressive pavilion. In the winter it was put to other uses, and three months previously had even hosted a Football League match, Woolwich Arsenal's Manor Ground having been closed following a crowd disturbance. (Some 4,000 spectators saw a 3-3 draw with Leicester Fosse.) The Leicestershire match was the 11th first-class match to be played at Leyton. The ground would eventually host 412 matches, the last in 1977. Essex were now captained by Hugh Owen. In 1894 he had become the first batsman to score a first-class fifty, and later in the season a century, for the county.

Twenty-one wickets fell on the first day. Leicestershire batted first in front of a Whitsun Bank Holiday crowd which was to reach a then near-record 8,000. Opening the bowling at the pavilion end Pickett found the fast pitch to his liking and in two hours, bowling unchanged, dismissed the visitors for 111. He was playing in his 19th first-class match, and had never taken more than four wickets in an innings before (although he had taken eight in an innings three times for the county in non-first-class matches). Leicestershire were not a strong batting side; only one batsman, William Tomlin, made a century for them during the season, which makes it even more remarkable that Walter Mead and Kortright were incapable of getting even one wicket at the other end. A spontaneous collection round the ground for the popular Pickett realised £20.

Pickett's analysis is one of the longest-standing county bowling records. Only the Lancashire innings record, set by Hickton in 1870, has greater longevity (although Tyler set the current Somerset record later in 1895). Pickett's figures have only been bettered three times in the Championship. Mark Ilott came close to beating Pickett's Essex record when he took nine for 19 against Northamptonshire at Luton exactly 100 years later, and Stan Nichols came close to equalling it in 1936 with nine for 32 against Nottinghamshire, the other wicket falling to a run-out. The only other all-ten for Essex was achieved by Trevor Bailey in 1949, but his wickets cost 90 runs.

Leicestershire's top-scorer, captain Charles de Trafford, was a famed hitter who seldom wore batting gloves and who captained the county from 1890 to 1906. Leicestershire's elevation to first-class status was mainly due to his drive and enthusiasm. On the other hand another specialist batsman Charles Stone, who was in the middle of a run (spread over two seasons) of six consecutive innings that yielded one run, completed the first half of a pair. The one batsman who evaded Pickett was 24-year-old left-hand allrounder John King who was making his first-class debut. Thirty years later he played the last of his 502 matches for the county, by which time he had scored nearly 23,000 runs (including a double-century against Hampshire at the age of 52) and taken 1,100 wickets for them. Pickett hit the stumps six times. The other wickets fell to catches, two of which were taken by wicketkeeper Tom Russell, whose pair later in the match followed a duck in his previous innings, against Middlesex.

Essex failed to pass Leicestershire's meagre score and the visitors were batting again by the end of the first day, losing an early wicket to Pickett. Despite Kortright's eight wickets they did better second time around and Essex were left 199 to win. De Trafford (44) again batted well, but top-scorer was Mat Chapman whose obdurate 56 was the highest score of his 28-match career. Pickett took no further wickets in the Leicestershire second innings and *The Times* commented that 'he had nothing like the pitch and spin that he possessed in the first stages of the game'. On a far from perfect pitch Essex slumped to 98 for five by the close. The remaining wickets soon fell on the next day with the only resistance to fast bowler Arthur Woodcock (seven for 62, and twelve wickets in the match) being provided by Charles McGahey's 54. Despite Pickett's all-ten his team had lost by 75 runs.

After their good start to the season Leicestershire lost form and finished equal twelfth (out of 14) in the Championship. *Wisden* commented that 'it was a matter of common knowledge that there was a lack of discipline among the professionals'. Essex on the other hand, after their poor showing in 1894, performed creditably to finish equal sixth.

Pickett's 1895 renaissance was soon over. Overweight and in his mid-30s, his tally of wickets fell in the next two seasons and he was not even in the team for his benefit match against Hampshire at Leyton. A rain-affected match yielded only £150, although collections by schoolboys of the county resulted in him being presented with a timepiece and a miniature bat, ball and stumps in gold and silver.

After leaving Essex Pickett umpired two full seasons and then coached at Clifton College. His end was tragic. At the end of September 1907, nearly penniless and with several children to support, he disappeared from his home. His body was found on the beach at Aberavon, South Wales six days later. His wife died the following March. Tragically, Arthur Woodcock, who had bowled Leicestershire to victory in the match in which Pickett had taken his all-ten, also died by his own hand, taking poison in May 1910 at the age of 44.

Edwin Tyler

Somerset v Surrey, 1895
County Championship

County Ground, Taunton on 22, 23, 24 August 1895 (3-day match)
Toss won by Somerset
Somerset won by 53 runs
Umpires: WF Collishaw, J Wickens
Somerset 168 (T Richardson 6-85) and 141 (T Richardson 7-67); Surrey 139
(EJ Tyler 10-49) and 117

Surrey first innings

R Abel	c Hedley b Tyler	34
JM Read	c Hedley b Tyler	21
TW Hayward	c Palairet b Tyler	34
W Brockwell	b Tyler	4
FC Holland	c Dunlop b Tyler	13
*WW Read	b Tyler	8
WH Lockwood	not out	11
HDG Leveson Gower	lbw b Tyler	0
GA Lohmann	c and b Tyler	0
+ C Marshall	c Newton b Tyler	6
T Richardson	b Tyler	4
Extras	(b 4)	4
Total	(all out, 69.3 overs)	139

Fall of wickets 1-44, 2-69, 3-93, 4-99, 5-113, 6-123, 7-123, 8-123, 9-135, 10-139

Somerset bowling : SMJ Woods 18-7-44-0, EJ Tyler 34.3-15-49-10, GB Nichols 14-4-28-0, WC Hedley 3-1-14-0

Somerset: LCH Palairet, G Fowler, WN Roe, CE Dunlop, WC Hedley, SMJ Woods (capt), WRR Smith, GB Nichols, AE Newton (wk), AH Westcott, EJ Tyler

Ted Tyler was a six-foot tall, very slow left-arm bowler. Tossing the ball high into the air, his clever flighting of the ball at a time when slow bowlers often bowled with a long on and long off lured many batsmen to their doom. In the fashion of the time as a slow bowler he usually opened the attack. Born in 1864 in Kidderminster Tyler played for his home county Worcestershire before joining the Somerset groundstaff, playing for Taunton while qualifying. He quickly established himself as a mainstay of the side and his bowling contributed greatly to Somerset's elevation to first-class status in 1891.

Tyler was calmly impervious to punishment. He had to be: in July 1895 he was the first bowler to concede 200 runs in a Championship innings when he took five for 215 against Essex, and in his next match he took one for 212 whilst Archie MacLaren made 424 for Lancashire. But he didn't spend all summer watching the ball disappear into the churchyard outside the Taunton ground, and the all-ten he took later in the season would have been consolation for this week of slaughter. It came towards the end of August against eventual Champions Surrey. Heavily reliant upon amateurs, Somerset often had difficulties in putting their best side out. Apart from Tyler the only other professional who played regularly was George Nichols, a hardworking fast-medium bowler who later went into business with Tyler, and also wrote plays. Somerset had started the season badly, but then redeemed themselves by winning five successive matches during August. Despite enduring a few hammerings Tyler had been taking wickets consistently.

A homely ground close to the centre of Taunton, the County Ground has hosted first-class cricket since 1882. Dominated by church towers at one end and the Quantock Hills at the other, it is one of the most attractive grounds on the circuit. It had originally had a cinder athletics track but, as part of ongoing development, by the 1890s this had been covered over.

Surrey needed to win to hold off Lancashire's challenge for the Championship. Earlier in the season they had comfortably beaten Somerset by nine wickets at The Oval (Tyler bowling 27 wicketless overs). Unlike Somerset the Surrey side was based on its professionals and the only amateurs at Taunton were Walter Read (standing in for Kingsmill Key as captain) and 'Shrimp' Leveson Gower. Somerset's first innings had been notable for a typically elegant 64 (the only fifty in the match) by Lionel Palairet against a powerful Surrey attack of Tom Richardson, George Lohmann and Bill Lockwood (albeit that Lohmann was just returning to the side having missed two seasons because of ill health and Lockwood was suffering a temporary loss of form). There was a good attendance and 'much enthusiasm was shown'.

Reaching 93 for two thanks to consistent contributions from Bobby Abel, Tom Hayward and Maurice Read, Surrey's response began well and a healthy lead looked likely. However after they were all caught off Tyler nobody stayed long and at the close they were 135 for eight. Both openers had been caught at mid off by Coote Hedley, a career soldier and useful fast-medium bowler, whose action was however under some suspicion. Abel had let Somerset off lightly. Four years later at The Oval he would carry his bat for a Surrey record 357 (out of 811). It was a match that Tyler was probably glad to miss. Curiously although Abel would make 74 first-class centuries, it was the only one he made in 28 matches against Somerset. 24-year-old Hayward had not yet scored 1,000 runs in a season (he was eventually to do so twenty times) but his promise had been noticed and he would make his Test debut the following winter in South Africa.

Tyler's overnight figures were eight for 45. Next morning he quickly had Surrey keeper Charles Marshall caught by his counterpart Arthur Newton and then bowled Tom Richardson. He had bowled unchanged. At the other end Sammy Woods, who of course already had an all-ten to his name, bowled 18 unrewarded overs. As his batting advanced he was not now the bowler he had once been.

Tyler's figures are still a Somerset record. As six of the Surrey side made centuries during the season and three would make Test centuries it was a considerable feat. A collection made for him on the ground produced over £35. Only one other bowler, J.C. White, another slow left–armer, has ever taken an all-ten for Somerset.

Richardson added another seven second innings Somerset wickets to the six he had taken in the first and Surrey were left 171 to win. Several Surrey batsmen reached double figures but none stayed long enough to enable their side to get close as Tyler took three more wickets. With three run-outs, including Abel (the season's top run-scorer apart from Grace), Surrey hadn't helped their cause.

Taking 14 Yorkshire wickets in the next match, Tyler passed 100 wickets for the third and final time in his career, finishing the season with 124 wickets in all matches; although they did cost 22.58 runs each, making him the most expensive of all the 15 bowlers who took 100 wickets in 1895. His efforts largely contributed to the county achieving a very creditable equal eighth place in the Championship. His reward was a trip to South Africa with Lord Hawke's team. Unsuited to the pitches, and handicapped by poor health, Tyler had a poor tour. He played in the Third Test, acquitting himself creditably with four wickets, but competition was too great for him ever to be picked again for England.

Unfortunately, Tyler had a doubtful action, likened by some to an athlete putting the shot. There were a number of other suspect bowlers playing around the turn of the century. Eventually umpires began to act and Tyler was one of a number called. The deed was done on 27 August 1900 towards the end the first day of the Surrey match at Taunton. Australian James Phillips, a fearless umpire who had already called Australian Ernie Jones in a Test, no-balled Tyler twice early in the Surrey innings. Walter Wright, the other umpire, disagreed with Phillips and in the second over in which no-ball was called refused to allow an extra delivery. There was much indignation that a professional who bowled too slowly to hurt anybody should be called, although others thought that slow bowlers shouldn't be exempt. Strangely Tyler bowled again next day coming on for just one ball at the end of the Surrey innings and dismissing Tom Richardson. His figures for the innings were one for 6 from 2.1 overs. He didn't bowl in the second innings and that was more or less the end of his career. He played a few matches unsuccessfully in 1901 and 1903. A last comeback at the end of 1907 was a little more successful. The team was short of bowling and he started with innings figures of nine for 83 against Sussex and six for 157 against Middlesex, but after that his season petered out and *Wisden* commented that 'for the most part his slows looked very harmless'. He finished his career with 895 wickets at an average of 22.09.

Although his cricket career finished early Tyler was already an entrepreneur with many other means of income including as a sports outfitter, tobacconist, insurance agent, travel agent and publican. And at Taunton School he coached Somerset's most successful ever bowler, J.C. White. A popular man, he died at Taunton in 1917 aged only 52.

Bill Howell

Australians v Surrey, 1899

Kennington Oval, Kennington on 15, 16, 17 May 1899 (3-day match)
Toss won by Surrey
Australians won by an innings and 71 runs
Umpires: RG Barlow, W Richards
Surrey 114 (WP Howell 10-28) and 64 (H Trumble 5-34, WP Howell 5-29);
Australians 249

Surrey first innings

R Abel	b Howell	22
W Brockwell	b Howell	29
EG Hayes	b Howell	12
DLA Jephson	c Darling b Howell	16
TW Hayward	b Howell	16
HB Richardson	b Howell	5
FC Holland	c and b Howell	2
*KJ Key	not out	4
HP Clode	b Howell	0
T Richardson	b Howell	2
+C Marshall	b Howell	0
Extras	(b 6)	6
Total	(all out, 60.2 overs)	114

Fall of wickets 1-39, 2-59, 3-80, 4-81, 5-99, 6-107, 7-108, 8-108, 9-110, 10-114

Australians bowling : MA Noble 7-1-25-0, H Trumble 22-8-44-0, WP Howell 23.2-14-28-10, CE McLeod 8-4-11-0

Australians: J Darling (capt), J Worrall, C Hill, SE Gregory, MA Noble, FA Iredale, VT Trumper, WP Howell, JJ Kelly (wk), CE McLeod, H Trumble

Bill Howell was a well-built Australian beekeeper who bowled at a brisk medium pace, cutting the ball sharply both ways. His sharply spun off break would grip even on the hardest Australian wickets. He was also a powerful left-hand hitter who occasionally produced something special. Born in New South Wales in 1869, he was the nephew of Edwin Evans who played six times for Australia (and provided Howell with 17 cousins!). Howell made his first-class debut for New South Wales against A.E. Stoddart's tourists in November 1894 having been spotted playing in the NSW Country Week. Picked as a batsman he made his mark as a bowler. Apparently his captain didn't know that the newcomer could bowl until Howell told him that he could dismiss the well-set Stoddart and John Brown. Coming on sixth change he did just that, bowling both, and three others, to take five for 44. He soon cemented his place in the side and was a regular for the next ten years.

Many thought that the 1899 Australian side was the best to tour England since 1882. (Umpire Dick Barlow who played in the famous Oval Test that year was in a good position to judge.) They would win the Test series one-nil, the second of four successive series victories. They had begun their tour with a number of matches in London, having the best of a draw against a strong South of England team at the Crystal Palace but then surprisingly losing to Essex at Leyton. Howell had not played in either match because of leg strain.

There was a crowd of about 8,000 at The Oval for their third match, some of whom sat in the impressive new £38,000 pavilion. Bobby Abel and Bill Brockwell opened the batting for Surrey on a soft pitch made relatively easy by rain which had prevented play until 1 pm and would threaten all day. Forty-one-year-old Abel was then one of the most prolific batsmen in the game and, apart from Ranjitsinhji, would be the season's highest run-scorer, whilst Brockwell had started the season well having already made two Championship centuries. The Australians' attack was opened by Monty Noble and Hugh Trumble. In 74 Tests these two Australian greats would take 262 wickets between them, but neither could make a breakthrough and with the score 39 the Australian captain Joe Darling turned to Howell. With his first ball in England he bowled Abel. After that nobody mastered him as, bowling with great accuracy and varying his pace skilfully, he hit the stumps eight times. The early batsmen all reached double figures and at 99 for four things weren't going too badly. However, with the exception of Surrey captain Kingsmill Key, who at least remained undefeated, the batsmen who followed provided little resistance.

England's Tom Hayward could make little of Howell and would be dismissed by him cheaply in both innings. In the five Tests that followed however, Hayward would easily be England's leading batsman while Howell would take eight expensive wickets. Further down the order slow left-arm bowler Harry Clode who had been playing in the Second Eleven with some success was rewarded for his promotion to the first-class game with a debut duck. He was followed to the wicket by Tom Richardson and Charles Marshall. Four years previously they had been the last two wickets to fall when Somerset's Ted Tyler had taken his all-ten against Surrey. The same fate now befell them again.

Howell's figures are still the best ever for any Australian team, and have only been bettered four times in cricket history: a remarkable performance for somebody who had never before taken more than six wickets in an innings. Surrey had now been on the receiving end of three all-tens in the last 11 seasons and Bobby Abel had played in all three games (and also played when Richardson took one). Two members of the Surrey side, Frederick Holland and Harry Clode, would still be alive 57 years and a day later when a Yorkshireman famously turned the tables on the Australians by taking all ten of their wickets on the same ground.

The Australians passed the Surrey total just before the close of the first day for the loss of four wickets. Surrey had opened their bowling with the pace of Richardson and the spin of Clode, the debutant soon compensating for his duck by bowling the Australian captain Joe Darling. Although Richardson, who had taken an all-ten five years before, took three good wickets his powers were on the wane, *Wisden* pointing out that he had put on quite a lot of weight. Next day heavy rain after lunch sent the 6,000 crowd home having seen little play (or a glimpse of the Prince of Wales who had been due to arrive at 5 pm).

There was a smaller crowd on the last day but at least the weather had relented. Although only wicketkeeper James Kelly reached fifty a number of batsmen made useful contributions as the visitors gained a lead that would prove too much for Surrey. Having been bowled by Howell, Hayward at least had the satisfaction of inflicting the same fate on the Australian, one of his three wickets in the innings. Bowling medium-pace off breaks he was a useful bowler in his early years and would finish his career with nearly 500 wickets.

By now the pitch had become difficult and Surrey had little hope of saving the match against Howell (five for 29) and Trumble (five for 34) who bowled unchanged. Howell started the rout by bowling Abel again, this time with no runs on the board, and the innings became a procession: in an all-out total of 64 only Ernie Hayes with 43 scored more than seven. Twenty-two-year-old Hayes was to become a Surrey stalwart, scoring his maiden century in the later return match with the Australians (which Surrey won with Howell taking just two wickets while Trumble took thirteen). In 1926, while Leicestershire coach, Hayes returned to the first-class game after seven years away and was run out for 99 in his first match.

Although he underperformed in the five Tests Howell had a good tour, together with Trumble and fast bowler Ernest Jones taking over 100 wickets. His final Test record was relatively modest (49 wickets in 18 matches) but he was playing in the same side as a number of fine bowlers. He was very economical, but only took five wickets in an innings once (five for 81 against South Africa on Cape Town matting on the short tour made by the 1902 Australians on their way home). He also had match figures of 17 for 54 against Western Province on this same tour. 1899 was the first of his three tours to England. He started the 1902 tour well, taking another 11 wickets against Surrey. However, his form fell away, no doubt affected by the sad experience of receiving the news that his mother and father had died within days of each other. He played no Tests in 1905, and after one match on his return to Australia his first-class career was over. When he retired only the great Charles Turner, with 263, had exceeded his 195 wickets for the state.

Bill Howell died in 1940 in Castlereagh, Sydney aged 70. He had lived long enough to see his son William play 14 matches as a right-arm off-break bowler for New South Wales during the 1930s.

Cyril Bland

Sussex v Kent, 1899
County Championship

Angel Ground, Tonbridge 5, 6, 7 June 1899 (3-day match)
Toss won by Kent
Sussex won by 112 runs
Umpires: WB Clarke, T Mycroft
Kent 278 (EH Killick 6-44) and 114 (CHG Bland 10-48); Sussex 154 and 350
(WM Bradley 8-122)

Kent second innings

*JR Mason	c Butt b Bland	12
A Hearne	not out	55
CJ Burnup	b Bland	1
WH Patterson	c Butt b Bland	0
HC Stewart	b Bland	0
W Rashleigh	c Butt b Bland	0
GJV Weigall	c Butt b Bland	0
F Martin	b Bland	15
SW Brown	b Bland	0
+FH Huish	lbw b Bland	28
WM Bradley	b Bland	0
Extras	(b 1, nb 2)	3
Total	(all out, 58.2 overs)	114

Fall of wickets 1-19, 2-21, 3-21, 4-21, 5-25, 6-25, 7-67, 8-67, 9-114, 10-114

Sussex bowling : FW Tate 16-9-21-0, CHG Bland 25.2-9-48-10, GR Cox 3-1-10-0, EH Killick 10-0-26-0, KS Ranjitsinhji 4-1-6-0

Sussex: G Brann, WL Murdoch (capt), A Collins, GR Cox, CB Fry, KS Ranjitsinhji, EH Killick, W Newham, HR Butt (wk), FW Tate, CHG Bland

Cyril Bland had a brief but successful career claiming 557 wickets in seven years. A fast bowler of wiry build, he is one of only 11 bowlers to have taken 100 wickets in his debut season. He was born in Lincolnshire in 1872 but obtained a Sussex residential qualification whilst playing for Horsham and made his first-class debut for them in 1897.

Bottom of the Championship in 1896, Sussex came sixth the following season. *Wisden* gave most credit for this advance to their new fast bowler. However Bland could be expensive, for example taking one for 165 at Sheffield whilst Yorkshire scored 681 for 5 declared, including 311 by John Brown. (Two years later he again had the pleasure of bowling to a triple-centurion, taking one for 170 at Hove whilst Victor Trumper scored 300 not out for the Australians.) He also had the unusual experience of being substituted in the match against Lancashire at Hove. He had bowled three overs before being taken ill. Archie MacLaren then allowed Ernest Killick to replace him, a sporting act which however met with some disapproval.

Kent were a peripatetic side. In 1899 they played home matches at six different venues. The Angel Ground, Tonbridge, with three games, of which the two in June were part of the town's cricket week, was the most frequently used. It was to be used regularly until 1939 before financial problems, brought to a head by the War with money not available to repair damage caused by military occupation, led to an end to county cricket at the ground. Its great claim to fame is as the site of the nursery which provided many players for the great pre-war Kent teams as well as some who shone elsewhere.

The 1899 Kent team could best be described as middling, probably stronger in batting than bowling. By early June they were without a win. Sussex on the other hand had started well and would finish fifth in the Championship. Bland had taken eight for 65 at the Angel two years previously and was no doubt looking forward to his return.

Captained by Jack Mason, who opened the batting and was run out for one, Kent batted steadily on a good pitch to make 278 in their first innings, Bland taking two wickets. Sussex were a strong batting side. Australian opener and Sussex captain Billy Murdoch was the first batsman to make a Test double-century (although he was now 45 and in poor form), C.B.Fry would score over 2,000 runs in the season, and K.S. Ranjitsinhji would become the first batsman to score 3,000. Fry and Ranji had just returned from playing in the First Test at Trent Bridge where they had been the only England batsmen to make fifties. However, Sussex made only 154. It would probably have suited Kent to bat again, but the option of whether or not to enforce the follow-on was not available under contemporary regulations. Sussex improved in their second innings: Fry made 85, a number of other batsmen scored well, and even Bland made 12, his highest Championship score of the season in 27 innings! Amateur fast bowler Bill Bradley, playing his first full season, took eight for 122 (to add to his four first-innings wickets). Next month he would take a wicket with his first ball in Test cricket.

At 19 without loss, chasing 227, Kent had made a steady start. At 25 for six it was clear that they weren't going to win. Led by Alec Hearne, who carried his bat for 55, they recovered partially. A ninth wicket partnership of 47 between Hearne and wicketkeeper Fred Huish (the season's leading wicketkeeper with 79 victims) took the score to 114 for eight and Kent had some hope of holding on for a draw. After a short rest however Bland came back, had Huish leg-before for what was, in his fourth full season, his highest first-class score, then clean bowled Bradley and Sussex had won with about half an hour to spare. *Wisden* commented that Bland 'bowled at a great pace and made the ball kick a good deal'. He took six wickets without help from the field; his other victims were all caught by Harry Butt, still the only Sussex wicketkeeper with over 1,000 victims for the county. There had been six ducks in the Kent innings, including a second in the match for William Rashleigh, a master at Tonbridge School and a previous victim of a W.G.Grace all-ten. The Reverend Rashleigh was a useful batsman who made nine first-class centuries, the last of which came later in the season against Warwickshire at Catford ('a marvel of cleanness and power', *Wisden*). Another runless batsman, Stevens Brown, would have no further chance to redeem himself. He was playing for Kent for the last time, a three-match career having yielded three runs and five wickets.

Medium pacer Fred Tate who took over 100 wickets in the season had failed to strike at the other end, and Murdoch even gave Ranji a few overs. The great batsman had his moments with the ball, eventually taking 133 first-class wickets. A week later his slow bowling would take five Nottinghamshire first-innings wickets, and dismiss Arthur Shrewsbury, still a fine batsman, twice.

Bland's figures remain a Sussex record, although Ian Thomson would come close to beating them at Worthing in 1964. They are the best innings figures in 106 matches at the Angel. As the ground is now a shopping centre they are unlikely to be beaten. The admirable magazine *Cricket* gave a long report of the match. Whilst giving considerable prominence to the batting performances (or lack of them) in the match it devoted minimum space to two outstanding bowling performances: 'Mr Bradley bowled very finely' ... and 'Kent collapsed...before the bowling of Bland'.

Hearne's single-handed battle with Bland deserves a mention. He was the first batsman to carry his bat during an all-ten, a feat only achieved twice since. Hearne was a genuine allrounder: only he and Frank Woolley have scored over 10,000 runs and taken over 1,000 wickets for Kent. His county had their revenge later in the season, beating Sussex in the return at Hove. Bland took one wicket in the match. Ironically it was Alec Hearne, the only batsman to elude him at Tonbridge.

Bland's form began to decline in 1901, *Wisden* cryptically referring to his 'decadence', and by 1904 his county career was over. Why, after taking 431 wickets in four seasons, did his career fall away so quickly? Perhaps as an out-and-out fast bowler coming into the first-class game at a relatively late age he was never going to last long. Also there was some suspicion about his action, although he was never called.

He continued to play club and league cricket. CricketArchive records him as late as 1913 playing for Stourbridge as their professional in the Birmingham and District Cricket League. Returning to his native Lincolnshire, he served in the Army Veterinary Corps in the First World War, and was for a time cricket coach at RAF Cranwell. His life ended tragically. At the beginning of July 1950 he drowned himself in the Maud Foster Canal, not far from his Old Leake birthplace. A heavy drinker, he had made a previous suicide attempt.

Johnny Briggs

Lancashire v Worcestershire, 1900
County Championship

Old Trafford, Manchester 24, 25, 26 May 1900 (3-day match)
Toss won by Worcestershire
Lancashire won by five wickets
Umpires: A White, W Wright
Worcestershire 106 (J Briggs 10-55) and 253 (HK Foster 113); Lancashire
205 (GA Wilson 6-63) and 156-5

Worcestershire first innings

*HK Foster	b Briggs	0
FL Bowley	c Eccles b Briggs	5
EG Arnold	c MacLaren b Briggs	1
GF Wheldon	c Radcliffe b Briggs	25
WH Hill	b Briggs	12
AW Isaac	c MacLaren b Briggs	3
A Bird	b Briggs	32
GA Wilson	lbw b Briggs	0
RD Burrows	b Briggs	17
AF Bannister	c MacLaren b Briggs	0
+T Straw	not out	7
Extras	(b 3, lb 1)	4
Total	(all out, 57.5 overs)	106

Fall of wickets 1-4, 2-6, 3-6, 4-36, 5-44, 6-46, 7-46, 8-70, 9-74, 10-106

Lancashire bowling : AW Hallam 10-5-16-0, J Briggs 28.5-7-55-10, WR
Cuttell 9-3-14-0, AW Mold 10-3-17-0

Lancashire: AC MacLaren (capt), A Ward, JT Tyldesley, CR Hartley, WR
Cuttell, J Briggs, A Eccles, JS Sharp, AW Hallam, L Radcliffe (wk), AW Mold

Johnny Briggs had been playing first-class cricket for 21 years before he
finally took an all-ten. Sadly, 1900 was to be his last season: just over a
year and a half later he died at the age of 39. He had taken 2,221 wickets in
first-class cricket (a total exceeded at the time only by W.G.Grace) including
118 in Tests. Just 5ft 5ins tall, Briggs was an inventive, hardworking slow
left-arm bowler with an easy action. He bowled off a very short run-up, and
could get through an over in less than a minute. (Bowlers at the
other end might not have always appreciated such haste.) A popular and
enthusiastic cricketer, Briggs was the first bowler to take 100 Test wickets,
a feat he achieved at Sydney in February 1895, just beating Australia's
Charles Turner to the target in the same match. He played twice against
South Africa in 1888/89, not a strong team, but somebody had to get them
out, and in the Second Test at Cape Town he took 15 wickets for 28. He
hardly needed any fielders: 14 of his victims were bowled and one lbw.
His batting never reached the heights of his bowling, but he was good for
over 500 runs most years, made a Test century, and in 1885, just two days
after his wedding, made 186 against Surrey at Liverpool, putting on a then-
world record 173 for the last wicket with Dick Pilling.

Briggs was born in Sutton-in-Ashfield, Nottinghamshire in 1862. The family moved to Lancashire and having qualified for the county young Briggs made his debut for them in 1879, coincidentally against Nottinghamshire at Trent Bridge. By 1900 he had taken nine wickets in an innings three times. He had come closest to an all-ten for Lord Londesborough's XI against the 1890 Australians when the one wicket to evade him was a run-out.

Lancashire nearly won the Championship in 1900 and it was not until mid-August that it became clear that they would have to settle for second place to a Yorkshire team that went through the season undefeated. Worcestershire on the other hand were not a strong team. Admitted to the first-class ranks the previous season they finished 12th out of 15 in the Championship, managing only three wins.

Not surprisingly Old Trafford had experienced a few changes since Hickton's all-ten there in 1870. It was now surrounded by spiked railings to stop the crowds spilling onto the ground, new stands had been added, there was a new scoreboard, and most noticeably there was a new pavilion, completed in 1895 at a cost of nearly £10,000. The pavilion had three bathrooms for the amateurs and one for the professionals! At least the professionals now changed in the same pavilion as the amateurs, rather than in their own more rudimentary accommodation elsewhere on the ground, even if it was two more years before paid and unpaid walked out side by side.

The first day, Thursday 24 May, was a holiday for the Queen's birthday, and there were some 7,000 present. It was perhaps remarkable that Briggs was playing at all. On the evening of the first day of the Headingley Test at the end of June the previous season the members of both the England and Australia teams had gone to the music hall. At about 10.15 Briggs, sitting in the front row, had a violent epileptic fit. He was admitted to Cheadle Asylum where he had remained until the end of March.

At the end of May 1900 the papers were reporting details of the Relief of Mafeking a few days earlier and this no doubt put the crowd in a good humour. Recovered from his illness, Briggs had not yet done a lot of bowling. However, heavy showers followed by sunshine provided him with helpful conditions which, opening the bowling, he wasted no time in exploiting. Henry Foster, the Worcestershire captain and their top run-scorer during the season, went for a duck and was quickly followed by Frederick Bowley (who played for the county until 1923, by which time he was their leading run-scorer with over 20,000 runs) and by Ted Arnold, the first Worcestershire player to achieve the season's double. Briggs' opening partner was medium pacer Albert Hallam. The following season Hallam would move to the county of his birth and in 1907 he and Tom Wass would bowl Nottinghamshire to their first Championship title since the great days of the 1880s. Extraordinarily the pair shared 298 wickets while John Gunn, the next most successful bowler, took 25.

Six for three wasn't a promising start for Worcestershire. Aston Villa's England football international George Wheldon, and W.H.Hill, playing in the first of his two matches for the county, put on 30 for the fourth wicket before another collapse left the score at 46 for seven. After that, 106 all out was something of a recovery. Long-serving fast bowler Robert Burrows, a useful hard-hitting batsman who would eventually make two first-class centuries, chipped in with a few runs, and a last wicket partnership between Albert Bird and wicketkeeper Tom Straw which added 32 was finally ended when Bird came down the pitch to Briggs and was bowled. 33-year-old off-spinner Bird, a stalwart of Worcestershire and Warwickshire pre-first-class cricket, was playing his fourteenth first-class match and made his highest score so far – a fine performance against a strong attack. A Nottinghamshire miner, Straw's greatest claim to fame is that he managed to get himself out 'obstructing the field' not once but twice in a 61-match first-class career.

Briggs bowled throughout the innings whilst Willis Cuttell and Arthur Mold, both England bowlers, who between them took over 200 wickets for the county in 1900, went wicketless. The Lancashire fielding had not been faultless, but Briggs had received considerable help from his captain, and then England captain, the imperious, and often impecunious, Archie MacLaren, who took three catches off his bowling. Over a 20-year playing career Walter Wright had appeared in two matches involving all-tens; after three matches as an umpire he had now stood in another.

Lancashire made a shaky start to their innings, but going in at 53 for four Briggs, with 33 in less than half an hour, got them going again and at 191 for seven at the close they were reasonably well placed. The visitors put on a much better display on the second day. Soon dismissing Lancashire they scored 253 (Briggs three for 63), and then reduced Lancashire to 82 for five still needing another 73 to win. Fortunately for Lancashire, Johnny (J.T.) Tyldesley was still there and, together with Alexander Eccles (with MacLaren and Charlie Hartley, one of only three amateurs in the side), he safely saw his side home, the remaining 48 runs being hit off without further loss in half an hour on Saturday morning.

Lancashire easily won the return at Worcester just over a month later, Tyldesley and Eccles both making centuries. This time Briggs only took one wicket, but it was a good one: Reginald (R.E.) Foster, who just over three years later would make the then-record Test score, 287, against Australia at Sydney. Dying in 1914, like Briggs he would not live to see his fortieth birthday.

Briggs' first-class career came to an end at Lord's in September playing for North against South. He took six wickets in South's first innings. Three of his victims (W.G.Grace, Trott and Bland) had also taken an all-ten, as had umpire Pickett. After that his health deteriorated and he was readmitted to the asylum in the following March. This time there was no recovery and he died in January 1902. More than 4,000 people were present at Stretford Cemetery to see him laid to rest: evidence of the esteem in which the ever popular Johnny was held.

Albert Trott

Middlesex v Somerset, 1900
County Championship

County Ground, Taunton 6, 7, 8, August 1900 (3-day match)
Toss won by Somerset
Middlesex won by one wicket
Umpires: J Moss, WAJ West
Somerset 89 (AE Trott 10-42) and 327; Middlesex 139 (B Cranfield 7-74) and 280-9

Somerset first innings

LCH Palairet	b Trott	12
CA Bernard	b Trott	23
E Robson	b Trott	0
CE Dunlop	b Trott	1
*SMJ Woods	lbw b Trott	4
AE Lewis	c and b Trott	8
J Daniell	lbw b Trott	0
VT Hill	b Trott	35
+AE Newton	c Warner b Trott	0
EJ Tyler	b Trott	2
B Cranfield	not out	2
Extras	(b 2)	2
Total	(all out, 29.2 overs)	89

Fall of wickets 1-12, 2-12, 3-25, 4-29, 5-41, 6-43, 7-70, 8-?, 9-?, 10-89

Middlesex bowling : JT Hearne 15-4-45-0, AE Trott 14.2-5-42-10

Middlesex: PF Warner, J Douglas, RN Douglas, CM Wells, BJT Bosanquet, G MacGregor (capt, wk), RW Nicholls, JT Rawlin, AE Trott, W Williams, JT Hearne

Albert Trott was another of cricket's tragic heroes. Born in Melbourne in 1873, after an impressive Test debut against A.E.Stoddart's 1894/95 England team he should have been a certainty for the 1896 tour to England led by brother Harry. Inexplicably he wasn't chosen, and so decided that if Australia didn't want him he would continue his career in England. Whilst qualifying for Middlesex he served on the MCC groundstaff (including fielding as a substitute for Australia in the 1896 Lord's Test). Once qualified he soon made his mark and for a few years was one of the best allrounders in the world: as a mainly medium pace off-spinner with a lowish action who could move the ball both ways, and cleverly vary his pace from fast to slow; as a hard-hitting, crowd-pleasing, but often injudicious, batsman, famously remembered for hitting a ball from Australian Monty Noble over the pavilion at Lord's in 1899; and as a brilliant fielder anywhere. He also played two Tests in South Africa for his adopted country. By all accounts he had a lot of fun off the field. Unfortunately however, and resorting to clichés, the popular Trott was a 'flawed genius' and 'his own worst enemy'.

Trott's all-ten at Taunton was achieved in an exciting game to which he contributed fully with both bat and ball. Captained by Gregor MacGregor, or in his absence by their best batsman Pelham Warner, Middlesex, who would finish halfway in the Championship, had a curious season. By the end of June they had won just once, but then picked up so much that in the second half of the season they were a match for anybody. Somerset finished below halfway. Two of the team, Sammy Woods and Ted Tyler, of course already knew what it was like to take all ten wickets. Woods wasn't bowling much now however, and the side was also weakened by the non-availability, because of the Boer War, of Coote Hedley, Frank Phillips and Henry Stanley (who lost his life in September), all of whom had performed usefully in 1899. Both teams still had a strong amateur representation, although the bowling was still mainly in the hands of the paid.

Woods won the toss and chose to bat. After morning rain play could not start until 3.15, by which time the pitch, drying under a hot sun and a strong wind, gave Trott considerable help. Few home batsmen withstood him for long as, varying his pace, he turned the ball sharply. With six batsmen bowled, two leg-before and one caught and bowled it was a virtually single-handed performance. The two leg-befores were captain Woods and future captain John Daniell. The two (possibly brave) umpires were John Moss and William West. Between them they played just six first-class matches, but by the time their umpiring careers finished in the 1930s they had each stood in over 650 matches, a total still only achieved by three others: David Constant, Tom Spencer and, top of the list, Frank Chester (774).

Initially while Lionel Palairet and Charles Bernard were at the wicket batting had not looked too difficult, but once the former left the only batsmen who put up a fight were Bernard who resisted for over an hour before being seventh out, and Vernon Hill who had gone in at 43 for six and hit a bright and breezy 35. He was last out having been missed by Richard Nicholls off a difficult skyer in Trott's previous over. Hill played 121 first-class matches for Somerset between 1891 and 1912. He only made two first-class centuries: one for Somerset (116 against Kent in 1898) and one for Oxford in the 1892 University Match. Born in Wales, he played an important role in cricket history by helping to arrange matches which provided funds for the campaign which eventually led to Glamorgan achieving first-class status. Edinburgh-born batsman Charles Dunlop (only five fifties in a 43-match career) just got off the mark. He would not do this well in the second innings.

Trott had bowled unchanged with J.T. Hearne. In helpful conditions the great J.T., one of only four bowlers to take over 3,000 first-class wickets, could not get even one while Trott enjoyed himself at the other end. *Wisden* said that he was not 'the Hearne of four years ago' (when he took 257 wickets). However he wasn't finished yet and ten years later, aged 43, topped the national averages with 119 wickets at under 13 apiece. Trott's figures were a county record and have only been bettered once (by Gubby Allen in 1929). There was still time for Middlesex to score 35 for two before the close. In good weather Somerset fought back on the second day, finishing off Middlesex for only 139, Beaumont Cranfield taking seven for 74, and then scoring 257 for six. Cranfield was being groomed to take over from Tyler as the side's slow left-armer. He could turn the ball more than Tyler but lacked his guile. At first he seemed a more than adequate replacement, taking over 100 wickets in three successive seasons, but his temperament was suspect and by 1905 he had lost his place in the side. He died in 1909 aged 36 having contracted double pneumonia at a local football match. Four months later J.C. White, one of the greatest of all slow left-armers (and another all-ten man), made his debut for Somerset.

On the final day Somerset extended their second innings to 327, mainly thanks to fifties from Palairet, Bernard and Ernest Robson (after a first innings duck). Taking two for 116 Trott had found things more difficult second time around. Middlesex, needing 278 to win, began well, but then slumped to 221 for seven before Trott (34 not out) skilfully marshalled the tail to see his side home with seven minutes left in front of a 'good company'. Remarkably, Middlesex had also won their previous match by one wicket, whilst Somerset had lost theirs by the same margin.

It was a busy season for Trott. Only he and the slower Wilfred Rhodes bowled more than 1,500 overs (with nobody else exceeding even 1,200). He could be expensive though, his 211 wickets costing 23.33 runs apiece. *Wisden* thought that this might be because the 'inexhaustible' Trott perhaps carried his variations of pace too far.

Sadly Trott's peak was all too short. He liked his drink and visiting the bookies, had begun to put on weight, and his marriage was breaking down. *Wisden*'s report on the 1901 season alludes to a 'deterioration' in form, and by 1905 he had gone from 'bad to worse' and needed 'a little hard training during winter and spring'. He still had his moments though, most notably in his famous benefit match against Somerset (again) in 1907 when he took four wickets in four balls (amazingly he almost got five in five, the next ball shaving the stumps and going for four byes) and then finished off the innings with a hat-trick. After the match Sammy Woods gave Trott a straw hat. Hand-painted on the band were seven rabbits bolting back to the pavilion.

Trott played his last first-class match in 1911. Of his 1,674 wickets, 946 had been taken for Middlesex, a total then only exceeded by Hearne. He umpired competently for two seasons, but illness forced him to give up in 1914. Suffering from dropsy (a swelling of the soft tissues due to water accumulation) and with heart and kidney problems, he had become a shadow of his former self. At the end of July 1914 he discharged himself from hospital and returned to his lodgings in Willesden, north London. Alone in his room, he shot himself. With few possessions his 'will' was scribbled on the back of a laundry ticket. Three years later brother Harry, who in his time had battled mental illness, died aged just 51.

Arthur Fielder

Players v Gentlemen, 1906

Lord's Cricket Ground, St John's Wood on 9, 10, 11 July 1906 (3-day match)
Toss won by Gentlemen
Gentlemen won by 45 runs
Umpires: J Moss, JE West
Gentlemen 167 (A Fielder 10-90) and 321 (RH Spooner 114, WS Lees 6-92);
Players 199 (NA Knox 5-73) and 244 (NA Knox 7-110)

Gentlemen first innings

RH Spooner	b Fielder	5
HK Foster	b Fielder	10
PA Perrin	lbw b Fielder	2
*FS Jackson	c Lilley b Fielder	40
BJT Bosanquet	c Lilley b Fielder	56
KL Hutchings	c Lilley b Fielder	2
JN Crawford	b Fielder	0
GL Jessop	b Fielder	12
+H Martyn	c Haigh b Fielder	26
NA Knox	not out	6
W Brearley	b Fielder	0
Extras	(b 6, nb 1, w 1)	8
Total	(all out, 58.5 overs)	167

Fall of wickets 1-13, 2-15, 3-28, 4-107, 5-109, 6-109, 7-127, 8-161, 9-167, 10-167

Players bowling : A Fielder 24.5-1-90-10, JR Gunn 13-5-15-0, S Haig 5-2-11-0, WS Lees 5-1-15-0, W Rhodes 11-3-28-0

Players: TW Hayward, FL Bowley, JT Tyldesley, D Denton, EG Hayes, W Rhodes, JR Gunn, AFA Lilley (capt, wk), WS Lees, S Haigh, A Fielder

Arthur Fielder is the only bowler to have taken an all-ten in the Gentlemen v Players match at Lord's, one of the great matches of the year, and in years when there were no Tests (such as 1906), *the* great match. Fielder was a strong, hardworking fast bowler, able to move the ball away and occasionally bring it back. He only played for England six times, but on his second tour to Australia took 25 wickets in four Tests and must be considered unlucky never to have been capped again.

Born near Tonbridge in 1877, he became a regular member of the Kent team at the advanced age of 26. In the wet summer of 1903 seventy wickets was a good performance for a fast bowler, and with England short of pace he was selected to tour Australia with Pelham Warner's MCC side the following winter. Back in England, Fielder had a good season in 1904 but struggled in 1905 and his quantum leap in performance in 1906 must have come as some surprise. The 172 wickets he took for Kent, at the time a county record, were largely instrumental in them winning the Championship for the first time.

1906 celebrated the centenary of the Gentlemen v Players series and the 40,000 spectators attracted to Lord's saw a memorable match. Despite the rich amateur talent available in this so-called Golden Age of cricket, the Players usually had the edge: since 1890 they had been victorious eight times to the Gentlemen's four. Two very strong sides had been assembled, although the injured C.B.Fry was unavailable for the Gentlemen, and the team did not include the two batsmen who finished top of the season's averages: Worcestershire's Reginald Foster who played two matches averaging 81, and Kent's Cuthbert Burnup who averaged 67 from 13 matches. For the Players, George Hirst had turned down an invitation to play in order to save himself for his county. As he would eventually complete a unique season's 2,000 runs-200 wickets double he probably deserved a rest, although his decision provoked some criticism. His presence might have affected the outcome of the match, although given his form he might also have spoiled Fielder's all-ten.

The Gentlemen were captained by Yorkshire's Stanley (F.S.) Jackson, the Players by Warwickshire wicketkeeper Dick Lilley. Jackson had retired at the end of the previous season (in which he had captained England to an Ashes victory whilst topping both batting and bowling averages), but had accepted an invitation to captain the Gentlemen. Their batting was very strong. Gilbert Jessop, a man with a famous Test century to his name, went in as low as number eight, and at nine wicketkeeper Henry Martyn, Somerset's only representative in the match, was a first-class centurion.

In humid conditions Lancashire's Reggie Spooner and Worcestershire captain Henry Foster opened for the Gentlemen against Fielder bowling from the Nursery End, and Nottinghamshire's John Gunn bowling left-arm medium pace from the Pavilion End. Seventeen wickets would fall on the first day. *The Times* commented that 'once more Lord's proved a paradise for fast bowlers', whilst *Cricket* suggested that the pitch had been over-watered. Fielder quickly dismissed both openers, Foster already having been dropped off him three times, and then Percy Perrin of Essex, to reduce the amateurs to 28 for three. Bernard Bosanquet, playing on home territory, joined Jackson, and a fighting partnership saw lunch taken with the score 102 for three. Fielder, having been rested, returned to have Bosanquet caught behind for 56, the partnership having put on 79 in 80 minutes. The only other significant contributions came from Jackson who, in his first innings of the year, scored 40 in two and a half hours, and Martyn whose brisk fifteen minute stay, which included three fours in an over in an attempt to knock Fielder off his length, ended when he skied a ball to Yorkshire's Schofield Haigh at mid on. Having taken nine wickets, Fielder must have been heartened to see one of cricket's natural number elevens, Walter Brearley (career batting average 5.89), coming to the wicket, and the excited spectators must have had high hopes of seeing an all-ten. They were not disappointed as the Lancashire fast bowler's stumps were uprooted second ball.

The pitch was obviously fast, *Cricket* commenting that Fielder's deliveries had come quickly off the pitch, although *The Times* partly contradicted its earlier assessment by saying that the 'wicket was not really difficult, nor did the ball get up unduly high'. Whatever the conditions, Fielder had achieved his success by bowling an unyielding length on or outside the off stump, six of his victims having been either bowled or leg-before and three more caught at the wicket. Lilley had used four bowlers at the other end. All had played for England, all would take over 100 wickets in the season, but all went unrewarded while Fielder set his record. Umpire John Moss having stood for an all-ten at Taunton six years before had now presided over the next one.

At the close of a pace-dominated first day the Players were 136 for seven, with only Tom Hayward (54) and Yorkshire's David Denton (48) withstanding the speed of Brearley and Surrey's Neville Knox. This was Hayward's great season. He scored 3,518 runs, a total famously only ever exceeded by Denis Compton and Bill Edrich in 1947. Knox was probably the fastest bowler in England at that time, and yet Martyn stood up to the stumps, taking the ball with ease. The Gentlemen used up most of the second day in scoring 321, Spooner (114), Foster (67) and Jessop (73 not out in an hour) contributing most of the runs. The fearless Jessop had been particularly severe on Fielder, more than once dropping on to one knee and pulling him into the Mound Stand. The 49 that the unlikely pairing of Brearley and Jessop added for the last wicket was to be the difference between the two teams. Fielder took another four wickets, but they cost 131 runs, his figures not helped by Jessop's onslaught.

Set 290 to win the Players lost three early wickets, all bowled by Knox. Surrey colleagues Hayward (34), Ernie Hayes (55) and Walter Lees (51), supported by John Gunn (42), started a fightback but nobody could last long enough against the intimidating pace of Knox whose seven for 110 bowled his side to victory. Knox's career was meteoric. He was in only his second full season of first-class cricket after leaving Dulwich College (a good breeding ground for quick bowlers: both Arthur Gilligan and Trevor Bailey are old boys). He appeared in two Tests in 1907, but because of acute shin soreness his career was more or less over soon afterwards.

Fielder was not much of a batsman but, as a number eleven, his name is associated with two famous last wicket partnerships. At Melbourne in January 1908 the 39 runs that he and Sydney Barnes scored is still England's highest last wicket partnership to win a Test, and the following year at Stourbridge he scored an unbeaten 112 in putting on a then-world record 235 with Frank Woolley (185). Fielder is one of only three batsmen to score a century batting at number eleven in the Championship.

He remained a key member of the Kent side that won four Championships in eight years.

The only pace bowler to have taken 1,000 wickets for Kent, in total he took 1,277 first-class wickets. Too old for county cricket after the War, for some years Fielder coached at Rugby School. He died aged 72 in south London in 1949. Two years previously his next door neighbour had commited suicide by gassing himself and some of the carbon monoxide had seeped into his accommodation, severely affecting his health.

George Dennett

Gloucestershire v Essex, 1906
County Championship

Ashley Down Ground, Bristol on 6, 7 August 1906 (3-day match)
Toss won by Essex
Gloucestershire won by nine wickets
Umpires: AE Clapp, FW Marlow
Essex 84 (EG Dennett 10-40) and 127 (EG Dennett 5-48, FB Roberts 5-69);
Gloucestershire 173 (JWHT Douglas 5-50) and 39-1

Essex first innings

*FL Fane	c Jessop b Dennett	11
JWHT Douglas	b Dennett	14
PA Perrin	c Brownless b Dennett	22
CP McGahey	c Brownlee b Dennett	17
WMF Turner	st Board b Dennett	0
FH Gillingham	c Spry b Dennett	4
AJ Turner	c Thomas b Dennett	3
W Reeves	c Brownlee b Dennett	4
CP Buckenham	lbw b Dennett	5
+AE Russell	not out	0
W Mead	c Goodwin b Dennett	2
Extras	(lb 2)	2
Total	(all out, 38.4 overs)	84

Fall of wickets 1-19, 2-47, 3-47, 4-47, 5-55, 6-70, 7-75, 8-81, 9-82, 10-84

Gloucestershire bowling : EG Dennett 19.4-7-40-10, FB Roberts 19-8-42-0

Gloucestershire: COH Sewell, EP Barnett, GL Jessop (capt), AFM Townsend, JH Board (wk), FE Thomas, LD Brownlee, HS Goodwin, FB Roberts, EJ Spry, EG Dennett

Along with Jack Newman of Hampshire and Glamorgan's Don Shepherd, George Dennett is one of only three bowlers to have taken over 2,000 first-class wickets but never play for England. He was a fine slow left-arm bowler, but he played at the same time as Wilfred Rhodes, Colin Blythe and Frank Woolley and with relatively few Tests staged then it was going to be difficult for him to get a cap. Cool even when under attack, with a quick arm action Dennett obtained considerable bounce and got many batsmen caught on the off side as they were unable to keep their drives on the ground. Strangely, as he delivered the ball he looked not at the batsman but up in the air.

Dennett was born in Upwey, Dorset in 1879. He began as a professional for the Grange Club in Edinburgh before being discovered by Gilbert Jessop playing in Bristol club cricket. He made his first-class debut in 1903 and took well over 100 wickets in every season up to the War. In 1907 he became the first Gloucestershire bowler to take 200 wickets in a season.

The Ashley Down ground had been laid out during the 1880s on open farmland to the north of Bristol. By the beginning of the century it was largely surrounded by residential streets and was overlooked on two sides by the grim grey buildings of Muller's orphanage, but despite this it still had a sense of spaciousness.

The match started on August Bank Holiday Monday. Gloucestershire and Essex were reasonably well matched, both eventually finishing around halfway in the Championship, both relying heavily on amateurs: Gloucestershire fielding eight and Essex seven. Dennett hardly failed during 1906, succeeding nearly every time he bowled, and finishing with 175 wickets, a total surpassed only by Arthur Fielder and George Hirst. Gloucestershire's reliance on him was remarkable. He took 160 Championship wickets; their next highest wicket-taker was Henry Huggins with 39. Essex, who went in first, were a decent batting side. *Wisden* commented that 'the team had run-getting power down to almost the last man'. However overnight rain had produced a bowler-friendly pitch on which 24 wickets fell on the first day. Essex made a steady start, reaching 47 before the second wicket fell. Frederick Fane and Johnny Douglas, both future England captains, had opened the batting. They were followed by 'The Essex Twins', Percy Perrin and Charlie McGahey. Between them the two were to make over 50,000 first-class runs but in this match they only made 48. Two years previously at Chesterfield Perrin had made 343 not out, still an Essex record. Despite this he never played for England, probably because he was a very slow fielder.

Dennett sent down seven overs before getting his first wicket, but after that he needed only another 12 to dismiss Essex before lunch for 84. He was supported by brilliant fielding, Leigh Brownlee in particular making three very good catches in the deep from hard-hit drives. An Oxford Blue and future editor of the *Daily Mirror* Brownlee's early career had shown some promise: in his sixth match, not yet aged 20, he made a century for Gloucestershire against a strong Kent attack. However, in a 82-match first-class career he never again reached three figures.

Cricket was not impressed by the Essex batting: 'No one played him [Dennett] with any confidence and the innings calls for no detailed description'. Looking at the scorecard it doesn't seem an unreasonable comment. The brothers Turner, Walter and Arthur, aggregated only three runs, although Walter would top score in the Essex second innings. Making 13 centuries between them in 128 matches they were both batsmen of considerable talent who, because of Army duties, were unable to play regularly. If they had they might well have gone further. Walter Turner was stumped by Jack Board, a fate that befell many batsmen: in a career that lasted a quarter of a century he stumped 359 batsmen, a total only exceeded by Kent's Les Ames and Fred Huish. Board's Essex counterpart, Edward Russell, who had succeeded older brother Tom behind the stumps, evaded Dennett's clutches and would be rewarded by promotion to nightwatchman in the second innings. The last Essex batsman Walter Mead did not make Dennett wait long for his tenth wicket. He was caught by Harry Goodwin whose undistinguished eleven-year first-class career (in 31 matches he never bowled or reached fifty) would finish the following season with a pair against the South Africans, bowled both times by Ernie Vogler, the next bowler to take an all-ten.

At least the Bristol public were impressed with Dennett's bowling, a collection around the ground raising over £25. Dennett's figures are still a county record, and beat the nine for 34 taken by the fast-medium Huggins against Sussex at Bristol two years previously.

Gloucestershire went in after lunch and scored 173 in just 43 overs. This healthy rate of scoring was due to the home side's captain Gilbert Jessop who scored 75 in 95 minutes before he was caught and bowled by Douglas. This would be a laudable rate of scoring for a conventional batsman, but was slow for a batsman who in recent years had four times reached 200 in less than 150 minutes. The great Jessop wasn't in particularly good form in 1906, but his rate of scoring illustrates the continuing difficulty of the conditions.

There was still an hour and three quarters left on the first day; time for Essex to lose four more wickets for 63 runs. Dennett took three of these, having Douglas caught for 25 and tempting both of the 'Twins' into being stumped by Board. The match was over by lunch on the next day. Although the wicket showed some improvement Essex could only get as far as 127, leaving Gloucestershire an easy task. Dennett took another five wickets to finish with fifteen for 88 in the match. Only Walter Turner (37) and the Reverend Frank Gillingham (20) resisted for long. The Reverend was an interesting character. Born in Tokyo, dying in Monaco, he scored just over 10,000 first-class runs and played his last match in 1928 aged nearly 53. He is perhaps most famous for making the first wireless cricket commentary in England: Essex against the New Zealanders at Leyton in 1927. He was later to fill in time during a rain delay at The Oval by commenting on the advertisements around the ground. The BBC's puritanical Director-General John Reith was not impressed!

Dennett had bowled unchanged in the match with fast bowler Francis Roberts who, wicketless in the first innings, was rewarded with five for 69 in the second. Roberts was an amateur playing only his second match for Gloucestershire since leaving Cambridge. He was only available to play in August, but was a regular until the First World War, which was to claim his life in February 1916 aged 33. This was his only five-wicket haul, but he was a useful bat, scoring five centuries for Gloucestershire. He always played in glasses.

Dennett had served in the Boer War and was commissioned from the ranks in the First World War. Still serving in India he couldn't return to cricket until 1920. Although Charlie Parker had now completed his post-war switch from fastish left-arm to slowish left-arm and begun to take wickets in vast numbers, there was still a place in the Gloucestershire side for Dennett. By the time he played his last match in 1926 at the age of 47, he had taken 2,082 wickets for the county, a total only exceeded by Parker and Tom Goddard. He became coach at Cheltenham College. In later years he suffered from Parkinson's Disease and he died at Cheltenham in 1937.

Ernie Vogler

Eastern Province v Griqualand West, 1906/07
Currie Cup

Old Wanderers Pirates Lower Back Ground, Johannesburg on 26, 27, 28
December 1906 (3-day match)
Toss won by Eastern Province
Eastern Province won by an innings and 301 runs
Umpires: AJ Atfield, WH Creese
Eastern Province 403 (DS Lumsden 103, GA Verheyen 5-122); Griqualand
West 51 (AEE Vogler 6-12) and 51 (AEE Vogler 10-26)

Griqualand West second innings

RHG Percy	b Vogler	0
SAL Olver	b Vogler	0
TA Eden	b Vogler	7
W Dickens	c and b Vogler	0
*AP Eland	b Vogler	0
GA Verheyen	lbw b Vogler	0
SW Windsor	b Vogler	2
GT Hitchman	not out	19
LG Wright	b Vogler	7
GF Fletcher	c Hibbert b Vogler	0
+HJ Druce	c and b Vogler	4
Extras	(b 12)	12
Total	(all out, 23 overs)	51

Fall of wickets 1-0, 2-1, 3-1, 4-1, 5-5, 6-5, 7-18, 8-42, 9-42, 10-51

Eastern Province bowling : AEE Vogler 12-2-26-10, AT Lyons 9-6-10-0, MA
Bell 2-0-3-0

Eastern Province: RP Hannam, DS Lumsden, MA Bell, C Fock, AEE Vogler,
FJ Hippert, AT Lyons, WA Glisson, HT Hibbert (capt), A Melvill (wk), J Loots

Having developed the googly to a level where it was lethal enough to
win Test matches, England's Bernard Bosanquet passed the baton to the
famous 'googly quartet' who toured Britain with the 1907 South Africans.
Opinions differed whether Aubrey Faulkner, Reggie Schwarz, Ernie Vogler,
or Gordon White was the best, but arguably for a brief period Vogler was at
least the second-best bowler in the world (after England's Sydney Barnes).
Following a stuttering run-up Vogler's stock ball was a leg break with, as
alternatives, a well disguised googly, a top spinner and a slow yorker. All
this he combined with accuracy and deceptive variation of flight and pace.
In South Africa the difficulties batsmen faced in countering these new-
fangled varieties were compounded by the extra bounce due to the use of
matting pitches. (Turf was not used for a Test in South Africa until 1931.)

Born in Cape Province in 1876, the young Vogler had moved around a
bit: his boyhood was spent in Durban, and he later moved to Pretoria. He
made his first-class debut, for Natal against Transvaal at Johannesburg,
on his birthday, 28 November 1903. Deciding that he wanted to become

a full-time professional he joined the MCC groundstaff in 1905. He might have been offered a Middlesex contract but the county already had two 'colonials' in Albert Trott and Frank Tarrant and there was a feeling a third would be a bit much. Instead he was found employment back home by South African tycoon Sir Abe Bailey.

Vogler made his Test debut after just six first-class matches, playing in all five matches against Pelham Warner's 1905/06 tourists. His return was modest, just nine wickets, but he was also a useful bat and in the final match of the series scored 62 not out, at the time a Test record for a number eleven batsman.

The Currie Cup had been first contested in 1889/90. Since its resumption after the Boer War it had been dominated by Transvaal and 1906/07 was no different. In order that the selection committee for the forthcoming 1907 tour could assess all possible candidates it had been decided to revert to concentrating the competition at one centre, and in addition that it would be played on a full league basis with each team playing the others once. The tournament was held over a two-week period starting on 26 December 1906. It was played at four venues at the Old Wanderers Ground, Johannesburg and at Berea Park, Pretoria. Six teams competed.

Vogler was now playing for Eastern Province. Despite his presence however, they were a very weak side. They won two matches, but only against the even weaker teams Griqualand West and Orange Free State, and their three defeats were all by an innings. None of the Griqualand West side that stepped onto the field on Boxing Day 1906 ever made a first-class century. Six were making their first-class debuts. (In view of their performance it is perhaps surprising that some weren't also playing their last match.)

Both umpires were British-born: Alf Atfield from Kent and Bill Creese from Monmouthshire. Atfield would be standing at Taunton 14 years later when Surrey's Tom Rushby took an all-ten. He spent his winters coaching and umpiring in South Africa, where he would stand in eight Tests involving England, although never officiating in a home Test. Creese umpired 16 first-class matches, all in South Africa (where he died) including one Test. In 1913/14 the MCC tourists played Border twice in a week. Baggage man Creese umpired the first match and played in the second.

Eastern Province batted first and made 403. In his second first-class match opener David Lumsden made 103, having made a pair in his first. In seventeen subsequent innings he never got past 24. Vogler second top scored with 79. Because of rain Eastern Province's innings took up most of the first two days, leaving the Griquas only time to make eight without loss before rain brought an early close. The following morning the Lower Back Ground was so wet it was ruled unplayable. However, the adjoining Top Back Ground was reasonably dry and so the venue was simply switched! The conditions suited Vogler. Play started late and Griqualand West quickly took their score to 20, aided by Vogler's first three balls which beat both batsman and wicketkeeper and produced twelve byes. However he soon got his range and at lunch, taken with the score 29 for five, his figures were four for 4. All out soon after for 51 (Vogler six for 12), the

Griquas followed on and with Vogler taking four wickets in his first two overs before long they were 18 for seven. Some tailend hitting revived things a little, and last man Henry Druce at last managed to break his first-class duck at his fourth attempt, but the end came at four o'clock with the score again 51. With thirteen ducks in the match, Griqualand West had been dismissed twice in less than two and a half hours. The only batsman not dismissed by Vogler at least once was Brixton-born George Hickman who had been run out without scoring on debut in the first innings. He had an interesting career, playing three matches in 1906/07, one more 14 years later at the age of 40, and then umpiring three in the 1930s, the last involving Walter Hammond's 1938/39 tourists.

The *Rand Daily Mail* called the proceedings 'a fiasco'. It was the first of three matches that the Griquas would lose in the tournament by an innings and over 300 runs, and they would become so disheartened that, rather than face the might of Transvaal in their last match, they conceded the match and went home.

Vogler's figures had improved on the previous record (jointly held by Moss and Howell) and have only been beaten three times since. It had been a bit of a one-man show: all but one of his 16 victims had been either bowled, leg-before or caught and bowled. Byes had contributed significantly in both Griqualand innings. Clearly wicketkeeper Arthur Melvill found Vogler's variations a bit of a handful. He had stood behind the stumps to him before, although to be fair he wasn't a regular keeper. Vogler had nearly taken an all-ten just two matches previously playing for MCC at Lord's against the 1906 West Indian tourists, the one wicket to evade him being a run-out. He later also played four (non-Cup) matches for Transvaal and finished 1906/07 as the season's leading wicket-taker with 55 victims.

Vogler peaked when South Africa met England in 1909/10 in a series won 3-2 by the home side largely thanks to Faulkner (545 runs and 29 wickets), and Vogler whose 36 wickets were a Test series record. After this high point his career quickly petered out. The following season the South Africans toured Australia, losing 4-1 in a series in which the Australian left-arm pace bowler Bill Whitty took 37 wickets to surpass Vogler's record. Away from the matting pitches of home, with the exception of Schwarz, the much vaunted South African attack failed against the batting power of Australia, Victor Trumper et al. Vogler particularly disappointed, *Wisden* referring to his 'deplorable failure'. After Australia Vogler played just two more first-class matches and as a professional for various clubs in Britain. Curiously his last first-class match was for Woodbrook Club and Ground, in Ireland, against the South Africans who were in Britain participating in the ill-fated 1912 Triangular Tournament. Of Vogler's 393 first-class wickets 64 had been taken in 15 Tests. Three years earlier in a remarkable two-day, non-first-class match, Vogler, playing for Woodbrook, had scored a century in an innings in which County Galway's William 'Budge' Meldon had taken ten for 126, and then taken his own all-ten (for 41) in Galway's second innings to add to the six wickets he had taken in their first.

Although there are suggestions that he drank heavily, Vogler lived to a reasonable age, dying in Pietermaritzburg in 1946. He was more fortunate than other members of the 'googly quartet': White died of wounds in Palestine just before the end of the First World War; Schwarz died a week after the end of the War, a victim of the influenza epidemic that swept the Western Front; and Faulkner died by his own hand in 1930.

Colin Blythe

Kent v Northamptonshire, 1907
County Championship

County Ground, Northampton on 30, 31 May, 1 June 1907 (3-day match)
Toss won by Kent
Kent won by an innings and 155 runs
Umpires: W Attewell, CE Dench
Kent 254 (W East 5-77); Northamptonshire 60 (C Blythe 10-30) and 39 (C Blythe 7-18)

Northamptonshire first innings

+WA Buswell	st Huish b Blythe	0
M Cox	st Huish b Blythe	0
CJT Pool	c Fielder b Blythe	0
WH Kingston	lbw b Blythe	2
GJ Thompson	b Blythe	0
W East	c Huish b Blythe	0
*EM Crosse	c Fairservice b Blythe	0
AR Thompson	c Seymour b Blythe	10
GAT Vials	not out	33
W Wells	c Humphreys b Blythe	0
LT Driffield	b Blythe	12
Extras	(b 1, lb 2)	3
Total	(all out, 31 overs)	60

Fall of wickets 1-0, 2-0, 3-1, 4-3, 5-4, 6-4, 7-4, 8-24, 9-26, 10-60

Kent bowling : C Blythe 16-7-30-10, WJ Fairservice 12-5-17-0, A Fielder 3-0-10-0

Kent: FE Woolley, HTW Hardinge, J Seymour, KL Hutchings, AP Day, EW Dillon, E Humphreys, FH Huish (wk), WJ Fairservice, C Blythe, A Fielder

Among a number of worthy contenders, many rate Colin Blythe the best left-arm spinner of all. A testing opponent in all conditions, he had a fluent action, bringing his arm from behind his back in a long sweeping arc, and the left-arm spinner's full armoury: the stock leg break, the arm-ball, and a medium-pace inswinger, all allied to perplexing changes of flight and pace. And if all this failed a few high full tosses might lure the batsman to destruction. He was also a fine violinist and this no doubt helped strengthen the long fingers which could extract turn on most surfaces.

Born in Deptford, south east London in 1879 the young Blythe (nicknamed Charlie because of his cheery cockney personality) was apprenticed at Woolwich Arsenal and played local cricket. In July 1897 he went to Rectory Field, Blackheath, to see Kent play Somerset and was spotted bowling a few balls before play to Kent veteran Walter Wright. This led to a successful trial at the newly-established Tonbridge nursery, and a first-class debut there two years later when his first ball bowled Yorkshire's Frank Mitchell. (Mitchell had played twice for England in South Africa and would captain South Africa in the 1912 Triangular tournament.) It was the beginning of a glorious career which ended fifteen years later with 2,503 wickets at a cost of 16.81, and four Championships for Kent.

Northampton's Wantage Road headquarters had been used for cricket since the 1880s and for the previous ten years it had also been used by Northampton Town Football Club. Over time a stand and terracing was constructed for the winter game, but it was always an uneasy fit and in 1994 the football club finally moved from its quirky three-sided home to a proper purpose-built (but less interesting) stadium. The match against Kent wasn't a meeting of equals. The visitors had won the Championship the previous season, and would do so three more times before 1914. Northants on the other hand had only entered the Championship two years previously and were still struggling to establish themselves. *Wisden* referred to 'a deplorable lack of resolution and stability in their batting' (best evidenced at Gloucester later in June where a promising first innings 10 for one became 12 all out). Northants no doubt viewed the game with some trepidation: their previous match, a fortnight before, had also been against Kent, at Catford, where they lost by an innings and 100 runs.

The game started on Thursday 30 May, Blythe's birthday. There was rain about and Northants didn't even begin their first innings until Saturday. Nevertheless Kent still had the match won by half-past four, dismissing Northants twice in three and a quarter hours. Conditions were so spinner-friendly that fast bowler Arthur Fielder (172 wickets in the season) only bowled three overs. Kent began by making made 254, mainly thanks to Wally Hardinge (73) and Ken Hutchings (52). Hardinge played 606 times for Kent, a total only exceeded by Frank Woolley. His last first-class innings (hit wicket bowled Leyland 19) against Yorkshire at Dover in 1933 denied the great Hedley Verity (nine for 59) a third all-ten. One of a small number of double-internationals, he was capped by England once at cricket and once at football (while playing with Sheffield United).

On a slow, soft pitch, the Northants innings began unusually, openers Walter Buswell and Mark Cox both being stumped by Fred Huish. Buswell gave great service to Northants behind the stumps, but in front of them his accomplishments were more limited: two fifties and a century in 327 innings. Things got worse and at 4 (including two leg-byes) for seven (Blythe seven for 1) the ignominy of a single-figure score seemed a distinct possibility, and would have been even more so if Blythe hadn't missed a George Vials caught and bowled chance with the score at nine. Double figures were eventually achieved, but at 26 for nine (Blythe nine for 13) things still didn't look too good. However, Blythe then had to sweat another twelve overs for his tenth wicket as Vials and Lancelot Driffield took the score to the dizzy heights of 60 before Blythe bowled fellow left-arm spinner Driffield soon after lunch. The youngest man in the team, the 20-year-old Vials would give Northants cricket great service, especially as captain in 1912 when the county were Championship runners up, and as president for twelve years from 1956. Both Vials and William Wells who followed him to the wicket would make two first-class centuries, a feat which six of the side failed to achieve even once.

The home crowd enthusiastically applauded both Blythe's feat, and their own side's 'recovery'. Blythe's analysis is still a Kent record. Seven batsmen had failed to score, including future Test cricketer George Thompson. When he retired after the War Thompson was his county's leading wicket-taker (and is still second highest) as well as having done the double twice. As he had failed to strike with his fast-medium bowling and would make only one run in the second innings, his contribution to 'Blythe's match' had been untypically modest.

Hot sun then began to make the wicket more difficult and unsurprisingly Northants, following on, did even worse making 39 (Blythe seven for 18). Any chances of another Blythe all-ten went quickly as Vials, opening this time, was bowled by Bill Fairservice for one, having been dropped by him off Blythe in the previous over. As Fairservice took 853 wickets for Kent, and was still scoring for the Second Eleven at the age of 87, he was well named. Cox, stumped off Blythe again, at least had the consolation of top scoring with 12. Blythe had bowled unchanged to become the first bowler to take 17 wickets in a day, a feat since repeated only by Hedley Verity and Tom Goddard. He had been well supported by his fielders, both close and further out, as batsmen tried to hit themselves out of trouble. Kent only just made it: the last few overs were played in drizzle, and soon after the last wicket fell heavy rain set in. Blythe had plenty of time to contemplate his great achievement as he missed the next two Kent games with a chill.

Blythe's career peaked in 1909 with 215 wickets, including 11 wickets against Australia in the First Test at Edgbaston. He had surpassed this achievement two years before at Headingley taking 15 wickets against South Africa. However, *Wisden* commented that he had 'bowled himself to a standstill'. Certainly, Blythe found the strain of Test cricket stressful. This may account for the fact that he only played 19 times for England, and not at all after 1910 even though the powers of left-arm rival Wilfred Rhodes had temporarily waned. However, it was a very successful Test career: exactly 100 wickets at 18.63, at the time only the fourth England bowler to reach this milestone (after Johnny Briggs, George Lohmann and Bobby Peel).

In August 1917 Blythe played in a one-day charity match at Lord's for Navy and Army against Australians and South Africans. He only took one wicket, albeit a good one: Charlie Macartney. It was Blythe's last appearance on a cricket field. By the end of the following month he was on his way to France, having already announced that he would be retiring from first-class cricket after the War. On the evening of 8 November near Passchendaele in Belgium, Sergeant Blythe attached to the King's Own Yorkshire Light Infantry was struck by shrapnel and killed instantly. He was the most distinguished of the many cricketers who died in the conflict. Schoolmaster Lancelot Driffield, his tenth victim at Northampton, had died of natural causes a month before. Every year as part of the Cricket Week a wreath is laid on Colin Blythe's memorial at the St Lawrence Ground, Canterbury.

Bart King

Gentlemen of Philadelphia v Gentlemen of Ireland, 1909

Merion Cricket Club Ground, Haverford on 17, 18 September 1909 (3-day match)

Gentlemen of Philadelphia won by an innings and 168 runs

Gentlemen of Ireland 111 (JB King 10-53) and 74 (HV Hordern 5-30); Gentlemen of Philadelphia 353 (FS White 118)

Gentlemen of Ireland first innings

WMJ Mooney	b King	1
GA Morrow	not out	50
O Andrews	b King	5
JM Magee	c Haines b King	16
*+FH Browning	b King	1
JG Aston	b King	0
HM Read	b King	16
WP Hone	b King	0
W Harrington	b King	11
WH Napper	lbw b King	0
JE Lynch	lbw b King	1
Extras	(b 6, lb 1, nb 1, w 2)	10
Total	(all out, 36.1 overs)	111

Fall of wickets 1-2, 2-16, 3-56, 4-61, 5-61, 6-85, 7-85, 8-109, 9-109, 10-111

Gentlemen of Philadelphia bowling : JB King 18.1-7-53-10, HV Hordern 11-2-38-0, PH Clark 5-1-8-0, W Graham 2-0-2-0

Gentlemen of Philadelphia: CC Morris, FS White, RH Patton, JL Evans, JB King, AM Wood, W Graham, HV Hordern, PH Clark (capt), HA Haines, CH Winter (wk)

In the quarter-century before the First World War the Philadelphians (a combined team of amateurs drawn from the city's clubs) could field a team well able to hold its own in first-class cricket. For a time cricket, rather than baseball, was the city's major sport, with a number of fine grounds on which big matches drew large crowds: for example 22,000 in 1891 to watch Lord Hawke's XI. The Philadelphians toured Britain five times between 1883 and 1908. They also received many visitors, including three Australian teams returning from Britain. And for a time a Philadelphian was one of the best bowlers in the world.

Born in Philadelphia in 1873, John Barton King played baseball when young but soon took up cricket. He progressed quickly, making his first-class debut in 1893 against Jack Blackham's Australians. With seven wickets in a match that the Philadelphians won easily, his impact was immediate. He would eventually play 65 first-class matches: 37 on three tours to Britain, the others in Philadelphia against a variety of teams on short autumn tours. He was also a decent bat. Against Surrey in 1903 he scored 98 (run out) and 113 not out (and bowled Tom Richardson with ten minutes left to complete a Philadelphian victory). This was his only first-class century, but he finished his career with a useful average of 20.51.

Tall, wiry, with powerful shoulders and long arms, King possessed considerable powers of endurance. In the final strides of his run up he held the ball above his head in both hands much like a baseball pitcher, although there was never any suggestion that he threw. A keen student of bowling technique, his most dangerous ball was the inswinger, but he could also deceive the batsman by making the ball go straight or move away a little. His stock pace was probably what we now call fast-medium.

King had already twice come close to an all-ten. In September 1897 against P.F.Warner's XI he had denied himself a tenth wicket by catching the visitors' captain, and in 1903 against, admittedly, a weakened Lancashire side, nine might have been ten if he hadn't been involved in running out the other batsman.

In 1909 the Irish were on a short tour of North America and were captained by their wicketkeeper 41-year-old Frank Browning who was playing the final two matches of an 11-match career. A barrister, Browning would be killed in Dublin during the 1916 Easter Uprising. Ireland only had a day's acclimatisation in Philadelphia, and it showed. Their match against the Philadelphians began in cool, cloudy conditions, although the sun would emerge later. The Merion Cricket Club had been founded in 1865 (and proudly celebrated its 150th Anniversary in 2015). It had been unlucky with clubhouse fires but now possessed an impressive brick and stone structure.

King opened the bowling on a green pitch with H.V.'Ranji' Hordern, who was studying dentistry at the University of Pennsylvania. Despite bowling 11 overs against weak batting Hordern would fail to strike. However he would later bowl his leg spin for his native Australia with great success, taking 46 wickets in seven pre-war Tests. The Philadelphia captain Percy Clark also went unrewarded. Finishing his career just one short of 200 wickets, like King he was a fine exponent of swing and like King he would live into his nineties.

Apart from a brilliant catch by Harold Haines at slip, King needed no help from his fielders. The Irish innings, such as it was, was held together by George Morrow who emulated Alec Hearne's earlier feat by carrying his bat throughout an all-ten (although he was a little fortunate as King bowled him with his only no-ball). This was Morrow's only fifty in an eight-match first-class career. A sizeable crowd had built up and he, and of course King, were enthusiastically acclaimed. Three Irish batsmen failed to score, including John Aston who would complete a pair on debut in the second innings (bowled King again). Aston would also be bowled twice by King when the two sides met again a week later, but at least he finally broke his first-class duck in the second innings. That might have been the end of a forgettable career, but 16 years later he played twice for Ireland, making a fifty against Scotland and achieving another duck against Wales, bowled by Jack Mercer (later himself to take an all-ten) but taking five wickets in an innings with his medium pace. Pat Hone also made a (first-ball) duck on debut. He later wrote *Cricket in Ireland*, published in 1955 it was the country's standard cricket history. In 1879 his wicketkeeping uncle Leland had become the first man to represent England in Tests who had never played for a first-class county. King's final victim, Joseph Lynch, was playing his only first-class match. He was killed in France in 1915 aged 35. It has to be recognised that the Irish team wasn't very strong. Five were making their first-class debut, some top players were unavailable, and it has been suggested that its selection was biased towards the south. In their careers the whole team played only 65 first-class matches between them, scoring 1,273 runs at an average of 11.68 with just four fifties but no centuries.

Philadelphia in turn also struggled for a while. Opener C.Christopher 'Christy' Morris went first. To honour his lifelong devotion to the game the famous Cricket Library and Collection housed in the Haverford College Library would later be named after him. However with opener Francis White batting three hours for 118 and the tail wagging vigorously, the home side eventually achieved a healthy lead (Morrow coming on late taking four for 42). The Irish did even worse second time around, King (four for 38) and Hordern (five for 30) sharing the wickets, with King this time legitimately dismissing Morrow, and then Browning and Aston, in an all-bowled hat-trick. The dinner dance laid on in the evening in the club house may have been some consolation.

Ireland did no better in the return match at Manheim, though Morrow shone again, top scoring in each innings with 35 out of 78 and 22 out of 68. Sadly he did not live to an old age, dying in a Dublin nursing home in 1914 aged 37.

How good was King? C.B. Fry thought him 'the best swerver I ever saw', Hordern said that he would be his first choice in a World XI, and Yorkshire's Rockley Wilson thought that around 1903 he was probably the best fast bowler in the world. King had a very good record on tour. The counties didn't usually field their strongest teams but on the other hand, playing for a relatively weak team, King often lacked consistent support at the other end. Some evidence is provided by King's record against a selection of the top batsmen of the period. For example, he bowled in 59 innings against one or other of Warner, Jessop, Hayward, Ranji, S.E.Gregory, G.Giffen, Darling and Hill, dismissing them 19 times (ie about 1 in 3 innings). Hugh Trumble, one of Australia's greatest bowlers, dismissed the same batsmen 49 times in 141 innings (again about 1 in 3). This comparison has many limitations, but does suggest that King's record against the best was good, lending weight to the high regard in which he was held.

Finishing with 415 wickets at 15.65 each, King's career ended in 1912 as it had begun, with two matches against Australian tourists. He continued to play club cricket, but Philadelphian cricket went into decline after the War due to the counter-attraction of other leisure opportunities. King's later career was in insurance. Elected an honorary life member of MCC in 1962, he died three years later in a Philadelphia nursing home two days short of his 92nd birthday.

Alonzo Drake

Yorkshire v Somerset, 1914
County Championship

Clarence Park, Weston-super-Mare on 27, 28 August 1914 (3-day match)
Toss won by Yorkshire
Yorkshire won by 140 runs
Umpires: A Millward, AE Street
Yorkshire 162 (JJ Bridges 5-59) and 112 (E Robson 5-38); Somerset 44 (MW Booth 5-27, A Drake 5-16) and 90 (A Drake 10-35)

Somerset second innings

BL Bisgood	c Dolphin b Drake	11
+H Chidgey	b Drake	4
E Robson	c Birtles b Drake	3
LC Braund	b Drake	9
BD Hylton Stewart	st Dolphin b Drake	3
W Hyman	st Dolphin b Drake	4
*ESM Poyntz	c Oldroyd b Drake	5
PP Hope	c and b Drake	19
HW Saunders	b Drake	0
JD Harcombe	b Drake	26
JJ Bridges	not out	1
Extras	(b 4, nb 1)	5
Total	(all out, 17.5 overs)	90

Fall of wickets 1-13, 2-20, 3-25, 4-28, 5-33, 6-38, 7-49, 8-52, 9-89, 10-90

Yorkshire bowling : MW Booth 9-0-50-0, A Drake 8.5-0-35-10

Yorkshire: MW Booth, BB Wilson, D Denton, R Kilner, W Rhodes, TJD Birtles, A Drake, P Holmes, GH Hirst (capt), E Oldroyd, A Dolphin (wk)

Another tragic figure of Edwardian cricket, Alonzo Drake was born in Rotherham in 1884. He bowled left-arm slow to medium pace. Swinging and spinning the ball, he could be irresistible when conditions favoured him. He was also an attacking left-hand batsman, twice scoring 1,000 runs in a season.

Drake made his county debut in 1909 at a time when Yorkshire needed to plan for the future. George Hirst and Schofield Haigh were nearing 40, and it was hoped that Drake and Major Booth in particular would help form the nucleus of the next Championship-winning team. A forward, Drake was also a talented footballer, notably for Sheffield United, but he also came down south to play for Queen's Park Rangers. It appears however that he gave up the professional game when his cricket career began to take off. His bowling continued to develop and in 1914 he took 158 wickets, a total only exceeded that season by Colin Blythe and Hampshire's Alex Kennedy. Just over a month before the Weston match he performed another rare feat, taking 4 wickets in 4 balls against Derbyshire at Chesterfield.

Clarence Park was staging its first cricket festival. By the time the seaside ground dropped off the circuit in 1996, holidaymakers had enjoyed 191 first-class matches there. However, the only all-ten in all that time was taken in the first match of that very first festival. The atmosphere wasn't very festive. The War to End All Wars had just begun and Sir John French's British Expeditionary Force was already suffering casualties in Belgium. County cricket struggled on until the end of the month when it was decided in the face of mounting criticism that it must end, leaving a few matches unplayed. Despite the shadow cast by the War the match was well attended. Somerset had been a poor side for some time, usually finishing around the bottom of the Championship and at Weston they were missing a number of key amateurs, notably J.C.White, their most successful ever bowler. Yorkshire on the other hand continued to be formidable opponents, finishing fourth in the Championship (won by Surrey). Their bowling depended almost exclusively on Booth, Drake and Wilfred Rhodes. They arrived at Weston from Bristol where they had heavily defeated Gloucestershire, Booth and Drake having bowled unchanged in both innings. Somerset must have feared the worst: the previous year at Bath Drake's match figures were a remarkable seven for 7 (four for 4 in the first innings, three for 3 in the second).

Yorkshire fielded an all-professional side. Their captain Sir Archibald White having joined his regiment, they were led by Hirst. Somerset, captained by Massey Poyntz, still relied considerably on amateurs. A combination of rain and a newly laid and poorly prepared pitch that cut up badly would make batting increasingly difficult in a match ending well inside two days. Yorkshire batted first in good weather. They wasted no time and after an hour had scored 90 for five, mainly thanks to a typically dashing 52 by David Denton. Drake going in at seven then batted steadily for an hour and a half, his 51 seeing his side through to what proved to be a match-winning 162. The Somerset batting was opened by amateur Bertram Bisgood and professional Len Braund. Bisgood had made a century against Worcestershire on his debut seven years before but had not done a lot since. Braund, one of the major figures of cricket's Golden Age, didn't bowl his leg spin much now, although he had taken three wickets, including Drake's, in Yorkshire's first innings. He could still bat though, the previous year making 257 not out against Worcestershire. Unfortunately neither stayed long. They were in good company as Booth and Drake, sharing the wickets, needed only 15 overs to skittle Somerset.

Twenty-seven-year-old Booth (Major was his first name, not a military rank) bowled medium-fast right-arm. He had a short, brilliant career: in just over four full English seasons (plus a tour to South Africa in which he was capped twice) taking 603 wickets. A useful bat he accomplished the 1,000 run-100 wicket double in 1913. Weston was his penultimate first-class match. Two years later he lost his life on the first day of the Battle of the Somme.

Yorkshire made 112 in their second knock, Drake making 12 before he became one of 44-year-old fellow Yorkshireman Ernie Robson's five victims. A great Somerset servant, allrounder Robson bowled fast-medium and is one of only four bowlers to have taken over 1,000 wickets for the county. Still playing in 1923, he was appointed to the umpires' list for the following season but died in May before donning the white coat.

Set an unlikely 231 to win, Somerset began batting just before lunch on the second day. This time wicketkeeper Harry Chidgey (final career record 99 matches, 717 runs), promoted from his first innings number eleven, opened with Bisgood. Like most of his colleagues, he didn't last long, although he helped put on 13, the highest opening partnership of the match. Somerset's puny final total might have been even worse if John Harcombe, going in at 52 for eight, had not hit Drake for 11 in an over on the way to a bright 26 before the Yorkshireman bowled him to finish the innings. Harcombe was a 31-year-old South African who had settled in the west and was playing his first match for nine years. He played a few matches for the county, but with little success. Bowled twice by Drake without scoring, Henry Saunders, another occasional amateur, would not have enjoyed his only Championship match. Drake needed only 53 balls to take all-ten (and in fact took the wickets in a spell of 42 balls). To this day no other bowler has performed the feat so quickly, or without bowling a maiden. Bowling within himself as the end drew close, Booth did his best not to spoil Drake's show. Drake had been well supported by Arthur Dolphin, Yorkshire's regular wicketkeeper since 1910, a position he would hold until 1927. Dolphin later became a respected first-class, and Test, umpire, standing bareheaded whatever the weather. One of Dolphin's victims, William Hyman, was playing in the penultimate match of a 38-match career in which he would make exactly 1,000 runs. His main claim to fame is an innings of 359 not out for Bath Cricket Association against Thornbury in 1902 (apparently made in less than two hours!).

Drake's figures beat Yorkshire's previous best, nine for 22 by left-arm spinner Bobby Peel in 1895, also against Somerset. A sign of Yorkshire's strength is that for various reasons three of its greats, all left-armers, were playing but didn't bowl. Still a formidable opponent, Wilfred Rhodes wasn't quite the bowler he used to be, or would become again; Hirst was coming to the end of his illustrious career; and Roy Kilner was played mainly as a batsman. As well as taking most wickets in the match Drake also scored most runs.

Drake was to play just one more match before his career ended with 480 wickets at 18.03 each. A rather brooding character, there were reservations about his temperament. If things did not go his way in the field he could become despondent, and his fielding could leave something to be desired. It is fairly clear now that these weaknesses were related to the illness that was to end his life prematurely. Turned down for military service his physical decline had been evident for some time, although he was still working as a wool operative in 1918 and playing cricket. A heavy smoker he probably had cancer although it was a heart attack that took him suddenly in 1919.

What might Alonzo Drake, and Major Booth, have achieved after the War if they had been spared? Yorkshire quickly developed some new stars and returned to their powerful best but England were initially outclassed by Australia and they might just have helped stem the tide. Who knows?

Frank Tarrant

Maharaja of Cooch-Behar's XI v Lord Willingdon's XI, 1918/19

Deccan Gymkhana Ground, Poona on 12, 13 August 1918 (2-day match)
Toss won by Lord Willingdon's XI
Match drawn
Lord Willingdon's XI 219 (FA Tarrant 10-90) and 132-4 dec; Maharaja of Cooch-Behar's XI 265 (FA Tarrant 182 not out, SM Joshi 6-56) and 22-4

Lord Willingdon's XI first innings

KO Goldie	c Gaekwad b Tarrant	64
TW Kirkwood	lbw b Tarrant	13
P Vithal	lbw b Tarrant	9
DK Kapadia	b Tarrant	43
SA Mirza	lbw b Tarrant	0
M Yusuf Baig	not out	34
*GA Laverton	c Dass b Tarrant	15
+PJ Chinoy	b Tarrant	4
CM Rigby	c Banerjee b Tarrant	0
SM Joshi	b Tarrant	14
PH Daruwala	b Tarrant	0
Extras		23
Total	(all out, 72.4 overs)	219

Fall of wickets 1-48, 2-72, 3-129, 4-153, 5-153, 6-181, 7-192, 8-192, 9-217, 10-219

Maharaja of Cooch-Behar's XI bowling: FA Tarrant 35.4-4-90-10, HW Lee 22-4-72-0, S Ghose 8-3-17-0, B Mukherjee 2-0-11-0, KHS Narayan 5-2-6-0

Maharaja of Cooch-Behar's XI: HW Lee, B Mukherjee, M Dass, P Banerjee (wk), FA Tarrant, D Gaekwad, P Ghosh, KHS Narayan, S Bose, S Aikut, S Ghose

One of the best cricketers never to play Test cricket, as an Australian playing most of his cricket in England the restrictive qualification rules of the time prevented Frank Tarrant playing at that level. If he had he would probably have been successful as both batsman and bowler. His first-class career lasted almost 38 years (only C.K. Nayudu, W.G. Grace, Lord Harris and A.W. Nourse played longer) and when he finally retired he had scored nearly 18,000 runs at an average of 36.41 and taken over 1,500 wickets at 17.49. An Australian who starred in England, he was the first man to take all-ten in India! He made himself into a very good batsman, at first a bit cautious but in later years hard hitting and aggressive. As a left-arm spinner he could vary his pace from slow to medium and at his best was surpassed at the time (probably only just) by Colin Blythe and Wilfred Rhodes. He was a true allrounder, his performances fit to rank with those of Giffen, Grace and other greats and when he had played his last match for Middlesex in 1914, only Pelham Warner had scored more runs for the county and only J.T.Hearne taken more wickets.

Tarrant was born in Melbourne in 1880. Having played three games for

Victoria and obtained employment as a ground bowler for the Melbourne Cricket Club he knew that if he wanted to make cricket his profession he had to play in England. A touring Pelham Warner, impressed with what he saw in the nets, arranged for him to be taken on the Lord's groundstaff so that he could qualify for Middlesex. Gradually coming to terms with English conditions Tarrant's performances improved each year before he leapt into prominence in 1907 with 1,552 runs and 183 wickets (curiously exactly the same number of wickets as fellow left-armers George Hirst and Colin Blythe). This was his first double, a feat he was to repeat (comfortably) in each of the following seven seasons.

Tarrant nearly achieved an all-ten at Bristol in 1907 when, having taken the first nine Gloucestershire second innings wickets for 41 on a treacherous pitch, the last one fell to J.T. Hearne. There was plenty of time left (the match finished at twenty to two) and Middlesex won by an innings. I wonder if Tarrant felt a bit aggrieved?

The First World War marked the end of Tarrant's English career; at the end of the 1914 season he moved to India, making it his base for most of the next 30 or so years, interspersed with visits to Australia. Wealthy princes had begun to provide coaching opportunities in India and as Tarrant had spent his past few winters coaching there it was a natural move. During the War he played a number of first-class matches in India with considerable success, but none more so than when he played for the Maharaja of Cooch-Behar's XI at the Deccan Gymkhana Ground in August 1918. First-class cricket in India was still in its relative infancy, although India was the only country where first-class cricket was played in every wartime season. In 1918/19 the season amounted to eight matches of which Tarrant played in four. Indian princes had begun to realise that involvement with the British national game could help further their political power, hence during 1917/18 and 1918/19 the Maharaja's team played a number of games now regarded as first-class, including two against a team representing the Governor of Bombay (Lord Willingdon). The Deccan Gymkhana is one of the oldest sporting institutions in India; initially a cricket club it slowly expanded to provide facilities for many sports. The Gymkhana Ground was used regularly for cricket from the end of the 19th century until the 1920s, mainly for the annual Europeans against Parsees match. It has been little used since for first-class cricket, although it is still used for other matches.

The Maharaja's team in August 1918 mainly relied on two players: Tarrant and county colleague Harry Lee, who was coaching at Cooch Behar College and would go on to have a long and successful career when he returned to England. The rest of the side were home-based players whose first-class careers would amount to a handful of unsuccessful matches each - most notably Susanta Ghose who in this his only first-class match batted once, at number eleven, making one run, and did not bowl. Although his Lordship's eleven did not include anybody of the quality of Tarrant and Lee, the talent that it did have was spread a bit more evenly throughout the team, some of whom would have at least some success on the cricket field.

The first day was a local holiday and Willingdon's XI, captained by George Laverton (ex Harrow School), batted first on a fast true pitch in front of a large crowd. They made a good start, reaching 129 for two thanks to Edinburgh-born Thomas Kirkwood, who in his sixth, and last, first-class match contributed 13 (his highest ever score) to an opening partnership of 48, Kenneth Goldie (64) and Dolly Kapadia (43). A punishing batsman, Goldie could only play in England when home on leave from service with the Indian Army. When he did, he found a place in a strong Sussex batting line up - Fry, Ranji et al playing 64 times and scoring three centuries. After Goldie and Kapadia went nobody apart from Mirza Yusuf Baig offered much resistance. Except for changing ends twice Tarrant bowled throughout the innings. He hit the stumps four times as well as persuading the umpires to judge three other batsmen leg-before. The previous best figures in India had been nine for 17 by Guy Napier (Cambridge University and Middlesex) for Europeans against Parsees, also at Poona, in September 1909. Napier lost his life six years later in the Battle of Loos.

After Lee, who opened for the Maharaja's side, went for only ten, wickets fell regularly and, although Tarrant was still there with 29 not out, a close of play score of 90 for eight did not bode well. However the following day Tarrant and S.Aikut (a number ten of no batting pretension) came together in an extraordinary partnership of 173 for the ninth wicket. It lasted 210 minutes and Aikut contributed just 5 before he was run out. Of partnerships between 150 and 199 runs only two other batsmen have exceeded Tarrant's 87 % share. After his 182 not out the next highest score was 12! Three batsman have scored a century and taken all-ten in the same match. Tarrant's was easily the highest individual innings of the three.

After this there was relatively little time left for play and the match petered out into a draw. Even allowing for the fact that the opposition weren't especially strong Tarrant's had been a remarkable allround performance.

Tarrant's association with the subcontinent was to prove lucrative. He became involved in trading racehorses for Indian princes, an activity that generated more income for him than cricket ever had, and enabled him to buy property in Australia. He still remained involved with cricket however, including playing in a few first-class matches, helping in the organisation of Indian cricket (especially managing the unofficial Australian tour of 1935/36), and umpiring, including standing in 1933/34 (together with Surrey's Bill Hitch) in the first two Test matches played in India. And finally, in 1936, he made his last first-class appearance, for Europeans against Hindus in the Quadrangular Tournament. At the age of 56 he bowled 43 overs taking four wickets, all Test cricketers, and made 78 and 18 against a strong Hindu attack.

Frank Tarrant spent his final years in Australia. He died in Melbourne in 1951 a very wealthy man.

Billy Bestwick

Derbyshire v Glamorgan, 1921
County Championship

Cardiff Arms Park, Cardiff on 18, 20 June 1921 (3-day match)
Toss won by Glamorgan
Derbyshire won by two wickets
Umpires: GP Harrison, JP Whiteside
Glamorgan 168 and 106 (W Bestwick 10-40); Derbyshire 83 and 193-8 (A Nash 5-56)

Glamorgan second innings

*TAL Whittington	b Bestwick	0
WN Gemmill	b Bestwick	2
WE Bates	b Bestwick	48
H Tomlinson	c Storer b Bestwick	20
+GE Cording	b Bestwick	4
HG Symonds	b Bestwick	1
WLT Jenkins	c Elliott b Bestwick	6
AE O'Bree	c Storer b Bestwick	16
JC Clay	b Bestwick	5
H Creber	b Bestwick	1
A Nash	not out	0
Extras	(b 1, lb 2)	3
Total	(all out, 37 overs)	106

Fall of wickets 1-0, 2-9, 3-48, 4-60, 5-71, 6-80, 7-89, 8-105, 9-106, 10-106

Derbyshire bowling: W Bestwick 19-2-40-10, WJV Tomlinson 6-0-17-0, H Storer 6-1-24-0, W Reader-Blackton 6-1-22-0

Derbyshire: GM Buckston (capt), W Carter, GR Jackson, G Curgenven, SWA Cadman, H Storer, JM Hutchinson, W Reader-Blackton, WJV Tomlinson, H Elliott (wk), W Bestwick

At 46 years 116 days, Billy Bestwick is the oldest man to take an all-ten. He played for Derbyshire from 1898 until 1925 with, remarkably, a five year first-class 'career-break' from 1910 until 1914. Born in Heanor in 1875, one of 14 children, Bestwick was a miner when not playing cricket. Well-built, bowling fast-medium off a short run-up, with a strong body action, usually making the ball move away after pitching, he could extract life from most wickets.

He made his first-class debut for Derbyshire in 1898 and, together with Arnold Warren, provided the cutting edge of the Derbyshire attack until he was released in 1909. Like many cricketers of the day he had a liking for drink, and the committee finally decided that they had had enough and that, fine bowler though he was, he had to go. Two years previously he had been involved in a pub brawl at Heanor resulting in the death by knife wound of a William Brown, but was acquitted of manslaughter on the grounds that he acted in self-defence. His first-class career apparently ended, Bestwick moved to south Wales in 1912 to find work in the mines and steelworks and to qualify for Glamorgan, for whom he played in 1914 before they joined the County Championship. After the War, Bestwick and Derbyshire made up their differences and in 1919 the returning veteran headed the county averages. Unable to agree terms for 1920 Bestwick was again back in south Wales but Derbyshire saw sense, improved their offer, and he returned to his home county for the following season. He had lost a little speed, but his skill was undiminished and even in 1925, his last season, he took seven for 20 against Leicestershire.

Derbyshire finished twelfth in the Championship in 1921, a seemingly modest achievement, but a considerable improvement on 1920 when they lost all their 17 matches. *Wisden* chiefly attributed this change in fortunes to Bestwick who took three times as many wickets as any other bowler. Glamorgan were in their first Championship season. They had won their inaugural match, against Sussex, in front of a wildly enthusiastic Cardiff crowd of some 7,000, but little went right after that and when the season ended the Welsh county had taken over from Derbyshire as wooden spoonists. The county ground was next to the famous Cardiff Arms Park: this was not yet the dominating presence it would become upon completion in 1934 of a new double-decker rugby stand along the southern boundary of the cricket ground. Despite his years Bestwick was back full-time. He had taken 1,024 first-class wickets in a 240-match career and had begun the season in fine form, adding another 56 wickets in just seven matches. With 147 wickets at less than 17 apiece Bestwick would eventually have his best season ever, and finish close to the top of the first-class averages.

Derbyshire were captained at Cardiff by 40-year-old George Buckston who had returned to the first-class game after a break of 14 years. Their western tour had not gone well so far with defeats against Somerset and Gloucestershire, and things weren't looking any better by close on Saturday. Missing their captain and leading batsman, Norman Riches, Glamorgan scored 168 (Bestwick four for 71, William Bates 67). Derbyshire began their innings against two Glamorgan bowlers at different stages in their careers, 23-year-old Johnnie Clay and 47-year-old Jack Nash. The young and the old soon reduced the visitors to nought for three, a catastrophic start from which they never recovered. With Bates achieving career-best figures of four for 17 with his left-arm spin Derbyshire's innings finished just before close of play, Bestwick making one of his 141 career ducks.

What to do on the Sunday rest day? Have a drink of course. For away matches, to ensure some moderation, one of the team was usually given the job of chaperoning Bestwick, the long-serving, and perhaps long-suffering, allrounder Arthur Morton often getting the job. Unfortunately, because of a motorcycle accident Morton was out of the side and the usual arrangements clearly failed because by Sunday evening Bestwick was 'hors-de-combat' after a heavy session with friends from Neath.

However, whatever condition he was still in on Monday morning clearly didn't affect his bowling. Opening the attack in overcast conditions, he bowled the Glamorgan vice-captain Tom Whittington in his first over and with the score nine William Gemmill shared the same fate. Leicestershire-born left-hander Harry Tomlinson then helped Bates take the score to 48 before he became Bestwick's third victim, caught by Harry Storer. Thirty-five-year-old local club professional Tomlinson had made his first-class debut in the previous match. He had started well, top scoring with 36 against Somerset, but he never surpassed this score and his first-class career would be over after eight matches. When he left Bestwick bowled with such devastating effect that he had taken all ten wickets before lunch, the last three in four balls, as the home side slumped to 106 all out. Bestwick's final victim, 49-year-old Harry Creber, was, like Nash, a key part of Glamorgan's pre-war Minor County success that led to the county's promotion to the first-class ranks. Bestwick hit the stumps seven times. Bates had top scored again but couldn't find anybody to partner him for long. He had played for Yorkshire before the War and as a reliable batsman and useful bowler would serve Glamorgan well for ten years. Sport was in his blood. His father played cricket 15 times for England in the 1880s; his son was Ted Bates, legendary Southampton Football Club manager.

Bestwick had a set a county record that still stands, beating William Mycroft's nine for 25 against Hampshire in 1876. It might have been his second all-ten. The previous month he dismissed nine Warwickshire batsmen for 65 at Edgbaston, but unfortunately Sam Cadman picked up the opener Leonard Bates (no relation) who had batted throughout most of the innings. *Wisden*'s match report makes no reference to Bestwick's nine wickets.

Given what had gone before, 192 to win was a considerable target, and at 116 for eight a Derbyshire defeat seemed inevitable. However, Watford footballer Bill Carter (50 not out) and wicketkeeper Harry Elliott (20 not out) then attacked the bowling so effectively that victory was achieved by 5 o'clock, a perhaps unexpected outcome given that neither Carter nor Elliott yet had a first-class fifty to his name, and both had failed to score in Derbyshire's first innings. Fortunately the number eleven batsman (W.Bestwick, final career average 4.71) was not required to bat! Elliott would eventually play 520 matches for the county and, returning in an emergency for four matches in 1947, was one of two players in the match to play after the Second World War. The other was Johnnie Clay who in 1948, aged 50, would appropriately take the final Hampshire wicket that sealed Glamorgan's first Championship title.

The Derbyshire Committee decided to reward Bestwick for his achievement at Cardiff with collections at the next two home games. As players then only received match fees in the summer he generously gave half of the sum collected to his minder, Arthur Morton, to help him out during his spell out of the side.

Bestwick finished his 323-match career with 1,457 wickets at 21 apiece, all but five of which were taken for Derbyshire, a total still only exceeded for the county by the redoubtable pair of Cliff Gladwin and Les Jackson. In 1922 he uniquely bowled in tandem with his son Bob while Warwickshire's Willie Quaife and son Bernard batted together.

Perhaps surprisingly in view of his apparent unreliability, Bestwick became a first-class umpire standing in over 200 matches (including three Tests). Ill health forced his retirement at the end of the 1937 season and he died in May 1938.

Jack White

Somerset v Worcestershire, 1921
County Championship

County Ground, New Road, Worcester on 18, 20, 21 June 1921 (3-day match)
Toss won by Worcestershire
Somerset won by 83 runs
Umpires: J Carlin, J Moss
Somerset 237 (E.Robson 111) and 364 (PR Johnson 163, CV Tarbox 7-55); Worcestershire 237 (JC White 10-76) and 281 (E Robson 5-83, JC White 5-99)

Worcestershire first innings

FL Bowley	c Lowry b White	1
FA Pearson	c and b White	74
RE Turner	b White	12
HL Higgins	lbw b White	16
*MFS Jewell	st Chidgey b White	66
WE Richardson	b White	7
CR Preece	c Daniell b White	27
CV Tarbox	b White	13
+CB Ponsonby	lbw b White	0
VW Humpherson	not out	2
HA Gilbert	c Hope b White	0
Extras	(b 14, lb 5)	19
Total	(all out, 91.2 overs)	237

Fall of wickets 1-4, 2-47, 3-81, 4-106, 5-127, 6-182, 7-222, 8-222, 9-237, 10-237

Somerset bowling: E Robson 25-4-71-0, JC White 42.2-11-76-10, GE Hunt 18-4-55-0, LE Wharton 6-2-16-0

Somerset: PR Johnson, J Daniell (capt), TC Lowry, LE Wharton, FE Spurway, E Robson, PP Hope, JC White, LH Key, GE Hunt, H Chidgey (wk)

Together with W.G.Grace and Trevor Bailey, Jack (J.C.) White is one of only three amateurs to have taken 2,000 first-class wickets. Born in 1891 in Holford, in north Somerset, he followed his father into farming. Fortunately he organised his life so that agriculture didn't cause him to miss too much cricket, and when he was away his father looked after business. At Taunton School he came under the influence of coach and fellow slow left-armer Ted Tyler, then the only bowler with an all-ten for Somerset. He made his first-class debut in 1909. Excused war service as a farmer, he took 100 wickets in a season for the first time in 1919, a feat he repeated annually until 1932. When he retired in 1937 he had taken 2,165 wickets for Somerset, a total nobody has got close to passing.

White had a ruddy complexion and hair which had turned from fair to silvery-grey. He didn't spin the ball much. He didn't need to. He had many other strengths: cunning flight, the ability to make the ball swerve and dip, unrelenting accuracy, and great perseverance. These attributes made him a formidable opponent on hard pitches where bowlers more reliant on spin struggled.

Somerset depended heavily on amateurs: in 1921 the names of 26 of the 30 players used in the Championship were prefixed by 'Mr' on the scorecard. In the early 1920s they consistently finished around mid-table in the Championship, a decent performance given their limited resources. They were led by the forceful ex-rugby union international John Daniell who captained them in all but two of the 15 seasons between 1908 and 1926, and who did much to hold the side together during difficult times. Worcestershire on the other hand consistently finished near to (or at) the bottom. They were led by Chile-born amateur Maurice Jewell, a moderate cricketer but another whose efforts to keep his county club alive should not be underestimated. The county had joined the Championship in 1899, playing then, as they still do, at the beautiful New Road ground. By mid-June 1921 White had already taken ten or more wickets in a match four times. And he liked bowling against Worcestershire. He would eventually take more wickets against them (218) than against any other opponents, including 16 in one day at Bath in 1919.

Batting first Somerset made 237, mainly thanks to a century by the 51-year-old Ernie Robson, one of the county's few professionals. The Somerset attack was then opened by workhorse Robson and White, who soon had Fred Bowley caught by Cambridge undergraduate Tom Lowry (a future New Zealand captain and brother-in-law of future England captain Percy Chapman). Bowley's 276 against Hampshire in 1914 was a Worcestershire record that would stand until 1982. The other opener was stalwart allrounder 'Dick' Pearson (who two years later would achieve the double for the only time in his career at the age of nearly 43). With only three wickets down just before the close Worcestershire were probably feeling pleased with their day's work. However, White then held one back to Pearson and caught and bowled him, and the sides ended the day evenly placed with Worcestershire 108 for four. White quickly took another wicket, his fifth, on Monday morning but Somerset were then held up by a captain's innings by Jewell who made 66 before being stumped by Harry Chidgey. At 222 for six the home team might have hoped for a first innings lead, but White quickly removed the tail and the two sides finished exactly level after their first innings. Last man in had been Humphrey 'Barmy' Gilbert, a barrister who had bowled with considerable success for Oxford University before the War. In 1909 he had been asked to be at Edgbaston for the First Test in case he was needed to play against Australia. He was no bat however and had soon been caught by Philip Hope who, together with Robson and Chidgey, was one of only three members of the Somerset side who been playing when Alonzo Drake had scythed his way through them seven years before.

White had bowled almost unchanged for 42 overs for his all-ten, light work for someone who would become well used to bowling over 50 overs in an innings and who would three times exceed 70. He had nearly achieved an all-ten at Bristol in August 1914, taking nine for 46, but missing Thomas

Langdon, the Gloucestershire opener, who had been run out early on. His all-ten was the second for Somerset and the first at Worcester. And long-serving umpire John Moss had seen his third all-ten, having previously stood whilst Trott and Fielder performed the feat.

Uniquely, on the same day, less than 100 miles away at Cardiff, Billy Bestwick was also taking his all-ten. With due deference to social status the headline in *The Times* read 'TEN WICKETS IN AN INNINGS. MR JC WHITE AND BESTWICK'

Somerset's second innings 364 was dominated by a brilliant 163 by the ever-elegant forty-year-old amateur Randall Johnson. Aged 29, medium pacer Charles Tarbox was in his debut season. He hadn't even bowled in Somerset's first innings, but this time he took seven for 55, improving on his previous best of two for 27. Worcestershire's target was tough: 365 in 280 minutes. At 199 for one they had a chance. However apart from Bowley (99) and Pearson (80), nobody else did much and they lost by 83 runs, Robson and White, five for 99 in 47 overs, sharing the bowling and the wickets. White was the first bowler to take 15 wickets in a match at Worcester, a feat only repeated there once, by Worcestershire's Reg Perks in 1937, five days before White at the age of 46 signed off his first-class career with second innings figures of six for 52 against Glamorgan.

The last Worcester wicket fell at 6.45 pm. Somerset then had to get to Derby where they were playing the next day, and where coincidentally Bestwick and White would be in opposition. Somerset were in the field again, the apparently inexhaustible Robson and White bowling another 57 overs and dismissing Derbyshire for 155. And even then White didn't get much of a rest. His batting was improving (he eventually made six first-class centuries), and promoted to number five he was quickly in at 26 for three. Next day he reached 80, at the time his highest first-class score, before he was bowled by Bestwick. He then bowled another 41 overs in taking eight Derbyshire second innings wickets.

White was in the middle of a purple patch: 57 wickets in five matches. With England two down against Warwick Armstrong's rampant Australians, the Test selectors could not ignore such form and White was one of four England debutants in the Third Test at Leeds. Although he took three second innings wickets for only 37, after another defeat the selectors were in no mood for continuity. They used 30 players in the series, and after one match White was out. He did not reappear for seven years, but when he did he performed famously and tirelessly on England's victorious 1928/29 tour of Australia, with 25 wickets finishing the leading bowler on either side. Nearing 40, White's remaining Test career was brief and he finished with 49 wickets from 15 matches.

A reserved, undemonstrative man it has to be said that he probably wasn't that popular with team-mates, but neither did he court popularity. He could be sparse in his encouragement of the younger professionals, arguably a failing in someone who captained his county from 1927 to 1931 (and occasionally his country). However, on his return from Australia the people of Taunton lined the streets to welcome their local hero.

'Farmer' White died in May 1961, soon after being appointed president of the County Cricket Club. A pair of wrought iron gates were erected in his memory at the entrance to the Taunton County Ground.

Tom Rushby

Surrey v Somerset, 1921
County Championship

County Ground, Taunton on 6, 7, 8 July 1921 (3-day match)
Toss won by Surrey
Surrey won by 229 runs
Umpires: AJ Atfield, JH Board
Surrey 236 and 264 (A Sandham 109, E Robson 6-84); Somerset 110 (T Rushby 10-43) and 161 (JW Hitch 6-59)

Somerset first innings

PR Johnson	c Hitch b Rushby	0
AES Rippon	lbw b Rushby	10
SGU Considine	b Rushby	0
LE Wharton	c Shepherd b Rushby	7
TC Lowry	b Rushby	18
E Robson	b Rushby	31
*J Daniell	lbw b Rushby	0
JC White	c Shepherd b Rushby	0
GE Hunt	c Strudwick b Rushby	1
WS Whiting	not out	18
+SL Amor	c Sandham b Rushby	19
Extras	(b 5, w 1)	6
Total	(all out, 35.5 overs)	110

Fall of wickets 1-2, 2-3, 3-10, 4-32, 5-41, 6-45, 7-51, 8-61, 9-82, 10-110

Surrey bowling: JW Hitch 8-1-21-0, T Rushby 17.5-4-43-10, PGH Fender 8-1-35-0, HA Peach 2-1-5-0

Surrey: A Jeacocke, A Sandham, A Ducat, TF Shepherd, HA Peach, JW Hitch, PGH Fender (capt), WJ Abel, JH Vincett, H Strudwick (wk), T Rushby

Soon after White's all-ten, the tables were turned as Somerset had two inflicted upon them in a three-week period, the first by Surrey's Tom Rushby. Born in Cobham, Surrey in 1880, Rushby was by trade a carpenter and so better placed than some to cope with the uncertainties of life as a professional cricketer. Making his first-class debut in 1903 he came to the fore in 1909, taking over 100 wickets and finishing close to the top of the national averages. But then in 1910 he left Surrey to play Lancashire League cricket. The issues are murky, but this seems to have been related to a rift between Committee and players which resulted in England's Jack Crawford leaving and the termination of the contract of Australian Alan Marshal. Fortunately Rushby's northern sojourn was brief and he was back in 1911. His tireless fast-medium bowling, often on fairly batsmen-friendly Oval pitches, made him a mainstay of the Surrey attack and in 1914, when they won the Championship for the only time between 1899 and the 1950s, he headed the county's averages. Unsurprisingly the circumstances were unusual. Because of the War Surrey, well clear at the top of the table, cancelled their last two matches. Some argued that they had forfeited the right to the title and that it should be held in abeyance.

However, common sense prevailed and an MCC Committee meeting held in November declared Surrey Champions. Minds were then of course on more serious matters.

Although nearing 40 when cricket recommenced in 1919, Rushby was still a force to be reckoned with. And Surrey certainly needed him. He and Bill Hitch carried the attack, in all matches bowling 1,900 overs and taking 251 wickets between them, with Rushby taking over 100 for the fourth and last time. But by 1921 his powers were waning and this proved to be his last season as he dropped out of the first-class game through illness, having taken 954 wickets (all for Surrey) at 20.58 apiece.

Led by the ever resourceful Percy Fender Surrey were a team to reckon with. Six of the side played for England against Warwick Armstrong's Australia, and Tom Shepherd, who didn't, was one of the season's leading batsmen. In the early 1920s they were always near to the top of the Championship, although never quite doing enough to reach the very top. They were to come so close in 1921. Going into their last match, at Lord's against leaders, and reigning Champions, Middlesex, they had won 15 matches. They needed just one more win to take the crown from their north London rivals. Unfortunately, having bowled the home side out for 132 in the first innings, they couldn't prevent them reaching 322 in their second to win by six wickets. For the second successive season Middlesex had won the Championship at Lord's in an exciting finale that would be mirrored there 95 years later.

At Taunton back in early July things had been a bit easier, although not at first as Surrey, with Hobbs out with appendicitis, slumped to 76 for six on the first morning, before recovering to make 236 thanks to 72 by William Abel and 49 by Fender. Abel was the son of Bobby Abel, whose unbeaten 357 still stands as Surrey's highest ever individual score. Not in the same class as his illustrious father, he was still a useful cricketer who played 170 times for the county. It is an interesting reflection on early 1920s cricket, or at least the Somerset attack, that the first dismissal in the match, with only ten runs on the board, was a stumping, Alfred Jeacocke falling to White's left-arm wiles.

Somerset would have been feeling some confidence that they would make a decent reply. In their previous match against Warwickshire, which they won by seven wickets, Randall Johnson and Louis Wharton had both made eighties, and Tom Lowry fifty. And the last time their opening pair had gone out together, against Glamorgan at Swansea in June, they had both made centuries and put on 189. This time however Johnson went first ball while his partner, Sydney Rippon, whose son Geoffrey, born three years later, would become a government minister, made just ten.

With Rushby taking advantage of a fast pitch wickets then fell at regular intervals with only the reliable Ernie Robson resisting for long. He was eventually bowled by Rushby just before close of play, which came with Somerset nine down for 89 (a slight improvement on 61 for eight). Rushby had taken all nine for 31 and, like James Lillywhite half a century before, would have a worrying night wondering whether he would achieve an all-ten. He did get his tenth wicket next morning, but he was made to wait a while, bowling another 17 balls before he had Stanley Amor, one of four wicketkeepers used by Somerset during the season, caught at mid on by Andy Sandham. The tenth wicket pairing of Amor and leg-spinner Walter Whiting had put on 28, the largest partnership of the innings. Amor was described by Peter Roebuck in his Somerset history as a 'big noise in Bath cricket'. In a 22-year career in which he played 29 matches he never got past 21, and so in the circumstances 19 was an impressive effort.

Rushby had bowled unchanged, whilst Hitch and Fender, both of whom played for England during the summer, bowled unsuccessfully at the other end. Three weeks after taking an all-ten, White had now himself been part of one. Another one of Rushby's victims was skipper John Daniell who was given out leg-before without scoring and would be given out caught behind in the second. As the umpires were then selected each season by the county captains themselves, these were arguably 'courageous decisions'. Both umpires however could no doubt stand up for themselves. Fifty-three-year-old Alf Atfield would eventually umpire 387 first-class matches. Gloucestershire's Jack Board, at the age of 54, was in his first season as a Championship umpire, but had previously played 525 first-class matches.

Surrey made 264 in their second innings, leaving Somerset 391 to win on a wearing pitch. Johnson again went first ball and, with the exception of Robson who made 50 out of a final total of 161, nobody provided much resistance, the match finishing early on Friday morning. This time Rushby took just one wicket, Bill Hitch with six for 59 doing the damage. The tireless veteran Robson had done his best to thwart Surrey, top scoring in each innings and taking ten wickets in the match.

Rushby's figures are still a county record, just beating Tom Richardson's ten for 45 against Essex in 1894. It was the sixth time he had taken five or more wickets in an innings against Somerset. The only other team against whom he had done it so often was the mighty Yorkshire. Returning to The Oval to play against Sussex he was, according to *The Cricketer*, 'given a rare reception' when he went out to bat. He took 70 wickets in 1921 and headed the Surrey averages, but *Wisden* commented that 'between his best days and his worst there was a great gulf', and he only played seven more matches in the season before his 229-match career was over. With the exception of one match for the Players he had appeared exclusively for Surrey. Only four other bowlers, Moss, Briggs, Drake and Shahid Mahmood (of whom more later), have taken all-ten in their final first-class season.

Variously described as enthusiastic, temperamental, and unpredictable, despite earlier problems Rushby's efforts were clearly highly regarded by his county, and he was granted a benefit in 1922, the Kent match yielding some £1,100. After retiring he became a private coach and died in Ewell, Surrey in 1962 aged nearly 82.

Charlie Parker

Gloucestershire v Somerset, 1921
County Championship

Fry's Ground, Bristol on 30 July, 1. 2 August 1921 (3-day match)
Toss won by Somerset
Gloucestershire won by one wicket
Umpires: J Blake, HI Young
Somerset 212 (CWL Parker 10-79) and 240 (PT Mills 5-92); Gloucestershire 248 and 205-9

Somerset first innings

PR Johnson	c Barnett b Parker	1
JCW MacBryan	c Williams b Parker	46
TC Lowry	c Smith b Parker	20
A Young	b Parker	34
SGU Considine	lbw b Parker	23
+LE Wharton	b Parker	12
*J Daniell	st Robinson b Parker	4
E Robson	c Smith b Parker	7
JC White	lbw b Parker	16
JJ Bridges	c Barnett b Parker	24
RC Robertson-Glasgow	not out	21
Extras	(lb 3, w 1)	4
Total	(all out, 80.3 overs)	212

Fall of wickets 1-3, 2-47, 3-87, 4-116, 5-139, 6-142, 7-143, 8-161, 9-176, 10-212

Gloucestershire bowling: CWL Parker 40.3-13-79-10, PT Mills 38-7-116-0, EG Dennett 2-0-13-0

Gloucestershire: AE Dipper, FJ Seabrook, EP Barnett, WH Rowlands, PFC Williams, H Smith, FG Robinson (capt, wk), JL Stanton, PT Mills, CWL Parker, EG Dennett

Well over 3,000 first-class wickets, but just one Test cap, for one of the best left-arm spinners ever? Many reasons have been suggested: there were a number of very good spinners playing; Gloucestershire were perhaps an unfashionable county; Parker wasn't that young; maybe his fielding wasn't very good. His outspokenness didn't help. If something needed to be said, he said it. A kindly man off the field, Parker was at times his own worst enemy. Accosting Pelham Warner in the lift of a Bristol hotel at the end of Gloucestershire's Annual Dinner in 1929 didn't help his cause. Parker clearly blamed the influential Warner for his stunted Test career.

Born in Prestbury, Gloucestershire into a large farm-labouring family in 1882, Parker attended Cheltenham Grammar School and continued his self-education after leaving. He established himself in the Gloucestershire side in 1908. George Dennett was the left-arm spinner in situ and so Parker bowled medium pace. Although he did all right he wasn't really happy and after the War informed the county that he would play as a spinner, or leave.

With Dennett still serving as an officer in India the county acquiesced and Parker repaid them by taking wickets in vast numbers.

Over six feet tall, Parker had a beautiful smooth action and spun the ball fiercely despite bowling quicker than most spinners. Near unplayable on difficult pitches, his accuracy, puzzling flight and bristling aggression still made him a formidable opponent even in less helpful conditions.

Gloucestershire were a middling team in 1921, in fact so middling that of 24 Championship matches played they won 12 and lost 12. They had four captains during the season, Foster Robinson leading in half their matches. He usually also kept wicket although Gloucestershire had a very efficient keeper in Harry Smith who would play once for England in 1928. Smith was a useful batsman and would play even when not keeping.

Gloucestershire had already beaten Somerset once in 1921, Parker taking ten wickets at Taunton back in May. They would also win the Bristol return, but it would be a much closer game and Parker would take even more wickets. He had been in good form coming into the match, reaching his 100 wickets for the season earlier in the month, just before appearing in his one and only Test. There was a good crowd for the first day of the traditional August Bank Holiday fixture with the neighbours. The ground had been purchased in 1915 by J.S. Fry and Sons Ltd (the chocolate manufacturers), giving the county some respite from its pre-war financial difficulties. Opening the bowling, probably wearing his cap as was often his custom, Parker quickly had Randall Johnson caught for one by Edgar Barnett. After that he worked his way steadily through the Somerset batting, eight batsmen reaching double figures but none scoring fifty. Only Jack MacBryan seemed comfortable, a fine performance given that as an amateur his availability in 1921 had been limited, his only Championship appearance so far being over two months before.

At 176 for nine Parker had no doubt hoped to wrap up the Somerset innings quickly and complete his all-ten. However, numbers ten and eleven, Jimmy Bridges and Raymond Robertson-Glasgow, then scored 36 for the last wicket in less than half an hour before the final wicket eventually fell, like the first, caught Barnett bowled Parker. Fast-medium bowler Bridges is one of those unfortunate individuals whose highest first-class score is 99 not out, remarkably made when going in at number eleven against Essex at Weston-super-Mare in 1919. In 348 first-class innings he scored just two fifties and never got near a hundred again.

Parker had bowled unchanged for three and a half hours and conceded just seven boundaries. A collection raised £53 for him. One of his victims was the Somerset captain and, more importantly, Test selector, John Daniell, stumped by Robinson for four. Surely this must have helped his future Test prospects? Evidently not. Robinson deserves a mention for keeping for 80 overs without conceding a bye. Perhaps surprisingly, fellow slow left-armer George Dennett, now back from India and who would take 107 wickets in the season, bowled only two overs in the innings, 42-year-old medium pacer Percy Mills being left to do all the hard work. A mainstay of Gloucestershire's attack for many years, the virtual retirement of Dennett in 1926 would give the popular Mills greater opportunities and, for the first time in a career that started in 1902, he took 100 wickets in a season. After his earlier all-ten White had now also been part of one twice, and all in the same season, a 'feat' nobody else has ever emulated. And six other members of the Somerset side had been playing three weeks before when Rushby took his all-ten against them.

Gloucestershire topped the Somerset score by 36, Edgar Barnett (95) making the highest score of his 64-match career. Sadly he died of meningitis the following January aged 37 and did not live to see the success achieved for county and country by his nephew Charlie. Somerset replied with 240 (Parker three for 78), MacBryan (49) top scoring again. Like Parker, he played just one Test – against South Africa in 1924. Parker at least got to bat and bowl. In a rain-affected game MacBryan, a small, neat batsman, particularly strong off the back foot, did neither, although he did field. He died in 1983 aged nearly 91, at the time England's oldest surviving Test cricketer. Gloucestershire were left a tricky 205 to win on a pitch affected by overnight rain. Recovering from 65 for five to 202 when the eighth wicket fell, they looked just about home. However, number ten Parker then managed to get run out for a duck, still leaving three to get! Fortunately history does not record Parker's words on his return to the pavilion. Smith however (a chanceless 62 not out) was still there to get the job done. It is interesting to note that play was apparently extended past half past six in order to get a result.

Parker had improved on his previous best figures, nine for 35 against Leicestershire the previous season, and the following year he would famously take nine for 36 against Yorkshire in his benefit match, hitting the stumps with five successive balls, although unfortunately the second was a no-ball (the only one he bowled in his 10.2 overs!). Three years later he would take 17 for 56 against Essex at the Wagon Works Ground, Gloucester, still the best ever match figures for Gloucestershire, and if Jack Russell hadn't been run out in the first innings it might have been another all-ten. Parker would eventually take exactly 300 wickets against Somerset, including five (or more) wickets in an innings no fewer than 30 times. Somerset would have some measure of revenge at Bristol in 1923 when they batted first and made 532 for nine declared while Parker conceded 231 runs for his six wickets.

Parker had had decent figures (two Australian wickets for 32 in 28 overs) on his Test debut at Old Trafford in 1921 but that was the end of his England career. By the early 1930s he had support at Gloucestershire from off-spinner Tom Goddard, another bowler who took wickets in vast numbers. Even as Parker approached, and then passed, 50, he still took wickets: 219 in 1931 and over 100 in every succeeding season until 1935 when he finally retired having taken 3,278 wickets. Becoming an umpire, Charlie Parker's last day on the circuit was also the last day of the 1939 season. It was a famous occasion, Hedley Verity taking seven for 9 at Hove; two great left-arm spinners leaving first-class cricket together. Parker also coached, both for the county and at Cranleigh, where he died in 1959.

Arthur Mailey

Australians v Gloucestershire, 1921

College Ground, Cheltenham on 20, 22, 23 August 1921 (3-day match)
Toss won by Australians
Australians won by an innings and 136 runs
Umpires: B Brown, A Millward
Australians 438 (W Bardsley 127, CG Macartney 121, CWL Parker 5-148);
Gloucestershire 127 and 175 (AA Mailey 10-66)

Gloucestershire second innings

CS Barnett	b Mailey	25
AE Dipper	b Mailey	4
RP Keigwin	c Mayne b Mailey	65
H Smith	c and b Mailey	0
WR Hammond	b Mailey	1
*+FG Robinson	b Mailey	4
WH Rowlands	b Mailey	23
FJ Seabrook	c and b Mailey	30
PT Mills	c Pellew b Mailey	3
CWL Parker	not out	8
JGWT Bessant	b Mailey	0
Extras	(b 5, lb 6, nb 1)	12
Total	(all out, 57.4 overs)	175

Fall of wickets 1-16, 2-34, 3-38, 4-47, 5-59, 6-109, 7-158, 8-164, 9-175, 10-175

Australians bowling: JM Gregory 12-2-38-0, AA Mailey 28.4-5-66-10, WW Armstrong 12-1-54-0, J Ryder 5-3-5-0

Australians: HL Collins, W Bardsley, CG Macartney, CE Pellew, JM Gregory, WW Armstrong (capt), ER Mayne, J Ryder, HSTL Hendry, H Carter (wk), AA Mailey

Three weeks after Charlie Parker's feat it was Gloucestershire's turn to be on the receiving end of an all-ten – a record fifth for the season. Together with fearsome pace pair Jack Gregory and Ted McDonald, and large leg-spinner Warwick Armstrong, Arthur Mailey was one of four bowlers who took 100 wickets for the 1921 Australian tourists. Mailey had made his Test debut the previous winter, taking 36 wickets, an Australian Ashes series record that stood for over 50 years. An attacking leg break and googly bowler, spinning the ball furiously and flighting it generously with consequent occasional adverse effects on his length, he could summon up an unplayable delivery on the best of pitches. In a strong Australian batting side he could afford to buy his wickets, and often did. A heavily spun ball can do funny things in the air and he twice bowled Jack Hobbs in a Test with a full toss.

A small man, philosophical and whimsical, Arthur Mailey was one of cricket's characters. He was no doubt particularly philosophical when he took four for 362 against Victoria in 1926/27 (figures never 'bettered' in first-class cricket). Born in Sydney in 1886 his early life was hard. He had many jobs, including glass-blowing, an occupation that usefully strengthened both fingers and lungs. His first-class debut for New South Wales in 1912/13 was followed by tours to North America and to New Zealand, and when cricket resumed after the War he soon became his country's premier spinner, albeit now in his mid-30s.

Having inflicted Test cricket's first five-nil whitewash the previous winter, Armstrong's 1921 Australians continued to steamroller English cricket. Between Tests many of the counties were simply overwhelmed. The final Test at The Oval had finished on a Tuesday, the game meandering farcically to a draw. The Australians' next opponents were Gloucestershire at Cheltenham (the third match of the 1921 Festival) but they were not due there until the following Saturday. They would have welcomed the break, since their tour, which lasted just over four months, involved 39 (mainly first-class) games, with few rest days built into the schedule. Beat Surrey at The Oval on Tuesday afternoon, start against Yorkshire at Bradford next morning, finish on Friday and immediately travel back down south to Portsmouth to play Combined Services on Saturday. The uncompromising Armstrong was not happy, and the situation caused much friction.

Nevertheless, a visit from the Australians was eagerly anticipated and attracted big crowds everywhere and the gate receipts at the beautiful College ground at Cheltenham beat all records, with a 10,000 crowd packing in on the first day. In the interests of safety children had to be accompanied by their parents. Gloucestershire went into the match in poor form, having lost both the two preceding Festival matches. They had made a few changes, including bringing in a promising 18-year-old named Walter Hammond, who was qualifying for the county.

Mailey had nearly achieved an all-ten earlier in the year at Melbourne: his nine for 121 in the second England innings of the Fourth Test is still an Australian record. He would go one better this time. The match went true to form. On Saturday on a fast pitch and in glorious sunshine the Australians made 425 for eight, mainly thanks to chanceless centuries from Charlie Macartney and Warren Bardsley, and a typically aggressive 78 from a gloveless Jack Gregory. Coincidentally when the Australians had played Gloucestershire earlier in the season at Bristol the same two batsmen had made centuries and Gregory had made an even quicker 78.

The last two wickets went quickly on Monday. Rain had now affected the pitch and the home side were at an immediate disadvantage and were following on by the middle of the afternoon. Four Australian bowlers shared the first-innings wickets, with Mailey coming on late to take three for 21. The only batsman who resisted for any time was Richard Keigwin who made 47 in just under two hours. Young Hammond, who later confessed how frightened he had been facing Gregory, failed to contribute, the bounding Australian quickly rearranging his stumps.

Mailey started the Gloucestershire second innings with 99 wickets for the season. He soon reached three figures, bowling the obdurate Alf Dipper with the score 16. Following his success in cleaning up the tail in the first innings, Armstrong had sarcastically thrown the ball to Mailey at the beginning of the second and suggested that he bowl at the good batsmen, and then he would come on and finish the tail. However it didn't work out like that. At 59 for five it looked like the match might be over in two days. However, Keigwin again batted well and took the score to 109 before his partner Harry Rowlands was bowled for 23 just before close of play. Mailey had so far taken all six wickets, five bowled (including a bamboozled Hammond who took ten minutes to score a single) and one caught and bowled. Next morning, after early rain, Keigwin found another stubborn partner in Frederick Seabrook and they took the score to 158 before he was finally caught for 65. Thirty-eight-year-old Keigwin had won a Blue in each of his four years at Cambridge, played for Essex and briefly for Gloucestershire after moving there to become a master at Clifton College. However, he had a modest career, averaging 19.79 from 74 matches, and so his success against a strong Australian attack must have been a bit of a surprise. An exceptional scholar-athlete, he won Blues at three other sports, played hockey for England, and was made a knight of the order of Danneborg for his services to Danish literature. Like all the amateurs, Keigwin emerged from a tent whilst the professionals came out from the gymnasium!

The last three wickets fell quickly and the match was over before lunch. Mailey had bowled unchanged. Charlie Parker was the one batsman to evade him, although he had dismissed him in the first innings, stumped by Sammy Carter, the only Yorkshireman playing in the match. Nearly one in five of Mailey's eventual 779 first-class wickets were stumped, but Parker was the only one of his 13 victims in the match to fall this way. And another umpire had achieved a hat-trick of all-tens. Remarkably Arthur Millward's first had been Sammy Woods back in 1890 (followed by Drake's in 1914).

An early finish gave the Australians a bit more time to get to Taunton next day for another innings victory. Still unbeaten, they famously then lost their next match against Archie MacLaren's England XI at Eastbourne, and then a second at Scarborough against C.I.Thornton's XI. Mailey was last man out in each match, but then he did go in at eleven.

Mailey toured Britain again in 1926, taking another 100 wickets and finishing his Test career with 99 wickets. Although he had a modest batting record his last wicket partnership of 127 with Johnny Taylor at Sydney in December 1924 was an Australian Test record that stood until 2013. Multi-talented, he was a particularly skilled cartoonist and his autobiography, memorably entitled *10 for 66 and all that*, contains many humorous examples of his art. In his last first-class appearance, at Melbourne in 1930 for The Rest against an Australian XI, a match played for the benefit of former colleague Jack Ryder, he dismissed Don Bradman in both innings in the great man's second match on return from his breakthrough tour of Britain. Journalism and cricket of a more leisurely nature took him abroad many times: in 1932 he organised, and played in, a very successful tour to North America, which was also Don Bradman's honeymoon.

Mailey ended his days in Cronulla, a Sydney beachside suburb, enjoying life on his boat, painting, writing and fishing. He died on New Year's Eve 1967 just before his eighty-second birthday.

George Collins

Kent v Nottinghamshire, 1922
County Championship

Crabble Athletic Ground, Dover on 16, 17, 18 August 1922 (3-day match)
Kent won by an innings and 69 runs
Umpires: B Brown, GA Fuller
Kent 351; Nottinghamshire 120 (GC Collins 6-18) and 162 (GC Collins 10-65)

Nottinghamshire second innings

G Gunn	b Collins	6
WW Whysall	lbw b Collins	2
JR Gunn	b Collins	4
*AW Carr	c Freeman b Collins	0
J Hardstaff	lbw b Collins	49
WRD Payton	c Hubble b Collins	42
GM Lee	c and b Collins	1
SJ Staples	b Collins	19
+TW Oates	c Ashdown b Collins	8
F Barratt	c Freeman b Collins	19
TL Richmond	not out	7
Extras	(b 2, lb 1, nb 1, w 1)	5
Total	(all out, 54.3 overs)	162

Fall of wickets 1-6, 2-12, 3-12, 4-13, 5-96, 6-98, 7-113, 8-130, 9-147, 10-162

Kent bowling: GC Collins 19.3-4-65-10, WH Ashdown 5-0-8-0, AP Freeman 20-7-55-0, FE Woolley 7-2-15-0, GJ Bryan 3-0-14-0

Kent: JL Bryan, HTW Hardinge, J Seymour, FE Woolley, AF Bickmore, GJ Bryan, WH Ashdown, GC Collins, JC Hubble (wk), LHW Troughton (capt), AP Freeman

Allrounder George Collins is one of the less august names among those who have taken an all-ten. In fact, going into the Nottinghamshire game, after 85 first-class matches he had taken fewer than 150 wickets and never taken more than five wickets in an innings. It's probably not too unreasonable to call him a journeyman cricketer – somebody who doesn't hit the heights too often, but makes valuable contributions when needed in support of some of the more talented players. Tall and heavily-built he was a versatile left-handed batsman who could bat anywhere and defend or attack as necessary. With the ball, after a long bounding run, he bowled right-arm fast-medium and on his day delivered a potent outswinger.

Collins was born in Gravesend, Kent in 1889 into a cricketing family, his grandfather, father and uncle all having played for the county. Joining the Tonbridge Nursery in 1908 he made his county debut in 1911 but couldn't cement his place in a powerful Kent team, and left the staff at the end of the 1913 season. Rejoining in 1919 he was a first-team regular from 1920 until 1926 before slipping out of the side.

Nottinghamshire, second in the Championship, went into the match needing a win to keep the pressure on leaders (and eventual Champions) Yorkshire. Kent, having a good run, were in fifth place. Collins had contributed relatively little recently: a few useful scores, but, after a good start with the ball, only six wickets since the beginning of July. To be fair, his opportunities were limited by the form of spinners 'Tich' Freeman and Frank Woolley who jointly took 336 Championship wickets in the season.

Carved into a hillside, the Crabble Athletic Ground was an interesting venue: on one side backed by steep terraces, on the other the land falling away into a wooded valley floor. Players leaving the field had to climb steep steps to the pavilion, with even more climbing to reach the professionals' dressing room on one floor, the dining room on another, and the amateurs' dressing room yet one storey higher. Sadly, the pitch declared unfit, the ground saw the last of its 106 first-class matches in 1976.

Kent batted first and were all out just before the close for 351, Jack Bryan and Wally Hardinge having opened with a stand of 158. Three of the first five Nottinghamshire batsmen had appeared for England, and the two others would soon do so. However, despite this apparent strength, the Midland county lost 16 wickets on the second day, 12 of them to Collins. Showers delaying play for about half an hour, Nottinghamshire began batting in overcast conditions. However, the pitch continued to favour batting and in no way explained their poor showing. Collins opened the bowling from the pavilion end, helped by a stiff breeze blowing down the pitch. He struck quickly: with the score 12 he had William Whysall well caught at mid off by Godfrey Bryan (Jack's brother) and then trapped the great George Gunn leg-before to a ball that kept slightly low. Nottinghamshire continued to struggle. At 71 for eight (Collins having taken six wickets) they faced the embarrassment of failing to reach three figures. Joe Hardstaff (18 not out) however helped to marshal the tail, but a final score of 120 still left them well adrift on the first innings. Collins had made the ball swing as well as break back quickly and in 17 overs achieved career-best figures of six for 18, and not a duff batsman among them.

Kent captain Lionel Troughton probably had little hesitation in asking the visitors to follow on. In the first innings Collins had opened the bowling with Woolley. Second time around he was partnered by Bill Ashdown who, 13 years later, would make 305 not out against Derbyshire at Dover, easily the ground's record score. Notts began again soon after 4 o'clock. They didn't start well. In the first over, George Gunn, in typically eccentric fashion, made six runs and then walked two yards down the pitch and lost his middle stump! Four wickets were soon down for 13, including Gunn's brother John bowled for 4, and Notts' captain Arthur Carr who skyed the ball to cover point and was caught by Freeman without scoring. A two-day finish looked possible, but the resolute Hardstaff found a like-minded partner in Wilfred Payton (42) and the two veterans stayed together almost until the close, when two wickets fell quickly leaving Nottinghamshire hopelessly placed at 98 for six. Little play was needed on Friday morning. Hardstaff went quickly, Collins pinning him in front of the stumps for a patient 49. Hardstaff's son, Joe junior, would himself be part of an Eric

Hollies all-ten 24 years later.

On past performance Notts' nine, ten and eleven wouldn't have been expected to contribute much, but they did at least do better than the top order. (Six years later, after many moderate seasons with the bat, fast bowler Fred Barratt suddenly more than doubled his previous best output and made 1,167 runs.) There was a little drama at the end of the innings. Collins could be rather slow in the field. With nine wickets down (all to Collins) the burly Barratt, facing Freeman, gave Collins a chance to which he was slow to move and failed to take. He was understandably concerned that the crowd would think this deliberate (although given the position of the match it was unlikely to have affected the result). And then in the next over it was Freeman himself who took a brilliant catch to give Collins his all-ten! A few years later the voracious Freeman would achieve the feat a record three times, but this time he had bowled 20 unrewarded overs.

Collins' figures (innings and match) were, and presumably always will be, a Dover record. At the time they were also the second best match, and third best innings, figures for Kent. Perhaps surprised by his success, *The Times* commented 'He certainly is quite one of our most extraordinary cricketers......he never appears to know quite what he is about to do'. *The Cricketer* said that he was 'a cricketer of moods, with the most tender heart imaginable'. They may have been right: five wickets in the Lancashire first innings in his next match ('good bowling by Collins': *The Times*), was followed by one for 85 against Middlesex when his bowling was 'the most amiable, stingless matter imaginable'.

Umpire Brown, only appointed to the county first-class list in 1921 after previously umpiring Minor County, mainly Durham, matches, had now already umpired his second all-ten, having stood the previous season when Mailey had performed the feat.

Collins' last match, perhaps appropriately, was against Nottinghamshire at Gravesend at the end of May 1928. For him it was a low-key affair as he injured his finger fielding on the first day, bowled only nine wicketless overs and was then unfit to bat as Kent stumbled to an innings defeat. He had never taken 100 wickets in a season, his best year being 1923 when he took 90, as well as scoring over 1,000 runs for the only time. The closest he came to representative cricket was touring the West Indies (before they attained Test status) with Freddie Calthorpe's MCC team in 1925/26. In the event he had little success and played only five matches on the tour. In all he took 379 first-class wickets at an average of 23.91 and scored just over 6,000 runs at an average of 22.11.

After retirement Collins became groundsman at the Officers Club, Aldershot (where he also umpired one first-class match: Army v South Americans in 1932). He died in Rochester in 1949 aged 59.

Harry Howell

Warwickshire v Yorkshire, 1923
County Championship

Edgbaston, Birmingham on 23, 24, 25 May 1923 (3-day match)
Toss won by Yorkshire
Yorkshire won by 84 runs
Umpires: WA Buswell, TM Russell
Yorkshire 113 (H Howell 10-51) and 162-6 dec; Warwickshire 110 (GG Macaulay 5-42) and 81

Yorkshire first innings

P Holmes	c Smart b Howell	1
H Sutcliffe	c Smart b Howell	8
E Oldroyd	c Smith b Howell	44
E Robinson	c Partridge b Howell	4
W Rhodes	c Smart b Howell	12
R Kilner	b Howell	6
M Leyland	lbw b Howell	3
*G Wilson	c Smith b Howell	14
GG Macaulay	b Howell	0
+A Dolphin	c Smith b Howell	6
A Waddington	not out	7
Extras	(b 8)	8
Total	(all out, 50.1)	113

Fall of wickets 1-2, 2-19, 3-27, 4-59, 5-67, 6-79, 7-88, 8-88, 9-94, 10-113

Warwickshire bowling: H Howell 25.1-5-51-10, NE Partridge 19-4-41-0, FSG Calthorpe 6-1-13-0

Warwickshire: LTA Bates, EJ Smith (wk), FSG Calthorpe (capt), WG Quaife, GW Stephens, JA Smart, FR Santall, RES Wyatt, NE Partridge, HA White, H Howell

The only bowler to have taken all-ten against Yorkshire in a county match, Harry Howell was, until Larwood emerged, probably the fastest bowler playing in England. Off a long run-up he had an easy action, which was just as well given the work he had to get through. Playing for a moderate Warwickshire team in the early 1920s, and lacking consistent support at the other end, his record was outstanding and perhaps deserved greater Test recognition. A cheerful man who enjoyed his cricket, his career was short: his first more-or-less full season was in 1914, and he played little after 1925.

Born in Birmingham in 1890, Howell didn't really get the chance to establish himself until after the War but began so well that, in order to keep him away from league cricket, the county signed him up for five years. 161 wickets in 1920 earned him a place on the tour to Australia the following winter but in his three Tests Howell suffered badly from missed catches and only took seven wickets for 468. He was not alone in finding Australia a cricketing culture shock. The Tests were played on perfect wickets in virtually unbroken sunshine and most of the England bowlers had figures they would rather forget. Later, when Warwickshire famously lost to Hampshire in 1922 after dismissing them for 15 in their first innings he had the contrasting figures of six for 7 (breaking a stump in the process) and three for 156 (his most expensive analysis ever).

The pre-war Warwickshire team that Howell had joined had a strong pace attack. Left-armer F.R. (Frank) Foster had helped bowl England to victory Down Under in 1911/12, Frank Field was genuinely fast taking nearly 1,000 wickets for the county, and Percy Jeeves was one of England's most promising younger bowlers. When Howell came back in 1919 things had changed. A motor-cycle accident prevented Foster returning to the game, Field was in his mid-40s, and Jeeves had been killed in action (at least his name is remembered, P.G. Wodehouse having used it for his famous fictional valet). Howell, approaching 29, rose to the challenge of being both shock and stock bowler. Yorkshire on the other hand, with a full hand of bowlers able to exploit any conditions, and batting to match, won the Championship every season from 1922 to 1925. Ten professionals captained by an amateur, Geoffrey Wilson, a modest bat but brilliant fielder, they were a hard team to play against and to captain. And there were rumours that Yorkshire fielders sometimes roughed up the pitch to help their bowlers, accompanied by excessive use of what we now call sledging.

By the time Yorkshire came to Birmingham in May 1923 they had already started the season well: three comprehensive victories and a rain-affected draw. Warwickshire's record was more modest: win, draw, loss, but with Howell already among the wickets. Although it occasionally hosted Test matches, Edgbaston was still wide open, largely uncovered, rather rural in appearance and with few spectator facilities. Major development of the ground would not follow until after the Second World War.

There was rain about on Wednesday 23 May, and little or no play in most matches, only the West Indian tourists down at breezy Brighton getting in a full day. Birmingham was no exception and the redoubtable Yorkshire pair Percy Holmes and Herbert Sutcliffe had to wait until twenty-five minutes to five before they could set out. Howell made the most of a pitch which was soft on top, firm underneath and on which he made the ball lift awkwardly. In the very first over Sutcliffe was struck a nasty blow on the jaw. He was able to continue after receiving attention but eventually became one of three batsmen caught in the slips by Jack Smart. By the close Yorkshire had struggled to 67 for five, Howell (five for 36) having all the batsmen in trouble except for Edgar Oldroyd (32 not out).

Twenty wickets fell next day as conditions continued to favour bowlers. The overnight break allowed the rested Howell to continue to bowl unchanged, and he needed less than an hour to polish off the Yorkshire batting. Oldroyd made 44 before he was caught behind by Tiger Smith, one of three catches taken in the innings by the former England keeper. All but one of Oldroyd's 384 matches were for the county. He was one of only three of the Yorkshire side who never played for England. He wouldn't have let them down if he had. A last wicket partnership of 19, the second highest of the innings, between Wilson and Abe Waddington had at least allowed them to limp to three figures. Howell's figures were a Warwickshire record, improving on the nine for 35 taken by the left-arm of Sam Hargreave twenty years before at The Oval. He is the last bowler (after Burton, Tyler and Bill Howell) to have taken all-ten against the eventual County Champions (see Appendix for further details).

After a great fight before a rapt crowd Warwickshire failed by three runs to match Yorkshire's total. They started well, but 72 for three became 72 for six, as fiery medium-pace off-spinner George Macaulay, perhaps incited by his first innings duck, took the first of his four hat-tricks for the county (a record shared with Fred Trueman), and there was no recovery. The only Warwickshire batsman who reached twenty was Len Bates, literally batting on his home ground as, son of the groundsman, he had been born there in 1895. Yorkshire again made a shaky start to their second innings. This time it was Warwickshire captain Freddie Calthorpe (four for 52) who did the early damage, Howell also chipping in with two more wickets. Sadly Calthorpe died prematurely, in 1935 aged only 43.

At 59 for five Yorkshire were again in trouble, but they had just the pair for a crisis, Roy Kilner (another early death, five years later) and a young Maurice Leyland, whose partnership of 84 enabled a declaration to be made at 162 for six. With more rain on the third day, Warwickshire were left only two hours and a quarter to make 166. At first a draw seemed likely, but nobody resisted Emmott Robinson, Macaulay and Kilner for long and just before half past six Yorkshire had won by 84 runs. Given the conditions, most of Warwickshire's wickets in the match fell, not surprisingly, to Yorkshire spin and it is ironic that it was his own county's lack of a quality spinner that gave Howell the chance to perform his great feat.

The 152 wickets that Howell took in 1923 were at the time a Warwickshire record. (Their next highest wicket-takers were Norman Partridge and Calthorpe who took just 56 and 55 wickets respectively with their medium pace.) The only fast bowler to have exceeded this total for the county is New Zealander Tom Pritchard who took an impressive 166 in 1948. England still needed a fast bowler and Howell went Down Under again in 1924/25. However, this time he got little opportunity and did not appear in any of the Tests.

Howell continued to be the mainstay of the Warwickshire attack but at the end of 1925 when, despite being handicapped by illness, he had taken over 100 wickets for the sixth successive year, he decided that the strain of regular county cricket was too much and that he could not undertake another season. He went into the Birmingham League, but still played a few more games for the county until 1928. He had also had a brief Football League career, mainly with Wolverhampton Wanderers. Like his former captain Calthorpe he died tragically early, in 1932 aged 41.

Alex Kennedy

Players v Gentlemen, 1927

Kennington Oval, Kennington on 6, 7, 8 July 1927 (3-day match)
Toss won by Players
Match drawn
Umpires: LC Braund, J Stone
Players 424-9 dec (EH Hendren 150); Gentlemen 80 (AS Kennedy 10-37) and 181-8

Gentlemen first innings

NVH Riches	c Durston b Kennedy	0
RES Wyatt	c Shepherd b Kennedy	18
A Jeacocke	c Sandham b Kennedy	7
NE Haig	c Hendren b Kennedy	19
CP Brutton	b Kennedy	0
*LH Tennyson	c Hendren b Kennedy	4
JP Parker	c Durston b Kennedy	2
M Falcon	c Hendren b Kennedy	16
+WB Franklin	c Mead b Kennedy	2
IAR Peebles	not out	3
RPH Utley	st Livsey b Kennedy	7
Extras	(lb 2)	2
Total	(all out, 44.4 overs)	80

Fall of wickets 1-1, 2-17, 3-32, 4-33, 5-45, 6-50, 7-51, 8-61, 9-72, 10-80

Players bowling: AS Kennedy 22.4-10-37-10, JA Newman 7-3-8-0, JW Hearne 15-5-33-0

Players: JB Hobbs (capt), A Sandham, JW Hearne, EH Hendren, CP Mead, JH Parsons, TF Shepherd, JA Newman, AS Kennedy, WH Livsey (wk), FJ Durston

Alex Kennedy took more wickets than any Hampshire bowler, even Derek Shackleton, and like the great Shack began life many miles from Hampshire. Shackleton was born in Yorkshire (just), whilst Kennedy was born in Edinburgh in 1891, his family moving south five years later.

Bowling at around medium pace with a smooth rhythmical action, Kennedy's stock delivery with the new ball was the inswinger but his most dangerous ball was the leg cutter, varied with an occasional off-spinner. Changes of pace, tireless accuracy, great stamina and patience meant that even in unfavourable conditions he was an unrelenting foe. He formed a great bowling partnership with Jack Newman, Hampshire's third highest wicket-taker. He was also a useful batsman, five times accomplishing the allrounder's seasonal double.

Making his first-class debut in 1907, Kennedy became a county regular two years later and took 100 wickets in a season for the first time in 1912, a feat he repeated another 14 times. He exceeded 200 wickets in 1922 (as well as scoring over 1,000 runs, a double only emulated by Albert Trott and Maurice Tate) and earned a place in F.T.Mann's team touring South Africa the following winter. He couldn't have done much better, taking 31 wickets in a closely fought series that England won 2-1. These were his only five Tests. By now an even greater medium pacer, Maurice Tate, had come along, and with Leicestershire's George Geary also available further international honours were always unlikely. Even in 1934, his last full season, aged 43, he finished only a few runs and wickets short of a sixth double. Only six bowlers have exceeded his 2,874 first-class wickets and his position near the top of the record-list of course remains assured for ever.

Having taken well over 100 wickets in every season since 1914, Kennedy lost form in 1926 and failed to achieve his usual three-figure haul. His benefit, which raised £1,095 from a rain-affected match against Surrey, will have provided some consolation. Things improved in 1927 and he was more or less back to his usual self with the ball. For The Oval Gentlemen v Players match the tradition was that no players would be selected from counties otherwise engaged. With twelve counties playing in the Championship (and Nottinghamshire playing the New Zealand tourists) the sides were far from representative and only five participants would reappear in the main match played at Lord's the following week. Having said that, with Surrey, Middlesex and Hampshire not engaged, the professionals could put out a team whose batting order began Jack Hobbs, Andy Sandham, Jack (J.W.) Hearne, Patsy Hendren and Phil Mead, and whose members scored 57 centuries during the season (compared with the amateurs' five!).

There were no fewer than four Hampshire players in each side. Captained by one of them, Lionel Tennyson, the Gentlemen also included two pre-war Cambridge Blues who never played first-class county cricket but who went on to have long and successful Minor County careers: Michael Falcon (Norfolk) and wicketkeeper Walter Franklin (Buckinghamshire). Both fine cricketers, Falcon had taken eight wickets in the famous match at Eastbourne when an England XI beat Warwick Armstrong's hitherto undefeated 1921 Australians. Hampshire fast bowler Richard Utley was making only his fifth first-class appearance. His first-class career lasted only two seasons, but with 90 wickets it was not unsuccessful. However he had a greater calling, entering the Benedictine Order and becoming a master at Ampleforth School.

An even more intriguing choice was a fellow countryman of Kennedy's, wrist-spinner Ian Peebles, who was actually making his first-class debut at the age of 19. In fact by the time he made his Test debut the following winter he had still not played county cricket. He had been coached by the great South African Aubrey Faulkner and much was expected of him. He had a short and successful Test career, but sadly his bowling lost its initial venom and his best days were soon over.

Batting first the Players lost their first wicket at 57, Peebles forcing Sandham to play on to his famous googly. After that the day's play was dominated by Hendren who made 150 before he became one of four wickets taken by Falcon. Batting at six Jack Parsons made a modest 29 before being dismissed by Warwickshire colleague Bob (R.E.S) Wyatt. A remarkable man who served both Army and Church with distinction, Parsons played for both Players and Gentlemen and would not have been out of place in an England team.

Having scored 424 for nine by the end of the first day, the Players immediately declared on Friday morning after rain had prevented any play on the second day. The Gentlemen now had to face Kennedy on a drying, wearing pitch. Hampshire's Scot took full advantage, consistently putting the ball in that difficult spot around leg stump that compelled the batsman to play at his awkwardly lifting leg cutter. First to go was dentist Norman Riches, who in 1921 had become the first Glamorgan batsman to pass 1,000 runs in first-class cricket. He failed to trouble the scorers this time, but at 44 he could still bat, as shown the following season when he scored centuries against Warwickshire and against a powerful Lancashire attack.

After that, although Kennedy's county colleague Charles Brutton was the only other batsman to make a duck, nobody could resist him for long. He received admirable support from his close fielders, particularly Hendren who snaffled three catches including Kennedy's own county captain Lionel Tennyson. Although without doubt Kennedy got considerable help both from the pitch and the batsmen, it is worth noting that the two bowlers who delivered 22 wicketless overs at the other end, Newman and Hearne, eventually took nearly 3,900 first-class wickets between them. Utley was the last to go, smartly stumped by Tennyson's valet Walter Livsey, a very capable keeper who despite the conditions kept for 45 overs without conceding a bye. Kennedy's figures will remain the best ever in a Gentlemen-Players match, and are also still the best ever by a Hampshire bowler in any match.

Following on, the Gentlemen began their second innings after lunch. The heavy roller had made the pitch a little easier and this time the amateurs were more resilient, most of them at least reaching double figures. Nevertheless, at 152 for eight and with half an hour left, defeat still looked likely, but a gallant unbroken stand of 29 between Falcon (11 not out) and Franklin (20 not out) saved the Gentlemen from the ignominy of being bowled out twice in a day. Kennedy took two more wickets, but this time it was the medium pace of Surrey allrounder Tom Shepherd with four for 20 that did most damage.

With the exception of the special circumstances of 1970, 1927 was the last peacetime season in which England played no home Test matches. The Gentlemen-Players match at Lord's a week later was therefore the most important match of the season. Unfortunately it was spoiled by rain. However, the Gentlemen were able to put out a much stronger side. Only Franklin would not play for England and, thanks particularly to a Jardine century, in the time available they gave a much better account of themselves. Kennedy did not appear for the Players.

On retirement from the county game Kennedy became coach first at Cheltenham College and then at King Edward's School, Johannesburg. His continued love of bowling meant that his young charges were never short of quality net practice. On his return, when not attending to his tobacconist and stationer's business in Southampton, he spent many hours at the county ground watching, and talking about, cricket. Alex Kennedy was clearly a much admired colleague and friend. John Arlott knew him as a sober and steady man, and team-mate Harold Day, on hearing of his death in 1959, expressed the opinion that there was never a greater-hearted trier nor a fairer bowler.

Gubby Allen

Middlesex v Lancashire, 1929
County Championship

Lord's Cricket Ground, St John's Wood on 15, 17, 18 June 1929 (3-day match)
Toss won by Lancashire
Match drawn
Umpires: LA Benwell, J Stone
Lancashire 241 (GE Tyldesley 102, GOB Allen 10-40) and 310-9 dec (JL Hopwood 106 not out); Middlesex 228 (HW Lee 124, RK Tyldesley 5-40) and 170-5 (HW Lee 105 not out)

Lancashire first innings

C Hallows	b Allen	12
FB Watson	b Allen	47
GE Tyldesley	b Allen	102
J Iddon	b Allen	0
JL Hopwood	c Price b Allen	48
TM Halliday	b Allen	0
+W Farrimond	b Allen	6
*PT Eckersley	not out	8
RK Tyldesley	b Allen	0
EA McDonald	st Price b Allen	1
G Hodgson	b Allen	0
Extras	(b 11, lb 5, nb 1)	17
Total	(all out, 111.3 overs)	241

Fall of wickets 1-23, 2-102, 3-102, 4-215, 5-215, 6-228, 7-239, 8-239, 9-241, 10-241

Middlesex bowling: NE Haig 29-8-48-0, FJ Durston 10-3-17-0, GOB Allen 25.3-10-40-10, RWV Robins 22-1-54-0, IAR Peebles 12-2-26-0, JW Hearne 8-1-28-0, JL Guise 5-1-11-0

Middlesex: JL Guise, HW Lee, JW Hearne, GOB Allen, Lord Aberdare, RWV Robins, NE Haig (capt), WFF Price (wk), JHA Hulme, FJ Durston, IAR Peebles

In club cricket captains are occasionally warned that a player might struggle to get to a game for the start because he has to work in the morning. But surely not in the first-class game? Not now, but it was possible when counties included amateurs in their ranks, many of whom, like Allen, had to earn a crust somehow or another. Working with Debenhams, Allen couldn't get to Lord's for the start of the match against Lancashire in 1929, but his captain's tolerance would be well rewarded.

One of the game's most influential figures (some might say too influential!), George Oswald Browning Allen was born in Sydney in 1902 (Uncle Reginald having played for Australia) and brought to England aged six. He was a genuine fast bowler whose classic side-on action enabled him to produce sharp outswing, a batsman who would make a Test century, and a brilliant fielder, usually close in. After Eton and Cambridge most of his cricket was for Middlesex. However, because of business he could never find the time to play regularly, and in a career lasting over 30 years never really had the chance to get close to 1,000 runs or 100 wickets in a season.

Lancashire were a very strong team, having won the Championship in each of the previous three seasons, and doing so again in 1930 following second place in 1929. They were captained by 25-year-old Peter Eckersley, the youngest member of the side (albeit that Thomas Halliday was only a day older). Leading the side for seven years until he became an MP in 1935, he was known as the 'cricketer-airman' because he often flew his own plane to matches. Together with Geoffrey Legge (Kent) and Robert Nelson (Northants) he was one of three former county captains to be killed in 1940.

Middlesex consistently finished in the top half of the table in the late 1920s, without ever really challenging for the top spot. They made considerable use of amateurs, but remarkably their main impact in 1929 was with the ball rather than the bat, three taking over 100 Championship wickets: captain Nigel Haig, who bowled fast-medium, and leg-spinners Walter Robins and Ian Peebles. The first two also did the allround double in all first-class matches. Allen couldn't play enough to get anywhere near 100 wickets but, thanks to a fine 155 against Surrey, he did top the county's batting averages.

Middlesex usually tried to recruit Allen for their strongest fixtures, and Haig was obviously keen that he should play against Lancashire, even if it meant starting without him. In fact he wasn't too late, and only missed about 20 minutes play. In front of a Saturday crowd of over 20,000 Lancashire had made a steady start thanks to Charlie Hallows and Frank Watson, each of whom had made over 2,500 runs the previous season. Allen was soon put on at the Pavilion End. The pitch was fairly easy, but he had a breeze to help him and at 23 he brought one back sharply to bowl Hallows. Lunch, taken at 90 for one, reinvigorated Allen, and with the score 102 he first took out Watson's middle stump and then Jack Iddon's off stump. Ernest Tyldesley and Len Hopwood then took the score to 215 until, just before tea, Allen was brought back for his final, and most devastating, spell. First he bowled Tyldesley who had just completed the 67th of his 102 first-class centuries, and then, immediately after the interval, Halliday for a duck. One of the lesser lights of the side, Halliday played 41 matches for the county, scoring just one century.

Hopwood helped to keep the innings going a little longer before he was caught behind by Fred Price for a gallant 48, the only catch in the innings. Lancashire's final wickets then fell in a clatter, Hopwood's being the first of four that Allen took in five balls spread over two overs. After bowling Richard Tyldesley he had fellow fast bowler Ted McDonald stumped. Some explanation is perhaps needed! McDonald had charged out of his ground and so Allen, who had seen him coming, simply bowled a slow, wide ball which enabled Price to run up and remove the bails. Allen then wound up the innings by bowling Gordon Hodgson. Born in South Africa (of English parents) Hodgson was no batsman, but a very useful fast bowler. His priority however was football. Only Ian Rush and Roger Hunt have scored more goals for Liverpool, and he was capped twice for South Africa and three times for England.

Maintaining pace and accuracy Allen had hit the stumps eight times, and in his last spell had taken seven for 13 in 11.3 overs. It is a measure of the quality of Allen's bowling against a powerful Lancashire batting line-up that Haig, Robins and Peebles, already referred to above, and Jack Hearne and Jack Durston, a pair who also performed prolifically with the ball,, bowled 81 overs at the other end without success. Allen's figures are still a Middlesex record, beating Albert Trott's ten for 42 against Somerset in 1900.

There was time for Middlesex to lose three cheap wickets, including nightwatchman Fred Price, on Saturday evening. However thanks to a century by nuggety opener Harry Lee they nearly reached first innings parity. Allen took just one wicket in the Lancashire second innings and with Hopwood making a century the northerners were able to set Middlesex 324 to win in three and a quarter hours. Thanks to another Lee century (none of his colleagues passed 40 in either innings) Middlesex came out of the match with a creditable draw. Lee's experience was a little better than that of 44-year-old Lord Aberdare who made a pair in his penultimate county match. A decent batsman with six first-class centuries to his name, he had acceded to his title in February, having previously played as Clarence Bruce.

Allen played six matches for Middlesex in 1929 and this was the only one in which he took more than three wickets in an innings. He made his Test debut against Australia the following summer and returned 'home' two years later to play in the infamous Bodyline series. His record in 1932 had been modest and his selection did not meet with universal approval but with 21 Australian wickets he vindicated his selection. He refused to bowl Bodyline, but as an amateur he was of course in a good position to defy his captain. And he was back in Australia four years later, this time as captain. England lost the series but, after the ill-feeling generated on the previous tour, at least he helped restore good relations. His Test career seemed to be over but in 1947/48, aged 45, he reluctantly came back to lead England in the Caribbean in an unequal struggle between an unrepresentative injury-hit England side and an emerging home side. Allen finished his Test career with a very creditable 81 wickets in 25 matches. His last match for Middlesex was in 1950 but, playing a match or two for Free Foresters each season, his career continued until 1954 and ended with 788 wickets.

Allen's career off the field was as impressive as it was on. At various times chairman of selectors, chairman of the MCC cricket committee, MCC president, and MCC treasurer, his influence was also felt in other ways: he led the move to make a number of professionals honorary MCC members, introduced decent coaching for boys who wanted it, and helped in stamping out the throwing epidemic of the late 1950s/early 1960s. Knighted for his services to the game in 1986, he died in his house overlooking Lord's in 1987 having been in poor health after an operation. The former Q Stand at Lord's had been renamed in his honour.

Tich Freeman

Not surprisingly, five foot two inches tall Alfred Percy Freeman was universally known as 'Tich'. His achievements with the ball were staggering. Technically he had everything. Unrelentingly accurate, off a short run-up (often preceded by a hitch of the trousers) his stock ball was the leg break, varied with a well-disguised googly or top spinner. And if that wasn't enough for the poor batsman to cope with, he varied pace and flight skilfully.

Born in Lewisham, South London in 1888 into a cricketing family many of whom played for Essex, Freeman actually appeared for Essex Club and Ground but, no doubt to their eternal regret, the county did not engage him. Joining the Kent staff in 1912 when, with Blythe, Woolley and the googlies of Douglas Carr, Kent were already well served for spin, it was difficult to break into the side and in effect his career only really started in 1919. His impact was immediate. Initially taking between 150 and 200 wickets in most seasons, Freeman's wicket-taking then moved up to extraordinary levels: a record 304 wickets in 1928, and more than 2,000 wickets in eight seasons - including a record three all-tens.

Kent v Lancashire, 1929
County Championship

Mote Park, Maidstone on 24, 25, 26 July 1929 (3-day match)
Toss won by Lancashire
Lancashire won by 189 runs
Umpires: A Morton, J Stone
Lancashire 347 (FB Watson 126, AP Freeman 10-131) and 305-6 dec (C Hallows 114); Kent 235 and 228

Lancashire first innings

C Hallows	c Ames b Freeman	13
FB Watson	lbw b Freeman	126
GE Tyldesley	st Ames b Freeman	66
J Iddon	st Ames b Freeman	30
JL Hopwood	lbw b Freeman	1
TM Halliday	b Freeman	5
L Warburton	c Todd b Freeman	14
+G Duckworth	c Ashdown b Freeman	4
*PT Eckersley	b Freeman	27
RK Tyldesley	not out	27
EA McDonald	c Watson b Freeman	18
Extras	(lb 15, nb 1)	16
Total	(all out, 107 overs)	347

Fall of wickets 1-28, 2-174, 3-234, 4-248, 5-254, 6-264, 7-274, 8-293, 9-311, 10-347

Kent bowling: AC Wright 21-3-81-0, WH Ashdown 17-5-43-0, AP Freeman 42-9-131-10, FE Woolley 13-6-35-0, HTW Hardinge 14-5-41-0

Kent: HTW Hardinge, GS Watson, FE Woolley, LEG Ames (wk), WH Ashdown, BH Valentine, LJ Todd, IS Akers-Douglas, GB Legge (capt), AP Freeman, AC Wright

By the start of the 1929 season Freeman already had many records under his belt, but he still hadn't taken an all-ten. He had come close, notably at Hastings in 1921 when Herbert Wilson declared the Sussex second innings closed leaving him with figures of nine for 87, and at Hove a year later when Frank Woolley took the last wicket after Tich had taken the first nine for a mere 11, robbing him of a world record analysis. However, he finally remedied the omission at beautiful Mote Park, Maidstone at the end of July.

Kent were captained by Geoffrey Legge who had scored a century against Lancashire at Maidstone two years before when he partnered Percy Chapman (260) in putting on 284 for the sixth wicket. With eleven wins from eighteen matches Kent went into the match leading the Championship. It was the second match of the Maidstone Week. In the first, Kent had beaten Sussex by an innings before lunch on the second day (Freeman thirteen for 105), but they were to win just one more match and finish the season a disappointing eighth.

Nine of the Lancashire team had been on the receiving end of Gubby Allen's all-ten the previous month. The two absentees were Bill Farrimond, replaced behind the stumps by George Duckworth, and Gordon Hodgson who was replaced by Leslie Warburton. Farrimond and Hodgson were both playing for the Second Eleven against Cheshire at Warrington where Eddie Paynter, not yet established in the Lancashire first team, top scored in both innings. Warburton had an unusual career. Aged 19 he played four matches for Lancashire in 1929. He next appeared in the 1936 Roses Match and, a fortnight later, on the strength of his fast-medium bowling in the Central Lancashire League, in the North v South Test Trial at Lord's. He then played two final matches in 1938, one for Lancashire and one for an England XI against the Australians at Blackpool.

Lancashire batted first in front of a good crowd, as usual opening with the stylish left-hander Charlie Hallows and the obdurate Frank Watson. Hallows had started the season well, carrying his bat for 152 in the Whitsun Roses Match, but had failed to reach three figures since. The pitch was fast and easy-paced and the outfield quick, and after the opening bowlers had failed to break through Freeman was given an early bowl and soon had Hallows caught behind. Watson had made 169 against Surrey in his previous innings and continued where he left off, making another century and holding the innings together before he was eventually trapped in front by a quicker top spinner. With Tyldesley also prospering Lancashire had been well placed at 234 for two but the remaining batsmen proved incapable of mastering Freeman's varied spin, seven wickets falling for 77 runs. With his ninth wicket Freeman set a record for the best-ever figures at Maidstone, previously held by Frank Woolley who took eight for 22 against Gloucestershire in 1921, but he then had to sweat a bit for the coveted tenth wicket.

Although they both had first-class centuries to their names, numbers ten and eleven, burly leg-spinner Richard Tyldesley and Australian fast bowler Ted McDonald, aren't particularly remembered for their batting. However, hitting out boldly they put on 36 before George Watson relieved the tension by holding a difficult catch at long on to finish the innings. Freeman's ten for 131 was the most expensive all-ten ever, just 'beating' Lillywhite's ten for 129 back in 1872. He was chaired back into the pavilion for his efforts. He had been excellently supported by keen Kent ground fielding and behind the stumps by Les Ames who made two stumpings, took a catch and conceded no byes in an innings of 347. Of Freeman's 267 wickets in 1929, thirty-five were stumpings by Ames who would retire over 20 years later having taken a world record 418 stumpings.

Freeman is the only bowler to have taken all-ten at Maidstone and as Mote Park saw the last of its 218 first-class matches in 2005 it may be a record that remains unbeaten. Umpire Jimmy Stone had officiated each of the last three all-tens, including Kennedy's and, earlier in the 1929 season, Allen's.

When Kent went in at the end of the day after a delay for rain, George Watson was quickly brought down to earth, caught behind without scoring by Duckworth. This would be the last of Watson's eight matches for Kent but he would later play over 200 matches for Leicestershire. Freeman had a modest career record as a batsman, but he had made a Test fifty against Australia, and next day it took a ninth wicket partnership of 63, the highest of the Kent innings, between Les Todd (52 not out) and Freeman (28) to avert the follow-on.

With only one wicket at a cost of 96, Freeman could not repeat his mastery of the Red Rose batsmen a second time around. Hallows finally got another century, *The Times* opining that he played Freeman as well as any batsman in the country, a score of 114 lending weight to this opinion. Freeman's only victim was Thomas Halliday, bowled for 4, the last innings of his 41-match career. Another four and he would at least have finished it with 1,000 runs. Set 418 to win Kent made only 228. Halliday made his final mark in the first-class game by catching Freeman (for 11) off the left-arm spin of Jack Iddon. Despite losing, Kent remained at the top of the table, just, but it wouldn't last.

Freeman had taken ten South African wickets for England earlier in the month at Headingley and immediately after Maidstone he travelled to Old Trafford where he took another twelve wickets. Not surprisingly in view of his form he retained his place for the final Test at The Oval, a match in which Ames, replacing Duckworth, began his successful 47-match England career with a duck. Unfortunately in South Africa's only innings Freeman took nought for 169, his worst ever first-class analysis, and he had played his last Test. One of the umpires was Billy Bestwick, who knew a bit about all-tens.

Freeman took 66 wickets in 12 Test matches, a decent record, but most of his success came against the 'lesser' nations, South Africa and the West Indies. In two Tests in Australia his eight wickets cost 57 each. He might have done better if he had been picked against them at home, but it never happened. He probably should have played more. Turning 40 in 1928, maybe he was thought too old. Or perhaps his personality told against him. Much-loved, he had a natural humility. There was no fuss, he just 'got on with it'.

Kent v Essex, 1930
County Championship

Southchurch Park, Southend–on-Sea on 13, 14, 15 August 1930 (3-day match)
Toss won by Kent
Kent won by 277 runs
Umpires: W Bestwick, WR Parry
Kent 122 (K Farnes 5-36) and 422-9 dec (AM Crawley 175; Essex 145 (AP Freeman 10-53) and 122 (AP Freeman 6-41)

Essex first innings

LG Crawley	lbw b Freeman	22
DF Pope	c Bryan b Freeman	38
J O'Connor	lbw b Freeman	19
CAG Russell	not out	47
JA Cutmore	c Knott b Freeman	6
MS Nichols	st Ames b Freeman	0
*HWF Franklin	c Bryan b Freeman	1
+JR Sheffield	st Ames b Freeman	0
K Farnes	b Freeman	1
TPB Smith	c Woolley b Freeman	1
HJ Palmer	b Freeman	0
Extras	(b 5, lb 5)	10
Total	(all out, 72.4 overs)	145

Fall of wickets 1-39, 2-68, 3-113, 4-127, 5-129, 6-137, 7-137, 8-139, 9-145, 10-145

Kent bowling: AC Wright 13-2-25-0, WH Ashdown 9-2-23-0, AP Freeman 30.4-8-53-10, CW Peach 6-1-14-0, HTW Hardinge 14-6-20-0

Kent: AM Crawley, HTW Hardinge, FE Woolley, LEG Ames (wk), WH Ashdown, JL Bryan (capt), CH Knott, LJ Todd, AC Wright, AP Freeman, CW Peach

Although Freeman's short Test career was over he continued to take first-class wickets in vast numbers. His second all-ten came just over a year later in the first match of the Southend Festival Week, against a decent Essex side that would finish the season sixth in the Championship, just one place below Kent. Essex still played most of their matches at their Leyton headquarters, but a couple of matches were played every year at spacious Southchurch Park, usually timed to take advantage of the holiday season. With its invigorating air and other seaside delights it was a popular venue. It was an interesting ground with two cricket pavilions (for the two clubs that used the ground), a large pond and of course, when the circus came to town, a number of bright marquees.

The official captains unavailable, both teams were led by deputies. For Essex Henry Franklin was standing in for Harold Morris and his usual deputy Charles Bray, whilst Kent were captained by Jack Bryan in place of Geoffrey Legge. Franklin and Bryan were both schoolmasters whose availability was mainly limited to the summer holidays. Franklin and Bryan died within a month of each other in 1985. Aged 88 Bryan was the oldest living Kent cricketer and the last surviving member of the MCC side to Australia in 1924/25 (although he never played Test cricket).

On a first day on which 17 wickets fell, Kent led off with a mediocre 122, nineteen-year-old future England fast bowler Ken Farnes taking five for 36 in only his second first-class match. The only real resistance came from 44-year-old opener Wally Hardinge who carried his bat for 49, the eleventh (and final) time he had performed this feat, and the third time against Essex.

The Essex openers Leonard Crawley, cousin of Kent opener Aidan, and Dudley Pope then gave their side a good start. Twenty-three-year-old Pope had recently made his maiden first-class century at Hove. Four years later, having established himself in the Essex side, he was returning from the last match of the season at Gloucester, where he had made a century against his former county, when the car he was driving collided with a lorry and he was killed instantly.

Just nine runs behind Kent's total with only two wickets down, and with Jack (C.A.G.) Russell, to this day one of the county's highest ever run-scorers, at the crease, Essex were probably hopeful of a decent first-innings lead. On the other hand Freeman had taken five wickets (at least!) in each of the last nine innings he had bowled against them, and the sequence wasn't going to end yet as the bamboozled middle and lower order failed against him completely. By the close he had taken seven for 49, reducing the home side to 137 for seven. The ever ready Ames had made two more stumpings, including Essex counterpart Roy Sheffield who surely should have known better. An interesting character, Sheffield loved to travel. This had its drawbacks, particularly in 1932/33. Whilst other cricketers were engaged in the Bodyline series he was being arrested on suspicion of being a Bolivian spy. After cricket he settled in New Zealand where he lived until the age of 90.

Freeman's cousin Jack Russell was 41 not out overnight but the Essex tail didn't stay with him too long on Thursday morning, Freeman needing only a quarter of an hour to finish off the innings. Both Farnes and leg-spinning amateur Harold Palmer would finish their careers with batting averages well below double figures, but 21-year-old leg-spinner Peter Smith would eventually make eight centuries (including a record 163 at number 11 against Derbyshire in 1947). He would be the only member of the Essex side who played 18 years later on the same ground when the Australians scored 721 in a day (Smith 38 overs four for 193). He finished his career with 1,697 wickets, a total only exceeded by five other leg-spinners, and is Essex's leading wicket-taker.

Russell had remained undefeated. Aged 43 and in his last season, he was one of cricket's unluckier batsmen. In only ten Test appearances he made five centuries: three against Warwick Armstrong's Australians and the other two in the same match against South Africa, after which he never played for England again! Perhaps the selectors didn't warm to his utilitarian style, perhaps he just played for an unfashionable county, perhaps competition for places was too great.

After that it was all Kent. Freeman's first victim had been Leonard Crawley. Cousin Aidan redeemed the family honour by hitting a brilliant 175 in just under three hours, no doubt taking advantage of an outfield made none too reliable by the passage of summer. Two years previously, captaining Oxford University, he had made a century against Kent. Crawley had a remarkable life becoming, among many other things, both a Labour MP and later a Conservative MP. Playing for Free Foresters against Oxford University in 1949, he was the last person to appear in a first-class match whilst still a serving member of the House of Commons.

Setting Essex 400 to win, Kent triumphed by 277 runs. Left all day to reach their improbable target, Essex lasted only two and a half hours. Deputy-deputy-captain Franklin had a modest career record, but he at least provided some leadership by top scoring with 38, albeit in a losing cause. Freeman took six more wickets and finished with sixteen for 94 in the match. Umpire Bestwick (again) no doubt looked on approvingly.

With the ground now off the county circuit after hosting 130 first-class matches, Freeman's innings and match analyses are Southchurch Park records unlikely to be beaten. The previous innings record had been set in the inaugural first-class match on the ground when J.W.H.T. (Johnny) Douglas took eight for 33 against Leicestershire in 1906, with Freeman's cousin Alf Russell the Essex wicketkeeper. Aged 48 Douglas would make his final first-class appearance a week after Freeman's feat, and tragically drown in a collision off the Danish coast four months later whilst attempting to save his father's life.

Freeman had now made it 11 successive five-fors against Essex, a sequence he would eventually extend to 17. He probably liked bowling against Essex; he took more wickets (269) against them than against any other team. To be fair he probably liked bowling against quite a few counties, taking over 200 against nine in all.

The day after the Southend match, Saturday, was the first day of the deciding Fifth Test at The Oval between England and Australia. The 14 players from whom the final England side would be selected included two wicketkeepers, Les Ames and Lancashire's George Duckworth. In the event, Ames had taken a blow on the knee on the last day at Southend and Duckworth played, unfortunately having a poor game by his high standards. Meanwhile the overlooked Freeman went on taking wickets for Kent, first innings figures of five (including Bradman and Ponsford) for 78 when the Australians came to Canterbury, again raising the question of the briefness of his Test career.

Kent v Lancashire, 1931
County Championship

Old Trafford, Manchester on 27, 28, 29 May 1931 (3-day match)
Toss won by Lancashire
Match drawn
Umpires: WA Buswell, A Morton
Lancashire 184 (AP Freeman 10-79) and 84-0; Kent 285-9 dec (FE Woolley
108, JL Hopwood 6-55)

Lancashire first innings

C Hallows	b Freeman	9
FB Watson	c Woolley b Freeman	19
GE Tyldesley	lbw b Freeman	70
J Iddon	st Ames b Freeman	4
JL Hopwood	b Freeman	2
E Paynter	c and b Freeman	39
*PT Eckersley	b Freeman	1
FM Sibbles	c Crawley b Freeman	8
+G Duckworth	not out	7
RK Tyldesley	c Valentine b Freeman	1
EA McDonald	b Freeman	20
Extras	(b 1, lb 1, nb 1, w 1)	4
Total	(all out, 88.1 overs)	184

Fall of wickets 1-11, 2-46, 3-62, 4-66, 5-146, 6-147, 7-148, 8-157, 9-159,
10-184

Kent bowling: AE Watt 11-3-19-0, WH Ashdown 18-7-37-0, AP Freeman
36.1-9-79-10, HTW Hardinge, 23-6-45-0

Kent: HTW Hardinge, AM Crawley, FE Woolley, LEG Ames (wk), APF
Chapman (capt), BH Valentine, LJ Todd, AE Watt, WH Ashdown, TA Pearce,
AP Freeman

1931, another season, another all-ten for Freeman – and once again against
Lancashire. After four wins out of four by the end of May, Kent were top
of the table as they travelled north to Manchester. Lancashire on the other
hand had begun their quest to retain the Championship title badly, and
after a season of deplorable weather and affected by loss of form and
illness of some of the side, eventually had to settle for sixth place in the
table. Unaffected by a long journey from Taunton where they had easily
beaten Somerset the previous day, Kent continued their good form, having
the better of a match unfortunately left unfinished because of heavy rain
which prevented any play on the second day.

Lancashire batted first in pleasant weather and in front of a large
crowd. Only three batsmen reached 20, and one of those was 40-year-
old Australian fast bowler Ted McDonald who went in at number eleven.
The Kent attack was opened by the medium-fast bowling of Alan Watt, a
23-year-old just making his way in the side, and the more experienced Bill
Ashdown, who is famous for having played first-class cricket in England
both before the First World War and after the Second. Both would finish
their careers with over 600 wickets, but once they had got the shine off

the ball Freeman was on, and he soon yorked Charlie Hallows, beaten in the air by the leg-spinner's deceptive flight. After this, the only resistance of any substance came from Ernest Tyldesley, who had seen it all before, and is still his county's highest run-scorer, and 29-year-old left-hander Eddie Paynter who was playing his first full season, hadn't yet made a first-class century (although he would remedy this omission twice in July) but would be an England Test player by the end of the summer. Their fifth-wicket partnership had reached 80 when Freeman, returning to the attack at 3.15 pm, dismissed both batsmen in the same over: first trapping Tyldesley in front of the stumps with a googly and then taking a brilliant return catch as Paynter drove the ball back hard to his left. Tyldesley would eventually be dismissed 22 times by Freeman, more times than by any other bowler. However, their paths often crossed and Tyldesley returned the compliment by scoring more runs against Kent than against any other team. Four wickets down for 146 soon became 159 for nine. A few tailender's blows from McDonald moved the score along, but at 184 he swung once too often, missed, and Freeman had become the only man to have taken three all-tens. It might never have happened: in the previous over, McDonald had been dropped at long off by Bill Ashdown off Wally Hardinge's left-arm spin. A great bowler, 40-year-old McDonald had lost form and was in his last season with his adopted county. He would return to Lancashire League cricket and six years later was killed on the road near Bolton as a result of a motor car collision.

Freeman had been supported by some brilliant fielding, but given the quality of the pitch 184 all out was a poor total for a team most of whom were (or would be) Test cricketers. Freeman had used his googly just enough to create uncertainty among the Lancashire batsmen, and with the possible exception of Paynter none of them had played him with any confidence.

Lancashire had been on the receiving end of an all-ten for the third time in three years, two of which had been inflicted by Freeman. Eight of the side had appeared in all three matches (see statistical appendix) and nine had appeared in both of the Kent matches.

Adventurous batting took Kent to 143 for two by the close, and with Frank Woolley 51 not out spectators planning to watch on the second day must have anticipated seeing the great left-hander reach another hundred. Unfortunately bad weather postponed this pleasure until the final day and left little opportunity for Kent to force a result, Lancashire easily playing out time on a placid pitch on which Freeman bowled 15 wicketless overs before more rain brought a premature close at four o'clock. The rest of the country had been similarly affected by the elements and only at Lord's, where Middlesex beat Essex, was a result reached.

Captained by the enterprising Percy Chapman whose Test career, like Freeman's, had recently come to an end, Kent were unable to maintain their early season form over the rest of the season but still finished a creditable third in the Championship behind Yorkshire and Gloucestershire, for whom spinners Charlie Parker and Tom Goddard totalled 327 Championship wickets.

The two teams played another draw in the return match at the Angel Ground, Tonbridge two weeks later. The visitors had a measure of revenge in their first innings, hitting Freeman's 48 overs for 179 runs. He did however take another seven wickets. In all he took 241 Championship wickets in 1931. He would probably have welcomed some support. Kent's next highest wicket-taker with 61 was Charles (Father) Marriott, a very skilful wrist-spinner, but who was only available during the school holidays.

Although Freeman twice took all-ten against Lancashire, not surprisingly given their strength his record against them was not as good as against most other counties: in all Championship matches he took a wicket every six and a half overs at 17.30 apiece, whereas against Lancashire he took his wickets every nine and a half overs at 24.70. In the three Test matches against New Zealand in 1931 England used three leg-spinners, all amateurs: Freddie Brown, Ian Peebles and Walter Robins. In total during 1931 these three took 270 wickets at 21 runs each, with a strike rate of 45 balls per wicket. All three were in their early/mid 20s and Brown and Robins were also good batsmen but the comparison with Freeman's season (276 wickets at 16 runs each, strike rate 35) is of interest.

The end of Freeman's career in 1936 was anticlimatic. He still got 100 wickets, but at the age of 48 physical exertion was taking its toll and to provide some rest, the Kent Committee suggested a match-to-match contract. Freeman declined and there was no re-engagement. Only Wilfred Rhodes has exceeded his 3,776 first-class wickets. Of bowlers taking at least 2,000 first-class wickets, his strike-rate (a wicket every 41 balls) is bettered only by Surrey's Tom Richardson and Yorkshire's Schofield Haigh.

In 1949 Tich Freeman was one of the first former professionals to be offered honorary MCC membership. Appropriately for somebody who loved to bowl all day, he retired to a house in Maidstone he named 'Dunbolyn'. He died in 1965. Later that year a plaque in his honour was unveiled at Canterbury.

George Geary

Leicestershire v Glamorgan, 1929
County Championship

Ynysangharad Park, Pontypridd on 14, 15 August 1929 (3-day match)
Toss won by Leicestershire
Leicestershire won by 15 runs
Umpires: TW Oates, F Parris
Leicestershire 102 (FP Ryan 5-38) and 141 (JC Clay 5-63); Glamorgan 160
(G Geary 6-78) and 68 (G Geary 10-18)

Glamorgan second innings

WE Bates	c Bradshaw b Geary	4
AH Dyson	lbw b Geary	0
D Davies	c Bradshaw b Geary	2
MJL Turnbull	b Geary	20
DE Davies	c Shipman b Geary	0
JJ Hills	b Geary	0
*JC Clay	c Berry b Geary	15
HRJ Rhys	not out	6
T Arnott	lbw b Geary	0
FP Ryan	b Geary	2
+T Every	b Geary	0
Extras	(b 9, lb 9, nb 1)	19
Total	(all out, 32.2 overs)	68

Fall of wickets 1-8, 2-8, 3-11, 4-13, 5-19, 6-55, 7-58, 8-66, 9-68, 10-68

Leicestershire bowling: G Geary 16.2-8-18-10, WE Astill 16-6-31-0

Leicestershire: EW Dawson (capt), AW Shipman, GL Berry, NF Armstrong, H Riley, JC Bradshaw, WE Astill, G Geary, TE Sidwell (wk), CAR Coleman, HA Smith

Tall and well-built, George Geary bowled fast-medium off a short run-up and with an easy action. He was persistently accurate and, like his great contemporary Maurice Tate, came quickly off the pitch. Moving the ball both ways he possessed a dangerous leg cutter, and if the conditions helped him could be near unplayable. He was also a useful batsman and a brilliant slip fielder.

The eldest of 16 children, Geary was born in Barwell, Leicestershire in 1893, his father a shoemaker. He made his first-class debut in 1912 but his career nearly ended during the War when his left shoulder and thigh had an encounter with a spinning propeller, the side effects of which he was still feeling when county cricket resumed. Deciding that he wasn't yet up to the rigours of first-class cricket, he played in the Lancashire League before resuming as a Leicestershire regular in 1922. His pre-war promise was soon confirmed and two years later he played the first of 14 Test matches that would yield 46 wickets. He made important contributions in the 1926 and 1928/29 Ashes-winning series, took twelve for 130 on Johannesburg matting in December 1927, and appeared twice against the

1934 Australians, dismissing Don Bradman in his penultimate match.

With 152 wickets Geary was at the height of his powers in 1929. An elbow injury meant that he had hardly bowled in 1928 and for a while his career was in jeopardy. However an operation fixed the problem and by the following winter he was fit enough to top the England bowling averages and in the final Test at Melbourne take five for 105 in Australia's first innings, bowling 81 overs, at the time a record for the most balls bowled in a Test innings.

Leicestershire finished ninth in the Championship in 1929, a good performance for a side including few top players. They were captained by Eddie Dawson whose brief five-match Test career would finish with a fifty at Eden Park, Auckland the following February. Glamorgan finished bottom, winning just three matches. *Wisden* thought that they had rarely had a much more depressing season. They had joint captains, Norman Riches and Johnnie Clay, but unfortunately on a number of occasions neither was available. Their batting was inconsistent and they were dismissed below 100 on eight occasions, including twice below fifty. Earlier in the season Leicestershire had beaten them by an innings at Loughborough, bowling them out for 98 in their second innings. Even so, given that they had won their previous match against Somerset at Weston-super-Mare chasing 247, they must have been confident of reaching just 84 to win in the fourth innings of the return match in August 1929. George Geary had other ideas.

Ynysangharad Park in the heart of Pontypridd had been opened in 1923 as the town's War Memorial. As well as being home to Pontypridd CC it would host many other sports and entertainments. Glamorgan had been playing there since 1926, their first such match away from the main centres of Cardiff and Swansea since they attained first-class status in 1921. Attendances were good, and in 1929 the ground was not only awarded two Championship matches but one against the South African tourists as well.

Leicestershire batted first and made only 102, with left-arm spinner Frank Ryan (five for 38) and off-spinner Clay (four for 30) doing most of the damage. It might have been worse: the score was only 79 when the ninth wicket fell but fast bowler Haydon Smith came in and hit 22 while Geary (8 not out) held up the other end. In a low-scoring match this would prove to be a crucial partnership. Glamorgan did better, being dismissed shortly before close of play for 160, Geary taking six for 78 and Ewart Astill, the only bowler to take more than 2,000 wickets for Leicestershire, four for 56 with his medium-pace spin.

Leicestershire's second-innings 141, Ryan and Clay again taking most of the wickets, left Glamorgan all the time in the world to make just 84 to win. The pitch wasn't easy, but it was still a very gettable target, although it was soon looking very ungettable. Early failures included William Bates (top-scorer in Bestwick's all-ten), whose 70 had held the first innings together, and Arnold Dyson and Joe Hills, two of five batsmen who made Championship hundreds for Glamorgan in 1929 but who both contributed nothing this time. With half the side gone for 19 runs two of Glamorgan cricket's greatest, Maurice Turnbull and the captain Clay, were united at the crease. Turnbull is one of Glamorgan's finest batsmen. Clay is one of Glamorgan's finest bowlers, but he also had two centuries to his name. They were Glamorgan's first two England cricketers but, even more importantly, in the 1930s the off-the-field fund-raising activities of these two friends ensured the survival of the poverty-stricken county. Killed in the War, Turnbull did not live to witness his county's greatest moment, but in 1948 off-spinner Clay, then aged 50, would play a key role in Glamorgan's first Championship title, taking nine wickets in the crucial match at Bournemouth at the end of August, and topping the national averages.

Any thoughts of titles were far from their minds in 1929, but at least the pair steadied the ship and the home crowd must have been hopeful of victory. However, with the score 55, Geary struck again, bowling Turnbull, then quickly having Clay caught by Les Berry and, without further help from the fielders, clearing up the tail. One of his victims was previous year's captain Trevor Arnott, trapped in front for his second duck of the match, and the fifth of the innings. Glamorgan's 68 would have been even poorer without a generous donation of 19 extras. Geary's last victim was 19-year-old wicketkeeper Trevor Every who was playing in his debut season. His career showed great promise but ended tragically. He had to pull out during the first match of the 1934 season against Kent because he could not pick up the flight of the ball and within a year his sight had gone.

The match was over in two days and Geary's analysis was a world record (beating Vogler's 10 for 26) which must have seemed unbeatable – until it was beaten three years later. His match figures, sixteen for 96, are also still a Leicestershire record. The early finish gave Geary all next day to get to The Oval where he was due to play in the Fifth Test against the South Africans.

Since 1929 only three teams have lost in the Championship whilst chasing fewer than 84 to win. And the next to achieve this feat? Well sadly for Johnnie Clay, Dai Davies, Emrys Davies and Arnold Dyson, who played in both matches, it was Glamorgan again: set 70 to win at The Gnoll, Neath in 1936 they were spun out for 61 by Worcestershire's Peter Jackson and Dick Howorth.

Together with Ewart Astill, Geary carried the Leicestershire attack for many years, finally retiring in 1938. In his second benefit match in 1936 he took six for 36 and seven for 7 against Warwickshire. He must have wondered if the £10 the rain-affected match yielded him was worthy recompense.

Because of injury Geary bowled relatively little in his last season but made three of his eight first-class centuries, finishing with 13,501 first-class runs to add to his 2,063 wickets. His county career over, he coached for 20 years at Charterhouse, where he fired Peter May with the ambition to reach the top, and then for another decade at Rugby.

The cheerful and universally-popular George Geary died in his home county in 1981, leaving Harold Larwood as the only surviving member of the victorious Ashes-winning England team at The Oval in 1926.

Clarrie Grimmett

Australians v Yorkshire, 1930

Bramall Lane, Sheffield on 10, 12, 13 May 1930 (3-day match)
Toss won by Yorkshire
Match drawn
Umpires: G Beet, TW Oates
Yorkshire 155 (CV Grimmett 10-37); Australians 320 (WM Woodfull 121)

Yorkshire first innings

P Holmes	b Grimmett	31
H Sutcliffe	c Walker b Grimmett	69
E Oldroyd	lbw b Grimmett	2
M Leyland	st Walker b Grimmett	9
*AT Barber	st Walker b Grimmett	1
A Mitchell	b Grimmett	3
E Robinson	c Bradman b Grimmett	2
+A Wood	c Richardson b Grimmett	17
GG Macaulay	st Walker b Grimmett	1
W Rhodes	not out	6
WE Bowes	b Grimmett	0
Extras	(b 4, lb 9, nb 1)	14
Total	(all out, 65.3 overs)	155

Fall of wickets 1-59, 2-84, 3-120, 4-125, 5-126, 6-130, 7-130, 8-132, 9-155, 10-155

Australians bowling: TW Wall 16-3-42-0, EL a'Beckett 12-6-11-0, PM Hornibrook 12-4-49-0, CV Grimmett 22.3-8-37-10, SJ McCabe 3-2-2-0

Australians: WM Woodfull (capt), WH Ponsford, DG Bradman, AF Kippax, SJ McCabe, VY Richardson, EL a'Beckett, CV Grimmett, CW Walker (wk), TW Wall, PM Hornibrook

Don Bradman was the star of the 1930 Australians but they could not have won the series against England without Clarrie Grimmett's 29 wickets. Slightly-built, Grimmett bowled from a short run, with a low arm action accentuated by his crouching delivery. His stock ball was a modestly turning leg break, varied with a sparingly used googly and a lethal top spinner which trapped many unwary batsmen. His length and direction were unwavering. Grimmett was the ultimate student of the game, constantly practising, constantly developing new deliveries. He had a number of nicknames, most commonly the Fox because he preyed on batsmen. He usually bowled in a cap, apparently worn to shade his eyes, not hide his baldness.

Born in New Zealand on Christmas Day 1891, Grimmett moved to Australia in 1914 to further his cricketing ambitions. Eventually the South Australians spotted his potential and an offer of cricket and a signwriter's job was too good to refuse. Grimmett played his first match for his new state in October 1924; four months later, already 33 years old, he was making his Test debut at Sydney. And what a debut. Australia were 3-1 up, but England had been gradually improving and were expected to put up a good fight. However, taking eleven for 82 Grimmett bowled Australia to an easy victory. It was a remarkable start to a Test career that would finish 11 years later with a record 216 wickets from only 37 matches.

Third in 1930, Yorkshire were entering a period up to the Second World War when they would dominate the Championship. Of the ten professionals in the side against the Australians, five had played for England and three would go on to do so. They were led by 25-year-old amateur Alan Barber of whom *Wisden* said that he was perhaps the first Yorkshire captain since Lord Hawke worth his place as a player.

The interwar Yorkshire sides are remembered for the power of their bowling, but they could also bat and wickets against them were well-earned. In 1930 eleven English batsmen made 2,000 runs in the season, and three of these were Yorkshiremen: Herbert Sutcliffe, Maurice Leyland, and 43-year-old Percy Holmes. Australian sides usually met Yorkshire twice during the season, with one of the matches played at Bramall Lane, Sheffield. The ground's urban location, and the dust and ash from the surrounding factories and foundries, gave it a distinctive atmosphere. And the outfield's many bare patches were a reminder that Sheffield United also played football there.

The illustrious opening pair Holmes and Sutcliffe began quietly in front of 'seven thousand cloth-capped Yorkshiremen' as the sun appeared 'through a pall of smoke'. Sutcliffe eventually became more aggressive and, after he had driven left-armer Percy Hornibrook for a six and a four in the same over, Grimmett was brought on at the Football Ground End with the score 46. He had begun the tour in fine form, taking 21 wickets in three matches, and it was perhaps surprising that he hadn't come on sooner. However, having got on it didn't take him long to get among the wickets, Holmes soon playing on for 31. On an easy-paced pitch Grimmett could only turn the ball slowly: most of the home batsmen would fall prey to his clever variations of pace and flight. Edgar Oldroyd had joined Sutcliffe but was not really comfortable, and soon after lunch with the score 84 Grimmett first beat him with a leg break outside the off stump and then whipped in a trademark top spinner and trapped him in front. Sutcliffe continued to bat confidently and, in partnership with the resolute Maurice Leyland, took the score to a solid looking 120 for two before he was caught behind for a chanceless 69. When he left the rest of the innings became a procession, with only wicketkeeper Arthur Wood and extras reaching double figures in Yorkshire's final total of 155. The last seven wickets had fallen in just over an hour, Grimmett conceding only 16 runs. He had hardly bowled a loose ball and his figures are still the best ever against Yorkshire, and a record for Bramall Lane that will never be beaten, Yorkshire having vacated the ground after the 1973 season and left it to the winter game. And after standing at Pontypridd umpire Thomas Oates had officiated his second all-ten in ten games.

Grimmett was ably helped by the young South Australian keeper Charlie Walker who made three stumpings and held a brilliant catch to dismiss Sutcliffe. His stumping of Barber was particularly special: the fraction of a second when the Yorkshire captain lifted his right leg gave him just enough time to whip off the bails. It all happened too quickly however for some of the crowd, and they let the umpire know in no uncertain terms what they thought of the decision. The unfortunate Walker toured England in both 1930 and 1938, but never played for his country. A bomber pilot during the Second World War, he was shot down over Germany in 1942 and died at the age of 33.

Grimmett had wrapped up the innings by dismissing Bill Bowes, bowled first ball, probably not an unusual experience for someone who in a 20-match first-class career had not yet once reached double figures, and whose final tally of runs would not match his 1,639 wickets. The one batsman who evaded Grimmett was 52-year-old Wilfred Rhodes, who had previously opened for England with some success but was now batting down the order and preparing the way for his equally great left-arm spin successor Hedley Verity, who would make his first-class debut a week later. The vociferous Bramall Lane crowd could sometimes be hostile to the opposition, but they knew their cricket and as Grimmett ran back to the pavilion they rose to him in sincere and hearty appreciation of his feat. Tim Wall had bowled 16 wicketless overs at the other end. Three years later, when he took all-ten for South Australia against New South Wales, Grimmett would be the one who was empty-handed.

When bad light and rain finally stopped play at 6.15 pm the Australians' score was 69 for one. Ominously, Bradman, who had begun the tour with scores of 236 and 185 not out, was on 24. More rain prevented play until after lunch on Monday, and Bradman 'only' scored 78, but the Australians still reached 320 all out just before the close, mainly thanks to 121 by captain Bill Woodfull. The visitors were well placed for victory, but rain came to Yorkshire's rescue by preventing play on the third day. In the return match at Bradford two months later Bradman scored one, Grimmett took 11 wickets, and the Australians won by ten wickets.

Grimmett never took all ten wickets in an innings again, but he took nine twice, including nine for 180 against Queensland in December 1934, still the most expensive ever nine (or ten) wicket analysis. After taking 44 South African wickets in 1935/36, still an Australian Test series record, Grimmett must have looked forward to more success against England back home the following season. Controversially however he had played his last Test, losing his place to Frank Ward, a good bowler but not in Grimmett's class. Even more surprisingly, given his previous success there, Grimmett was not selected for the 1938 tour of the British Isles. Bill O'Reilly called the decision a 'shameful omission'.

Grimmett was still bowling well enough at the age of 48 to take 73 wickets in 1939/40. He retired at the end of the following season having taken 1,424 first-class wickets, still a record for bowlers who have never played county cricket.

Grimmett had many strings to his bow. He wrote three instructional books, coached, played golf to a good standard and later in life sold insurance. He died in Adelaide in 1980 aged 88.

Hedley Verity

Hedley Verity followed in the tradition of the great Yorkshire left-arm spinners. However, usually bowling at around slow-medium pace and relying on changes of pace rather than flight to deceive batsmen, he was dissimilar in style from his incomparable predecessor Wilfred Rhodes. Tall with an easy run-up and smooth high action, he was able to make the ball lift uncomfortably on most wickets and give his close fielders plenty of work. His accuracy and control meant that on helpful wickets he was devastating, whilst on batsmen-friendly ones he was still a formidable and unyielding opponent. In the words of Don Bradman 'there's no breaking point with him'. And he should know: Verity dismissed him ten times, a total only equalled by Clarrie Grimmett. A useful batsman with a first-class century and three Test fifties to his name, he was even pressed into service as an England opener at Adelaide in 1937.

Born in Leeds and biding his time in the Lancashire League until Rhodes retired, Verity was 25 when he came into the first-class game in 1930. In a short career he took 1,956 wickets. His average, 14.90, was easily better than that achieved by any other 20th-century bowler taking as many wickets. Together with another Yorkshire great, Bill Bowes, he bowled his county to seven Championships. When war came only Clarrie Grimmett, Sydney Barnes and Maurice Tate had exceeded his 144 Test wickets. Among many great feats, one in particular stands out: his 15 for 104 at Lord's in 1934 when he became the second bowler after Rhodes to take 15 Australian wickets in a Test. Fittingly, the great Wilfred was present to see his successor's feat. It would be a long time before England beat Australia at Lord's again.

Yorkshire v Warwickshire, 1931
County Championship

Headingley, Leeds on 16, 18 May 1931 (3-day match)
Toss won by Warwickshire
Yorkshire won by an innings and 25 runs
Umpires: W Bestwick, JH King
Warwickshire 201 and 72 (H Verity 10-36); Yorkshire 298 (JH Mayer 6-76)

Warwickshire second innings

*RES Wyatt	c Holmes b Verity	23
AJW Croom	c Greenwood b Verity	7
LTA Bates	c Mitchell b Verity	19
N Kilner	c Mitchell b Verity	0
JH Parsons	c Leyland b Verity	9
WA Hill	c Wood b Verity	8
+JA Smart	c Mitchell b Verity	0
DG Foster	st Wood b Verity	0
CF Tate	lbw b Verity	0
GAE Paine	c and b Verity	0
JH Mayer	not out	6

Extras   0
Total   (all out, 45.4 overs)   72
Fall of wickets 1-16, 2-33, 3-33, 4-51, 5-59, 6-59, 7-59, 8-59, 9-59, 10-72

Yorkshire bowling: WE Bowes 5-1-7-0, E Robinson 4-1-9-0, H Verity 18.4-6-36-10, GG Macaulay 18-11-20-0

Yorkshire: P Holmes, H Sutcliffe, M Leyland, E Oldroyd, A Mitchell, FE Greenwood (capt), E Robinson, A Wood (wk), GG Macaulay, H Verity, WE Bowes

Verity took all-ten twice. The first occasion, 18 May 1931, was his 26th birthday. Having played first-class cricket for just less than a year he was the only one of the Yorkshire eleven still uncapped. Under their new captain Frank Greenwood Yorkshire would go on to win the Championship in 1931 whilst Warwickshire, a county for whom Verity had once had a brief unsuccessful trial, would finish comfortably in mid-table. Yorkshire included eight current or future England players. Warwickshire only had two, Bob Wyatt and George Paine, but they did have a few other famous names: Norman Kilner and Cecil Tate were the younger brothers of Yorkshire's Roy and the great Maurice respectively.

Although the Championship season was two weeks old Yorkshire were playing their first home match. It began unremarkably, Yorkshire's first innings 298 heading Warwickshire's 201 (Verity three for 61 in 32.3 overs). Warwickshire's second innings began at a quarter to four on the second day in unpleasant 'two sweaters' weather. However, the 4,000 spectators present were no doubt glad that they braved the cold and stayed until six o'clock to see a remarkable and unexpectedly sudden end to the match.

The roller had enlivened the pitch and Greenwood, having quickly got Verity into the attack, helped start the eventual rout with a smart running catch at mid on to dismiss opener Alfred Croom with the score 16. With six centuries and over 1,500 runs, 1931 would be the long-serving Croom's best season, but it would be another six years before, aged 41, he made his only century against Yorkshire. Warwickshire's captain Bob Wyatt played aggressively with some success, but with the score 33 was caught in the covers, to be followed in the same over by Kilner who was caught at backward point by Arthur Mitchell. Eventually dismissed by him 14 times, Wyatt would become one of Verity's favourite victims: only five batsmen would fall to him more often.

Bates and Parsons hung on until tea, but two more wickets fell quickly after the interval and at the beginning of Verity's 16th over Warwickshire were struggling at 59 for five. Six balls later they were 59 for nine with Jack Smart, caught at backward point, and Derek Foster falling to the first two balls of the over, and Cecil Tate and George Paine, (a smart left-handed caught and bowled) to the fifth and sixth. Having previously played for Derbyshire Tate was making his Warwickshire debut. Although he had made a good start by dismissing Sutcliffe when Yorkshire batted, Warwickshire already had a very good left-arm spinner in Paine, and Tate would play just seven not very fruitful matches for the county.

The first ball of Verity's 17th over was uneventful and a first hat-trick had just evaded him twice. The omission would be remedied the following season. Verity had to wait another three overs before the historic tenth wicket fell: Aubrey Hill, who had come in at number six and watched the earlier carnage from the other end, caught behind. At 21 Hill was the youngest player in the match. Born in Carmarthen, he had started as an amateur but now played as a professional. Apart from Paine who played one match in 1947 (taking five Lancashire wickets in an innings) Hill was the only member of the Warwickshire side who played for the county after the Second World War.

Only Wyatt and Bates had reached double figures. Verity had received great support from his fielders: apart from one stumping and a leg-before all the wickets had fallen to catches, three at backward point by Arthur 'Ticker' Mitchell, a determined batsman and one of the most brilliant close fielders of the day. And on a pitch doing a bit, wicketkeeper Arthur Wood hadn't conceded any byes. Amazingly, in conditions that must have suited him, another Yorkshire great, medium-pace off-spinner George Macaulay, bowled 18 unrewarded overs at the other end. However, Verity himself had done his bit to try and get him a wicket, a diving attempt at short leg resulting in an injury that required his right arm to be bandaged for the rest of the innings. A fiery opponent, as befitted a former fast bowler, Macaulay's first-class record, 1,837 wickets at 17.65, was almost as remarkable as Verity's. Like Verity he would lose his life on active service during the War.

Verity had failed by one run to equal Alonzo Drake's analysis as the best ever figures for Yorkshire, another omission that would be remedied the following season, but they are still the best ever by anybody against Warwickshire. Having stood during Freeman's all-ten at Southend the previous season, Billy Bestwick had now been involved in three all-tens.

Strangely Warwickshire and Yorkshire met again less than a fortnight later at Edgbaston. In a rain-affected draw Verity bowled 12 wicketless overs after Sutcliffe (129) and Holmes (250) had opened the match with a partnership of 309.

Verity was brought down to earth later in the month with figures of 12 overs none for 70 at Bradford against Kent, as he came up against the great Frank Woolley in superb form. Consolation soon followed however with a county cap in June and a first Test cap against New Zealand at the end of July. In his first full season he would finish with 188 wickets, a total exceeded only by Tich Freeman and Charlie Parker who both took over 200.

Yorkshire v Nottinghamshire, 1932
County Championship

Headingley, Leeds on 9, 11, 12 July 1932 (3-day match)
Toss won by Nottinghamshire
Yorkshire won by ten wickets
Umpires: HG Baldwin, W Reeves
Nottinghamshire 234 and 67 (H Verity 10-10); Yorkshire 163-9 dec (H Larwood 5-73) and 139-0

Nottinghamshire second innings

WW Keeton	c Macaulay b Verity	21
FW Shipston	c Wood b Verity	21
W Walker	c Macaulay b Verity	11
*AW Carr	c Barber b Verity	0
A Staples	c Macaulay b Verity	7
CB Harris	c Holmes b Verity	0
GV Gunn	lbw b Verity	0
+B Lilley	not out	3
H Larwood	c Sutcliffe b Verity	0
W Voce	c Holmes b Verity	0
SJ Staples	st Wood b Verity	0
Extras	(b 3, nb 1)	4
Total	(all out, 47.4 overs)	67

Fall of wickets 1-44, 2-47, 3-51, 4-63, 5-63, 6-63, 7-64, 8-64, 9-67, 10-67

Yorkshire bowling: WE Bowes 5-0-19-0, GG Macaulay 23-9-34-0, H Verity 19.4-16-10-10

Yorkshire: P Holmes, H Sutcliffe, A Mitchell, M Leyland, W Barber, AB Sellers (capt), A Wood (wk), AC Rhodes, H Verity, GG Macaulay, WE Bowes

Records are meant to be broken but Verity's next, and even greater, all-ten will take some beating. Headingley wasn't looking its best as the double-fronted rugby and cricket stand was in the throes of being rebuilt following a fire three months earlier. Nottinghamshire were a strong side; County Champions three years before they would finish fourth in 1932. Ten of the team were already first-class centurions, and the eleventh, Charlie Harris, would make the first, and second (a double), of his eventual 30 centuries the following season. However, batting first, they entertained the Headingley crowd by taking up the whole of Saturday in scoring 234 in 132 overs against aggressive Yorkshire outcricket, Harold Larwood top scoring with 48. Verity took a modest two for 64, and it was another slow left-armer, England batsman Maurice Leyland, who had the best figures, running through the tail to finish with four for 14 from 8.2 overs. A more than useful bowler the burly Leyland might have bettered his nearly 500 first-class wickets had he played for a less well-endowed county.

Yorkshire faltered in turn against the pace of the England pair Larwood and Voce. Sutcliffe, easily the season's leading run-scorer, went for a duck, and Yorkshire were struggling at 163 for nine when a thunderstorm halted play at 4 o'clock on Monday. Play could not start again until 12.30 on Tuesday and in a daring move Brian Sellers immediately declared, still 71 behind. One of county cricket's outstanding leaders, Sellers was deputising for the unavailable Frank Greenwood and would be officially appointed captain the following season, a position he held with great success until 1947.

Notts settled in to play for a draw and openers Walter Keeton and Frank Shipston were not parted until after lunch with the score 44. Seven years later Keeton would score 312 not out against Middlesex, still the only triple-century scored for the county. Shipston had a less eminent career, but lived until 2005, dying a few days short of his 99th birthday, an anniversary that remarkably Willis Walker, the Notts' number three, did live to see (although without quite making his century).

The sun having come out on a drying pitch the ball was beginning to bite and Verity, bowling from the building site end, had brought up more close catchers. Two more wickets fell quickly, but with the score 63 for three and a Notts' lead of 134, a draw still looked a good bet. However, in an echo of Verity's all-ten the previous season, a collapse of epic proportions then ensued. It started with a hat-trick in Verity's 18th over. The first two victims were Walker and Harris, both caught in the slips, followed by George (G.V.) Gunn, leg-before to a well disguised faster arm-ball. G.V. was the son of the great George, still his county's leading runs-scorer, who the previous week at the age of 53 had played his final match for them.

After this the wickets fell in such a rush that the excited 2,000 crowd had hardly had the chance to discuss the possibilities of another Verity all-ten when, by 3.30 pm, it had happened, Sam Staples overbalancing first ball, Wood doing the rest. Scenes of wild enthusiasm followed. The last seven wickets had fallen for four runs, and Verity had taken ten wickets in just 52 balls. He conceded just five scoring shots and his is still the only all-ten to include a hat-trick.

Interestingly, as with Verity's previous all-ten, eight batsmen were caught, one stumped and one leg-before. Another similarity was that again it was Macaulay who bowled at the other end and went wicketless in helpful conditions, although it wasn't for the want of trying. He did however contribute to the record by taking three sharp slip catches. He didn't always field there, but regular slipper Mitchell had retired from the match with a damaged hand, courtesy of a Larwood bouncer. Three batsmen had failed to score in either innings, Bill Voce, Sam Staples and skipper Arthur Carr, who was twice caught just in front of the sightscreen by Wilf Barber as he attempted to open his account with a six. A fine attacking batsman who made 45 first-class centuries, the combative Carr had captained the county since 1919 and would go on to do so until 1934 before being deposed in controversial circumstances related to his uncompromising support for the county's Bodyline bowlers Larwood and Voce. It wasn't a good match for the captains with the bat: in his only innings Sellers also failed to open his account.

The only batsman to evade Verity was wicketkeeper Ben Lilley, who had also been undefeated, with 46, in Nottinghamshire's first innings. As he had made 200 not out for Notts Second Eleven in 1925 against a Staffordshire attack that included Sydney (S.F.) Barnes, he already had some experience in resisting great bowlers. Verity would take five or more wickets in an innings 164 times in his career, but would only do so three times in 14 matches against Notts. With the exception of Somerset (against whom he only played four times) Verity took fewer wickets against Notts than against any other county.

Yorkshire needed 139 to win but Notts didn't really have the bowlers to take advantage of the helpful conditions and Holmes (his second fifty of a low-scoring match) and Sutcliffe, putting on 100 together yet again, comfortably reached the target in 100 minutes with an hour to spare. At the end of the match scorecards as souvenirs were much in demand, as was Verity to autograph them.

Verity again finished as one of the season's leading wicket-takers and his form had booked him a trip to Australia and New Zealand the following winter where he took 11 Australian wickets and came second in the Test averages.

Poignantly, the last time Verity bowled in a first-class match, at Hove on 1 September 1939, with war certain, he gave a final demonstration of his remarkable skills, taking seven for 9 as Sussex were skittled for 33 on a drying wicket. Nearly four years later, in a sad parallel with the death of another great left-arm bowler, Colin Blythe, in the First World War, Captain Hedley Verity of the Green Howards died in a military hospital in Caserta, Italy 11 days after being seriously injured in Sicily. A popular, dignified and caring man, he was only 38 and might have contributed fully to the English game when hostilities ended.

Vallance Jupp

Northamptonshire v Kent, 1932
County Championship

The Nevill Ground, Tunbridge Wells on 6, 7, 8 July 1932 (3-day match)
Toss won by Kent
Kent won by an innings and 188 runs
Umpires: EF Field, EJ Smith
Kent 360 (LEG Ames 149, VWC Jupp 10-127); Northamptonshire 97 (AP Freeman 8-44) and 75 (AP Freeman 8-38)

Kent first innings

WH Ashdown	c Bakewell b Jupp	43
LJ Todd	lbw b Jupp	7
FE Woolley	lbw b Jupp	52
+LEG Ames	c MHD Cox b Jupp	149
AM Crawley	b Jupp	7
HTW Hardinge	c Bakewell b Jupp	0
IS Akers-Douglas	b Jupp	2
TA Pearce	b Jupp	83
*BH Valentine	not out	0
AE Watt	b Jupp	0
AP Freeman	st Bellamy b Jupp	2
Extras	(b 13, lb 2)	15
Total	(all out, 121 overs)	360

Fall of wickets 1-28, 2-81, 3-124, 4-140, 5-140, 6-164, 7-358, 8-358, 9-358, 10-360

Northamptonshire bowling: ADG Matthews 28-6-80-0, RJ Partridge 33-9-81-0, VWC Jupp 39-6-127-10, AL Cox 13-4-39-0, MHD Cox 6-1-17-0, JE Timms 2-1-1-0

Northamptonshire: AH Bakewell, AW Snowden, AL Cox, JE Timms, VWC Jupp, KJ Rymill, MHD Cox, WC Brown (capt), ADG Matthews, BW Bellamy (wk), RJ Partridge

Born in Burgess Hill, Sussex in 1891, and educated privately, Vallance Jupp made his debut for his home county in 1909. Short and broad-shouldered he was a doughty and skilful cricketer who began as a medium-fast bowler, switching to off spin after the War. He made steady progress and the first of eight Test caps came against Warwick Armstrong's Australians in 1921.

After the War Northamptonshire needed to appoint a paid secretary for the first time. Jupp (still then with Sussex and having switched from professional to amateur) got the job. It was a good move all round: Jupp had an electrical goods business in Northampton, and the county got a very good cricketer. Jupp performed the double ten times, a total only exceeded by the great Yorkshire pair Hirst and Rhodes. And, for a variety of reasons, he missed four full seasons when he might have increased that tally. Given that he spent most of his career playing for a desperately weak Northamptonshire side, it is an impressive record.

He was appointed county captain in 1928. Although his tenure was not without some success, he was not a great leader. His relations with the Northamptonshire committee, and even some of the team, were not good and, after his side had finished bottom of the table in 1930 and 1931, he agreed to resign. He was not afraid of confrontation, although others have attested to his underlying kindness.

Jupp's all-ten came against a side including Frank Woolley and Les Ames, two of the only 25 batsmen who made 100 hundreds in their careers. He then top scored in both innings against an attack that included Tich Freeman, a bowler who took more first-class wickets than anybody except Wilfred Rhodes. And still he finished on the losing side.

Relieved of the cares of leadership Jupp had an outstanding season in 1932: taking 130 wickets and scoring 1,700 runs, at the age of 41 he was easily the oldest of the five players who did the double. His skills were displayed to no better effect than against Kent in the rural beauty of Tunbridge Wells, a ground far removed from the more basic urban charms of the County Ground at Northampton.

In a match in which every wicket bar two fell to spin, Kent went in first and were dismissed for 360 just before the close. It was an uneven innings. Northants were missing the incisive left-arm pace of their eventual all-time leading wicket-taker, E.W. (Nobby) Clark, who was not playing regularly because of league commitments. Lunch was taken at 120 for two, and with Frank Woolley and Les Ames (both of whom reached 1,000 runs for the season during their innings) together and looking comfortable, a large score seemed possible. However, Jupp dismissed the great left-hander leg-before and, helped by a second brilliant catch at short square leg by Fred Bakewell, his post-lunch spell of four for 18 reduced the home side to 164 for six. In the previous match, against Middlesex, Ames and Alec Pearce had rescued the Kent second innings, taking the score from 163 for seven to 283 for eight. Remarkably, coming together at 3 o'clock, they did the same trick again, this time putting on 194 before Ames was well caught in the deep having batted just over four hours. It was the only catch Mark Cox made in a three-match career. Pearce went next ball, bowled Jupp. His off driving had been excellent. England wicketkeeper Ames would eventually make 102 centuries. Pearce's career would be more modest: one century and three fifties in 55 matches, but he did become club president in 1978.

After that, Jupp rapidly completed his all-ten. Given his record-breaking association with all-tens it was perhaps appropriate that Tich Freeman was Jupp's final victim. He had got away with one wild swing but didn't escape twice and was stumped next ball by long-serving keeper Ben Bellamy. Jupp had taken the last four wickets in one over for two runs. Kent vice-captain Bryan Valentine, standing in for captain Percy Chapman, and a very useful batsman to come in at number nine, could only watch as the innings subsided.

Flighting the ball skilfully and making it turn quickly, Jupp had toiled patiently for his success, bowling 39 overs off a short run-up that didn't take too much out of him. His figures are still a Northants record, beating the nine for 30 taken by the medium pace of Albert Thomas, a Welsh recruit, against Yorkshire at Bradford in 1920. They are also still a record for the Nevill Ground. The previous record-holder was Worcestershire's Fred Root who had taken nine for 81 two years previously and, like Jupp, still finished on the losing side. Kent's total of 360 was the highest at the time in which a bowler had taken an all-ten. Only Lillywhite in 1872 and Freeman in 1929 had taken an all-ten while the opposition made 300, and Ames' 149 is still the highest individual score in an all-ten innings.

Northants were 4 for one overnight. Thundery rain next day prevented any play after one o'clock, by which time they had staggered to 93 for nine. For a while it had looked as if Tich Freeman might emulate Jupp's feat. However, after he had taken the first six wickets, the slow left-arm of Wally Hardinge (one of only 12 English double football cricket internationals) broke the spell. The last wicket fell quickly the next morning; Jupp top scored with 34 out of 97 and Freeman, who had bowled unchanged, finished with eight for 44 in 21.1 overs.

Jupp had a wide range of strokes but often had to moderate the enterprise of his early days to help stabilise the Northants batting. His county's performance at Tunbridge Wells illustrated why. Following on in bright sunny conditions, Northants were once more soon in trouble. Going in at eight for 3 Jupp (32), late cutting particularly skilfully, was again the only batsman to play the sharply turning spin of Freeman with any confidence, the little man bowling unchanged again in a Northants innings of 75 that was all over by lunch. The Northants captain William Brown had a modest record for the county, just one century and two fifties in 127 matches, but going in with six wickets down in each innings and remaining undefeated with six and 12 he at least provided some leadership by resisting the irresistible Freeman.

Kent's win enabled them to remain at the top of the Championship table. However, again they faded towards the end of the season, winning only five more matches out of 12 and slipping to third place, whilst Yorkshire's run of 11 wins out of 12 would see them finish well clear at the top. Northants would finish 16th, just above Worcestershire. It was a position they would only improve upon once in the next ten seasons.

In 1935 tragically Jupp became the first of three Northants Test cricketers whose careers were blighted by automobile accidents. In 1936 Fred Bakewell was so severely injured that he never played again, and 33 years later Colin Milburn lost an eye. They were both gifted openers whose careers were in effect ended at the age of 27. The consequences of Jupp's accident were even more serious. Just before midnight on Saturday 12 January, near to his Northamptonshire home, the car he was driving was in collision with a motorcycle, killing the 19-year-old pillion passenger. Found guilty of manslaughter Jupp was sentenced to nine months' imprisonment. He returned to county cricket in 1936 and finally retired in 1938 with over 23,000 runs and nearly 1,700 wickets to his name.

In July 1960, aged 69, Vallance Jupp collapsed and died in his garden at Spratton, a village only a few miles from the site of the fateful accident 25 years earlier.

Tim Wall

South Australia v New South Wales, 1932/33
Sheffield Shield

Sydney Cricket Ground, Sydney on 3, 4, 6 February 1933 (4-day match)
Toss won by New South Wales
New South Wales won by 98 runs
Umpires: GE Borwick, WG French
New South Wales 113 (TW Wall 10-36) and 356; South Australia 114 (WH Howell 5-31) and 257 (HC Nitschke 105, WJ O'Reilly 5-56)

New South Wales first innings

JHW Fingleton	b Wall	43
WA Brown	c Whitington b Wall	0
DG Bradman	c Ryan b Wall	56
SJ McCabe	c Walker b Wall	0
RC Rowe	b Wall	0
FS Cummins	c Walker b Wall	0
*+HSB Love	b Wall	1
CJ Hill	b Wall	0
WH Howell	b Wall	0
WJ O'Reilly	b Wall	4
GL Stewart	not out	2
Extras	(lb 1, nb 5, w 1)	7
Total	(all out, 28.4 overs)	113

Fall of wickets 1-12, 2-87, 3-87, 4-88, 5-88, 6-99, 7-105, 8-105, 9-106, 10-113

South Australia bowling: TW Wall 12.4-2-36-10, BJ Tobin 5-0-23-0, CV Grimmett 11-0-47-0

South Australia: VY Richardson (capt), HC Nitschke, AR Lonergan, AJ Ryan, RS Whitington, BJ Tobin, AG Shepherd, PK Lee, CV Grimmett, TW Wall, CW Walker (wk)

After George Giffen's feat nearly fifty years before, the second all-ten in Australia, and the first in the Sheffield Shield, was a long time coming. Tim (christened Thomas) Wall had only previously taken five or more wickets in an innings six times, with a best of six for 40 in a non-Shield match against Western Australia, and so a full hand of wickets was heady heights for the 29-year-old fast bowler.

Adelaide-born Wall made his first-class debut in 1924, aged 20, and after a number of useful performances was selected to play in the final Test of the 1928/29 series. Four down, Australia desperately needed some pace to replace the menacing Jack Gregory (85 wickets in 24 Tests) who had retired after damaging his knee during the First Test at Brisbane. Australia averted a whitewash, and with eight wickets Wall contributed significantly to his side's five-wicket victory in a timeless match that went into the eighth day. A consistent performer, Wall would eventually take 56 wickets in 18 Tests, and 330 in all first-class matches, in an era largely dominated by spin and played on good pitches. He toured the British Isles in 1930 and 1934 with Australia's Ashes winning teams. Tall and with a long run-up (spectators apparently enjoyed heckling him as he walked slowly back to his mark), he had a good action, and the stamina to bowl accurately for long spells. Not super-fast like, for example, Larwood, he could however move the ball, and also inconvenience batsmen with sharp lift.

New South Wales were playing their last match of the season. Having won four matches out of five they had already retained the Sheffield Shield. They were captained by wicketkeeper Hammy Love, the visitors by Vic Richardson. A noted allround sportsman, Richardson was one of only three Australian batsmen who would play in all five matches of the Bodyline series, standing up well against the fearsome attack before making a pair in the Fifth Test. Wall was also in good form: he would take his 50th Test wicket in the Fourth Test at Sydney a week later, and with 16 wickets in the series was the only Australian pace man to make any impact. He had taken five for 72 in the first England innings of the Third Test at Adelaide, a match played before a total attendance of 172,000.

The spectators three weeks later at Sydney for the first day of the South Australia match, a more modest 7,000, must have been surprised to see the powerful New South Wales batting line-up routed in conditions which, apart from a cross-breeze helping Wall's swerve, were good for batting. Bill Brown went quickly, caught by Richard 'Dick' Whitington for a duck. Neither was yet 21. Whitington would eventually become a prolific writer of cricket books, whilst the following year Brown would score a century at Lord's in his second Test.

As Test opener Jack Fingleton was then joined at the wicket by Don Bradman, and Stan McCabe was to follow, the home supporters must have expected that their team would put together a formidable total as they had already done several times in the season. At first all seemed to be going well. Fingleton and Bradman were still together at lunch and Wall had the unremarkable figures of one for 31 from seven eight-ball overs. At the beginning of Wall's second over after lunch New South Wales were a comfortable 87 for one. At the end of it, in a Verity-like collapse, they were 88 for five, with Fingleton the first to go. The last time next man in Stan McCabe had appeared at the Sydney Cricket Ground he had played one of cricket's great innings, 187 not out in the First Test against the ferocious attack of Larwood and Voce. This time he was caught behind first ball. He was followed by Sheffield Shield debutant Raymond Rowe, and then by Frank Cummins, playing the last match of a first-class career that was decidedly less successful than that of his illustrious cousin Charlie Macartney.

Don Bradman managed to stay a little longer, seeing the score to 106 before he became Wall's ninth victim, mishitting a hook and skying a catch to square leg. His 56 was made in the relatively slow time, for him, of 109 minutes. When the innings closed soon afterwards Wall had taken nine for 5 in 5.4 overs after lunch. He had hit the stumps six times and, amazingly, the only batsman apart from Bradman and Fingleton to reach four was last man out Bill O'Reilly! Six others failed to score and Bill Howell, who had taken all-ten for the Australians at The Oval in 1899, would have noted that his son William was one of them. Clarrie Grimmett was the second highest wicket-taker in Australia in the season (behind O'Reilly), and had dismissed 13 Queenslanders in his previous match, but while Wall created havoc at one end he went wicketless for the first time in the Sheffield Shield for seven years.

The match continued to surprise when South Australia went in and by the close they had also been dismissed, with a lead of just one. The damage was mainly done by Howell who took a career-best five for 31 with his off breaks and outshone the great O'Reilly. Wall was not usually expected to get many runs; in 135 first-class innings he made just one fifty, but going in at 77 for eight he made a useful 13 and in partnership with 20-year-old Alan Shepherd just took his side ahead before he was dismissed. In the next over Shepherd, who top scored with 32, then fell to Bradman's occasional leg spin.

Next day, Saturday, the crowd doubled and the match reverted to some sort of normality. New South Wales eventually made 356 second time around, with Wall (two for 91 in 22 overs) performing more modestly. Bradman top scored (obviously not that unusual, he did it in 128 of his 338 innings) with 97 (more unusual, he was dismissed in the 90s only six times).

South Australia never really looked like reaching their 356 target. Left-handed opener Jack Nitschke made a dashing 105 in 132 minutes, but nobody else reached forty. Later a very successful racehorse breeder, Nitschke played two Tests and might have played more if Australia had not been so well endowed with batting at the time. He was splendidly christened Homesdale, and also known as 'Slinger'. This time leg-spinner O'Reilly (five for 56) and left-armer spinner Clement Hill (four for 61) took most of the wickets. Hill shared a famous name but was unrelated to the great pre-war batsman. Finishing top of the season's averages with 22 wickets at 15.27, like the great O'Reilly he bowled at a brisk pace for a spinner. As in the first innings, Bradman took the last wicket and, perhaps appropriately, his victim was Wall, stumped by Love who was playing his final Shield match (although curiously he played his only Test the following week). Among Bradman's 36 first-class wickets the name Wall appears three times and he probably qualifies as his 'rabbit'. To even things up a bit, Wall did dismiss Bradman five times.

Wall retired after the end of the 1935/36 season, his 22 wickets that season helping South Australia win the Sheffield Shield for only the second time since the First World War. A school teacher like a number of his team-mates, he was later involved in coaching and cricket administration. Tim Wall died in Adelaide in March 1981 aged nearly 77. He had suffered for some time from Parkinson's disease. There were suggestions that he had taken his own life, but David Frith points out in *Silence of the Heart* that his death certificate does not support this.

John Wisden
Didn't need any help from
his fielders.

Teddy Walker
All ten and a century in the same
match, and another all-ten.

Alfred Shaw
An early finish enabled spectators
to go to The Derby.

Edward Barratt
One of only two bowlers to take
all ten against Australian tourists.

George Giffen
Set records that even WG couldn't
emulate, and took Australia's first
all-ten.

Albert Moss
10 for 28: a first-class debut
to remember.

Harry Pickett
10 for 32 in 1895. Record figures
for an Englishman that stood for
12 years, and still an Essex record.

Bill Howell
The first of two Australian tourists
to take an all-ten in England

Cyril Bland - The only all-ten at the Angel ground, Tonbridge.
It's the Angel shopping centre now.

Albert Trott
Nine of his wickets needed no help from the field.

Ernie Vogler
Started the match on one ground,
finished it on another by taking
South Africa's first all-ten.

Alonzo Drake
Only needed 53 deliveries to
dismiss Somerset.

Billy Bestwick
46 years 116 days: the oldest
bowler to take all ten.

George Collins
Outbowled Tich Freeman.

Tich Freeman
Three all-tens in successive seasons.

Clarrie Grimmett
All ten against Yorkshire for the other star of the 1930 Australian tourists.

George Geary
10 for 18: an unbeatable record,
beaten three years later ...

... by Hedley Verity,
whose 10 for 10 has stood as the
most economical all-ten for 85 years
and counting.

Vallance Jupp
All ten, and top scored in
both innings. Still finished
on the losing side though.

Tim Wall
The only all-ten to include
Bradman, and the first in the
Sheffield Shield.

Eddie Watts
The last all-ten before the Second
World War.

Ken Graveney
Aged 24, photographed just four
months before his all-ten.

Bob Berry
All ten for the first of his three counties against his second.

Jim Laker
63 wickets against the Australians in one memorable season.

Tony Pearson
The only Oxbridge Freshman
to take all ten.

Richard Johnson
At 19 years 185 days the
youngest Englishman to take
all ten, here receiving the
Middlesex Player of the Month
award for July 1994.

Shahid Mahmood stands with the 1962 Pakistan touring team to the British Isles.
Back row: Mohammad Farooq, Munir Malik, Ijaz Butt, Afaq Hussain, Intikhab Alam, Antao D'Souza, Haseeb Ahsan, Mushtaq Mohammad, Shahid Mahmood, Asif Ahmed. Front row: Nasim-ul-Ghani, Wallis Mathias, Saeed Ahmed, Hanif Mohammad, Javed Burki (captain), Imtiaz Ahmed, Mahmood Hussain, Alimuddin.

Anil Kumble
Waited while the openers put on 100, then took Test cricket's second all-ten.

Tommy Mitchell

Derbyshire v Leicestershire, 1935
County Championship

Aylestone Road, Leicester on 15, 17, 18 June 1935 (3-day match)
Toss won by Leicestershire
Match drawn
Umpires: WR Parry, EJ Smith
Derbyshire 140 (HA Smith 5-51, G Geary 5-46) and 227 (WH Marlow 5-69);
Leicestershire 123 (TB Mitchell 10-64) and 111-3

Leicestershire first innings

AW Shipman	c Worthington b Mitchell	10
GL Berry	b Mitchell	11
NF Armstrong	c Worthington b Mitchell	13
FT Prentice	lbw b Mitchell	10
GS Watson	b Mitchell	0
CAR Coleman	b Mitchell	8
*WE Astill	b Mitchell	18
G Geary	b Mitchell	16
HA Smith	c Worthington b Mitchell	8
WH Marlow	st Elliott b Mitchell	14
+P Corrall	not out	6
Extras	(b 5, lb 4)	9
Total	(all out, 43.1 overs)	123

Fall of wickets 1-21, 2-30, 3-39, 4-39, 5-56, 6-57, 7-85, 8-92, 9-110, 10-123

Derbyshire bowling: WH Copson 16-3-30-0, TS Worthington 2-0-6-0, TB Mitchell 19.1-4-64-10, LF Townsend 6-2-14-0

Derbyshire: AE Alderman, H Storer, TS Worthington, LF Townsend, E Carrington, GF Hodgkinson (capt), AF Townsend, AV Pope, H Elliott (wk), TB Mitchell, WH Copson

Coal mining didn't just provide Derbyshire with fast bowlers, it also provided the county's best ever spinner. Tommy Mitchell was born in Creswell in 1902 where he worked for the local colliery and played for its cricket team. Spotted bowling his sharply turning leg spin when Derbyshire played the colliery during the 1926 General Strike, he was late coming to the county game, and didn't make his debut until 1928. It might not have happened: Mitchell initially turned down the county's offer of £3 a week, arguing that he could earn more in the pits. It took £4 to get him. His round dark-rimmed spectacles gave him a slightly comical appearance belying his hard coalmining background. With sleeves buttoned at the wrist he had a lively twirling action and got through his overs quickly, googlies and conventional off breaks adding to the batsman's problems. He was also a fine cover fielder. Not much of a batsman (412 innings yielding only one fifty), he did however contribute to one major batting record when he lent Walter Hammond his brand new bat to make the then-record Test score, 336 not out against New Zealand at Eden Park in April

1933. Popular and humorous he was nevertheless unafraid to speak his mind, a trait which more than once got him into trouble. And he could be temperamental, which probably prevented a successful career from being even more successful.

Mitchell made his England debut in the fourth Test of Douglas Jardine's tour of Australia in 1932/33. As Derbyshire historian John Shawcroft has pointed out it was ironic that Derbyshire, a club with seam bowling traditions, should provide a leg-spinner for a series dominated by English pace. He did well, taking three cheap wickets, including bowling the 'unbowlable' Australian captain Bill Woodfull in the first innings and getting him caught at slip in the second. Unfortunately the rest of his Test career was less successful and he took only another five more wickets in four more matches.

Mitchell's all-ten came at another ground no longer on the county circuit. Leicestershire had been playing at Grace Road since 1878, but it was thought to be too far from the city centre and a move to Aylestone Road was made in 1901. Eventually hosting 399 first-class matches it was a ground not without attractions, although emissions from nearby chimneys and the building of an electricity works nearby could make it difficult for players and spectators to stay clean throughout the day! Used by the services during the Second World War, it was unfit for first-class cricket when peace returned and Leicestershire went back to Grace Road (although playing two matches at the old ground in 1957, and one in 1962). A stone's throw from Leicester City's King Power Stadium, Aylestone Road is still used for local sport, including cricket.

Derbyshire were one of the strongest county sides in the 1930s: second in the Championship in 1935 they famously went one better for the only time the following season. In contrast, over the same period, with one exception, Leicestershire always finished well below halfway. However, that exception was 1935 when, led by Ewart Astill, one of its great names and its first professional captain, they climbed to sixth. Unfortunately Astill's tenure lasted only that one season. He was a stopgap appointed until the New Zealand amateur Stewie Dempster (who to be fair was a very good batsman) could take over, whereupon Leicestershire reverted to the depths of the Championship. In the absence of Arthur Richardson, Derbyshire's ten professionals against Leicestershire were captained by Gilbert Hodgkinson, a 22-year-old amateur playing his third first-class match. Severely injured during the Second World War, his death was reported in *Wisden*. Happily this was a mistake and he returned to captain the county in 1946.

Put in to bat in bowler-friendly conditions Derbyshire made only 140, Haydon Smith and George Geary taking five wickets apiece. Geary of course knew what it was like to take an all-ten and at the age of 42 was having one of his best-ever seasons. Leicestershire began their innings just after 5 o'clock on a pitch that had been further livened by rain. By the close they were in trouble at 68 for six, all six wickets falling to Mitchell. One of his victims was George Watson whose catch for Kent at Maidstone six years previously had completed Tich Freeman's first all-ten. Mitchell had varied both spin and flight skilfully, although *The Times* suggested that he was flattered by feeble batting.

Picking up the remaining four wickets on Monday morning, with five batsmen bowled and one leg-before he hadn't needed a lot of help from the field, except from Stan Worthington who snapped up three sharp catches at silly point. Another product of the mining community, Worthington had been spotted whilst an electrician at Bolsover Colliery. He played for England nine times, and the following season his 128 against India made him the first Derbyshire batsman to score a Test century.

It had been a curious Leicestershire innings: apart from Watson everybody got a start, but nobody stayed long. Having stood while Freeman had spun out Essex at Southend in 1930 umpire William Parry had supervised his second all-ten. Parry, who had lost a leg during the War, never played first-class cricket, but umpired over 200 matches, including five Tests.

Mitchell's figures are another ground record that clearly won't be beaten. His three bowling partners at the other end, England players all (eventually), would between them take over 2,500 first-class wickets but were all wicketless this time.

Two of the Derbyshire team, Harry Elliott and Harry Storer, had also played 14 years previously at Cardiff when Billy Bestwick had taken Derbyshire's first all-ten. Only post-war allrounder Derek Morgan has exceeded Elliott's 520 appearances for the county, and nobody has got near his 292 stumpings for them – one of which helped Mitchell complete Derbyshire's second all-ten. Thirty-seven-year-old Storer was a determined batsman and useful bowler who came from a sporting family. He was an England soccer international and the following year would perform a remarkable double: appearing in Derbyshire's Championship-winning side and managing Coventry City to the Championship of the Third Division North.

Going in again with a lead of 17 Derbyshire made 227. Worthington (37) again top scored, but unfortunately his captain completed a pair. Chasing 245 with over a day left Leicestershire (51 for one) were well placed at the close but rain returned on Tuesday, preventing any play until 3.30 pm and ending the game at tea with the score 111 for three. Mitchell took another two wickets, including Frank Prentice who managed to hit his wicket attempting a late cut.

Mitchell finished the season with 171 wickets. Only Freeman, Verity, Goddard and Bowes took more, but none bettered his strike-rate of 32 balls per wicket. Just over four years later at the end of August he played his last first-class match, appropriately again against Leicestershire at Aylestone Road. Facing a side that included four of his all-ten victims he bowled little and took no wickets, whilst this time George Watson top scored for Leicestershire. Mitchell finished his career with 1,483 wickets, at the time Derbyshire's second highest wicket-taker just behind Billy Bestwick. He is still their most successful spinner. After the War he declined the terms offered by the county, returning to the pit and playing league cricket into his fifties.

Tommy Mitchell died in 1996 aged 93, England's oldest Test cricketer at the time, and the last survivor of Douglas Jardine's 1932/33 touring party.

Jack Mercer

Glamorgan v Worcestershire, 1936
County Championship

County Ground, New Road, Worcester on 29, 30, 31 July 1936 (3-day match)
Toss won by Worcestershire
Match drawn
Umpires: E Cooke, JA Newman
Worcestershire 143 (J Mercer 10-51) and 163-5 dec; Glamorgan 151 and 56-4

Worcestershire first innings

RDM Evers	c Smart b Mercer	3
CH Bull	c Brierley b Mercer	22
SH Martin	c Turnbull b Mercer	4
HHIH Gibbons	c Turnbull b Mercer	2
*+BW Quaife	c D Davies b Mercer	2
J Horton	b Mercer	0
RHC Human	not out	59
AP Singleton	st Brierley b Mercer	29
R Howorth	b Mercer	3
RTD Perks	lbw b Mercer	0
PF Jackson	c Lavis b Mercer	1
Extras	(b 6, lb 9, w 3)	18
Total	(all out, 51 overs)	143

Fall of wickets 1-14, 2-20, 3-30, 4-40, 5-42, 6-59, 7-113, 8-121, 9-121, 10-143

Glamorgan bowling: J Mercer 26-10-51-10, GH Reed 12-2-38-0, D Davies 6-1-9-0, DE Davies 7-0-27-0

Glamorgan : AH Dyson, DE Davies, D Davies, VGJ Jenkins, RG Duckfield, CC Smart, MJL Turnbull (capt), G Lavis, TL Brierley (wk), J Mercer, GH Reed

Glamorgan's second highest wicket-taker behind Don Shepherd, Jack Mercer was one of the best swing bowlers between the Wars. Unfortunately his best years coincided with those of the great Maurice Tate and, with other good fast-medium bowlers also around, he never won a Test cap. A fine craftsman, from an easy action he swung the ball both ways at medium pace, and when necessary could slow down and bowl off cutters. He was the cheerful mainstay of the Glamorgan attack, bowling long accurate spells, even well into his 40s: indeed his all-ten came at the age of 43, the oldest player in the match. A colourful character and man of many parts, he had travelled to Russia before the First World War, returning to serve with distinction before being wounded in France, was a decent linguist who could converse in French and Russian, and became a member of the Magic Circle.

Born in Southwick, Sussex in 1893 Mercer made his first-class debut for his home county in 1919 but opportunities on the south coast were limited and he moved to Glamorgan. He soon made an impact and his 136 wickets in 1926 brought him the honour of being the first Glamorgan cricketer to become one of *Wisden*'s Five Cricketers of the Year. It was a quality quintet, the other four being Harold Larwood, George Geary, and Australians Bill Woodfull and Bert Oldfield. The following winter he was selected to tour the subcontinent with Arthur Gilligan's (non-Test playing) MCC side, apparently learning of his selection when reading the *Daily Mail* whilst on a horse-racing holiday in France!

Worcestershire and Glamorgan were two of the 1930s' weakest sides, both spending most of the decade in the lower reaches of the Championship. The home side at Worcester in 1936 was captained by wicketkeeper Bernard Quaife, son of Warwickshire great Willie Quaife; Glamorgan by the inspirational Maurice Turnbull.

After overnight rain play could not begin until midday. Mercer had taken five Worcestershire wickets in each innings at The Gnoll, Neath the previous month and was probably anticipating the return match with some relish. If so he was soon proved to be right, The pitch gave him little help but the humid conditions did, as he moved the ball sharply either way, reducing Worcestershire to 59 for six by lunch, which he no doubt enjoyed as he reflected on a morning well spent, including a fifth wicket which gave him 100 for the season. One of his victims had been Harold 'Doc' Gibbons who, when he played his last match for the county ten years later, would be Worcestershire's then leading run-scorer.

Over his career Mercer had not always received the best of support from his fielders, but this time he had been well served by sharp work by the close catchers. Opener Charlie Bull had resisted solidly until just before lunch when he was caught by wicketkeeper Tom Brierley. A peripatetic cricketer, Brierley appeared for Lancashire after the War and then, having emigrated, returned as a member of the 1954 Canadian tourists. Bull's career did not last as long. Three years later he was killed in a motor accident on the Sunday evening of the Whitsuntide match with Essex at Chelmsford.

Resuming after more rain the bowlers had to use a wet ball, and Roger Human and Alexander (Sandy) Singleton took full advantage, putting on 54 in just over an hour before the aggressive Singleton swung once too often and was stumped. Still with one more year at Oxford University Singleton, who would captain Worcestershire in 1946, was playing his first Championship game of the season.

Mercer must have had high hopes of polishing the tail off quickly. Reg Perks, who went in at number ten, was a fine bowler, but he was also a record-breaking batsman of the wrong sort who, in a long career, would finish with an unsurpassed 156 ducks to his name. Mercer quickly helped him on the way to his record. To be fair Perks was not a complete duffer with the bat: he would eventually make 14 fifties. Peter Jackson who followed him was even less effective: in a 549-innings career he never passed 40. However he did hang around for a while in a last wicket partnership of 22 before Mercer had him caught in the outfield by George

Lavis who juggled with the ball before completing the catch, to everybody's relief, especially that of Emrys Davies who had been deliberately bowling wide of the stumps at the other end. Human, the only batsman who really mastered Mercer, had batted 100 minutes for his undefeated 59. Sadly he was to lose his life on active service in India just over six years later.

Among the many congratulatory telegrams Mercer received was one from Arthur Gilligan, his former touring captain. Mercer's previous best figures had been nine for 24 for Wales against Scotland on the spacious North Inch, beside the River Tay at Perth in 1923. The previous Glamorgan record, Johnnie Clay's nine for 54 against Northants, had lasted just a year. Mercer, who bowled unchanged, is still the only bowler to have taken all-ten for Glamorgan. Since then eight bowlers have fallen one wicket short of repeating the feat (including Clay, Mike Kasprowicz, Len Muncer and Don Shepherd who all 'failed' twice). Left-armers Jim Pressdee and Malcolm Nash might have completed a full house if it hadn't been for a run-out, whilst off-spinner Muncer, having taken the first eight wickets, caught the ninth batsman. Remarkably, Pressdee and Shepherd performed the nine-for feat in the same match, and Kasprowicz did it twice in 2003, each time against Durham.

Worcestershire had a good attack and bowled Glamorgan out for 151 on the second day. The wickets were shared by Dick Howorth, Reg Perks, Peter Jackson and Sid Martin (uncle of the great South African spinner Hugh Tayfield), all of whom would take over 100 first-class wickets the following season. At 65 for seven it might have been worse, but the tail wagged, including a dozen from Mercer, and Glamorgan ended with a lead of eight. Heavy rain over Thursday night prevented play on the final day until mid-afternoon. Worcestershire batted on for an hour and then declared at tea leaving Glamorgan 95 minutes to make 156 to win. They had a go, even promoting Mercer, a useful tailend hitter, to number four. However he was bowled by Martin for just one and the chase was given up soon afterwards.

Having taken ten wickets in his previous match, and then an all-ten, Mercer was on a roll. In his next match, at Swansea against the Indian tourists, he took a first-innings seven for 48, Glamorgan beating the visitors by an innings in two days. Openers Vijay Merchant and Mushtaq Ali had just put on 203 against England at Old Trafford. This time their partnership lasted no longer than Mercer's second over. Fittingly 1936 was Mercer's benefit year. However attendances at his given match, the Bank Holiday fixture with Sir Julien Cahn's XI, were affected by poor weather and his benefit yielded only £729.

Mercer played regularly for Glamorgan until his last game in 1939, but even then his first-class career had not finished. After the War, spent working in intelligence, he joined Northamptonshire as coach and when his new county had injury problems turned out for them at Southampton in June 1947 taking two for 100 in 26 overs. Not bad for a 54-year-old! He finally finished with 1,591 first-class wickets. Mercer would eventually spend 36 years with Northants, becoming scorer after nearly two decades of coaching. He was even still scoring for the Seconds at the age of 90.

Unsurprisingly he was a fine bowling coach: for example, much of the success achieved by Alf Valentine, the great West Indian spinner of the 1950s, was due to Mercer's encouragement.

Jack Mercer died aged 94 in Marylebone in 1987, just as the cricket season was drawing to a close.

Tom Goddard

Gloucestershire v Worcestershire, 1937
County Championship

College Ground, Cheltenham on 7, 9, 10 August 1937 (3-day match)
Toss won by Worcestershire
Gloucestershire won by three wickets
Umpires: GM Lee, FI Walden
Worcestershire 310 (TWJ Goddard 6-68) and 202 (TWJ Goddard 10-113);
Gloucestershire 196 and 317-7 (WR Hammond 178)

Worcestershire second innings

CH Bull	st Watkins b Goddard	24
+JS Buller	c Hammond b Goddard	12
E Cooper	b Goddard	18
HHIH Gibbons	not out	72
*BW Quaife	b Goddard	4
SH Martin	c Hammond b Goddard	4
RCM Kimpton	c Parker b Goddard	6
RHC Human	c Allen b Goddard	9
R Howorth	c Parker b Goddard	4
RTD Perks	c Crapp b Goddard	33
PF Jackson	c Crapp b Goddard	3
Extras	(b 6, lb 7)	13
Total	all out, 60,4 overs)	202

Fall of wickets 1-25, 2-59, 3-62, 4-66, 5-70, 6-80, 7-94, 8-98, 9-185, 10-202

Gloucestershire bowling: CJ Barnett 2-1-5-0, BH Lyon 2-0-9-0, EK Scott 3-0-8-0, RA Sinfield 25-7-54-0, TWJ Goddard 28.4-4-113-10

Gloucestershire : CJ Barnett, GW Parker, BO Allen (capt), WR Hammond, JF Crapp, EK Scott, RA Sinfield, BH Lyon, WL Neale, TWJ Goddard, BTL Watkins (wk)

A career change can often be beneficial, and it certainly did the trick for Tom Goddard. Twenty-one-year-old Gloucester-born Goddard made his first-class debut in 1922 as a fast bowler. Six feet three inches tall and well-built he had all the necessary physical attributes. However he never really made it and eventually joined the MCC groundstaff at Lord's. Experimenting with off breaks, his new-found ability was noticed in the nets by Gloucestershire captain Beverley Lyon who persuaded the county to re-engage him. Success was immediate: 184 wickets in 1929, an England cap in 1930. Competitive, attacking, his massive hands enabled him to spin the ball sharply and with any help from the pitch he was often virtually unplayable. His height was an added advantage as batsmen tried to keep the lifting ball out of the hands of the waiting short legs. Even in batsmen-friendly conditions his accuracy and flight still made him a difficult proposition. He was helped by the change to the lbw law in 1935 that enabled a batsman to be dismissed by a ball pitching outside the off stump. And of course he played his cricket on uncovered pitches, and with no restrictions on the placing of leg side fielders, giving bowlers conditions which those playing today can only dream about.

Off-spinners weren't very fashionable between the Wars and with fewer Tests and Hedley Verity established as England's main spinner, Goddard only played for England eight times. He did at least stamp his name on cricket history when he took a hat-trick in the Johannesburg Test on Boxing Day 1938. He added another later on the tour, and eventually finished his career with six, a total only exceeded by the seven taken by Kent's Doug Wright.

The Worcestershire side at Cheltenham, eight of whom had been on the receiving end of Mercer's all-ten the season before, probably knew what to expect, Goddard having taken 13 wickets against them earlier in the season at Dudley. In Gloucestershire's previous match, against Lancashire at Old Trafford, he was wicketless for the only time in a very successful season. Someone would pay.

Gloucestershire relied heavily on Goddard. With no bowler of pace, and his great partner Parker having retired, the only significant support came from fellow off-spinner Reg Sinfield. The pair took 337 Championship wickets between them in 1937; the next highest contribution came from Walter Hammond with 33. The visitors made a good start on Saturday, the opening day of the Cheltenham Festival. Batting first they made 310 in four hours, and then took four Gloucestershire wickets for 113 by the close of a lively first day. Curiously Goddard had not come on until the Worcestershire score had reached 167 for two, but when he did he immediately got among the wickets, finishing with six for 68 in 18 overs. Australian Roger Kimpton top scored, last out for 92. An Oxford cricket (and golf) Blue who liked to get on with things Kimpton only batted for an hour and a quarter. The previous season, batting with a runner, he had made a century against Lancashire in just 70 minutes. He liked batting against Gloucestershire - three of his eight first-class centuries came against them. Returning to Australia at the outbreak of war he won a DFC as a fighter pilot in the Pacific.

The game moved on apace on Monday. It began with two Cornish-born batsmen at the wicket: Jack Crapp and nightwatchman Edward Scott. Both would play for England after the War: Crapp at cricket, Scott at rugby union. Scott, a 19-year-old leg-spinner who had just left Clifton College, was playing the first match of his short first-class career.

Gloucestershire's first innings was over fairly quickly leaving them 114 behind. Worcestershire then made a bright start the second time around, Charlie Bull and Syd Buller putting on 25 before Buller, who had hit three fours, was caught by Hammond fielding in the (for him) less customary position of short leg. No fielder (apart from Goddard himself) took more catches off Goddard's bowling than Hammond (116). Two years later Yorkshire-born wicketkeeper Buller would be badly injured in the car crash that took Bull's life. Finding fame as a fearless umpire after the War, he collapsed and died during a break for rain in a Championship match at Edgbaston in 1970. With 81 in the first innings Bull had had a good match. He had been stumped in both innings, the only two of Goddard's 16 wickets in the match to fall that way.

For a while the batsmen scored freely. Buller's wicket had cost Goddard 20 runs in two overs and with the 50 going up in only 35 minutes Worcestershire seemed set for a good score. However once the second wicket went at 59 a collapse quickly set in as Goddard, well supported by his fielders, took out the middle order. At 98 for eight the end seemed close. However Harold Gibbons who had so far batted steadily for ten runs in 50 minutes found help, perhaps surprisingly, from Reg Perks who made 33 before he swung once too often and was caught on the boundary. Together the pair had put on 87 in just over an hour, hitting a six apiece. Goddard's figures had of course suffered a bit during this stand. However, he now had all nine wickets and he didn't have to wait long for the tenth as just over a year after becoming Jack Mercer's tenth victim Peter Jackson did the same for Goddard, leaving Gibbons, who had gone in second wicket down, undefeated and easily top-scorer. Goddard had paid a high price for his wickets, but he could afford to attack, and be attacked, whilst Sinfield kept things quiet at the other end. Goddard had previously taken nine wickets in an innings twice, with best figures of nine for 21 against Cambridge University in 1929 in a match also played at Cheltenham, but at the Victoria Ground, not the College Ground.

Gloucestershire would need to make the highest score of the match to win, a tricky 317 on a wearing pitch. By the close they were 91 for two, with captain Basil Allen on ten and, ominously for the visitors, Hammond on 62. These two continued the next day, putting on a match-winning 269 at over a run-a-minute on a pitch giving the spinners considerable help. Hammond eventually went for a typically hard-hitting 178. Allen who had largely concentrated on defence went soon after for 78. There was a late flurry of wickets and when the seventh fell three more runs were still required. However these were scored without further loss, Goddard, a modest batsman, fittingly being at the wicket at the time.

Gloucestershire's win left them fifth in the Championship table. They finally finished fourth, some distance behind Champions Yorkshire. Remarkably the official list of County Champions still doesn't include Gloucestershire. The Cheltenham pitch continued to help spin. In the second match of the Festival Goddard (12 wickets) and Sinfield dismissed all 20 Derbyshire batsmen. Goddard finished the season with 248 wickets, a total never since exceeded, and of course now never likely to be. He would eventually take at least 200 wickets in a season four times. And he wasn't finished with records yet. Two years later at Bristol, against Kent, he took 17 wickets in a day, a feat only emulated by Blythe and Verity.

Goddard was commissioned in the RAF during the War, but despite being in his mid-40s when cricket resumed continued to take wickets in vast numbers. When his career finally finished in 1952 he was just 21 wickets short of being the fifth man to take 3,000 first-class wickets. After cricket he set up a successful furniture shop in Gloucester in which he was active until about a year before his death in 1966.

Frank Smailes

Yorkshire v Derbyshire, 1939
County Championship

Bramall Lane, Sheffield on 24, 26, 27 June 1939 (3-day match)
Toss won by Yorkshire
Yorkshire won by 276 runs
Umpires: HG Baldwin, H Elliott
Yorkshire 83 (GH Pope 6-44) and 310 (W Barber 100); Derbyshire 20 (J Smurthwaite 5-7) and 97 (TF Smailes 10-47)

Derbyshire second innings

D Smith	b Smailes	8
AE Alderman	c Smurthwaite b Smailes	0
TS Worthington	c Mitchell b Smailes	32
LF Townsend	b Smailes	0
GH Pope	lbw b Smailes	1
AEG Rhodes	b Smailes	18
*TD Hounsfield	not out	21
AV Pope	b Smailes	4
C Gladwin	b Smailes	0
+H Elliott	b Smailes	6
TB Mitchell	st Fiddling b Smailes	6
Extras	(b 1)	1
Total	(all out, 34.1 overs)	97

Fall of wickets 1-0, 2-19, 3-19, 4-21, 5-56, 6-61, 7-71, 8-71, 9-79, 10-97

Yorkshire bowling: TF Smailes 17.1-5-47-10, J Smurthwaite 14-5-43-0, NWD Yardley 2-0-5-0, EP Robinson 1-0-1-0

Yorkshire : H Sutcliffe, A Mitchell, W Barber, M Leyland, NWD Yardley, GA Wilson, AB Sellers (capt), TF Smailes, EP Robinson, J Smurthwaite, K Fiddling (wk)

Although he played only nine full seasons (following occasional appearances in 1932 and 1933), Frank Smailes, the last man to take an all-ten for Yorkshire, and the only right-arm bowler to do so, appeared in seven Championship-winning sides. Like many colleagues he lost some of his best years to the War. Six feet tall with a high action he swung the ball late at around medium-fast and later developed into a very good off-spinner. He was also a good enough left-hand batsman to be classified as an allrounder, performing the double in 1938, the first Yorkshireman to do so since Roy Kilner and Wilfred Rhodes back in 1926.

Born in Ripley, North Yorkshire in 1910, his father a cattle dealer, Smailes was educated at Pocklington School. He began playing with Ilkley at the age of 16, and after spells with Harrogate, and then as a professional with Forfarshire and with Brighouse, became a Yorkshire regular in 1934, the imminent ending of George Macaulay's career leaving a vacancy in the side. Four years later he was named among the 13 players from whom the England side to play Australia at Old Trafford would be selected.

Sadly rain prevented any play at all. No doubt the selectors had been impressed by his match figures of ten for 137 for Yorkshire against the Australians at Bramall Lane the previous week, when he dismissed a well-set Don Bradman in both innings and outbowled Bill Bowes and Hedley Verity. After the 1938 disappointment, Frank Smailes did eventually get an England cap. He was probably past his best when cricket resumed in 1946, but in the First Test against India at Lord's, although overshadowed by Alec Bedser's 11 wickets on debut, he scored 25 and took three good wickets for only 44 runs in India's second innings.

Smailes' all-ten came in the middle of a season in which his appearances were limited by injury and in which he took just 50 wickets. It was an important match. Championship winners in 1936, Derbyshire were one of the strongest counties and were fourth in the table. Unsurprisingly Yorkshire were top. They would still be there at the end of the season, whilst Derbyshire would drop to ninth, mainly because of a weakness in their batting. England were playing the West Indies at Lord's and Yorkshire were missing Len Hutton, Arthur Wood (wicketkeeper), Hedley Verity and Bill Bowes, whilst Derbyshire's Bill Copson was also playing, making a successful Test debut with nine wickets. At the time, Copson, Verity and Bowes were the top three bowlers in the national averages.

With rain around bowlers took advantage at a number of grounds, no more so than at Bramall Lane on Saturday 24 June where the aforementioned trio weren't really missed. Play could not start until half past two. Two and half hours later Yorkshire had been bowled out for 83 by the Pope brothers, George and Alf, who bowled unchanged for 35.3 overs. (In 1939 overs were of eight balls. The experiment was not a success and when first-class cricket resumed in England in 1946 the over reverted to six balls.) It might have been even worse but captain Brian Sellers (31) and future England captain Norman Yardley (21) steadied the ship for a while by putting put on 31 for the sixth wicket after half the side had gone for 32.

Derbyshire's enjoyment of their success was short-lived. They went in, and were out three quarters of an hour later after a mere 67 balls. On a rain-damaged pitch, soft on top and hard underneath, Smailes and Jim Smurthwaite shared nine wickets (the other wicket to fall was Stan Worthington's, who was run out without scoring). It was in effect medium pacer Smurthwaite's Championship debut. He had played at Leicester the previous season but had neither batted nor bowled. He would play a few more matches but his first-class career would end with a modest 12 wickets in seven matches. Derbyshire's score is still their second lowest ever, and since the War had only been 'beaten' by Hampshire's famous winning 15 against Warwickshire in 1922. The first day then returned to some sort of normality as Herbert Sutcliffe and Arthur Mitchell took the score to 13 without loss before the close.

The second day went all Yorkshire's way. First, aided by five dropped catches, they took their score to 310 all out, Wilf Barber top scoring with a graceful 100. And then, having set Derbyshire a very improbable 374 to win, they reduced them to 31 for four by the close. Smailes no doubt slept happily having taken four for 14 in ten overs. It only needed about an hour the next morning to wrap things up. At first the overnight pair Worthington and Bert 'Dusty' Rhodes settled in well, but when they went 56 for four quickly became 79 for nine, top-scorer Worthington (32) having been brilliantly caught one-handed at slip by Arthur Mitchell. Tommy Mitchell (no relation) is the sort of batsmen most bowlers like to see coming in at number 11. However Smailes had to wait a while for his all-ten as Mitchell helped his captain, Thomas Hounsfield, put on 18. With plenty of time to spare, captain Sellers could afford to instruct Smurthwaite, bowling at the other end, to do his best not to take the final wicket. Smailes finally got his man off the first ball of his eighteenth over when the Derbyshire leg-spinner was stumped by Wood's stand-in Ken Fiddling, who conceded just one bye in the match on his Championship debut. After the War Fiddling, like many Yorkshiremen, would move on to find regular cricket elsewhere (with Northamptonshire).

The official Derbyshire captain in 1939 was Robin Buckston, but on occasions when he wasn't available another amateur was needed to do the job and Hounsfield was brought in. A batsman of limited achievement who made one fifty and seven ducks in a 16-match career, Hounsfield nevertheless did well to outscore most of his more illustrious colleagues. Swinging the ball both ways Smailes had taken full advantage of a pitch made faster by hot morning sunshine. Hitting the stumps six times and dismissing George Pope leg-before he hadn't needed too much help from his fielders. Not surprisingly he had bowled unchanged throughout the match. The full attendance for the match had been 12,000, but unfortunately only 500 were there on the last morning to applaud Smailes' feat. The match finished at 12.15. According to the *Sheffield Daily Telegraph*, Smailes was playing bowls by 1.15!

One of Derbyshire's greatest, Cliff Gladwin, was making his first-class debut in the match. With 0-36 in eight overs and two ducks it was an inauspicious start. He would play three more wicketless games before the War, but when he returned to the county game in 1946 aged 30 his impact was immediate and he remains his county's second highest wicket-taker. He took nine wickets in an innings three times. And one of them was so near to being an all-ten. At close of play on 21 June 1947 at Buxton, he had figures of nine for 119 as Lancashire finished on 350 for nine, with batsmen 10 and 11 at the wicket. Unfortunately the visitors' captain, Ken Cranston, declared first thing next morning.

Herbert Baldwin, one of only seven umpires to stand in over 600 matches, had seen his second all-ten, after officiating whilst Verity took his famous ten for 10 seven years earlier.

Smailes saw active service in the Mediterranean as a captain in the Royal Artillery. It was fitting that, together with Phil King, a Yorkshireman who played for Lancashire and Worcestershire, he located Hedley Verity's grave at Caserta and arranged for the erection of a monument on it.

Having taken 822 first-class wickets at an average of 20.81 Smailes retired from county cricket at the end of the 1948 season, partly because varicose veins were affecting his form. It had been an interesting last season: he occasionally led the side when Norman Yardley and Brian Sellers were unavailable, he took nine wickets in the match at Bradford as Yorkshire came close to defeating the eventually undefeated Australians, and his benefit yielded over £5,000 although his chosen match, against Surrey at Bramall Lane, was over in two days.

After Yorkshire Smailes became a professional at Walsall for five years and for a time kept the 'Sportsman's Arms' at Wath near Ripon. After a long illness he died in 1970 aged only 60.

Eddie Watts

Surrey v Warwickshire, 1939
County Championship

Edgbaston, Birmingham on 19, 21, 22 August 1939 (3-day match)
Toss won by Surrey
Surrey won by an innings and 1 run
Umpires: J Hardstaff, CWL Parker
Surrey 336; Warwickshire 115 (FR Brown 6-46) and 220 (EA Watts 10-67)

Warwickshire second innings

AJW Croom	c Gregory b Watts	12
WA Hill	c Gregory b Watts	31
FR Santall	c Squires b Watts	2
RES Wyatt	c Mobey b Watts	59
HE Dollery	c Garland-Wells b Watts	41
*P Cranmer	c Dickinson b Watts	3
NA Shortland	c Fishlock b Watts	3
+J Buckingham	lbw b Watts	22
WE Hollies	c Garland-Wells b Watts	1
JH Mayer	lbw b Watts	13
CWC Grove	not out	13
Extras	(b 12, lb 3, nb 3, w 2)	20
Total	(all out, 62.1 overs)	220

Fall of wickets 1-24, 2-33, 3-62, 4-147, 5-153, 6-161, 7-162, 8-166, 9-190, 10-220

Surrey bowling: AR Gover 12-0-36-0, EA Watts 24.1-8-67-10, FR Brown 17-2-78-0, JF Parker 5-2-7-0, HS Squires 4-1-12-0

Surrey: RJ Gregory, LB Fishlock, EW Whitfield, HS Squires, JF Parker, FR Brown, GS Mobey (wk), HM Garland-Wells (capt), PJ Dickinson, EA Watts, AR Gover

Born in Peckham, London, Eddie Watts played for Thames Ditton CC and made his first-class debut as an amateur in 1933, aged not quite 21, against Warwickshire, a county who would have good reason to remember him six years later. Turning professional he quickly became a regular member of the Surrey team. Strongly-built he bowled tirelessly at a lively fast-medium, swinging the ball both ways.

Watts usually opened the bowling with his brother-in-law Alf Gover who as spearhead of the attack got choice of ends, usually leaving Watts to bowl into the wind. Gover took 200 wickets in 1936 and 201 in 1937, the last fast bowler to reach this total. The following winter, touring India with Lord Tennyson's side, he injured his knee and was much less effective the following summer. Watts, however, rose to the challenge of the extra responsibility consequently thrust upon him and took over 100 wickets in a season for the first time, a target he achieved again in 1939.

By the middle of August 1939, with international tension rising, many thoughts were elsewhere. Surrey and Warwickshire were both below halfway in the Championship. Surrey, with future England captain Freddie Brown in the side, were captained by Monty Garland-Wells, a positive cricketer and fine allround sportsman whose name, according to *Wisden,* was informally used during the War as code word in North Africa: Garland-Wells = Monty = Montgomery. The home side, with past England captain Bob Wyatt in its ranks, was captained by Peter Cranmer, a brilliant rugby player who played 16 times for England. *Wisden* referred to him as 'a golden boy of English sport in the 1930s'. Wyatt's long career with Warwickshire was coming to an end; after the War he would play for, and captain, Worcestershire. The umpires were Charlie Parker (he of the all-ten in 1921) and Joe Hardstaff, whose son Joe was playing against the West Indies in the Third Test at The Oval and becoming the third Nottinghamshire batsman to complete 1,000 Test runs.

On a good pitch and before a crowd of some 4,000, Surrey used up the whole of Saturday compiling 336. England opener Laurie Fishlock top scored with 91, whilst leg-spinner Eric Hollies finished with four for 118, his final wicket giving him 100 for the season. Watts made 21 before he was stumped off the occasional off breaks of the 43-year-old Warwickshire opener Arthur Croom whose three for 22 were the only three wickets he took in this, his final, season. Scoring 55 not out, Surrey wicketkeeper Gerald Mobey, in his first fairly full season after spending most of the 1930s understudying Ted Brooks, was finally getting a chance to display his skills both sides of the stumps and earned selection for the abortive 1939/40 MCC tour to India. A collection for the testimonial fund of Worcestershire's Charles Bull (killed in a car crash earlier in the season) was held among the crowd and produced £38 15s 7d.

Warwickshire collapsed badly on the second day, future captain Tom Dollery (25) top scoring in an all-out first innings of 115. Most of the damage was done by the leg breaks of Brown (six for 46) who was in a good run of form having taken a career-best eight for 34 in the first innings of the previous match against Somerset.

Watts had hardly been needed in the first innings, bowling just four wicketless overs, but was soon contributing in the follow-on. The Warwickshire openers Croom and Aubrey Hill had both played against Yorkshire eight years before when Verity took the first of his two all-tens. Croom and then Reg Santall, both of whom were in their last seasons, went quickly. Croom had been playing for Warwickshire since 1922, whilst Santall had played in every season between the Wars (having made his debut at the age of 16) and would neatly finish his career with exactly 500 first-class appearances. Hill went at 62, having had the satisfaction of reaching 1,000 runs for the season for the first time during his innings. 123 for three at the close was something of a recovery but if Warwickshire were to have a chance of saving the match they needed the fourth-wicket partnership between past and future England players Wyatt and Dollery to continue to prosper. Unfortunately neither lasted long the next morning. The pitch still favoured batting, but a heavy atmosphere helped the ball to swing considerably and with a devastating spell of six for 4 Watts scotched any chance of recovery as a succession of batsmen were caught behind the wicket. With the score 190 for nine the last man, Charlie Grove, came out to join wicketkeeper Jack Buckingham, another member of the side appearing in his last season. Watts had been well served by his close fielders who took eight catches, but he nearly scuppered his chances of an all-ten by dropping a return catch off Grove. Fortunately the other bowlers, including Brown and Gover, who took over 200 wickets between them in 1939, couldn't (or perhaps wouldn't?) take the final wicket and after the last pair had put on 30 Watts pinned Buckingham in front of the stumps, only the third Warwickshire wicket in the match not to fall to a catch. Watts' all-ten was the last of the 23 between the Wars.

One of Watts' victims was Eric Hollies. Seven years later he would be the next bowler to take an all-ten. One of cricket's great rabbits Hollies would finish his long and successful career in 1957 with a batting average of 4.99, having exceeded 25 just once in 617 innings. Surprisingly he batted at number nine against Surrey, although to be fair by the end of the season his career average had reached the heady heights of 5.66.

Watts' season finished with three more matches. In the first two he took just two wickets, but he came back to form with five for 60 in the first Lancashire innings of the final game at Old Trafford. This turned out to be the home side's only innings as when the teams reached the ground on the third morning it was agreed that because of the worsening international situation the match would be abandoned. Strictly this was a Surrey home game, but with The Oval not available it had been transferred to Manchester. Eighteen-year-old Bernard Constable, one of the stars of the great post-war Surrey team, made his Championship debut in the match. He would still be playing for the county 25 years later. Edgbaston too would host one more match before war came. At least Warwickshire supporters had a victory against Gloucestershire, and a Dollery century, to savour.

Watts never received representative honours; in fact all but four of his 244 first-class matches were played for Surrey. The other four were played on tours he made to South America in 1937/38 with Sir Theodore Brinkman's team and to New Zealand the following winter with Sir Julien Cahn. A commissioned officer during the War, he returned to the Surrey side in 1946 and, although suffering with a knee injury, still contributed 58 Championship wickets to the cause as he provided support to Gover and the emerging Alec Bedser. Watts' career faded after his immediate post-war swansong and following knee surgery he played irregularly until retiring at the end of 1949, a season in which his benefit yielded £5,000 - then a Surrey record. His 729 career wickets cost him just over 26 runs apiece; a good record for somebody who did half his bowling at The Oval. A good striker of the ball he also made 6,000 runs at a respectable average of 21.

Watts later played in the Birmingham League, coached at Whitgift School at Croydon, and ran a sports shop. He died in Cheam, south London in 1982, aged nearly 70.

Eric Hollies

Warwickshire v Nottinghamshire, 1946
County Championship

Edgbaston, Birmingham on 24, 25 July 1946 (3-day match)
Toss won by Warwickshire
Nottinghamshire won by seven wickets
Umpires: A Skelding, CN Woolley
Warwickshire 170 and 113; Nottinghamshire 135 (WE Hollies 10-49) and 150-3

Nottinghamshire first innings

WW Keeton	b Hollies	40
CB Harris	b Hollies	10
RT Simpson	lbw b Hollies	14
J Hardstaff	lbw b Hollies	0
TB Reddick	b Hollies	1
*GFH Heane	lbw b Hollies	4
FW Stocks	not out	37
A Jepson	b Hollies	7
HJ Butler	b Hollies	8
+EA Meads	b Hollies	0
FG Woodhead	b Hollies	8
Extras	(b 4, lb 2)	6
Total	(all out, 53.4 overs)	135

Fall of wickets 1-47, 2-52, 3-54, 4-58, 5-62, 6-89, 7-109, 8-125, 9-125, 10-135

Warwickshire bowling: FR Mitchell 6-2-19-0, RH Maudsley 7-3-19-0, WE Hollies 20.4-4-49-10, WE Fantham 20-3-42-0

Warwickshire: P Cranmer (capt), R Sale, RH Maudsley, HE Dollery, JM Mills, KA Taylor, JS Ord, WE Fantham, FR Mitchell, CC Goodway (wk), WE Hollies

Eric Hollies is one of only three leg-spinners (with Kent's Tich Freeman and Doug Wright) to have taken 2,000 first-class wickets. In a career that lasted from 1932 to 1957 his 2,201 wickets for Warwickshire are easily a record for the county. He usually bowled off an eight pace run-up, varying his stock leg break with a top spinner or well-disguised googly. He also occasionally bowled off breaks or away swingers. A genial and much loved character, fair-haired and of medium height, his sturdy build and powerful legs gave him the stamina to maintain unerring accuracy over many long spells of bowling

Hollies was born in Old Hill, Staffordshire in 1912, in the so called 'Black Country', the hard industrial landscape west of Birmingham. After three seasons in the Birmingham League, and serving the appropriate residential qualification, Hollies made his Warwickshire debut in 1932. After a pasting by Walter Hammond he decided that a change of style was needed: he would bowl a flatter, straighter line in order to dictate where the batsman played the ball. The change yielded results: by 1935 he was making his

Test debut at Bridgetown, Barbados, under his county captain Bob Wyatt. He topped England's bowling averages in the series, but played no more Tests until after the War. Employment in a reserved occupation during the War, working for an engineering company, gave Hollies the chance to get in some cricket, and when competition resumed in 1946 he was prepared for battle. This was fortunate for Warwickshire since their next highest Championship wicket-taker after Hollies' impressive tally of 175 was Jack Marshall, another leg-spinner, with just 43. Fortunately reinforcements arrived and in 1951 Warwickshire won their second Championship, Hollies leading the way with 145 wickets. He was probably helped by an ankle injury which necessitated a shorter run-up and led to him giving the ball more air than usual. Five years later he stepped into the breach as county captain when MCC failed to approve M.J.K. Smith's special registration. It was not an experience he enjoyed.

As a batsman he failed to reach the heights, scoring fewer runs than he took wickets, although he could sometimes stick around when necessary and took part in ten last wicket stands of 50 or more.

The return of county cricket in 1946 was enthusiastically received despite appalling weather and amenities at some grounds which left much to be desired. Record attendances were set at many grounds and the counties fared well financially. Inevitably on the field however it was a season of rebuilding and none more so than for Warwickshire who used 31 players in the Championship, many of whom were amateurs who could not appear regularly. Hollies recalled that the composition of the team was often not known until a few hours before the game. Given their problems they did well to win seven matches. Yorkshire would eventually win the Championship for the fourth season in succession, a remarkable performance for a county that scored fewer runs than any other.

The Warwickshire side that met Nottinghamshire at the end of July included just three players who had played when Eddie Watts had taken his all-ten against them seven years before: captain Peter Cranmer, Tom Dollery and Hollies. Batting first Warwickshire were dismissed for 170. Recovering from 69 for six they were mainly indebted to off-spinner Bill Fantham who, going in at number eight, made 51, his highest score in a 63-match career, before he was dismissed by the Notts captain George Heane (whose other victim was Hollies, deservedly going in at number eleven).

Notts would finish the season only 13th in the Championship, one place above Warwickshire. They did however have a number of very good batsmen, but on a good wicket with the ball hardly turning at all Hollies had dismissed the lot by the close of the first day. And it's not unreasonable to say that he did it single-handedly, given that he hit the stumps seven times and dismissed the other three batsmen leg-before - the only bowler after John Wisden to take an unaided all-ten.

Notts had made a good start against the not particularly fearsome opening pair of Frank Mitchell and Ron Maudsley who between them eventually took only 74 first-class wickets in 84 matches. With 361 League appearances for Birmingham City, Chelsea and Watford, Australian-born Mitchell found greater fame on the football field. Maudsley, later a law professor, was Warwickshire captain in 1948 (a post shared with Dollery) and three years later in his final first-class match scored a century, his fourth, for Warwickshire against his alma mater Oxford, in the first of three first-class matches to be played at Stratford-upon-Avon.

Walter Keeton and Charlie Harris (both victims in Verity's record ten for 10 in 1932) put on 47 before Hollies switched from the pavilion to the city end and soon induced Harris to play on. The pair were one of county cricket's most prolific opening partnerships, reaching a hundred 46 times (the record is held by Yorkshire's Holmes and Sutcliffe with 69). The only batsmen who made scores of substance were Keeton and Freddie Stocks. Two months earlier left-hander Stocks had made a century on his first-class debut, and the following month he had Lancashire's Winston Place caught at the wicket with his debut first-class ball. Two of Hollies' victims were Joe Hardstaff, who the previous month had made 205 not out for England against India at Lord's, but this time was trapped by a googly second ball, and Reg Simpson. Twenty-six-year-old Simpson had made his Nottinghamshire debut earlier in the month (but had played first-class cricket in India during the War) and so far his highest county score was 29. Hollies later recalled that, in all the excitement, when last man Frank Woodhead came in after he had taken two wickets in two balls, he forgot to call in all the fielders, customary practice when a hat-trick was on. And Warwickshire keeper Cyril Goodway maintained that Hollies had taken all-eleven because he was sure that he had also stumped Stocks, unfortunately just as the sun suddenly broke through a gap in the clouds thereby (by his own admission) preventing umpire Alec Skelding from seeing what had happened.

Warwickshire struggled to 113 in their second innings. Hollies made four before he was bowled by Stoke City goalkeeper and future Test umpire Arthur Jepson, failing by one run to equal his highest score of the season! Nottinghamshire needed 149 to win, a tricky task given what had gone on before. However, they did have plenty of time, and used up 73 overs, reaching their target just before the end of the second day, achieving victory mainly thanks to Harris (80 not out) and Hardstaff (41). Clearly their main objective had been to keep out Hollies who bowled 31 overs in taking one for 29. The disappointment of defeat would have been slightly softened by the £100 that a collection yielded in recognition of his great feat the previous day. Curiously the return match with Nottinghamshire was played at Trent Bridge just one week later. Hollies again dismissed Simpson, but this time not before he had made his maiden century – a little matter of 201! The stylish Simpson would go on to score over 30,000 runs and play in 27 Tests.

Hollies' success helped revive his England career, and of course in 1948 he famously bowled Don Bradman for a duck in his final Test innings. He toured Australia with Freddie Brown's side in 1950/51, but the conditions didn't suit him, and he failed to add to his 13 caps and 44 wickets (a modest tally which did at least include five 5-fors).

After leaving the first-class game Hollies played briefly for Staffordshire and in the Birmingham League, appearing in his last match at the age of 62. He died suddenly after a heart attack in 1981. His ashes were scattered at Edgbaston, and the popular Rea Bank Stand renamed after him.

Jim Sims

East v West, 1948

Leyland Motors Ground, Kingston-upon-Thames on 8, 9, 10 September 1948 (3-day match)
East won by 223 runs
Umpires: SA Hipple, GS Mobey
East 392 (HA Pawson 128, RO Jenkins 5-84) and 304-8 dec (LJ Todd 107); West 294 and 179 (JM Sims 10-90)

West second innings

GM Emmett	b Sims	35
RO Jenkins	c Barling b Sims	8
F Cooper	c Gray b Sims	16
JF Crapp	b Sims	28
+AE Wilson	b Sims	2
C Cook	st Brown b Sims	2
R Howorth	not out	37
*BH Lyon	st Brown b Sims	10
MF Tremlett	st McIntyre b Sims	32
AE Nutter	b Sims	0
GEE Lambert	b Sims	0
Extras	(b 7, lb 2)	9
Total	(all out, 45.4 overs)	179

Fall of wickets 1-26, 2-61, 3-66, 4-83, 5-90, 6-101, 7-113, 8-173, 9-173, 10-179

East bowling: LH Gray 9-1-16-0, R Smith 4-1-13-0, JM Sims 18.4-2-90-10, TPB Smith 8-1-36-0, HA Pawson 6-1-15-0

East: LJ Todd, TC Dodds, HT Barling, SM Brown, HA Pawson (capt), AJW McIntyre (wk), R Smith, TPB Smith, JM Sims, RR Dovey, LH Gray

Tall and slim and renowned for his witty asides, Sims was one of cricket's most popular characters. Bowling with a high arm and pushing the ball through, his googly was as good as anybody's. The Middlesex 1947 Championship-winning side is particularly remembered for the power of its batting, the dynamic Denis Compton and Bill Edrich following prolific openers Jack Robertson and Syd Brown. However it also needed to get wickets, and although opener Laurie Gray (84 wickets) bowled accurately and unluckily, and Compton and Edrich did their bit, it relied particularly on Sims, who took 100 wickets despite missing some matches with a broken finger, and the left-arm spin of Jack Young (122).

Born in Leyton, Essex in 1903 Sims came late to first-class cricket. He made his debut in 1929 but it was two more years before he became a Middlesex regular. Able to call on Walter Robins, Ian Peebles, Greville Stevens and Jack Hearne Middlesex weren't short of wrist spin, and initially Sims was more a batsman who bowled. However, the emphasis gradually changed and by 1935 he was bowling for England. His four-match Test career would include two on Gubby Allen's 1936/37 tour of Australia and New

Zealand, but like many good English wrist-spinners he never made it at the top level, and Kent's Doug Wright is still the only one who has taken 100 Test wickets (albeit at a pricey 39 runs apiece). At county level however Sims was one of the mainstays of a Middlesex side that between 1935 and 1949 never ended outside the Championship top three. He had intended to retire at the end of the 1948 season but in view of his good form he accepted a new contract. He played on until 1952, and even in 1951 at the age of 48 he took 90 wickets in all first-class matches. Sims finished his career with 1,581 wickets and only Fred Titmus and the Hearnes, JT and JW, have exceeded the 1,257 he took for Middlesex.

Back in 1948 the first-class fixture list was so much different from today's. The first match (Worcestershire v Australians) didn't start until 28 April, and the Championship season ran from 8 May until 31 August (compared with 7 April until 28 September in 2017). What a waste! All those lovely balmy early autumn days (sometimes) and no cricket. As some consolation, festival matches were played in early September which at least allowed holidaymakers to see some cricket. In 1948 seven matches in all were played at Hastings, Scarborough and Kingston-upon-Thames. Holidaymakers, Kingston-upon-Thames? Well all right, the Kingston festival in south-west London wasn't exactly played beside the seaside, or as famous as some others, or as long lasting, but the 16 matches played there between 1946 and 1953 produced some good cricket, and I expect Jim Sims had fond memories of it. The ground belonged to aircraft manufacturers Hawkers and was located at one of their two Kingston factories. In 1928 it had been leased to Leyland, the motor vehicle manufacturers, for 20 years, with Hawker taking it back in 1948. Hence the ground was first called Leyland Motors Ground and later Hawker's Sports Ground. The factory was demolished in the 1990s but the ground survived providing a range of sporting activities.

Tony Pawson, Kent and Oxford University, the youngest member of the side, captained an East team that comprised players from Kent, Essex, Surrey and Middlesex. Pawson was a man of many parts: among other things he would play football for the England amateurs and for Charlton in the First Division, and become world fly-fishing champion. West were led by Bev Lyon, hard-hitting batsman and inspiring captain of Gloucestershire in the early 1930s. Lyon had played relatively infrequently since, but came back this one last time at the age of 46 to end a 267-match career. Worcestershire and Gloucestershire made up the majority of the West side, with in addition one player each from Northamptonshire and Somerset. The teams were reasonably well matched, but East always had the edge with Sims' bowling on the last day giving them the final decisive advantage.

In true festival fashion 498 runs were scored on the first day. East made 392, Pawson leading from the front with a stylish 128. Sims, batting number nine, remained 30 not out, resisting the wiles of fellow wrist-spinner Worcestershire's Roly Jenkins who took five for 84. Jenkins had a fine season, his 1,356 runs and 88 wickets earning selection for the tour of South Africa where he topped the England averages with 16 wickets, a precursor to an even finer season in 1949 when he took 183 wickets (and didn't play in any Tests!). West were 106 for three at close of play, Sims having picked up two wickets including Jenkins, caught by Pawson for 26.

Festival-style batting saw another 492 runs scored on the second day. First West took their score to 294 all out (Sims three for 82), and then East closed on 304 for eight, Kent's left-hand opener Les Todd top scoring with 107 and Pawson making 51.

An overnight declaration left West a stiff, but potentially gettable, 402 to win. They actually had a useful batting side. Apart from Sam Cook, a famous batting incompetent who strangely batted at six in the second innings, they were all, or would be, centurions (although some only managed one). However they never got close to their target.

Jenkins was the first wicket to fall, caught by Tom Barling who was appearing in the last of his 391 first-class matches, all but two of which had been played for Surrey. By lunch Sims had taken seven for 69 and with Pawson going on with his very occasional off breaks he was given every opportunity to complete the full set – a feat he soon accomplished. He hit the stumps five times, and three batsmen were stumped, two by Middlesex's Syd Brown, a brilliant outfielder who shared the keeping with Surrey's Arthur McIntyre. They were the only stumpings of his 329-match career. Sims had troubled everyone, only three batsmen reaching 30. All had played for England since the War: Gloucestershire's George Emmett, a fine county batsman who two months earlier had controversially replaced Len Hutton for the Third Test against Australia; Somerset's Maurice Tremlett, father of Hampshire's Tim and grandfather of England's Chris; and Worcestershire's left-hand allrounder Dick Howorth. Sims had gone into the match with 91 wickets for the season. His performance enabled him to reach his 100, a feat he had performed every year since 1935 (apart from 1938 when he was handicapped by minor injuries).

The Essex cousins Smith, Ray and Peter, who took 196 wickets between them during the season, bowled twelve wicketless overs in the second innings. Peter, another wrist-spinner, took nine wickets in an innings four times in his career, including twice in 1948 when his cousin picked up the other wicket each time; but an all-ten eluded him. One of the umpires was Gerald Mobey, who had kept wicket for Surrey when Watts had taken his all-ten in 1939. He had played the last of his 81 first-class matches just a month before, and would later officiate in the Championship for five years.

At 45 years 120 days Sims was the second-oldest bowler (after Bestwick) to take all-ten. His durability would earn him a second benefit in 1950, his first in 1946 having been ruined by the weather. Middlesex to the end, after he had finished with the first-class game he looked after the Second Eleven, giving sage advice to many young players, became coach and, in 1969, scorer. He was staying in a Canterbury hotel in April 1973 when he died the night before a Benson and Hedges Cup match.

Ken Graveney

Queen's Park, Chesterfield on 3, 4, 5 August 1949 (3-day match)
Toss won by Gloucestershire
Gloucestershire won by 184 runs
Umpires: E Cooke, HW Parks
Gloucestershire 198 (C Gladwin 5-53) and 302 (DB Carr 6-111); Derbyshire
149 (C Cook 5-40) and 167 (JKR Graveney 10-66)

Derbyshire second innings

R Sale	b JKR Graveney	7
CS Elliott	c Crapp b JKR Graveney	1
AC Revill	b JKR Graveney	0
JD Eggar	c Allen b JKR Graveney	14
DB Carr	c and b JKR Graveney	0
AEG Rhodes	c TW Graveney b JKR Graveney	65
+GO Dawkes	c Lambert b JKR Graveney	9
*DA Skinner	c Goddard b JKR Graveney	39
C Gladwin	b JKR Graveney	8
WH Copson	c Emmett b JKR Graveney	2
HL Jackson	not out	5
Extras	(b 10, lb 1, nb 2, w 4)	17
Total	(all out, 41.4 overs)	167

Fall of wickets 1-8, 2-10, 3-13, 4-13, 5-88, 6-108, 7-118, 8-137, 9-158, 10-167

Gloucestershire bowling: GEE Lambert 16-2-51-0, JKR Graveney 18.4-2-66-10, TWJ Goddard 5-0-21-0, C Cook 2-0-12-0

Gloucestershire: GM Emmett, TW Graveney, BO Allen (capt), JF Crapp, CA Milton, AE Wilson (wk), CI Monks, JKR Graveney, GEE Lambert, TWJ Goddard, C Cook

Gloucestershire's Ken Graveney only took 172 first-class wickets, but he took ten of those all in one go. A wholehearted bowler who swung the ball away at a lively fast-medium, remarkably he had two separate county careers 12 years apart.

Graveney was born in Hexham, Northumberland in 1924, two and a half years before famous brother Tom. His father died when they were young and the family followed their stepfather to Bristol. At the Grammar School Ken was a left-handed batting star (brother Tom fancied himself as a quick bowler!). After serving as a Royal Marine Commando during the War, and taking part in the Normandy landings, local cricket led to a successful trial with Gloucestershire and a first county career that lasted from 1947 to 1951. As a bonus Ken introduced Tom to the county.

Gloucestershire finished seventh in the Championship in 1949, the performances of the two Graveneys and Arthur Milton promising well for the future. Let down by unreliable batting Derbyshire however had a disappointing season, slipping from sixth to fifteenth place in the table. The sides had met earlier, Tom Goddard's second-innings nine for 61 at Bristol bowling Gloucestershire to an innings victory. Graveney had only been required to bowl ten overs in the match. The only wicket he took, the first to fall in the second Derbyshire innings, prevented Goddard taking another all-ten.

Batting first in the return match at Chesterfield's beautiful Queen's Park ground, Gloucestershire were soon in trouble with opener Tom Graveney bowled without scoring by Cliff Gladwin and captain Basil Allen leg-before to veteran Bill Copson, his only wicket of the match. Although George Emmett and Jack Crapp both reached 30, in a ten-over post-lunch spell Gladwin, who swung the ball awkwardly in a strong crosswind and took four for nought, reduced them to 91 for eight, Ken joining his brother as one of five ducks. Twenty-one-year-old Milton however stood firm and his 92 not out saw Gloucestershire to 198 all out. It was his highest first-class score so far. He would eventually make 56 centuries in a 26-year career, although the first was still two years away. He was also the last man to play both football and cricket for England. He received unlikely support from Tom Goddard (20) and left-arm spinner Sam Cook whose then career-best 18 was a score he would rarely surpass despite eventually batting 611 times.

Derbyshire also struggled in turn and conceded a first-innings lead of 49. Graveney took the first wicket, bowling Repton schoolmaster Dick Sale (who had been playing for Warwickshire in the match when Eric Hollies took his all-ten), but after that spinners Goddard and Cook did the damage.

Gloucestershire fared much better second time around. Gladwin's four for 90 gave him nine wickets in the match, while the six for 111 that Oxford University's Donald Carr took with his occasional slow left-arm spin (the first of his five 5-wicket hauls in a 446-match career) will have been some compensation for the two first-ball ducks he made in the match.

Derbyshire set off late on the second afternoon to chase 352. It was a difficult target and the expectation was that Gloucestershire's two main bowlers, Goddard and Cook, would spin their side to victory, after the opening bowlers Graveney and George Lambert (future father-in-law of Test umpire David Constant) had had a couple of overs to get the shine off the ball. Graveney upset the plan by dismissing Charlie Elliott with the fifth ball of his second over. Elliott, Derbyshire's top-scorer in 1949 and whose uncle Harry had kept wicket when Tommy Mitchell had taken his all-ten, would go on to umpire in 42 Test matches. Graveney added more wickets in his third, fourth and fifth overs (the unfortunate Carr brilliantly caught and bowled) by which time Derbyshire were 13 for four. However he failed to strike in his sixth and so had to come off! By close of play Derbyshire had recovered to 69 for four, mainly thanks to Dusty Rhodes who was 48 not out. It was the school holidays but history does not record whether his 13-year-old son, future England fast bowler Harold, was watching. Making good use of a wearing pitch Graveney had the satisfying overnight figures of four for 5.

Goddard and Cook took 243 Championship wickets between them in 1949 and so Graveney needed to keep getting wickets next morning in order to stay on. Fortunately he did, with Rhodes soon caught by the younger Graveney at extra cover for 65 and wickets six and seven following quickly after. A stubborn eighth wicket partnership then developed, led by the Derbyshire captain David Skinner. As Skinner was to average below 14 in a first-class career that lasted just 23 matches, his 39 was a commendable performance. Graveney was about to be rested but Allen decided that as he had all seven wickets he had better keep going, and he took two more wickets in the next five overs. With nine wickets down, another nuisance partnership developed, this time between Bill Copson and Les Jackson, not two of cricket's greatest with the bat (848 innings between them, no fifties!). Allen told Graveney that he had three more overs to get his tenth wicket. Fortunately soon after, with the score 167, Copson lofted a shot into the safe hands of George Emmett at extra cover and the deed was done. Goddard and Cook had hardly been needed.

Graveney is still the only non-spinner to have taken all-ten for Gloucestershire, and the only bowler to have done so at Chesterfield. As he had previously taken just 38 wickets in his 16-match career his success must have caused some surprise.

Although he played less than a full season in 1949 Graveney took 59 wickets and scored 505 runs. Gloucestershire seemed to have found a promising allrounder. However, despite much treatment he had never fully recovered from a back injury sustained while he was with the Commandos and only two years later to his great regret he had to give up. But he would be back.

By the early 1960s the county's captaincy had been a bit of a problem for some time. Tom Graveney had been captain in 1959 and 1960 but had been controversially deposed and after 13 years' service left to join Worcestershire. The Committee really still wanted the side to be led by an amateur and appointed Old Etonian Tom Pugh who had been playing for the county with modest success for two seasons. Leadership was in his blood, his uncle Peter Eckersley having twice led Lancashire to the County Championship in the 1930s. And as one of the best racquets players in the world he didn't lack competitive spirit. However, although a commendable fourth place was achieved in 1962, Pugh's batting was not up to standard and after two seasons it was decided that a change was needed. The appointment of Ken Graveney in 1963 at the age of 38 was surprising. Having made a successful career in the catering business, he was still playing cricket locally and had been captaining the Second Eleven, but was he up to the first-class game again? Unfortunately the move wasn't a success and in his two seasons in charge the county slipped from fourth to eighth to last. Graveney himself only contributed 39 wickets and just over 800 runs in the two seasons and he returned to business, handing over the reins to off-spinning allrounder John Mortimore.

Graveney would later go on to perform further service for Gloucestershire as chairman and as president. His son, slow left-armer David, would also captain the county, and later Durham in their early years as a first-class county, and go on to become a leading figure in English cricket as chairman of the England selectors and Chief Executive of the Professional Cricketers' Association.

Ken Graveney died in Texas in October 2015, a week before his famous brother.

Trevor Bailey

Essex v Lancashire, 1949
County Championship

Vista Road Recreation Ground, Clacton-on-Sea on 24, 25 August 1949 (3-day match)
Toss won by Lancashire
Lancashire won by ten wickets
Umpires: K McCanlis, CN Woolley
Lancashire 331 (TE Bailey 10-90) and 3-0; Essex 164 (JHG Deighton 5-53) and 169 (WB Roberts 6-29)

Lancashire first innings

C Washbrook	c Wade b Bailey	18
JT Ikin	b Bailey	42
W Place	c Wade b Bailey	28
GA Edrich	c Vigar b Bailey	82
KJ Grieves	c Wade b Bailey	11
*ND Howard	c Vigar b Bailey	66
P Greenwood	c Vigar b Bailey	2
JHG Deighton	c Pearce b Bailey	1
R Tattersall	not out	34
WB Roberts	b Bailey	15
+A Barlow	b Bailey	12
Extras	(b 10, lb 9, w 1)	20
Total	(all out, 106.4 overs)	331

Fall of wickets 1-26, 2-84, 3-104, 4-228, 5-256, 6-264, 7-265, 8-268, 9-297, 10-331

Essex bowling: TE Bailey 39.4-9-90-10, R Smith 33-8-107-0, TPB Smith 12-3-26-0, FH Vigar 7-1-27-0, EJ Price 8-1-29-0, WB Morris 3-1-12-0, TN Pearce 4-0-20-0

Essex: TC Dodds, SJ Cray, FH Vigar, R Horsfall, TE Bailey, TN Pearce (capt), WB Morris, R Smith, TPB Smith, TH Wade (wk), EJ Price

A true allrounder, Trevor Bailey's performances graced Lord's, Wembley and both Old Traffords. A shrewd, competitive cricketer, he always contributed, whether winning a match with his fast-medium bowling, saving it with his slow-medium batting or turning it with a brilliant catch. Born in 1923 in Westcliff-on-Sea, Bailey came to notice during the War playing for Dulwich College and when first-class cricket restarted was soon in the Essex side as well as getting his Blue at Cambridge.

For ten years from 1949 Bailey was more or less a regular in the England side (although curiously in 61 Tests he never played against India). He played a major role in England's 1950s pre-eminence and would become, after Wilfred Rhodes, the second player to score 2,000 runs and take 100 wickets for them. Because of the role he had to play for England, Bailey is often remembered as an ultra-defensive batsman, but to be fair to him he had begun his career as an attractive strokemaker.

Essex were still a nomadic side, spreading themselves around the county in a series of cricket weeks, achieved by turning the side into a travelling circus with a convoy of lorries bringing everything needed to convert a club ground into a county ground. In 1949 the Vista Road Recreation Ground, home of Clacton-on-Sea Cricket Club, was one of six venues where the circus came to town. Essex played their last game there in 1966, although the ground is still used by Clacton-on-Sea. To attract holidaymakers matches were played in late July or August. The pitch had a reputation for unpredictability, perhaps because, like other seaside grounds, its performance could seemingly be affected by the state of the tide. Playing two matches there each season Essex had not found Clacton to be a very successful venue for them since the War, and in the match just finished there they had lost by an innings, Bailey taking one for 133 as Somerset piled up 488. Essex and Lancashire, their opponents in the second match of the Clacton week, would both finish in the middle of the Championship in 1949. However, the following season Essex would fall to the bottom of the table for the first time ever whilst Lancashire, with a number of good young bowlers coming to the fore, would share the title with Surrey.

Lancashire had a useful batting side, starting with three England batsmen: Cyril Washbrook, Jack Ikin and Winston Place. Journeying from Liverpool they had not arrived in Clacton until 3.00 am and were no doubt glad to bat first. The main contributors were Geoff Edrich (82) and Nigel Howard (66). Howard was the son of influential administrator Rupert. He was in his first year as Lancashire captain, a position he would hold until 1953, and also captained a second string England on the 1951/52 tour of India and Pakistan.

It was apparently not until the eighth wicket fell at 268 that Bailey, or anybody else, realised that an all-ten was possible. Numbers nine, ten, jack were not renowned batsmen and he must have anticipated finishing the visitors off quickly and completing the job, especially as captain Tom Pearce helped by putting on two (very) occasional bowlers, including himself. The tail took advantage of this largesse before Bailey eventually bowled both slow left-armer Bill Roberts and wicketkeeper Alf Barlow, but only after their contributions in support of Roy Tattersall's 34 not out had seen Lancashire through to a match-winning score.

Bailey had swung the ball away at a lively pace, as well as bringing the occasional ball back, and many of his wickets came from tentative shots outside the off stump. He was particularly well served by allrounder Frank Vigar at slip and wicketkeeper Tom Wade, who each took three catches. On a good pitch Bailey had had to work hard for his wickets, bowling nearly 40 overs on a warm day taking three wickets by lunch and another three by tea. Once again the cousins Smith (186 wickets in the season) had bowled without reward whilst somebody cleaned up at the other end.

In time-honoured fashion the ball was mounted and inscribed, and later presented to Bailey by club president Lt-Col Hubert Ashton MP. Bailey would eventually play 28 matches against Lancashire but never took five wickets in an innings against them again, although he achieved the feat at least twice against each of the other counties. He is the only bowler to have taken an all-ten (or even a nine-for) in the 60 first-class matches played at Vista Road. He probably liked the ground, even though he made a pair against Yorkshire there in 1952. No other Essex player has scored more runs there or taken more wickets.

Essex batted feebly on the second day losing 19 wickets and the match. According to *The Times* some batsmen had been handicapped by a thick sea mist obscuring part of the ground. (And was the problem compounded by the proximity of the nearby railway line from which John Arlott had once recorded engines had 'belched a fog of smoke over the ground'?) In their second innings Essex were confounded by the spin of Roberts. Almost thirty-five, Roberts had had considerable success since the War, but his career was nearing its end; kept out of the side by the burgeoning talent of Lancashire's younger spinners, he died of cancer in 1951. Umpire Claud 'Dick' Woolley, an older brother of the great Frank, had also officiated just three years before when Eric Hollies had taken his famous all-ten. It was Woolley's penultimate Championship match: having played in 365 first-class matches (all but three for Northants), he then umpired another 281.

Achieving the first of his eight seasonal doubles and appearing in all four Tests against Walter Hadlee's New Zealanders, 1949 had been a breakthrough year for Bailey. The Clacton Week was not without interest for him the following year. He was injury prone, and in the first match bowled six overs and then went off for a massage. On return, as he prepared to bowl, Sussex captain James Langridge objected. After consultation it was agreed he would not bowl for an hour. In the second match he bowled his side to victory with a second-innings eight for 70 against Kent.

Essex captain from 1961 to 1966, Bailey retired at the end of the 1967 season. For a time he had seemed to be heir apparent to Len Hutton as England captain. However, the claims of Peter May, and the dim view taken by the establishment of the newspaper serialisation of his book *Playing to Win,* put an end to that. Only Peter Smith and Stan Nichols exceeded (just) Bailey's 1,593 wickets for Essex, and neither got near his 21,000 runs for them.

Bailey was always a busy man, even when playing cricket full-time. In 1948 Essex had offered him the post of assistant secretary, in effect paying him to play whilst retaining his amateur status. In 1955 he was appointed county secretary, a more onerous role. For a few seasons Bailey, a pacy forward, had a successful football career with Leytonstone and then Walthamstow Avenue (both sadly now defunct clubs) at a time when the amateur game attracted big crowds. It climaxed with an Amateur Cup winners' medal at Wembley in April 1952 before a crowd of 100,000, and a visit to Old Trafford the following season which saw Avenue hold Manchester United to a 1-1 draw in the fourth round of the FA Cup. He wrote, was engaged in various business and promotional activities, and of course was a long-serving and much-admired member of BBC's *Test Match Special* team. Tragically, in 2011 he died in a fire at his flat in Westcliff-on-Sea.

Bob Berry

Lancashire v Worcestershire, 1953
County Championship

Stanley Park, Blackpool on 29, 30, 31 July 1953 (3-day match)
Toss won by Lancashire
Lancashire won by 18 runs
Umpires: E Cooke, TW Spencer
Lancashire 265 (RTD Perks 7-115) and 262-8 dec; Worcestershire 191 and 318 (R Berry 10-102)

Worcestershire second innings

D Kenyon	lbw b Berry	51
PE Richardson	c Ikin b Berry	33
LF Outschoorn	b Berry	25
*RE Bird	c Ikin b Berry	3
G Dews	c Wharton b Berry	5
RG Broadbent	c Howard b Berry	92
LN Devereux	c Ikin b Berry	67
+H Yarnold	c Grieves b Berry	13
RTD Perks	c Tattersall b Berry	12
JR Ashman	not out	6
GH Chesterton	c Ikin b Berry	0
Extras	(b 7, lb 4)	11
Total	(all out, 94.2 overs)	318

Fall of wickets 1-84, 2-89, 3-99, 4-105, 5-153, 6-258, 7-286, 8-300, 9-318, 10-318

Lancashire bowling: JB Statham 19-4-54-0, A Wharton 10-1-36-0, R Tattersall 24-6-91-0, R Berry 36.2-9-102-10, JT Ikin 5-1-24-0

Lancashire: C Washbrook, JT Ikin, GA Edrich, W Place, KJ Grieves, ND Howard (capt), A Wharton, FD Parr (wk), JB Statham, R Tattersall, R Berry

Bob Berry was a diminutive and popular slow left-armer relying more on variations of flight than excessive spin. After league cricket he made his first-class debut for Lancashire in 1948 aged 22. Two years later, after only 23 first-class matches, he was playing for England against the West Indies on his home ground at Old Trafford. The selectors had tried a few slow left-armers since the War but nobody had really set the world alight, although Yorkshireman Johnny Wardle's time would come, and so the relatively inexperienced Berry was given a go. Taking nine wickets Berry had a good first Test. He had less success at Lord's in the Second Test, failing to strike as West Indies secured their first Test win in England. He played no more in the series but had impressed the selectors enough for him to be on the boat to Australia the following winter. He had a poor tour however and his brief Test career was over. Wardle and Surrey's Tony Lock were now the main contenders for the England side, and even Berry's Lancashire place was no longer certain because of the form of Malcolm Hilton (left-arm like Berry, but pushing it through and relying more on sharp spin than subtle variations of flight).

After playing only 26 matches in 1951 and 1952 and taking just 62 wickets, Berry had greater success in Coronation Year. He took advantage of the opportunities afforded by Hilton's temporary loss of form to take 98 wickets, the closest he ever got to 100 in a season. Writing in *The Cricketer* Trevor Bailey thought that he had recovered his deceptive flight and was spinning the ball more. His great day was the culmination of a three-match purple patch in which he would take 35 wickets. The game would have an exciting climax, and Berry would be in the thick of the action.

The tussle for the 1953 Championship was tense. Surrey won it, for the second successive year, but success was not assured until their penultimate match. At the end of July the table was topped by Sussex, who would not win their first title for another fifty years, with Surrey fourth and Lancashire, who would eventually finish equal third, their efforts seriously handicapped by rain, in sixth place. They probably took some consolation from the plight of their White Rose rivals across the Pennines who finished 12th, their then-lowest ever placing (although to be fair their players did contribute significantly to England's long awaited recovery of the Ashes that summer). Worcestershire meanwhile, led by Ronnie Bird and still awaiting their first Championship, would finish a lowly 15th.

Stanley Park is Blackpool's main public park covering an area of some 260 acres. The cricket ground is home to Blackpool CC. An attractive seaside ground with an impressive pavilion, it hosted the last of its 99 first-class matches in 2011 but is still used occasionally for List A matches. It is probably best remembered for Warwickshire's Jim Stewart battering a record 17 sixes in a match there in 1959, a total only exceeded three times since.

Until the last day the cricket in the Worcestershire match in 1953 had been unexceptional. Lancashire, with a side including eight players who had appeared for England, led off with 265, forty-two-year-old Reg Perks, Worcestershire's leading all-time wicket-taker, finishing with seven for 115 from 33 overs of accurate fast-medium swing bowling. Worcestershire replied with 108 without loss by the close; Don Kenyon, who had played in the first two Tests against Australia, and was to become his county's highest ever run-scorer, was 60 not out, and left-hander Peter Richardson, who would begin a successful Test career against the Australians three years later, was on 32. Earlier in the season they had put on 290 against Gloucestershire at Dudley.

Kenyon went without addition next morning and, apart from Richardson (62), nobody else stayed long as Berry (four for 23), Brian Statham and Roy Tattersall, sharing the wickets, dismissed Worcestershire for 191. Lancashire batted consistently in their second innings, reaching 262 for eight at the close. Chief contributors were Alan Wharton (58 not out), his second fifty of the match, and Australian Ken Grieves (66) whose skills as a fielder (he held more catches (555) for Lancashire than anybody else) were put to good use as a goalkeeper, first for Bury, and then Bolton Wanderers and Stockport County.

Lancashire declared overnight, setting Worcestershire 337 to win. It was a tough target, but Worcestershire made a gallant effort to achieve a surprise victory. That they got so close was partly due to a number of dropped catches – Berry himself the guilty party on two occasions. Kenyon and Richardson again began well, taking the score to 84, but after Berry had prised them out the Worcestershire middle order failed again and at 153 for five a win for the visitors looked unlikely. However, Bob Broadbent and Louis Devereux counter-attacked in a partnership of 105 to rekindle hopes of victory. Broadbent was particularly severe on Roy Tattersall, lifting him over the boundary four times, as well as hitting twelve other boundaries. Berry however kept pegging away to take advantage of Worcestershire batsmen hitting out in a bid to win their fifth match of the season. As he began his 37th over the situation was tense: two wickets left and only 19 runs needed. However he only needed two balls to move Lancashire up to fifth in the table, just four points behind Surrey.

Despite the transgressions in the field, eight of Berry's victims had fallen to catches, and it was fitting that the final wicket should be a catch, his fourth of the innings, by Jack Ikin, a brilliant fielder who would take 329 catches for Lancashire, mainly at short leg. The wicketless bowlers at the other end included two who had played for England against Australia earlier in the summer: fast bowler Brian Statham, one of England's greatest, and off-spinner Roy Tattersall whose 164 wickets during the season were exceeded only by the 172 taken by Nottinghamshire's Australian wrist-spinner Bruce Dooland. A month later Tattersall, with nine for 40 against Nottinghamshire, might have taken his own all-ten if the ninth wicket, Arthur Jepson, hadn't fallen to Berry.

Two participants at Blackpool had been involved 17 years previously when Glamorgan's Jack Mercer had taken all-ten against Worcestershire: Reg Perks, a victim of both all-tens (and also a Tom Goddard victim in 1937) and umpire Ernest Cooke, who had also stood for Graveney's all-ten in 1949.

Despite his achievements in 1953, followed by a successful winter tour to India with a Commonwealth XI led by Australia's pre-war wicketkeeper Ben Barnett, Berry played little in 1954 and was given permission by Lancashire to look elsewhere. Worcestershire, in need of another spinner to support Roly Jenkins, and remembering Blackpool, signed him on. Berry served his new county well for four seasons before the emergence of Doug Slade, a promising slow left-armer not yet aged 18, again restricted his opportunities and he joined Derbyshire, where he would stay another four seasons.

Without consistently hitting the heights, Berry had had a reasonably successful career, finishing with 703 wickets at just under 25 apiece. He was the first man to be capped by three counties, and appropriately had five-wicket hauls for both his adopted counties against Lancashire (having previously taken five wickets in an innings for Lancashire against them). He later became a publican and restaurateur and remained involved in the game as president of Farnsfield CC (near Mansfield in Nottinghamshire) and of the Lancashire Players' Association. Although he and Malcolm Hilton were cricketing rivals, they had also been long-time friends. Hilton died in 1990 aged only 61, and after Berry's wife died two years later he married Hilton's widow. They remained together until his death in Manchester in 2006 aged 80.

Fergie Gupte

Bombay v Pakistan Combined Services and Bahawalpur XI, 1954/55

Brabourne Stadium, Bombay on 3, 4, 6 December 1954
Toss won by Pakistan Combined Services and Bahawalpur XI
Bombay won by an innings and 125 runs
Umpires: JR Patel, KA Pradhan
Pakistan Combined Services and Bahawalpur XI 152 (SP Gupte 10-78) and
145; Bombay 422 (GS Ramchand 101)

Pakistan Combined Services and Bahawalpur XI first innings

+Imtiaz Ahmed	b Gupte	28
Alimuddin	st Tamhane b Gupte	11
*AH Kardar	c Umrigar b Gupte	13
Maqsood Ahmed	c Sunderam b Gupte	8
Shujauddin	lbw b Gupte	56
Raees Mohammad	b Gupte	5
Mohammad Ramzan	st Tamhane b Gupte	4
Zafar Ahmed	lbw b Gupte	1
Zulfiqar Ahmed	not out	14
Baseer Shamsi	c Rele b Gupte	9
Khan Mohammad	lbw b Gupte	0
Extras		3
Total	(all out, 63.2 overs)	152

Fall of wickets 1-33, 2-53, 3-54, 4-65, 5-79, 6-107, 7-127, 8-132, 9-132,
10-152

Bombay bowling: GR Sunderam 4-2-3-0, GS Ramchand 7-3-15-0, HT Dani
5-2-12-0, SP Gupte 24.2-7-78-10, MH Mankad 23-8-41-0

Bombay: P Roy, YK Rele, VL Manjrekar, PR Umrigar, HT Dani, GS Ramchand,
CG Borde, NS Tamhane (wk), SP Gupte, MH Mankad (capt), GR Sunderam

Subhash Gupte was the first Asian to take an all-ten. A slightly-built wrist-
spinner fit to rank with the best, he played during a period when Indian
cricket was not at its strongest, and his figures would probably have been
even better if he had not at times been overbowled. Born in Bombay in
1929 he was nicknamed 'Fergie' after Trinidad leg-spinner Wilf Ferguson
who had toured India with the West Indies in 1948/49. Four years after his
first-class debut in 1947 he was selected for the Third Test against Nigel
Howard's visiting England side. Although he didn't do enough to go on the
1952 tour of England, he soon became a regular member of the side. His
form on the 1952/53 tour of West Indies was a revelation: his 27 wickets,
on perfect pitches against a home side for whom the Three Ws scored
1,571 runs, were only eight fewer than the rest of the attack took between
them. A big spinner of the ball with a high arm action, Gupte achieved a
mesmerising variety of spin without compromising on accuracy and in 36
Tests would eventually take 149 wickets at 30 runs apiece. At the time,
among leg-spinners, only Clarrie Grimmett and Richie Benaud had more
victims.

After his West Indian success Gupte maintained his form the following year in India, taking another 27 wickets in five unofficial Tests against the touring Commonwealth XI, and then at the beginning of the next season becoming the first Indian to take an all-ten, in a match which was among those arranged to mark the Silver Jubilee of the India Cricket Board of Control. The Brabourne Stadium was at the time one of the few grounds on which at least three triple-centuries had been scored (the tally there now stands at five), and apart from Gupte nobody has yet taken nine or more wickets in an innings there. It was India's premier Test ground with an impressive clubhouse whose upper floors contained luxurious rooms where visiting cricketers could stay. Cricket politics would lead to its loss of Test status in the mid-1970s, although one match was played there against Sri Lanka in 2009.

Holders of the Ranji Trophy, Bombay were a powerful side. Only one of the eleven would never play Test cricket: opener Yatin Rele who nevertheless averaged a healthy 51 in a 12-match career. The visitors also had a strong side, seven of them having played for Pakistan, six of them at The Oval four months earlier when the fledgling cricketing nation had become the first to win a Test in its first rubber in England. Their captain Abdul Kardar had also appeared three times for India before Partition. He was, according to his *Wisden* obituary, an idiosyncratic and fearless cricketer and the father figure of Pakistani cricket, although 'diplomacy may not have come easily to him'.

Batting first the combined side didn't give a very good account of themselves, with Shujauddin the only batsman to get a decent score whilst the rest of the side struggled against Gupte's varied spin. He was on early and struck soon, luring Alimuddin out of his crease with the score 33 (the best partnership of the innings). Narendra Tamhane would play his first match for India on New Year's Day the following month, and when his 21-match Test career ended six years later he was India's leading wicketkeeper with 51 victims. The other opener, wicketkeeper Imtiaz Ahmed, one of the ground's triple-centurions, was the only other batsman to get into the 20s, before Gupte bowled him. The following October, batting at number eight against New Zealand, he made 209, the first of his three Test centuries. Only Wasim Akram (257 not out against Zimbabwe 41 years later) has also made a Test double-century from such a lowly position. The only batsman who failed to score was Khan Mohammad, a feat he would emulate in his second innings.

The Bombay attack comprised Test bowlers Gupte, Vinoo Mankad, Gulabrai Ramchand, Bal Dani, and a future international Gundibail Sunderam, and yet apart from Gupte none managed a wicket. Most surprisingly slow left-armer and Bombay captain Vinoo Mankad went without despite bowling 23 overs, although no doubt his steadiness helped Gupte at the other end. Mankad was one of Test cricket's true allrounders, worth his place in the side both as batsman and bowler. He finished his Test career in 1959 with 162 wickets and 2,109 runs. At the time he was India's highest wicket-taker, and held the record for his country's highest score (231) and highest score against England (184).

There was enough time left for Bombay to reach 107 for one by the close of the first day, a score that they would eventually extend to 422, mainly thanks to Ramchand (101), Vijay Manjrekar (99) and Pankaj Roy (88). Roy and Manjrekar, together with Mankad, would all have sons who also played for India. The hard-worked Shujauddin toiled for 50 overs with his left-arm spin to take four for 127, and then completed a fine allround match by scoring 74, his second fifty of the game, in another poor performance by the visitors. This time neither Gupte nor Mankad was required to turn his arm over. In fact, so inconsequential was most of the batting that Manjrekar, who only took 20 wickets in a career lasting 23 years, had the best figures (four for 21), albeit that most of his victims were in the lower order.

The match had been scheduled for three days but was extended to four as there was no play on 5 December as a mark of respect following the death of Sir Girija Shankar Bajpal, the Governor of Bombay.

Gupte might have had another all-ten four years later. In 1958/59 he took 22 wickets in five Tests against the touring West Indians captained by wicketkeeper Gerry Alexander. The West Indies were building another great team and, with Garfield Sobers, Rohan Kanhai and Basil Butcher all scoring heavily, they 'swept through the subcontinent on a flood tide of runs' (*Wisden*). Gupte paid a high price, 42 runs each, for his wickets, but he had little support at the other end, with nobody else taking more than five wickets in the series. In the first innings of the Second Test he took nine for 102 on Kanpur's jute matting, the first time a bowler had taken nine wickets in an innings for India. As he had taken the first seven wickets there was a time when it looked as if his performance might have been even more historic. And it probably would have been if Tamhane had not dropped Lance Gibbs, the one wicket that Gupte missed out on. Surprisingly the *Wisden* match report makes no reference to Gupte's historic feat.

Gupte toured England just once, with the 1959 Indian side that lost all five Tests. He was the side's leading wicket-taker with 95 in all matches. However, as he was familiar with English conditions, having played in the Lancashire League, and as the fine summer and consequent hard wickets should have suited him, his performance in the Tests - 17 wickets at 35 each - was a disappointment. Often used as a defensive stock bowler he never looked like a match-winner and seemed to lose heart, possibly because of the poor support he got from his fielders.

Gupte's Test career ended in unfortunate circumstances just over two years later after he had played in the Third Test against Ted Dexter's England side. A receptionist complained that Kripal Singh, Gupte's room-mate in the Delhi team hotel, had tried to make a date with her. A flimsy investigation was carried out and Gupte was reprimanded for not trying to stop Kripal Singh, and consequently omitted from the Indian tour of the West Indies that took place in early 1962. The disillusioned Gupte's first-class career was nearly over, although happily he was not totally forgotten by Indian cricket and a benefit match was held for him in Sharjah in 1982.

Having settled and worked in Trinidad, where he had met his wife, and where he played in three first-class matches, Fergie Gupte was suffering from diabetes when he died in Port of Spain in 2002.

Jim Laker

With great respect to Anil Kumble, the only other bowler to take a Test all-ten, Jim Laker's all-ten at Old Trafford in July 1956 is probably still the most famous bowling feat of all time. It is difficult to believe that there has ever been a better orthodox off-spinner (which precludes comparison with more unorthodox off-spinners such as Murali or Saqlain Mushtaq). He seemed to have everything. He spun the ball sharply, varied pace and flight consummately, was equally at home bowling over or round the wicket, and from a short relaxed run-up had a good balanced action which enabled him to maintain control at all times.

Born in Bradford, Yorkshire in 1922 (a city where he would take eight for 2 in a 1950 Test trial), Laker made a bit of a name for himself before the War in the Bradford League, but first really attracted attention playing cricket during war service in the Middle East having changed his bowling style from quickish to off spin. Before demobilisation he was billeted in South London and, joining Surrey, soon impressed and was chosen to tour the West Indies with Gubby Allen's side in 1947/48. However, there were a lot of good spinners around at the time and he did not become an England regular until 1956. Consequently, although he took 193 wickets in 46 Tests, he never took more than 18 wickets in a series apart from the spectacular 46 that he took in the 1956 Ashes series. Handicapped by an arthritic finger he retired at the end of 1959, although prompted by Trevor Bailey he returned to the game in 1962 as an amateur and played with some success for Essex. His final career tally was 1,944 wickets at 18.41 apiece. No post-war spinner has taken so many wickets at so low a cost. He was also a useful batsman with two centuries to his name.

Surrey v Australians, 1956

Kennington Oval, Kennington on 16, 17, 18 May 1956 (3-day match)
Toss won by Australians
Surrey won by ten wickets
Umpires: LH Gray, K McCanlis
Australians 259 (JC Laker 10-88) and 107 (GAR Lock 7-49); Surrey 347 (B Constable 109, IWG Johnson 6-168) and 20-0

Australians first innings

JW Burke	lbw b Laker	28
CC McDonald	c Swetman b Laker	89
KD Mackay	c Surridge b Laker	4
RN Harvey	c Constable b Laker	13
KR Miller	not out	57
+LV Maddocks	b Laker	12
RR Lindwall	b Laker	0
*IWG Johnson	c Swetman b Laker	0
AK Davidson	c May b Laker	21
WPA Crawford	b Laker	16
JW Wilson	c Swetman b Laker	4

Extras	(b 4, lb 8, nb 3)	15
Total	(all out, 107 overs)	259

Fall of wickets 1-62, 2-93, 3-124, 4-151, 5-173, 6-173, 7-175, 8-199, 9-217, 10-259

Surrey bowling: PJ Loader 15-4-30-0, WS Surridge 8-2-8-0, JC Laker 46-18-88-10, GAR Lock 33-12-100-0, DF Cox 5-0-18-0

Surrey: DGW Fletcher, TH Clark, B Constable, PBH May, KF Barrington, R Swetman (wk), DF Cox, JC Laker, WS Surridge (capt), GAR Lock, PJ Loader

At the end of the 1956 season many people would probably have given Laker the accolade of the best off-spinner ever. Remarkably however, at the beginning of the year, having played in only two of England's previous 16 Tests, he was still not even certain of his place in the national side. In a career that had started eight years before he had only played 24 times for England, taking a creditable, but not outstanding, 86 wickets.

Surrey were in the middle of a record-breaking seven successive seasons as County Champions, while the Australians were led by Victorian off-spinner Ian Johnson. Touring sides then really toured, and the visitors would eventually travel to all corners of Britain, playing 35 (mainly first-class) matches. By the time they came to The Oval in mid-May they had already played four first-class matches but were still looking for a win. In fact their first win against a county would not come until the beginning of July, although to be fair, in a dismally wet summer, many of their matches were badly affected by rain.

The match began on a grey, cold morning according to Peter West's book about the tour, although according to Alan Hill's biography of Laker it was 'a sweltering day'. The Australians saw off a Surrey opening attack lacking the injured Alec Bedser and then resisted Laker shakily for 40 minutes until, after 95 minutes and with the score 62, he switched to bowling round the wicket and immediately dismissed opener Jim Burke leg-before playing no shot. It was the highest partnership of the innings.

Burke's partner Colin McDonald, who had made 195 in his previous innings against Nottinghamshire, went on to top score with 89 before, at 151 for three, driving at Laker he was caught at the third attempt by juggling wicketkeeper Roy Swetman (standing in for Arthur McIntyre). After the openers went only Keith Miller resisted for long, but even this great cavalier was subdued for long spells as Laker took three wickets in the first two overs after tea, Ray Lindwall and Johnson both failing to score, to leave the Australians 175 for seven. The crowd had now built up to 10,000 as word got around that history might be made, and every wicket was heartily cheered. Alan Davidson and Pat Crawford countered with some lusty hitting, swinging Laker three times over the leg-side boundary, but at 217 for nine and with the incoming number eleven a 35-year-old slow left-armer Jack Wilson, whose eventual top-score in a 78-match career would be 19 not out, Laker's all-ten seemed inevitable. At the same score Miller gave a chance to Dennis Cox at cover off Tony Lock, which was fortunately, and probably with good intent, put down. It was a costly kindness because Miller then shepherded his partner whilst 42 runs were added before, to his great surprise, Wilson was adjudged caught behind to give Swetman his third victim, and the tiring Laker his all-ten. Starting at twenty past 12 and relieved only by lunch and tea he had bowled unchanged from the Pavilion End for four hours and 20 minutes. A few minutes later, in front of a cheering crowd, the ball with which he had achieved the feat was presented to him on the field by Surrey president Lord Tedder. The Club also gave him a cheque for £50.

Laker had scarcely bowled a loose ball. The pitch had been dry and dusty, but not unduly helpful, and five of his victims had fallen to the arm-ball. At the other end Lock had bristled ineffectively whilst conceding 100 runs. Laker's feat might never have happened. Having had a sleepless night after helping to nurse a sick daughter he only played after persuasion from his captain.

Led by Bernard Constable who made a steady 109, Surrey batted consistently to reach 347 just before the close of the second day. Laker did his bit with 43, including hitting Johnson for 16 in one over. After Laker's success Johnson was convinced that spin would do the same for the Australians. However, good bowler as he was, his slow flighty style was not best suited to English conditions, as evidenced by his figures: 60.3 overs six for 168. At the other end he was supported by 44 overs of left-arm spin from Alan Davidson who was on the way to becoming a great quick bowler, but as a spinner was no more than useful, and 19 overs from Wilson. Neither could match the turn extracted by Lock and Laker. The great Lindwall was given just two overs!

The Australians began well on the last morning in front of a large crowd hopeful of witnessing more history, but just before half past 12 with the score 56 Burke played too early at Lock and gave him a return catch which was jubilantly taken. McDonald had again batted well but half an hour later he went for 45, caught at second slip by Laker and an Australian collapse gathered momentum against a rampant Lock, supported by a cluster of close fielders. Lunch was taken with the score 89 for six and the innings was over 18 runs later at 2.40 pm leaving Surrey the formality of scoring twenty to win and become the first county to beat the Australians since 1912. This time Laker (two for 42) had played the supporting role to the fizzing left-arm spin of Lock who had been accorded the advantage of the, now apparently more helpful, Pavilion End. Lock had taken the first six wickets and so for a while an extraordinary double had seemed possible, until Laker broke the spell by dismissing Mackay leg-before offering no shot. (In 1939, 14-year-old Mackay, playing for Virginia State School against Sherwood State School, had taken all ten opposition wickets, and then scored 367 not out!) There was little rest for cricketers in those days: the Australians were playing Cambridge University next day, whilst Surrey travelled to Trent Bridge and lost heavily, off-spinner Ken Smales and Australian leg-spinner Bruce Dooland sharing 19 wickets!

England v Australia, 1956

Old Trafford, Manchester on 26, 27, 28, 30, 31 July 1956 (5-day match)
Toss won by England
England won by an innings and 170 runs
Umpires: DE Davies, FS Lee
England 459 (PE Richardson 104, DS Sheppard 113); Australia 84 (JC Laker 9-37) and 205 (JC Laker 10-53)

Australia second innings

CC McDonald	c Oakman b Laker	89
JW Burke	c Lock b Laker	33
RN Harvey	c Cowdrey b Laker	0
ID Craig	lbw b Laker	38
KD Mackay	c Oakman b Laker	0
KR Miller	b Laker	0
RG Archer	c Oakman b Laker	0
R Benaud	b Laker	18
RR Lindwall	c Lock b Laker	8
*IWG Johnson	not out	1
+LV Maddocks	lbw b Laker	2
Extras	(b 12, lb 4)	16
Total	(all out, 150.2 overs)	205

Fall of wickets 1-28, 2-55, 3-114, 4-124, 5-130, 6-130, 7-181, 8-198, 9-203, 10-205

England bowling: JB Statham 16-10-15-0, TE Bailey 20-8-31-0, JC Laker 51.2-23-53-10, GAR Lock 55-30-69-0, ASM Oakman 8-3-21-0

England: PE Richardson, MC Cowdrey, DS Sheppard, PBH May (capt), TE Bailey, C Washbrook, ASM Oakman, TG Evans (wk), JC Laker, GAR Lock, JB Statham

Laker's all-ten at The Oval was completed in a day. His all-ten at Old Trafford just over two months later took a bit longer, starting on Friday afternoon and finishing four days later as Manchester's weather lived up to reputation. The last Ashes match at the ground to produce a result had been in 1905. The series stood one all: after a draw at Trent Bridge Australia had won at Lord's, and Lock and Laker had bowled England to victory at Headingley. The pitch apparently breaking up early, the Australians weren't best pleased by the conditions at Old Trafford but England had no complaints reaching 459 on the second day, with Peter Richardson making his first Test century and the Reverend David Sheppard his second. Johnson's only consolation was that Cyril Washbrook became his hundredth Test victim. With Colin Cowdrey, Peter May, and Trevor Bailey completing the top order, the first five batsmen were all amateurs, a throwback to the Golden Age. It was a good series for the selectors: Cyril Washbrook, recalled after five years, had turned the series with a fighting 98 in the Third Test; Sheppard, who had given up regular cricket to take Holy Orders, was returning for the Fourth Test having played only four matches in 1956; and Denis Compton would be brought back successfully for the Fifth having recovered from a winter knee operation.

The Old Trafford pitch had already shown evidence of turn, and the Australians viewed with concern the clouds of dust enveloping it as the groundstaff swept it between innings (although much of this was of course from the footholds). They began well enough in their first innings on Friday afternoon, reaching 48 without loss before the game changed dramatically when Laker switched to the Stretford End, from where he would take all his wickets. Just before four o'clock a sharply turning ball found the edge of McDonald's bat and Lock picked up the Victorian at backward short leg. Four balls later Laker pitched a ball on left-hander Neil Harvey's leg stump that clipped off. Laker reckoned that that one ball went a long way to winning the match. Tea came with the Australians in difficulties at 62 for two, but nobody was prepared for the capitulation that followed as Laker took seven wickets for 8 runs in 22 balls. His nine for 37 was a short-lived Ashes record. He had bowled brilliantly but, apart from the openers, none of the Australians demonstrated the technique or application needed to counter a class off-spinner in helpful conditions. Lock, who had picked up his only wicket, Burke caught at slip, from the first ball after tea, was getting used to toiling with little reward while Laker prospered at the other end.

Following on Australia again began well, closing at 53 for one. The wicket that fell was neither of the openers. With the score 28 McDonald, hit on the knee by Statham earlier in the match, limped off for attention. He was replaced by Harvey who hit his first ball, a rare Laker full toss, straight to Cowdrey at short midwicket. The great left-hander, having made a same-day pair, threw his bat in the air in despair. Australia were facing a three-day defeat, but the weather had other ideas. Manchester was hit by a violent storm over Friday night and less than an hour's play was possible next day. England at least made some progress, the obdurate Burke, who had failed to add to his overnight 33, edging to Lock at leg slip. In a series in which no Australian made a century Burke was the only one who averaged 30 (just), and as he also scored more first-class runs than any other tourist *Wisden* made him one of its Cricketers of the Year. In February 1979 the 48-year-old Burke added his name to the tragically long list of first-class cricketers who have taken their own lives.

With more wind and rain once again only an hour's play was possible on Monday, in conditions so bad that it was necessary to use heavily weighted bails. Australia had still lost only two wickets; any more rain and on an uncovered pitch the chances of play and a home victory would be gone. Fortunately, at least for England, play started only ten minutes late on the final day. McDonald and Ian Craig were still together at lunch, Australia 112 for two and four hours left, and then the sun finally came out and enlivened a damp pitch. Craig went first, leg-before on the back foot after nearly four and a half hours resolute defence. Just 21, Craig was already on his second England tour. One of a number of batsmen unfortunate to be labelled 'the new Bradman', he had a useful career but had retired by the time he was 27.

 A disastrous half hour then left Australia 130 for six, Mackay (again), Miller and Archer all making ducks, but then the sun disappeared once more, the pitch eased, and with the usually aggressive Benaud and McDonald still there at tea, England were worried again. Benaud's pugnacious 97 at Lord's was Australia's highest score of the series. This time he was in defensive mode. However, the sun reappeared and at 181 McDonald's great vigil was finally ended, a lifting off break providing Sussex's 6 foot 5 inch Alan Oakman at short leg with his fifth catch of the match. This was the second time in the summer that the courageous McDonald had top scored with 89 whilst Laker ran through his team-mates. Could Laker get another all-ten? With Johnson complaining about the sawdust blowing in his eyes the Australians were time-wasting ingeniously, and there was no let up at the other end from the attacking Lock. Benaud and Lindwall who had resisted for 105 and 40 minutes respectively, were eventually prised out and just before five thirty, and with an hour to go, Laker hitched up his trousers and licked his fingers for the umpteenth time before jogging in to Len Maddocks who, hemmed in by three short legs, fatefully played back and umpire Frank Lee raised his index finger. Laker's final twisted-ankle appeal is one of cricket's most famous images. Outwardly unemotional as ever, he then slung his jersey over his shoulder, exchanged a few handshakes and strolled off. They knew how to celebrate in those days.

So many new world records: 19 wickets in a match, all-ten in a Test innings, all-ten twice in a season and an eventual Ashes record 46 wickets in a series. Poor Lock, who himself had taken an all-ten at Blackheath earlier in the month, had repeatedly beaten the bat, but with no luck. And of course two other greats, Brian Statham and Trevor Bailey, also had nothing to show for their labours.

Laker drove south after the match. He was playing for Surrey at The Oval next day. His opponents - the Australians! In seven matches that year he would take 63 wickets against them. Famously he stopped on the way back for a beer and sandwich and, whilst other customers discussed the Test, nobody recognised him.

It's fair to say that the Australians, who had come to Britain with a side picked to counter the menace of Frank Tyson whose pace had devastated them eighteen months before, were a weak batting side who on uncovered pitches didn't play off spin well. Laker himself thought that his best ever bowling had been his five for 88 from 65 overs in gruelling Bombay heat for the Commonwealth XI against a powerful Indian batting line-up in December 1950.

Feeling hard done by the conditions that they encountered in 1956, the Australians vowed revenge on Laker when England came out in 1958/59 to play on their pitches. However, although Australia won the series easily, their batsmen never got on top of Laker who finished England's leading bowler with 15 wickets at 21.20 in four Tests.

Laker was unafraid to air grievances and in 1960 his, ghost-written, second autobiography *Over to Me* caused considerable offence to the establishment, and his honorary MCC and Surrey memberships were withdrawn. They were later restored and he would become Chairman of Surrey's Cricket Committee. He also became a popular and knowledgeable cricket commentator with a great clarity of expression. Jim Laker died in April 1986, following complications after what should have been a minor operation. His ashes were scattered at The Oval. According to Alan Hill 'The deceptively aloof manner concealed a warm heart and a generous man'.

Ken Smales

County Championship

Erinoid Ground, Stroud on 9, 11, 12 June 1956 (3-day match)
Toss won by Nottinghamshire
Gloucestershire won by nine wickets
Umpires: LH Gray, K McCanlis
Nottinghamshire 122 and 137 (FP McHugh 6-41); Gloucestershire 214 (K Smales 10-66) and 46-1

Gloucestershire first innings

*GM Emmett	b Smales	33
W Knightley-Smith	c Rowe b Smales	34
RB Nicholls	c and b Smales	15
JF Crapp	c Winfield b Smales	0
+P Rochford	b Smales	2
CA Milton	not out	70
JB Mortimore	c Poole b Smales	45
DR Smith	lbw b Smales	0
BD Wells	lbw b Smales	4
C Cook	c and b Smales	0
FP McHugh	b Smales	0
Extras	(b 5, lb 5, nb 1)	11
Total	all out, 103.3 overs)	214

Fall of wickets 1-45, 2-76, 3-76, 4-78, 5-95, 6-198, 7-200, 8-204, 9-206, 10-214

Nottinghamshire bowling: AK Walker 25-8-50-0, A Jepson 8-3-20-0, B Dooland 29-13-67-0, K Smales 41.3-20-66-10

Nottinghamshire: RT Simpson (capt), RJ Giles, HM Winfield, CJ Poole, FW Stocks, EJ Martin, B Dooland, AK Walker, K Smales, A Jepson, EJ Rowe (wk)

Off-spinner Ken Smales was the 'other bowler' to take all-ten in 1956. His career didn't hit the heights achieved by the illustrious Surrey spin twins, but he is the only bowler to have performed the feat for Nottinghamshire, and he would achieve considerable renown in another sporting field.

Like Laker, Smales was a Yorkshireman who found fame outside his county of birth. Born in 1927 he was spotted by Yorkshire after playing for his home club Horsforth and then Keighley. But competition for places was great, and after 13 matches and 22 wickets for Yorkshire he moved to Nottinghamshire in 1951, not an obviously good career move given the then-famed unresponsiveness of Trent Bridge pitches. Nottinghamshire had struggled since the War: 15th in 1950, bottom of the Championship in 1951, reinforcements were obviously needed, especially bowlers. At the time there was an unofficial rule that allowed only players born in the county, or with long associations with it, to play for Nottinghamshire. In view of their parlous position the Committee decided to abandon the rule, and Smales was the first cricketer to be engaged following this change of heart. He initially performed steadily without setting the world alight, and then in 1955 took 117 wickets. No doubt Nottinghamshire's Australian import Bruce Dooland was glad of the help. The previous year he had taken 179 wickets in the Championship, the rest of the attack taking 210 between them. In five years in England Dooland would take 805 wickets with his quickish wrist spin (and do the double twice) and perform wonders in rejuvenating his adopted county.

The Erinoid at Stroud was a small, narrow ground in hilly terrain, laid out after the War thanks to the efforts of the managing director of the plastic-manufacturing company after which it is named. The match was its first-class debut and a grand occasion, attracting a good crowd. Local firms helped provide seating, a band played, the local MP attended, and there was a dance in the evening. Stroud would eventually host 14 first-class matches. Unfortunately the pitch wasn't that good and many of them didn't last the distance, and with falling attendances the county called it a day after 1963. A few years later the ground had disappeared under concrete.

Nottinghamshire were on a southern tour which included visits to Gravesend, Cardiff and Bath. They would finish eighth in the Championship, a position they had only bettered once since the War. Twelfth the previous summer, the home team would do much better, finishing third just behind runners-up Lancashire. In a wet summer they were particularly indebted to Sam Cook's left-arm spin and the off breaks of Bomber Wells. Unfortunately their best batsman Tom Graveney was absent on Test match duty.

In cold damp conditions Nottinghamshire never recovered from the early loss of their leading batsman, and captain, Reg Simpson, brilliantly run out from short midwicket by Arthur Milton. Gloucestershire began their reply well against Arthur Jepson and Alan Walker (a compatriot of Dooland, who later in the month would take four wickets in four balls against Leicestershire with his left-arm pace). Nobody has surpassed 40-year-old Jepson's eventual post-war total of 968 wickets for the county, but he had often had little experienced new-ball support and Smales himself sometimes had to help out at the other end.

The introduction of spin changed things, Smales causing Gloucestershire's 43-year-old captain George Emmett to play on with the score 45. Bill Knightley-Smith was joined by Ron Nicholls and, with the pair carefully taking the score to 76 just before the close, Gloucestershire could feel satisfied with their day's work. However, Smales struck again, tempting Nicholls into hitting a return catch. Nicholls would eventually play no fewer than 534 first-class matches, and remarkably every one was for Gloucestershire. Smales wasn't finished for the day yet: he had Cornish left-hander Jack Crapp, another long-serving 43-year-old, caught at short leg and then bowled nightwatchman, and fellow Yorkshireman, Peter Rochford. The home side closed precariously at 78 for four.

Although Smales had overnight figures of four for 12, with Dooland bowling at the other end he can hardly have dreamt of an all-ten. However, that is what happened on the second day, although not before a considerable fight by Gloucestershire's batsmen. The weather had improved and the Monday crowd numbered some two thousand. Knightley-Smith went quickly, caught by wicketkeeper Eddie Rowe. A couple more wickets and Notts would be through to a very weak tail which comprised three 'batsmen', Wells, Cook and Yorkshireman Frank McHugh, who, in a combined career total of 903 first-class matches, would accumulate one fifty between them. However before Smales could get at them, Arthur Milton and John Mortimore came together in a sixth wicket partnership of 103 that contributed considerably to eventual victory. Once Mortimore went however the Gloucestershire tail didn't disappoint, Smales sweeping it away without help from the field while Milton, whose Test debut was still two years away, hit ten fours in his undefeated 70. Smales, flighting the ball skilfully, had bowled with great accuracy, conceding fewer than two runs an over. Although the slowish pitch didn't help him the dangerous Dooland might have prevented his all-ten, but he had a number of catches dropped. After Giffen, Mailey and Graveney, Smales had become the fourth bowler to pay 66 runs for his all-ten.

There was however to be no happy ending for Smales as, despite a classy 70 by Simpson, Notts failed again and Gloucestershire completed victory before lunch on the third day. The match had marked the first-class debut, with pen and pencil, for the *Stroud News*, of a young Frank Keating, who would later become an eminent and much-admired sports journalist. He later recalled Jack Crapp's less-than-complimentary comments about the pitch. Smales must have thought that he was in line for Brylcreem's £100 award for the best bowling of the season. It was not to be. Tony Lock and then Jim Laker pipped him; but he didn't lose out too much because wisely he had covered himself at the bookmakers. Remarkably, umpires Laurie Gray and Kenneth McCanlis had also stood together the previous month when Jim Laker had rolled over the Australians. And having watched Trevor Bailey's all-ten in 1949, McCanlis, in his last Championship season, had completed his hat-trick.

Sixty years later Frank McHugh recalled that on seeing him come in at number eleven Smales had told him that he realised that he had a reasonable chance of getting all-ten. It was a shrewd judgement: McHugh would finish his 95-match career with significantly fewer runs, just 179 at an average of 2.63, than his 276 wickets. As McHugh took eight wickets in the match with his fast-medium bowling and Freddie Stocks the only wicket that fell in Gloucestershire's second innings, 19 of the 31 wickets that fell in the match were taken by Yorkshire exiles. In his next match, back in his own county, McHugh had match figures of eleven for 112. Remarkably, struck down by tuberculosis, it was to be his last first-class match. As he also made a pair and was part of a Bob Appleyard hat-trick, it was a final match to remember.

Smales only took 28 wickets in his next 19 matches but then in the return with Gloucestershire at Trent Bridge he had another inspired spell, taking seven for 48 in the visitors' first innings of a match that was eventually drawn.

Smales retired after the 1958 season with a final career total of 389 wickets at 31 runs each, to become assistant secretary of Nottingham Forest Football Club (FA cup-winners in 1959), although he continued to play club cricket. *Wisden* described his retirement as a severe loss. Eventually serving Forest for over 35 years, he would become full-time secretary three years later, a position he held during the club's great years under manager Brian Clough. He put his signature to many famous transfers including that of Trevor Francis, Britain's first million pound footballer. In 1991 he published a club history *Forest: the first 125 years*. He also ran a fascinating website about the club's history. He died in Cornwall in 2015.

Tony Lock

Surrey v Kent, 1956
County Championship

The Rectory Field, Blackheath on 7, 9, 10 July 1956 (3-day match)
Surrey won by an innings and 173 runs
Umpires: H Elliott, WFF Price
Surrey 404-4 dec (TH Clark 191, PBH May 128 not out); Kent 101 (GAR Lock 6-29) and 130 (GAR Lock 10-54)

Kent second innings

AH Phebey	b Lock	12
MC Cowdrey	lbw b Lock	8
RC Wilson	b Lock	32
+TG Evans	c and b Lock	19
AE Fagg	c AV Bedser b Lock	21
AL Dixon	b Lock	2
DG Ufton	not out	17
F Ridgway	c Stewart b Lock	7
DJ Halfyard	c Barrington b Lock	0
JCT Page	b Lock	0
*DVP Wright	b Lock	0
Extras	(b 6, lb 5, nb 1)	12
Total	(all out, 71.1 overs)	130

Fall of wickets 1-20, 2-29, 3-60, 4-84, 5-101, 6-104, 7-130, 8-130, 9-130, 10-130

Surrey bowling: PJ Loader 8-3-7-0, AV Bedser 16-5-41-0, GAR Lock 29.1-18-54-10, EA Bedser 18-10-16-0

Surrey: TH Clark, MJ Stewart, KF Barrington, PBH May, REC Pratt, EA Bedser, R Swetman (wk), WS Surridge (capt), GAR Lock, AV Bedser, PJ Loader

Tony Lock might have been a left-arm slow(ish) bowler, but he had a fast bowler's temperament. 'Always in the game', the title of an article written about him for the *Playfair Cricket Monthly* by Neville Cardus, aptly sums up his career, the most remarkable feature of which was that he reinvented himself as a bowler not once (a difficult enough feat) but twice, achieving record-breaking figures after both reincarnations. If that wasn't enough, he was one of the greatest close fielders ever, a useful batsman and, later in his career, inspired Leicestershire and Western Australia to levels of achievement never attained before, both by his forceful captaincy and his own performances on the field.

Born in Limpsfield, Surrey in 1929 he made his first-class debut against Kent just a week after his 17th birthday – still Surrey's youngest-ever player. Although he didn't take any wickets his first over was a maiden. Appropriately he also took the first of many brilliant catches, diving at backward short leg to pick up Arthur Phebey from an Alf Gover bouncer. After National Service Lock became a Surrey regular. A flighty bowler with minimal spin he had been doing well enough, but it was clear that he needed to be more penetrative to reach the next level and in 1952 a new Tony Lock returned to The Oval. Now spinning the ball sharply at a pace approaching medium, if his stock ball didn't do the trick he could unleash a lethal faster ball. The transformation came about because Lock spent his winters coaching at Alf Gover's South London indoor cricket school. It had a low roof and so he had to lower his arm and push the ball through. This enabled him to impart more spin, albeit with a changed action that now caused considerable concern, especially when he bowled his quicker one. The effect was immediate. A first Test cap soon followed and by early June 1956, aged 26 years 11 months, he took his 1,000th wicket. Only fellow Surrey bowlers George Lohmann and Tom Richardson, and Yorkshire's Wilfred Rhodes, had achieved this feat at a younger age. Later in the month he took ten wickets in the match against Kent at The Oval. By a quirk of the fixtures, which I'm not sure the Kent batsmen appreciated, the return was at Blackheath a week later.

Kent had been one of the weakest counties for a number of seasons: in 1956 only Leicestershire would finish below them. They were captained by 42-year-old England leg-spinner Doug Wright who was nearing the end of a long and successful career. The Rectory Field, Blackheath in south-east London had been hosting first-class cricket since 1887, usually one match a season, and usually Kent against neighbours Surrey. The ground lost its county cricket status after 1971 because the facilities for players, spectators, and their cars were not considered up to modern requirements. In its early years a number of England rugby internationals were played there and the ground is still the home of Blackheath Rugby Club.

In excellent conditions on the first day Surrey made 404 for four in 103 overs, mainly thanks to opener Tom Clark who, off driving crisply, made a career-best 191, and England captain Peter May who was 128 not out at the close. Clark made 190 in his next innings, against Gloucestershire, but never made a double century. Colin Cowdrey, a promising leg-spinner in his youth, conceded just three runs in his only over of the season. After weekend rain Stuart Surridge declared first thing on Monday morning. Kent's task was fairly hopeless and by the end of the day they had lost 16 wickets. They began well enough, reaching 55 before Lock bowled Arthur Phebey for 22. Cowdrey, the other opener, who eventually top scored with a fighting 49, was going in first because England needed him to do so, although it was a position he disliked, and the selectors would eventually decide that his talents were usually better employed in the middle order. Three years later Cowdrey, by now county captain, would make 250 against Essex at Blackheath, his highest-ever score in England. With Lock taking six wickets Kent struggled to three figures in their first innings and were batting again soon after lunch. Although Kent had batted poorly, Lock had had to work hard for his wickets, using his extra pace to extract life from a pitch that was taking spin only slowly.

Kent batted no better the second time around, only Bob Wilson and Arthur Fagg reaching twenty. England wicketkeeper Godfrey Evans batted at number four and made 19 before he hit a return catch to Lock, who would eventually take a remarkable 202 catches off his own bowling, a total equalled by J.C.White and exceeded only by W.G.Grace with 222. When Lock bowled Alan Dixon with the score 104 Stuart Surridge had hopes of a day off and claimed the extra half-hour. However, Derek Ufton and Fred Ridgway held on until the close which came with the score 128 for six and with Lock having taken all six for 54 in 26 overs (and twelve for 83 in 47 overs in the day). Ufton was Evans' understudy behind the stumps, but was playing as a batsman. A fine footballer, he played centre half for Charlton Athletic and had been capped once by England. To bowl at the other end Surrey had a choice of Eric Bedser, a very capable off-spinning deputy for Jim Laker (who was resting a sore spinning finger), the great Alec Bedser, and fast bowler Peter Loader, who had taken nine for 28 in Kent's first innings at Blackheath three years before (the previous best figures on the ground), and so Lock's all-ten was not a foregone conclusion. Whatever happened, the match obviously wasn't going to last much longer and the 100 or so spectators who turned up on Tuesday saw only 25 minutes cricket, although they at least had the compensation of seeing history made. Ufton (bowled by Lock for a duck in the first innings) added two to his overnight score and then, with Loader carefully bowling wide at the other end, Lock swept away the last four wickets without further score on a pitch that was even more difficult than the day before. Ridgway, the first to go, was caught by Micky Stewart, a future Charlton footballer, future Surrey captain, and future holder of the record for most career catches for the county. Having been involved in three all-tens as a player (Bestwick, Mitchell, Smailes) umpire Harry Elliott had now been involved in a fourth.

Lock had become the first bowler to take 16 wickets in a match for Surrey. Martin Bicknell has since repeated the feat (at Guildford in 2000), but at a greater cost. Although the spectators stood and clapped Lock back into the pavilion, the lack of a decent crowd meant that the usual level of excitement associated with an all-ten was missing. Four years later at Guildford against a strong Oxford University batting side Lock would nearly do it again, taking the first nine second-innings wickets before Alec Bedser bowled the last man. As the last wicket partnership had put on 21, perhaps captain Bedser had decided enough was enough?

Lock continued to take wickets in large numbers, in 1957 becoming the last bowler to take 200 in a season. And then at the end of the 1958/59 MCC Australasian tour he saw a slow motion film of his action. The throwing controversy was at its height and shocked by what he saw he knew he had to change, again. With his remodelled action he would become a left-arm spinner in the classical mould, using both spin and flight and able to perform successfully in all conditions.

Lock's last season with Surrey was 1963. Emigrating to Perth he played for Western Australia and, appointed captain in 1967/68, led them to the Sheffield Shield title for the first time since they began competing on equal terms with the other states. In nine seasons, before retiring after 1970/71, he took 316 wickets, a then-state record. And he was not yet finished with English cricket, returning to play for and captain Leicestershire for just over two seasons. His short stay was a great success: besides taking 272 wickets he led the county to third in the Championship in 1967, a position they had only previously achieved once, in 1953.

The following winter Lock's career took another twist. Fourteen years after his last Test in the West Indies he played two more there, replacing Fred Titmus who had lost four toes in a boating accident. In the final Test he made a belligerent 89, his best ever first-class score and his third Test fifty, all of which had been made against powerful West Indies attacks.

Lock's final career record was outstanding: 2,844 wickets at 19.23, a total exceeded by only seven bowlers, of whom only Derek Shackleton began his career after the Second World War; 1,713 wickets for Surrey, a total only exceeded by Tom Richardson; 174 Test wickets - only one English spinner, Jim Laker, had taken more; 10,342 runs with the bat - nobody has scored so many runs without a century; and 830 catches - only Frank Woolley and WG Grace took more.

After leaving Leicestershire, Lock returned Down Under and became a naturalised Australian. As well as coaching in Perth, Lock was employed as a cricket professional at Mill Hill School in north London. Dying in Perth in March 1995 his final years saw much sadness. Tried and acquitted of indecent assault, he was re-arrested on a second offence but the charge was eventually dropped. Whilst this was going on he was diagnosed with cancer, and had to bear the loss of his wife. It was a tragic end to the life of a wholehearted cricketer.

Premangsu Chatterjee

Bengal v Assam, 1956/57
Ranji Trophy

National Sports Council of Assam Ground, Jorhat on 26, 27, 28, 29 January 1957 (4-day match)
Bengal won by an innings and 206 runs
Bengal 505 (SK Shome 122, SK Girdhari 7-157); Assam 54 (PM Chatterjee 10-20) and 245 (SK Girdhari 100, DG Phadkar 7-65)

Assam first innings

A Guha Roy	c Shome b Chatterjee	4
KK Baishya	lbw b Chatterjee	1
MP Barua	b Chatterjee	2
*D Barua	lbw b Chatterjee	2
A Hazarika	b Chatterjee	0
SK Girdhari	lbw b Chatterjee	14
S Gogoi	b Chatterjee	4
TK Barua	b Chatterjee	5
A Rajbanshi	b Chatterjee	0
+M Talukdar	not out	2
G Das	b Chatterjee	0
Extras		20
Total	(all out, 38 overs)	54

Fall of wickets 1-4, 2-8, 3-12, 4-12, 5-15, 6-29, 7-45, 8-45, 9-54, 10-54

Bengal bowling: PM Chatterjee 19-11-20-10, DG Phadkar 14-12-10-0, KK Biswas 4-2-4-0, SK Shome 1-1-0-0

Bengal: P Roy (capt), SM Basu Thakur, R Sanyal, DG Phadkar, PK Sen (wk), RM Chanda, K Mitter, SK Shome, SN Ghoshal, KK Biswas, PM Chatterjee

Premangsu Chatterjee's ten for 20 is statistically the third best bowling performance ever in first-class cricket, and the best ever outside the UK. He was a slim, bespectacled left-armer who bowled medium-pace inswing, alternated with a ball that moved away off the pitch. He could also slow down and bowl useful spinners.

Born in Cuttack, Orissa, Chatterjee captained Calcutta University, and then as a 19-year-old made a promising first-class debut in 1947 with 14 wickets in his first two matches. He was sent to Alf Gover's Cricket School in London in 1952, and whilst in England he played as an amateur for Royton in the Central Lancashire League, and received an offer to turn professional with Worcestershire. However, by the end of 1955 his first-class career had still been only a modest one: 48 wickets in 15 matches. But the 1955/56 season saw him enter the record books when, playing for Bengal against Madhya Pradesh at Eden Gardens, Calcutta, he became the first bowler to take 15 wickets in a Ranji Trophy match. This was the beginning of a purple patch that saw Chatterjee take 32 wickets in three games. In his next match, the Trophy final against a strong Bombay side, for whom the prolific Test batsman Polly Umrigar made a century, he took seven first innings wickets for 101 runs from 52 overs. And then came more history in his next match the following season.

The national championship of India, the Ranji Trophy had been launched in 1934/35 in memory of the great batsman K.S.Ranjitsinhji who had died in April 1933. Teams competed on a zonal basis, the winners of each group then contesting for the Trophy on a knockout basis. Bombay would win the tournament in 1956/57 and monopolise it for the next 20 years. Bengal, led by India's Pankaj Roy, had won the Trophy just once, 18 years before, as well as being runners-up four times. Assam, in north-east India, generally one of the weaker states, have never won the Trophy.

The Jorhat cricket ground was surrounded by grass banks and large leafy trees. The trees cast long shadows later in the day and so close of play was usually 4.30 pm. The ground would host ten first-class matches between 1953 and 1974, and Assam would lose all ten.

Given that they really only had two bowlers Assam must have been quite pleased to take the first seven Bengal wickets for 257. Unfortunately the visitors' tail then wagged to good effect and, mainly thanks to Sunit Shome, who extended his only ever fifty to 122, batting nearly two days they reached 505 all out, the highest-ever total on the ground. The two aforesaid bowlers were Aswani Rajbanshi (62.4 overs, three for 213) and Surjuram Girdhari (72 overs, seven for 157). Given that he entrusted them with only 29 overs, the Assam captain clearly had little faith in the five other bowlers who constituted his 'attack'!

Assam's first innings then lasted just 38 overs and if it hadn't been for 20 extras, the details of which are not recorded, the final total would have been even sorrier. After his prodigious spell with the ball off-spinner Girdhari, down to bat at No. 6, must have been hoping for a rest. However it was not to be and he was soon back on the field again, going in with the score 12 for four. Making 14 he was the only batsman who passed five, and he helped effect what might be seen as some sort of recovery. Chatterjee's final victim was Gangaram Das. Having bowled 11 wicketless overs he had now begun his three-match first-class career with a duck, albeit that it had contributed to a piece of cricket history.

Bowling six batsmen and trapping three in front Chatterjee had come close to emulating Wisden and Hollies in taking all-ten without help from the field. It is stating the obvious to say that the Assam batting wasn't very strong. None of the side would play Test cricket, and in an eventual total of 202 first-class appearances its members would make just six centuries, and four of these were by Girdhari. Three were making their first-class debuts. For Siba Gogoi, who didn't bowl, it was his only match. And 54 was a score Assam would fail to better four times in their ten matches at the ground. Given all this it is surprising that, while Chatterjee bowled unchanged, at the other end Dattu Phadkar had bowled 14 overs without reward. Medium pacer Phadkar was a genuine allrounder who had been a mainstay of the Indian side for a decade after the War. He finished his career with 62 Test wickets, a total exceeded at the time by only three other Indians.

Assam followed on 451 runs behind. They were never going to get close to saving the match, but at least 245 was a respectable score. K.K. Baishya made 42 and extras added a useful 43, but the main contribution came again from the hardworking Girdhari who made exactly 100 and whose impressive, almost single-handed allround performance had unfortunately been in a losing cause. The only Assam batsman to score a century on the ground, Girdhari was coming towards the end of a 19-year, 48-match career that had begun in 1940. His best however was yet to come. In his next match, against Orissa, he scored 229 not out, and then two years later, again against Orissa, but now playing for Bengal, he had first-innings figures of six for 37 and then followed this by scoring 129 not out. Curiously, after his record-breaking first-innings performance, Chatterjee bowled 28 overs in Assam's second innings without taking any wickets, although he did take a couple of catches. The damage was done this time by Phadkar's seven for 65.

Chatterjee's figures were of course a Ranji Trophy record, beating the previous record which had stood for just two months since Vasant Ranjane, bowling fast-medium, had taken nine for 35 for Maharashtra against Saurashtra. Unlike Chatterjee who had made his first-class debut ten years before, it was 19-year-old Ranjane's first match. And his performance might have been even more remarkable if Bapu Nadkarni hadn't taken the last wicket after Ranjane had taken the first nine and prevented him becoming the second bowler, after Albert Moss, to take an all-ten on debut.

Indian Cricket made Chatterjee one its five Cricketers of the Year. He was in good company. The other four were Australians Richie Benaud, Jim Burke, Neil Harvey and Ray Lindwall who had all impressed in the three Tests that they had played on the way back from their unsuccessful tour of Britain.

After the group stage, Bengal qualified for the Ranji Trophy semi-final where they came up against Services at Eden Gardens. Unfortunately rain interfered and the match was decided on the toss of a coin, won by Services, an unlucky outcome for Bengal who had made 302 for four (Pankaj Roy 159 not out) in response to Services' 399 (Chatterjee four for 141 from 61 overs) and were thus denied the chance of a victory on first innings, which would have taken them through. It would be over 30 years before they won the Trophy for a second time.

Chatterjee played his last first-class match in January 1960. The previous season had been his most prolific (32 wickets in six matches) and included figures of seven for 17 in a zonal Ranji Trophy match against Bihar and, in the Final, first-innings figures, in an eventual losing cause, of six for 76 against Bombay. In a 13-year career he only played 32 matches, but his record of 134 wickets at 17.75 runs apiece is a creditable one. He might have played more first-class cricket but for the dictates of his professional career. He served as a college professor and university examiner before going to England, where he did a postgraduate course in personnel management at Manchester University, returning to India to become Industrial Relations Officer with Reckitt and Colman.

Chatterjee died in Kolkata in 2011 aged nearly 84. In 2005 he had received the Kartick Bose Lifetime Achievement Award from the Cricket Association of Bengal.

Jack Bannister

Warwickshire v Combined Services, 1959

Mitchell's and Butler's Ground, Birmingham on 27, 28 May 1959 (3-day match)
Toss won by Warwickshire
Warwickshire won by nine wickets
Umpires: D Davies, N Oldfield
Warwickshire 328-4 dec (WJP Stewart 151) and 17-1; Combined Services 114 (JD Bannister 10-41) and 229

Combined Services first innings

A Jones	c Khalid Ibadulla b Bannister	20
B Roe	c Hitchcock b Bannister	10
DS Williams	c Fox b Bannister	0
RJ Langridge	c Fox b Bannister	4
*GG Tordoff	lbw b Bannister	15
EMP Hardy	c Cartwright b Bannister	0
JHG Deighton	c Carter b Bannister	0
+J Fawkes	c Khalid Ibadulla b Bannister	4
PJ Phelan	c Fox b Bannister	41
D Meakin	not out	14
RL Pratt	c Khalid Ibadulla b Bannister	0
Extras	(b 4, lb 1, w 1)	6
Total	(all out, 46.3 overs)	114

Fall of wickets 1-25, 2-27, 3-32, 4-35, 5-39, 6-47, 7-50, 8-68, 9-114, 10-114

Warwickshire bowling: JD Bannister 23.3-11-41-10, RG Carter 12-2-31-0, TW Cartwright 2-1-4-0, Khalid Ibadulla 9-4-32-0

Warwickshire: Khalid Ibadulla, WJP Stewart, TW Cartwright, BE Fletcher, RE Hitchcock, MJK Smith (capt), WB Bridge, GH Hill, JG Fox (wk), JD Bannister, RG Carter

Jack Bannister spent a lifetime in cricket. After National Service, and three seasons with Mitchells and Butlers in the Birmingham League, Wolverhampton-born Bannister's first-class career began at Swansea in August 1950 three days after his 20th birthday. When it finished 18 years later all but six of his 374 matches had been for Warwickshire, and his fast-medium bowling had brought him 1,181 wickets for the county, a total only exceeded, just, by Sydney Santall's pre-First World War medium pace and, of course by a considerably larger margin, by Eric Hollies' wrist spin.

Between the Wars the armed services separately played a number of first-class matches. A combined team also occasionally came together, but after the Second World War it played more regularly, competing in another 57 matches until 1964, by which time the end of National Service had meant the end of a steady supply of promising young cricketers into the forces, many of whom would go on to shine for county or country. In addition to the counties, Combined Services sometimes played Oxford and Cambridge

Universties or the tourists, as well as meeting the Public Schools annually at Lord's (non-first-class), a match which must have had a slight element of Players versus Gentlemen about it. Although they fielded decent teams they weren't usually a match for their more experienced opponents and won just six matches (Northants, Glamorgan twice and Worcestershire three times) after the War, and none after 1952. They mostly met their opposition away, but if not, 'home' was military grounds at Portsmouth, Aldershot, Gillingham, Catterick, or Uxbridge.

Bannister soon established himself in the Warwickshire side but back injury threatened his career. After remodelling his action he slowly regained form, but competition for places in the side had intensified and by the time of the Combined Services match at the end of May 1959 he had played just one Championship match in the season. In a glorious summer Warwickshire captain Mike Smith was to become the first batsman in ten years to score 3,000 runs in a season and, against expectations, Warwickshire rose to fourth in the Championship, only 20 points behind Yorkshire who had finally broken Surrey's seven-year hold on the title.

Mitchells and Butlers was a local brewery. The ground was familiar territory for Bannister. Having hosted first-class cricket during the 1930s it had dropped off the circuit after the War before returning briefly in 1957. The Services were led by Yorkshireman Lieutenant-Commander Gerry Tordoff, a talented amateur sportsman who had also played for Cambridge University and Somerset. In 1955 the navy had allowed him to answer Somerset's call for an amateur captain. However the venture was not a success. They finished in last place (for the fourth successive season!) and he returned to the navy, playing for the Services until 1962. The Combined Services team was not a strong one. Four of the side never played first-class county cricket. All four were making their first-class debuts (including England rugby international Evan Hardy for whom it was his only only match).

On the opening day the Services' attack was put to the sword by the Warwickshire batsmen, especially by opener Jim Stewart who scored a run-a-minute 151. He hit five sixes, a modest total for someone who two months later would clear the boundary 17 times in the match against Lancashire at Blackpool. After an early declaration the Services, struggling against Bannister's sharp lift, finished the day on an unpromising 64 for seven.

Talking to the *Birmingham Post*, Bannister recalled the match: 'It was a wet wicket, right up my street. I had taken seven overnight but the footholds had gone. You could hardly stand up in them. But I knew the groundsman, Ray Weston, from when I played for Combined Services (sic) and I had a word and he put some new sods in for me. Strictly speaking it was against the rules but Dai Davies, who was umpiring at my end, let it go and the opposition didn't mind. It was a big help but I knew that, even with the new sods, the footholds wouldn't last long.'

Bannister took another wicket with the second ball next day, leaving Services 68 for eight. As well as Tordoff they had some useful batsmen, notably Glamorgan's Private Alan Jones who would score 36,000 first-class runs but never play for England (except in a 1970 Rest of the World series whose Test status was retrospectively removed; he kept the cap and blazer though!) and Aircraftmen Brian Roe and Richard Langridge, Somerset and Sussex respectively. However on this occasion the main contribution came from Essex off-spinner Aircraftman Paddy Phelan who hit 41 before he was caught behind, an edged drive fumbled then held by Jackie Fox, having added 46 for the ninth wicket with debutant Sergeant Douglas Meakin. Meanwhile Billy Ibadulla had been bowling at the other end and according to Bannister hadn't given up trying: 'Jack you wouldn't want a cheap wicket, would you?'. However Bannister got his man, and it was Ibadulla who took the catch at short leg! Last man, Senior Aircraftman Rodney Pratt had so far batted 22 times in first-class cricket with a highest score of nine. Not surprisingly he didn't stay long. More surprisingly, two months later he made 80, for Leicestershire, against Essex.

Improving on Hollies' figures, Bannister's figures are still a Warwickshire record. Interestingly he never hit the stumps, and apart from one lbw all his wickets fell to catches: three by Ibadulla and another three by County Durham-born wicketkeeper Fox who was standing in for Dick Spooner, another son of County Durham, who was in the last year of an outstanding career. Fox was playing in his third first-class match, but these were his first victims.

The match was over in two days, but the Services made a slightly better fist of it second time around mainly thanks to a captain's innings of 75 from Tordoff. Bannister took three more wickets (for 43) as the spoils were shared around a bit more evenly. The only wicket that Warwickshire lost knocking off the handful of runs needed for victory was the first-innings hero Stewart, who was bowled by Meakin for 151 runs fewer than he made in the first innings.

And Bannister's reward for his all-ten? He was dropped. 'M.J.K. Smith came over and said "Well done but hard lines". I had no problem with that because Ossie Wheatley and Roly Thompson were our first choices'. He got back later in the year, became a fixture in the side, and took over 100 wickets in each of the next three seasons.

Bannister missed most of 1963 with injury, but there was consolation the following season with an £8,847 benefit, and an appearance in the second Gillette Cup Final at Lord's, albeit that Warwickshire slumped to a disappointing defeat. He was back again two years later, this time on the winning side against local rivals Worcestershire. Warwickshire returned once more in 1968, but unfortunately without Bannister whose pulled calf muscle in the quarter-final had virtually ended his season and his first-class career (although he played a few limited-overs matches the next season).

Bannister's contributions off the field were considerable. In 1953 Warwickshire had started direct broadcasting of play at Edgbaston to local sanatoria and Bannister was one of several players who volunteered their services. The experience was invaluable as he later commented on

England matches for BBC on radio and television, and then for Talksport radio (while watching the game on television from his home in Brecon!). He was also cricket correspondent for the *Birmingham Post* for 29 years and wrote for the *Wisden Cricket Monthly*. No less importantly he served as secretary, chairman, and president of the Professional Cricketers' Association, which he had set up in 1967 to look after the interests of first-class cricketers in England and Wales. Sadly in 2009 he felt compelled to sever his honorary life membership of Warwickshire because of the county's apparent support for the England and Wales Cricket Board over its decisions regarding the sacking of the England captain and coach, Kevin Pietersen and Peter Moores, and in the Stanford affair. In later years his mobility was seriously affected by hip problems. He died in 2016 aged 85.

Tony Pearson

Cambridge University v Leicestershire, 1961

Brush Ground, Loughborough on 5, 6, 7 July 1961 (3-day match)
Toss won by Leicestershire
Cambridge University won by six wickets
Umpires: R Aspinall, F Jakeman
Leicestershire 283 (MR Hallam 115, D Kirby 5-76) and 160 (AJG Pearson 10-78); Cambridge University 337-5 dec (EJ Craig 101) and 109-4

Leicestershire second innings

*MR Hallam	b Pearson	64
DFX Munden	b Pearson	5
S Jayasinghe	b Pearson	41
LR Gardner	c Brearley b Pearson	0
J Birkenshaw	b Pearson	5
+J Mitten	b Pearson	0
RL Pratt	c Brearley b Pearson	12
CT Spencer	c Goodfellow b Pearson	11
RJ Barratt	c Brearley b Pearson	5
JS Savage	not out	9
BS Boshier	c Willard b Pearson	6
Extras	(lb 2)	2
Total	(all out, 62.3 overs)	160

Fall of wickets 1-27, 2-79, 3-79, 4-95, 5-95, 6-109, 7-131, 8-137, 9-154, 10-160

Cambridge University bowling: AJG Pearson 30.3-8-78-10, MJL Willard 19-6-41-0, D Kirby 11-1-30-0, NSK Reddy 2-1-9-0

Cambridge University: EJ Craig, A Goodfellow, JWT Wilcox, AR Lewis, NSK Reddy, JM Brearley (wk), D Kirby (capt), MJL Willard, RH Thomson, PD Brodrick, AJG Pearson

Tony Pearson is one of the lesser lights of the all-ten fraternity. His first-class career lasted three seasons, he only took 138 first-class wickets, and apart from his Cambridge University career he played just half a dozen matches for Somerset. Nevertheless, to take all-ten against a county side was a considerable achievement for a 19-year-old university freshman.

Born in Pinner, north-west London, Pearson attended Downside, a Catholic public school south-west of Bath whose most famous cricketing alumnus is Glamorgan's Maurice Turnbull. Pearson was tall and strongly-built and made good use of his height to bowl outswingers at a lively fast-medium. In his last season at school he had also headed the batting averages, but this prowess with the bat did not transfer to the first-class game as his career total of 355 runs in 51 innings attests.

For the Universities, victories against first-class counties were particularly welcome. In 1960, Cambridge had beaten three county sides, a record equalled in post-war years only in 1955. The following year however was one of rebuilding. Only five of the team that had drawn with a strong Oxford side at Lord's the previous summer were still available, and with a shortage of senior talent they had looked to the newcomers. Fortunately a number of them rose to the challenge. On the batting front, two 19-year-olds made over 1,000 runs in their debut seasons: Mike Brearley, who also kept wicket, and Edward Craig, who had scored prolifically at Charterhouse. Of the new bowlers, *Wisden* commented that 'Jefferson and Pearson soon emerged as the best new-ball pair, displaying stamina and accuracy above the ordinary.' Six foot seven inches tall Richard Jefferson would go on to have a useful county career, taking over 200 wickets for Surrey, and sire 6ft 10in county cricketer Will Jefferson. Cambridge bowlers had of course to spend much of their time trying to flog life out of batsmen-friendly Fenner's pitches.

As usual Cambridge had started their season with a run of home games at Fenner's until mid-June, before playing a series of matches away from home comforts, and finishing up at Lord's against the old enemy in early July. Having played 15 matches by the time they arrived at Loughborough, of which only two had resulted in victory, as against ten defeats, they would not have had high hopes of beating the home side. And neither of the wins had been against a county, both having come against the moderate opposition provided by Free Foresters and Col L.C. Stevens' XI. Leicestershire were, for once, having a good season. Bottom of the Championship the previous year they would finish ninth in 1961 (before picking up the wooden spoon again in 1962). They didn't have their strongest team out. Although their main bowlers were playing, they were notably missing their captain Willie Watson, who had made a successful move from Yorkshire, Alan Wharton, who had likewise come from Lancashire, and allrounder Jack van Geloven. They were led by Maurice Hallam, one of the best batsmen of his time never to play for England, whilst Cambridge were led by David Kirby who had already played for Leicestershire, and would be county captain the following season.

Like many outgrounds, facilities at the Brush Company's sports ground were basic and, apart from the pavilion, there was no permanent seating. Cars could however be parked around the perimeter. Cambridge would have been pleased with their first day performance, especially as they were without Jefferson. Leicestershire were mainly indebted to Hallam (115) and another Yorkshire import Jack Birkenshaw (61) for their 283, whilst for Cambridge off-spinner Kirby took the only five wicket haul of his 117-match career. Fifty-six without loss overnight, Cambridge had the luxury of being able to declare next day. Craig made 101, fellow opener Anthony Goodfellow 81, a score he would never exceed in a 21-match University career, and future England captain Tony Lewis, 55.

Leicestershire having lost one second innings wicket for 73 by the close, an interesting final day looked possible. However there was no hint that a record was in the offing. In his first ten first-class matches Pearson had only once got as many as four wickets in an innings, and in the match so far had taken one for 87 from 27 overs. However, as Scarlett O'Hara memorably said in *Gone With the Wind*, 'tomorrow is another day'. And it certainly was for Pearson who bowled another 19.3 overs and took the remaining nine wickets at a cost of 39 runs to become only the second bowler after Sammy Woods to take all-ten for Cambridge University.

He had soon got among the wickets on Friday morning, first breaking the overnight partnership by bowling Stanley Jayasinghe, a belligerent batsman who had played for Ceylon, and then in quick succession having Robin Gardner caught behind without scoring, and then bowling Birkenshaw and 20-year-old wicketkeeper John Mitten, who was making his first-class debut. Mitten's first-class career would be a short one. He had greater success as a professional footballer, although not as much as his more famous father Charlie, a skilful left winger who found post-war fame with Manchester United before controversially defecting to play in Colombia in 1950. Hallam did his best to hold the innings together but when he eventually played on all hopes of a decent total were gone. Unsurprisingly the Leicestershire tail didn't last long. The last three batsmen would eventually play nearly 600 matches between them, but didn't share one fifty. Only two other batsmen reached double figures, one of whom, Rodney Pratt, had been Jack Bannister's last victim when he took his all-ten two years before.

Pearson hit the stumps five times, all top order batsmen, and was well supported by Brearley who took three catches (in a season in which he would finish with a career-best haul of 47 catches plus three stumpings), and didn't concede a bye in either innings.

The ground would eventually host 16 first-class matches, the last in 1965. Only Pearson, and Hampshire's Butch White, with seven in each innings in 1963, ever took more than six wickets in an innings there.

Although Cambridge only needed 107 to win, the pitch was by now taking considerable spin and the University players apparently thought that off-spinner John Savage, who would take 122 wickets in the season, might be too good for them. In the event, although Savage took four cheap wickets, Cambridge knocked off the runs needed for victory fairly easily thanks to another dominant display from Craig (80 not out). Meanwhile Oxbridge was also having a good day in the Third Test at Headingley with Raman Subba Row, Colin Cowdrey, Peter May and Ted Dexter, plus Lancashire professional Pullar, all scoring solidly to help England to a first-innings lead over Australia for the first time since 1956.

Pearson performed modestly in the rain-affected University match in July with just one wicket in the only Oxford innings but, replacing the injured Ken Biddulph, he made an impressive debut for Somerset later in the month taking seven Worcestershire wickets in their second innings for 63 runs. In his few appearances for Somerset that season he took 23 wickets and headed their bowling averages. However, despite this promising beginning, his first-class county career was already nearly over, ending with just one more match against Kent two years later. He remained a mainstay of the Cambridge attack during his three years there, eventually taking 112 wickets for them, although never again taking five wickets in an innings.

Pearson had been studying medicine at Cambridge and went to Bristol for clinical studies where he played for his old club Clifton, an experience enhanced by the presence of Barry Richards and Mike Procter who had just come over from South Africa. He took up squash, and when he moved to London in 1969 applied to join Hampstead Cricket Club as a squash member. Finding that a number of the cricket team were Oxbridge contemporaries and that they had just won the national club cricket championship, he played with them for three summers before giving up after an injury.

Speaking to the author, Tony Pearson recalled cricket at Cambridge as a privilege in terms of the time off to play, the facilities at Fenner's and the standard of cricket that cricketers recently out of school were now able to play. He found it great fun, although initially rather intimidating, and recognised that although there were a number of good individual performances the side was often not quite good enough to push home an advantage. At Somerset the quality of the close catching in particular highlighted the missed opportunities at Cambridge. He modestly acknowledges the part that the batting of Craig and Goodfellow played in Cambridge's victory over Leicestershire, and the element of chance in an all-ten: in his case dropped catches off other bowlers - and the near run out of the last batsman off a ricochet!.

Ian Thomson

Sussex v Warwickshire, 1964
County Championship

The Manor Sports Ground, Worthing on 6, 8, 9 June 1964 (3-day match)
Toss won by Warwickshire
Warwickshire won by 182 runs
Umpires: J Arnold, AE Fagg
Warwickshire 196 (NI Thomson 10-49) and 129 (NI Thomson 5-26); Sussex
120 and 23 (JD Bannister 6-16)

Warwickshire first innings

NF Horner	c and b Thomson	0
RW Barber	c Suttle b Thomson	57
Khalid Ibadulla	c Buss b Thomson	17
*MJK Smith	lbw b Thomson	42
JA Jameson	b Thomson	7
TW Cartwright	st Gunn b Thomson	54
RE Hitchcock	lbw b Thomson	2
+AC Smith	b Thomson	2
JD Bannister	c Gunn b Thomson	1
R Miller	b Thomson	7
DJ Brown	not out	0
Extras	(b 2, lb 3, nb 2)	7
Total	(all out, 78.2 overs)	196

Fall of wickets 1-10, 2-48, 3-107, 4-122, 5-133, 6-151, 7-155, 8-163, 9-181, 10-196

Sussex bowling: NI Thomson 34.2-19-49-10, A Buss 12-1-42-0, JA Snow 16-2-52-0, ASM Oakman 5-2-11-0

Sussex: KG Suttle, RJ Langridge, LJ Lenham, ASM Oakman (capt), GC Cooper, FR Pountain, NI Thomson, A Buss, JA Snow, RV Bell, T Gunn (wk)

I Do Like To Be Beside The Seaside! Although many no doubt echo the sentiments of the popular music hall ditty, batsmen leaving The Manor Sports Ground in June 1964 probably didn't share the same enthusiasm.

Just over six feet tall, Staffordshire-born Ian Thomson made his Sussex debut in 1952 at the age of 23 and, after taking 101 wickets in the following season, remained the backbone of his county's attack for over a decade. From a high delivery, following a rather shuffling approach to the stumps, he bowled a sharp inswinger and on occasions a telling leg cutter.

Warwickshire came to Worthing at the top of the Championship table, level on points with neighbours Worcestershire. By the end of the season the neighbours would be on the top of the pile, leaving Warwickshire with the consolation that second place was their best effort since they won the title in 1951. Finishing halfway, Sussex's impact on the Championship would be minimal, but at least they retained the Gillette Cup in a one-sided Final against Warwickshire at Lord's, a match that started in warm, hazy, early-autumn conditions that suited the medium pace of 35-year-old Thomson whose four for 23 earned him the Man of the Match award.

Back in June there had been rain around aplenty. On Saturday 6 June play was impossible in five Championship matches, whilst at Trent Bridge, where Geoff Boycott was making his Test debut, England and Australia were similarly becalmed. The Worthing ground was council-owned, and thanks to the efforts of its staff who had cleared some 100 gallons of water off the square on Friday, a start was possible.

In the absence of England captain Ted Dexter Sussex were led by Alan Oakman. His first action was to lose the toss and in view of the unpromising weather forecast Warwickshire would have been pleased to bat first and to reach 103 for two before the heavens opened and brought an early end to proceedings. Left-hander Bob Barber, who had moved from Lancashire in 1963 and transformed himself into an adventurous opening batsman, was 57 not out. However, he failed to add to his score on Monday as Thomson collected his third wicket thanks to a catch at slip by Ken Suttle, who was getting on for three-quarters of the way through a remarkable sequence of 423 consecutive County Championship appearances. Sunshine and a drying wind on a rain-affected pitch had produced bowler-friendly conditions in which, the top surface having gone, the bounce of the ball had become totally unpredictable. Mike Smith, the Warwickshire captain, 27 not out overnight, had clearly decided that he would try to score runs as quickly as possible before conditions worsened further. However, after hitting two fours and a six off slow left-armer Ronnie Bell he fell leg-before to Thomson to a ball that kept wickedly low. After this only Tom Cartwright showed any ability to resist. Cartwright had done the double in 1962, but as he developed into one of England's very best medium-pace bowlers his batting became a secondary skill. Nevertheless, farming the bowling cleverly, he nearly saw his side through to 200 before, at one o'clock and with nine wickets down, having already swung Thomson for six, he tried again and was stumped by Terry Gunn, stand-in for England's Jim Parks. In the circumstances Yorkshireman Gunn, who would play 41 matches for Sussex in seven seasons, had done well to concede just two byes.

Thomson, having taken eight for 30 in the morning session, returned to the pavilion to a standing ovation and 'a triumphant fanfare of car horns'. At the other end Tony Buss (who would eventually take over 900 wickets for Sussex) and John Snow (soon to embark on a major England career) were unrewarded, probably because they bowled too short. Thomson however, putting the ball in the right place, had skilfully used the seam to take advantage of the conditions and come within one run of equalling Cyril Bland's county record figures from 1899.

The Times referred to the 'cheerful crowd'. It must have been Thomson's bowling and the sunny weather that perked them up. It certainly wasn't the Sussex batting, with the only decent first-innings resistance coming from opener Suttle (33), and then the tail as Snow and Bell added 39 for the ninth wicket. Warwickshire didn't do much better in their second knock, Thomson bowling unchanged for 25 overs to take another five wickets.

Set 206 to win on a worsening pitch Sussex adopted a policy of hit and hope. As they made only 23, clearly it didn't work as David Brown (two for 7), Jack Bannister (six for 16) and Cartwright (two wickets in two balls) enjoyed themselves, taking the last nine wickets for eight runs; Gunn concluding proceedings with his second duck of the match. Only Hampshire, at Burton in 1958, had made such a low score in England since the War. As an illustration of the difficulty experienced by the Sussex batsmen, Les Lenham was first hit on the chest by Bannister, and then, from a ball pitching in the same area, leg-before to a shooter!

The next match at Worthing, starting the following day, was no better, at least for batsmen. It was over in two days. Thomson wasn't complaining however. He took eight Nottinghamshire wickets and finished the match top of the national averages. With concerns about the pitch, and the size of the crowds, that was the end of first-class cricket at Worthing, 43 matches having been hosted since the first one in 1935.

Apart from flying out as a replacement on MCC's 'A' tour of Pakistan in 1955/56, Thomson had never really been in contention for representative honours as there were just too many good bowlers around. So his selection at the age of 35 to go to South Africa in the winter of 1964/65 with Mike Smith's side was a bit of a surprise. The England pace attack was in a state of transition. Fred Trueman and Brian Statham (both younger than Thomson!) were coming to the end of their great careers, John Snow hadn't yet quite come to the fore and Thomson, to his surprise, was selected to replace Yorkshire's Tony Nicholson who had dropped out injured from the originally selected squad. As a stock bowler, while off-spinners David Allen and Fred Titmus bowled England to a one-nil victory, he sent down 248 overs in five Tests, taking just nine wickets on pitches not made for English seamers. At the time of the First Test he had already taken 1,497 first-class wickets, a total unequalled by any other Test debutant. It was fortunate that he managed to stay fit because England's bowlers had been so beset by injuries that Somerset's Ken Palmer, who was coaching locally, was brought in for the last Test, and even Geoff Boycott was pressed into regular action (taking five wickets and finishing second in the averages!).

Thomson's exertions left him tired when the 1965 season began and he retired at the end of the year, although he came back for a few mainly List A matches in the early 1970s. Chairman Arthur Gilligan had approached him about succeeding Dexter as captain, but he preferred to make the break and return to his father's garage, before later becoming a teacher. Only Maurice Tate, George Cox and Albert Relf have exceeded the 1,527 wickets that Thomson took for Sussex.

By mid-August 2017 the top six oldest living England cricketers were Don Smith (94), Hubert Doggart (92), Ian Thomson (88), Alan Oakman (87), Alan Moss (86) and Jim Parks (85). All but Moss had played for Sussex. *Good Old Sussex by the Sea*!

Peter Allan

Queensland v Victoria, 1965/66
Sheffield Shield

Melbourne Cricket Ground, Melbourne on 7, 8, 10, 11 January 1966 (4-day match)
Toss won by Queensland
Victoria won by three wickets
Umpires: KR Butler, WK Collicoat
Queensland 180 (KR Stackpole 5-38) and 336 (DFE Bull 167 not out); Victoria 130 (PJ Allan 10-61) and 387–7 (IR Redpath 180, GD Watson 109)

Victoria first innings

IR Redpath	lbw b Allan	20
GD Watson	c Trimble b Allan	8
DJ Anderson	c Bizzell b Allan	45
*J Potter	c Cooper b Allan	5
KR Stackpole	b Allan	1
+RC Jordon	b Allan	27
AP Sheahan	c Cooper b Allan	0
JD Swanson	c Crane b Allan	0
JW Grant	c Crane b Allan	0
KW Kirby	c Trimble b Allan	18
AN Connolly	not out	0
Extras	(lb 4, nb 2)	6
Total	(all out, 30.6 overs)	130

Fall of wickets 1-15, 2-41, 3-53, 4-61, 5-100, 6-100, 7-100, 8-100, 9-123, 10-130

Queensland bowling: PJ Allan 15.6-3-61-10, JRF Duncan 5-0-31-0, JRE Mackay 1-0-12-0, FR Crane 9-5-20-0

Queensland: DFE Bull, SC Trimble (capt), WH Buckle, GM Bizzell, FR Crane, KP Ziebell, JRE Mackay, LD Cooper (wk), PJ Allan, JRF Duncan, DJ Lillie

Peter Allan played only one match for Australia and then was dropped. However, he had the consolation that in his next match a month later he became only the second bowler, and the first Queenslander, to take all-ten in a Sheffield Shield match. Tall and strong with great stamina, he bowled outswingers at a lively fast-medium.

Allan was born in Brisbane on New Year's Eve 1935. On the same day, in faraway Launceston, future captain of Australia Ian Johnson was one of nine Victorians making their first-class debuts against Tasmania. Allan made his own debut in 1959/60, playing three matches for Queensland, but then work took him to Melbourne for three years where, although he made the State squad, he could not break into the first team.

Returning home to take up a position with tobacco company WD & HO Wills (although he was a non-smoker!), he reappeared for Queensland. The State no longer had the cutting edge provided by West Indian Wes

Hall who had taken 76 Shield wickets in the previous two seasons, and Allan's return to the side at Brisbane in October 1963 wasn't that promising. Queensland took up most of the first two days scoring 613, Peter Burge contributing a State record 283 (since beaten only by Martin Love's undefeated 300 against Victoria in 2003/04). Allan ended the day well, quickly trapping opener Grahame Thomas in front of the stumps for two, but that was as far as his success went. New South Wales amassed 661(Bobby Simpson 359) and he finished with one for 144 from 25 overs. Things looked up after that and with 23 wickets Allan finished the season as his side's most successful bowler. Another 36 wickets the following season and Allan had booked himself a place on the Australian tour of the West Indies in the spring of 1965. Unfortunately illness restricted him to only four appearances, and five wickets.

Back in Australia Allan was clearly still in the selectors' thoughts and, having begun the season well, he was picked to share the new ball with Neil Hawke in the First Test against England at Brisbane in December 1965. Graham McKenzie had dropped out of the Australian 12 with back trouble, but then surprisingly appeared for Western Australia in the match being played at the same time in Adelaide. Allan took two wickets, including bowling the England captain Mike Smith for 16, but it was not enough to keep him in the side for the Second Test.

Victoria and Queensland weren't the strongest teams in the Shield when they met at the beginning of 1966. In fact at the end of the season they occupied the bottom two places in the table. (Victoria would win the Shield the following season but Queensland would once again finish last.) Victoria were missing Bill Lawry and Bob Cowper, both playing in the Third Test (which England would win by an innings and 93 runs). Having said that, they still had a decent batting line-up, including Ian Redpath, Keith Stackpole and Paul Sheahan, who would go on to score over 9,000 Test runs between them. Queensland were similarly missing captain Burge, wicketkeeper Wally Grout and allrounder Tom Veivers.

The visitors batted first and were dismissed for just 180, Keith Stackpole taking a career-best five for 38 with his leg breaks. Only three batsmen reached double figures: Des Bull (78), Bill Buckle (44), and the splendidly-named wrist-spinner Dennis Lillie (13). Victoria were 76 for four by close of play, Allan having taken all four for 32. After having Graeme Watson caught by stand-in captain Sam Trimble and then picking up Redpath leg-before, he struck two further important blows just before the close. First he had Victoria's captain Jack Potter, who had made 221 against New South Wales in his previous match, caught by wicketkeeper Lewis Cooper, and then bowled the powerful Stackpole.

Next morning Queensland reached 100 without further loss but then a spectacular collapse, which began when Allan bowled wicketkeeper Ray Jordon, reduced them to 100 for eight. On his first-class debut slow left-armer John Swanson was the middle man in a trio of ducks. He would even things up a bit next day by making Allan the first of his 36 first-class victims. David Anderson, who had gone in first wicket down and top scored with 45, went at 123 after batting resolutely for more than two hours, and Allan picked up his historic tenth wicket when he had wrist-spinner Keith Kirby caught by Trimble. Allan had taken the last six wickets in a spell yielding only 14 runs, and five of these were overthrows.

Bowling unchanged from the Northern end in a Victoria innings that had lasted only 30.6 (eight-ball) overs he had shown superb control and frequently caused the batsmen to play and miss at his outswinger. He had been aided in particular by a steady spell of off spin from Bobby Crane at the other end. Allan no doubt derived some satisfaction from the fact that his all-ten had come against the State who hadn't selected him when he was based in Melbourne. Meanwhile in Sydney in the Third Test England were closing their first innings with 488 on the board. Given his form the selectors might have been wishing that they had chosen Allan. Surprisingly, although it was his 30th first-class match, he had never before taken more than five wickets in an innings. Some 3,000 had been present to see Allan complete his feat, a reasonable crowd for a Shield match, but somewhat lost in a ground that had accommodated 90,000 on day two of the final Test against the West Indies five years before.

In taking the first all-ten in Australia since 1932/33, Allan had broken a number of long-standing records. The previous best figures at the MCG had been nine for 30 by South Australia's slow left-armer Joe Travers on New Year's Eve 1900 (he took the first eight wickets, so it was close to an all-ten). Like Allan, Travers played just one Test. Allan's figures were the best ever for Queensland, improving on the eight for 35 by leg-spinner Richard Wilson on his first-class debut against Auckland on the state's 1896/97 New Zealand tour. Queensland's best figures in the Sheffield Shield were eight for 148 by Brian Flynn, another leg-spinner, in November 1953 against a strong New South Wales batting line-up. At the time of writing nobody, apart from Allan, has taken more than eight wickets in an innings for Queensland.

Bowlers had a harder time in the second half of the match. First Queensland made 336 and then, left a difficult 387 to win in seven and a half hours, Victoria accomplished their task with three wickets and 48 minutes to spare. Redpath (180) and Watson (109, making his maiden century), both benefited from dropped catches, and this time Allan's figures were a disappointing nought for 63 from eleven overs. The selectors were impressed however. McKenzie had had a poor Third Test and Allan was picked in his place for the Fourth (the match in which one of his ten victims, Keith Stackpole, made his Test debut). Unfortunately Allan then had to withdraw because of acute shin soreness and a recalled McKenzie took six England first innings wickets. Allan's chance had gone. In March Allan took another all-ten, this time playing for South Brisbane in a local club match.

While not hitting such heights again, Allan continued to take wickets steadily. In 1968/69, his final season, he topped the Australian bowling averages with the impressive figures of 46 wickets at only 16.36 apiece, finishing his Queensland career with 199 wickets, a figure then only exceeded by medium-pace off-spinner Ron Oxenham (but since bettered by a number of bowlers, including Mike Kasprowicz at the top of the list with 505). He later served on the Executive Committee of the Queensland Cricket Association, managed Queensland teams on tour, and became manager of the Queen Elizabeth II Stadium, the 1982 Commonwealth Games Complex. He finished his career working as a civil marriage celebrant on tropical Hamilton Island.

Ian Brayshaw

Western Australia v Victoria, 1967/68
Sheffield Shield

Western Australia Cricket Association Ground, Perth on 21, 22, 23, 24 October 1967 (4-day match)
Toss won by Western Australia
Western Australia won by 136 runs
Umpires: JM Meachem, NE Townsend
Western Australia 161 and 371; Victoria 152 (IJ Brayshaw 10-44) and 244 (GAR Lock 5-36)

Victoria first innings

*WM Lawry	c Becker b Brayshaw	47
IR Redpath	b Brayshaw	21
KH Eastwood	c Vernon b Brayshaw	6
RM Cowper	b Brayshaw	7
J Potter	b Brayshaw	0
KR Stackpole	c Irvine b Brayshaw	0
GD Watson	c Inverarity b Brayshaw	37
JW Grant	b Brayshaw	24
+RC Jordon	c Becker b Brayshaw	9
BC Bitmead	not out	0
AN Connolly	c Inverarity b Brayshaw	0
Extras	(lb 1)	1
Total	(all out, 49.6 overs)	152

Fall of wickets 1-22, 2-28, 3-37, 4-37, 5-37, 6-104, 7-138, 8-151, 9-152, 10-152

Western Australia bowling: JM Hubble 7-0-36-0, GD McKenzie 17-4-42-0, IJ Brayshaw 17.6-4-44-10, RJ Inverarity 1-0-2-0, GAR Lock 7-1-27-0

Western Australia: WR Playle, R Edwards, GC Becker (wk), MT Vernon, RJ Inverarity, IJ Brayshaw, JT Irvine, AL Mann, GD McKenzie, GAR Lock (capt), JM Hubble

Just like the proverbial London buses, having waited a long time for one Australian all-ten, another one came along soon after, courtesy of the right-arm medium pace of Western Australian allrounder Ian Brayshaw. And again it was Victoria who were on the receiving end, with seven Victorians on both buses.

Western Australia had won the Shield at their first attempt in 1947/48, albeit that they only played each of the other States once (and had to guarantee the eastern States the return rail fares to Perth!). They eventually started playing all the States twice, home and away, in 1956/57, but it wasn't until 1967/68 under the inspiring leadership of new captain Tony Lock that they won the Shield again. Victoria, the previous year's winners, would finish in second place, and so matches between the two States had a particular importance that season.

Lightly-built and hence nicknamed 'Sticks', the competitive Brayshaw was a great team-man and a key member of the Western Australia side that won the Sheffield Shield five times during the 1970s. Born in South Perth in 1942 he had progressed from playing for Perth's Scotch College and then grade cricket with Claremont Cottesloe, to becoming a state regular in 1965/66. He also spent two seasons with Bacup in the Lancashire League. He was probably unlucky not to have played Test cricket.

The Western Australia Cricket Association Ground (the WACA) wasn't yet the major ground it was to later become. However, change was on the way. It would host its first Test match just over three years later (or maybe its second, a Women's Test having taken place there in 1958), for which the John Inverarity Stand (originally known as the Test Stand), replacing the 1897 pavilion, was built. Other developments would follow. One constant has been the Fremantle Doctor, the cooling early afternoon breeze from the direction of the port of Fremantle which provides welcome relief from the excessive summer heat, and help to bowlers with the skill to use it.

Only two batsmen prospered in Western Australia's unimpressive first innings: John Inverarity (76 not out in three and a half hours), and Bill Playle (30), both of whom it would be not unfair to call 'dour'. By the time Inverarity played his last first-class match, in 1985 at the age of 41, he was the highest ever run-scorer in the Sheffield Shield (9,341 runs at 38.44), a record now held by Darren Lehmann. A useful left-arm spinner, unexpectedly in his final season he took as many as 43 wickets. He led Western Australia to four Sheffield Shield wins, and on moving to Adelaide as a deputy headmaster in 1979 played for South Australia for six more seasons. Opener Playle had played eight Tests for New Zealand before moving to Western Australia where he served the State side with some success.

Victoria had a strong batting line-up and would have been optimistic of getting a decent first-innings lead as they began their defence of the Shield. Bill Lawry, Ian Redpath, Bob Cowper, Keith Stackpole and Graeme Watson were all Test players and Ken Eastwood would play once three years later; while twelfth man Les Joslin would play his only Test three months later. On the other hand, Western Australia did have two world-class bowlers in the contrasting fast right-arm of Graham McKenzie and slow left-arm of Tony Lock. Between them they would take over 4,000 first-class wickets, including 420 in Tests.

Despite the strength of their batting however, Victoria would fail by nine runs to equal Western Australia's score, but it wasn't McKenzie and Lock who scuppered their hopes, but 25-year-old Ian Brayshaw. He had played just two full seasons for Western Australia and as he had only taken five wickets in an innings twice, and with only ten expensive wickets in the previous season, his decimation of the Victorian batting came as a bit of a surprise. McKenzie opened the bowling with Jim Hubble. Left-armer Hubble never played Test cricket although he had been chosen to tour South Africa the previous season after only six first-class matches and 20 wickets. Redpath dominated an opening partnership of 22 with Lawry before Brayshaw, coming on first change, picked up Redpath and

Eastwood in his first two overs. At the close Victoria were 35 for two, of which Lawry had made just two.

Next morning, in front of a crowd of over 4,000, Brayshaw soon added to his haul, quickly bowling Cowper and Potter, and then having Stackpole caught by Jock Irvine, all within the space of five balls. Lawry and Watson took the score to 104 before Brayshaw induced Watson to give a catch to Inverarity at slip. Having batted 203 minutes for 47, the obdurate Lawry was finally prised out at 138, brilliantly caught by wicketkeeper Gordon Becker. The tail didn't hang about, the last three wickets falling for one run with Brayshaw completing the full house by dismissing Alan Connolly for a duck courtesy of another sharp Inverarity slip catch. A fine bowler for state and country, in 201 first-class matches Connolly never made a fifty.

Helped by a strong breeze, humidity and a lively wicket, Brayshaw had bowled with fine control of swing and cut and had been well supported by his close fielders. Like Peter Allan, he had broken some long-standing records. The previous best figures at the WACA were by Denijs Morkel who had followed up his 150 not out for the 1931/32 touring South Africans by taking eight state wickets (including John Inverarity's father) for 13, whilst the previous best figures for Western Australia were eight for 28 against Victoria by medium pacer Bobby Selk in March 1910 in the last of five matches played at the Fremantle Oval.

Western Australia made 371 in their second innings, with main contributions coming from Becker (95) and Inverarity (82). Brayshaw failed to score, dismissed again by Watson. For the second time in the match wicketkeeper Ray Jordon prevented any byes. When he retired three years later 'Slug' Jordon was Victoria's then most successful wicketkeeper with 260 victims. He never played for Australia, although, like Irvine, he toured India and South Africa in 1969/70.

Set an almost impossible 381 to win in five hours, Victoria fell well short. This time Lock (five for 36) did most of the damage. Brayshaw's contribution was a more modest two for 46. However one of his wickets was the key one of Lawry, bowled for 53 just when he was getting set for a long stay.

The return match at the Melbourne Cricket Ground at the end of the season was the Shield decider. Victoria went into it leading Western Australia by two points, but a ten wicket defeat saw the Shield go west. Brayshaw's performance this time was more modest: just one wicket and an innings of 29. However, as an ever-present, with 268 runs and 24 wickets his contribution over the whole season had been considerable.

Remarkably, after taking his all-ten it would be another eight years before Brayshaw took five in an innings again (well, actually six for 48 against Queensland). And then two seasons later, his final one, he not only came second in the national averages with 35 wickets at 18 apiece but scored 491 runs at an average of 38. In 101 first-class matches, all played for Western Australia, his final tally was 4,325 runs (including three centuries) at 31.80, 178 wickets at 25.08, and 108 catches, mainly in the slips.

Brayshaw was also a fine Australian Rules footballer and a member of the Claremont team that won the Western Australian premiership in 1964. After retirement he became a coach, was director of cricket at Kent CCC in 2002 and 2003, and a respected journalist, commentator and author with many cricket books to his name. His son Jamie also had a useful Shield career, mainly with South Australia, scoring nearly 5,000 runs in 75 matches.

Shahid Mahmood

Karachi Whites v Khairpur, 1969/70
Quaid-e-Azam Trophy

National Stadium, Karachi on 5, 6 September 1969 (3-day match)
Toss won by Khairpur
Karachi Whites won by an innings and 56 runs
Umpires: Badshah Shirazi, Shujauddin
Khairpur 93 and 146 (Shahid Mahmood 10-58); Karachi Whites 295

Khairpur second innings

Abdul Hameed	b Shahid Mahmood	15
Zafar Iqbal	c Aftab Alam b Shahid Mahmood	0
Shakoor Rana	b Shahid Mahmood	14
Aslam Sanjrani	b Shahid Mahmood	5
+Razaullah Khan	c Aftab Alam b Shahid Mahmood	27
Mohammad Akram	c Abdul Kadir b Shahid Mahmood	5
Zafar Mahmood	b Shahid Mahmood	23
Talat Iqbal	c Abdur Raqib b Shahid Mahmood	2
Tahir Ali	not out	38
*Abdul Aziz	c Aftab Alam b Shahid Mahmood	6
Ghulam Sabir	c Hasan Pervez b Shahid Mahmood	4
Extras		7
Total	(all out, 55 overs)	146

Fall of wickets 1-25, 2-33, 3-52, 4-68, 5-88, 6-92, 7-93, 8-105, 9-117, 10-146

Karachi Whites bowling: Mufassir-ul-Haq 3-2-6-0, Hasan Pervez 2-1-15-0, Shahid Mahmood 25-5-58-10, Saleem Jan 9-4-11-0, Abdur Raqib 7-3-18-0, Akram Ali 3-2-14-0, Aftab Alam 6-1-17-0

Karachi Whites: Amin Ashraf, Shahid Mahmood, Aftab Alam, Abdul Kadir (wk), Wallis Mathias (capt), Akram Ali, Waheed Yar Khan, Saleem Jan, Abdur Raqib, Hasan Pervez, Mufassir-ul-Haq

The next all-ten also came out of the blue. By September 1969, in a career that had started 13 years previously, 30-year-old left-hand allrounder Shahid Mahmood had taken 74 wickets in 63 matches with his medium-pace bowling, including five wickets in an innings just twice. Born in 1939 in Lucknow, India, his family moved to Pakistan in the early 1950s. He made the first of five centuries, a double (220), for Karachi University against Peshawar University shortly before his 20th birthday. Three seasons later he made a second century, 174 for Karachi against a fairly strong North Zone attack. Three other fifties and 23 wickets earned him place on the second Pakistan Test-playing tour to the British Isles in 1962.

The tour contrasted unhappily with the first in 1954 when Pakistan had drawn the rubber with an historic win at The Oval. This time an inexperienced team, unused to the conditions, was completely outplayed, losing the series four-nil. Shahid already had some experience of the country having toured with the Pakistan Eaglets in 1958 (taking an all-ten and scoring a century against Isle of Wight CA), but in common with a number of other members of the party the tour wasn't a great success for him: in 13 first-class matches he scored 369 runs at an average of 16.04, and took eleven wickets at 26.72. Playing in fewer than half of the tourists' matches he suffered from lack of opportunity. Still, he did at least get his one and only cap, albeit that he wasn't in very good form when he stepped onto the field at Trent Bridge at the end of July for the Fourth Test with the series already lost. Shahid performed modestly in a rain-affected draw. Opening in the first innings his 16 was 16 more than his illustrious partner Hanif Mohammad managed, and dropping down the order second time around he made nine before becoming the only wicket taken in the match by England captain Ted Dexter. He was given little chance with the ball, and although England piled up 428 for five declared he bowled just six wicketless overs (in two spells of five and one!). The star performer for Pakistan, among a number of modest performers, was Hanif's 18-year-old brother Mushtaq (who had been playing Test cricket since he was 15) who made 55 and 100 not out.

After his one Test Shahid was given little further opportunity to impress - just one county match, and festival matches at Hastings and Scarborough. Back home he had his moments over the next few seasons, but not enough of them to force himself into the selectors' thinking. And then came a remarkable swansong.

The Quaid-e-Azam Trophy, Pakistan's premier domestic first-class competition, was instituted in 1953/54. Quaid-e-Azam means 'The Great Leader', the title given to Mohammad Ali Jinnah, the founder of the state of Pakistan. In 1969/70 twenty teams took part. Because of their strength, Hyderabad and Karachi (both with sides named Blues and Whites), and Lahore (A and B) were allowed to enter two teams. The tournament started with the teams playing in groups in order to decide who would play in the semi-finals. So far, Karachi teams had dominated the Trophy winning it ten times. Khairpur first entered the competition in 1958/59, but had never reached the semis.

Mushtaq Mohammad had made a triple-century at the National Stadium two years previously, and the ground would go on to see four more triples (including Aftab Baloch's 428), but the match in September 1969 wasn't one for connoisseurs of big scores. None of the Khairpur side ever played Test cricket. Their best known player, eventually, was probably Shakoor Rana. Less successful than his two Test match-playing brothers, in an 11-match career he made just 226 runs and took 12 wickets. However, as an umpire 18 years later he was involved in the infamous spat with England captain Mike Gatting that led to a Test match being suspended while they tried, with limited success, to sort out their differences.

So far in their group Karachi had drawn one match and only won the other as a result of a walkover, whilst Khairpur had won one and lost one. However, as the stronger side, Karachi would have been expected to win. Their attack though was limited. Left-arm spinner Abdur Raqib would go on to take 643 first-class wickets, but his career was only just beginning and, whilst Mufassir-ul-Haq and Shahid would share 194 wickets, the four other bowlers used by skipper Wallis Mathias would eventually take just

25 between them. Having said that, Khairpur's batting was even weaker. Only one batsman, Mohammad Akram, had a first-class century to his name. He would later add one more, and Zafar Mahmood would also make one, but none of the others would ever reach three figures.

Only two batsmen even reached double figures in Khairpur's first innings, one of whom was the aforementioned Shakoor Rana with 24. Shahid bowled nine overs, picking up a couple of tailenders at a cost of 19 runs. He then opened the batting and made 22 before he was stumped off Khairpur's captain Abdul Aziz bowling off breaks (which were of course leg breaks to left-handed Shahid).

Batting steadily Karachi built up a sizeable first-innings lead by the time the innings closed in the middle of the second day. Khairpur did a little better the second time around, but their innings, and the match, was still over before the end of the day, the captains having agreed to play an extra half-hour. Left-arm opening bowler Mufassir-ul-Haq had played one Test five years before, but he was soon off, Shahid coming on first change and bowling throughout the rest of the innings. Shakoor Rana again stayed for a while before Shahid bowled him, but the only batsman who got past 30 was slow left-armer Tahir Ali who made 38 not out, going in at 93 for seven and helping guide his side to a slightly more respectable total. In putting on 29 with Ghulam Sabir for the last wicket, the highest stand of the innings, he at least ensured that Mahmood had to work hard for his all-ten. Having taken four for 79 in Karachi's innings Tahir Ali had had a good match in a hopeless cause. Sabir was caught by debutant Hasan Pervez who had thus caught the first batsman dismissed in the match and the last. Shahid hit the stumps four times, whilst three of the six catches taken off his bowling were pouched by Aftab Alam, the older brother of Pakistan's wrist-spinning allrounder Intikhab. In a 46-match career Alam hit seven centuries, one of which was a career-best 154 against Khairpur the previous season.

Two matches, and two months, later and Shahid's career was over. In the first, the Quaid-e-Azam semi-final, Karachi Whites came up against the rather powerful Pakistan International Airways (PIA) side, nine of whom had played for Pakistan, whilst the other two, Younis Ahmed and Zaheer Abbas, would soon do so. The match was drawn, but PIA went through to the Final (which they won) by virtue of their first innings lead. Shahid had a good match. He made 15 not out in Karachi's first innings, bowled 54 overs while PIA scored 531 for five declared, dismissing Hanif Mohammad and Younis at a cost of 75 runs, and then opening the batting made 110 not out. The match eventually petered out to a draw, enabling Hanif to bowl 22 overs of occasional off breaks, the longest spell of his career. One more wicket in his final match took Shahid's final career total to 89 wickets in 66 matches, from 990 overs. Of all bowlers who have taken an all-ten only Albert Moss (26 in four matches) has taken fewer wickets.

Shahid subsequently settled in New Jersey where he ran a successful advertising business, served the Pakistani community, and advised Presidents Reagan and Bush Senior on matters relating to the USA's Islamic community.

Eddie Hemmings

International XI v West Indies XI, 1982/83

Sabina Park, Kingston, Jamaica on 25, 26, 27, 28 September 1982 (4-day match)
Match drawn
Umpires: LU Bell, D Sang Hue
International XI 262 (ST Clarke 5-26); West Indies XI 419 (EE Hemmings 10-175)

West Indies XI first innings

CG Greenidge	c Ghavri b Hemmings	43
DL Haynes	c AR Butcher b Hemmings	96
G Powell	c Richards b Hemmings	16
LG Rowe	c sub (OW Peters) b Hemmings	47
+PJL Dujon	c Jesty b Hemmings	19
*CH Lloyd	c Jesty b Hemmings	60
MD Marshall	c sub (OW Peters) b Hemmings	40
RC Haynes	c Wright b Hemmings	15
AME Roberts	st Richards b Hemmings	34
ST Clarke	b Hemmings	6
MA Holding	not out	3
Extras	(b 18, lb 11, nb 10, w 1)	40
Total	(all out, 113.3 overs)	419

Fall of wickets 1-98, 2-137, 3-198, 4-254, 5-261, 6-353, 7-359, 8-400, 9-414, 10-419

International XI bowling: PJW Allott 24-6-70-0, KD Ghavri 17-1-70-0, EE Hemmings 49.3-14-175-10, KBS Jarvis 16-2-45-0, TE Jesty 7-1-19-0

International XI: GD Mendis, G Fowler, AR Butcher, RO Butcher, JG Wright (capt), TE Jesty, CJ Richards (wk), EE Hemmings, PJW Allott, KD Ghavri, KBS Jarvis

Born in Leamington Spa in 1949 Eddie Hemmings played for local works team Lockhead before making his Warwickshire debut in 1966. Beginning as a medium pacer, he eventually found success as an off-spinner who, with a lively, orthodox action, could deceive batsmen both in the air and off the pitch. His comfortable build did not prevent him having a 518-match career that lasted 29 years. To this substantial output would be added almost as many limited-overs matches.

His breakthrough came in 1974, eighty-four wickets and 645 runs earning him his county cap. After a couple more good seasons his performances waned and in 1979, his attributes not always appreciated at Edgbaston, he moved to Trent Bridge. Two years later he was a key member of a County Championship-winning side, and the summer after that he was a Test cricketer, initially getting his chance because John Emburey had been banned for going on a rebel South African tour. Hemmings' final Test figures in 16 matches, spread over nine years, were fairly modest, 43 wickets and 383 runs. However, his career was not without interest.

It is probably best remembered for Lord's 1990 when Kapil Dev decided that the best way to avoid the follow-on was to hit him for four successive sixes. He had his revenge in the second innings, picking up Kapil cheaply and helping bowl England to victory.

The first proper all-ten in the West Indies was a long time coming. Fitz Hinds had taken ten for 36 for A.B. St Hill's team against Trinidad in January 1901 but this was a 12-a-side match and fast bowler Henry Simmons chipped in late with a solitary wicket that prevented Hinds achieving an all-eleven,

With the West Indian first-class season largely held in the early months of the year a number of territories took the opportunity to arrange special matches in the period between the end of the English season and the start of the Australian one. In 1982 the Jamaican Cricket Board of Control's second International Cricket Festival, sponsored by Shell, Air Florida and the Jamaica Pegasus Hotel, comprised two matches between a West Indies Eleven captained by Clive Lloyd and an International Eleven under the New Zealander John Wright. The first, a 45-overs-a-side match played under lights at the National Stadium, Kingston, was the first night match contested in Jamaica. It was a great success, a crowd of more than 20,000 seeing an exciting finish and a win for the West Indies by three runs.

Hemmings' figures of nought for 41 from nine overs in this first match contrasted with those in the second match, which was played at Sabina Park. The match was preceded by an emotional ceremony, watched by many former West Indies stars, which saw 73-year-old Jamaican great George Headley open the new 7,000 seat south stand named in his honour. The West Indies side was almost at its awesome full Test strength, while Wright's side included seven Englishmen supplemented by Sri Lankan opening batsman Gehan Mendis, Indian left-arm opening bowler Kharsan Ghavri, and Barbados-born Roland Butcher.

Heavy rain before the match had affected part of the pitch and if hadn't been a festival match it might not have started. The visitors' first innings 262 wasn't a bad effort given that the West Indies' pace attack comprised Sylvester Clarke, Andy Roberts, Michael Holding and Malcolm Marshall, and that of their team only Roland Butcher had previously played first-class cricket in the West Indies. Clarke had the best figures (five for 26), whilst Lancashire's Graeme Fowler (63) and Surrey's Jack Richards (62) would have been well pleased with their performances against such a fearsome foursome. Kent's Kevin Jarvis was probably also feeling happy with his 14 not out, a total he had never reached before in 160 first-class matches. Hemmings himself was a useful batsman who had made his maiden, and only, first-class century two months before. This time however Clarke trapped him in front before he had scored.

Ghavri and Lancashire's Paul Allott opened the bowling against the West Indies side but could make little headway against Gordon Greenidge and Desmond Haynes, and it took the introduction of Hemmings to effect a breakthrough by having Greenidge caught by Ghavri, although not before the famous opening pair had put on 98. Jamaica's left-hand batsman

237

George Powell came in next, but didn't stay too long before Hemmings had him caught behind by wicketkeeper Richards. Together with fellow Jamaican Robert Haynes he was the only member of the West Indies XI not to play Test cricket, although wrist-spinner Haynes would later go on to play eight one-day internationals. After that the West Indians batted consistently, with every batman down to Andy Roberts at number nine reaching double figures (and extras chipping in with 40).

The tail didn't keep Hemmings waiting too long, but it was no foregone conclusion: Clarke had a first-class century to his name and Holding would eventually make six Test fifties. Two of Hemmings' wickets had fallen to particularly fine boundary catches by Trevor Jesty. Two more were taken by Ordelmo Peters, a young Jamaican batsman fielding substitute for the visitors. Some of the locals apparently weren't too impressed and pelted him with beer bottles. For his own safety he was moved to a part of the ground where the occupants were a little more sober. Peters made 82 and 79 on his first-class debut against Trinidad and Tobago later in the season, but after this promising start, in a 21-match career, never made a century. The West Indian batsmen had gone for their shots and Hemmings had paid a high price for his success - nobody has ever conceded as many as 175 runs in taking an all-ten, and only Jim Laker at Old Trafford had bowled more balls. Nevertheless it was a considerable achievement to take all-ten against such a strong batting side, and on first-class debut in the West Indies at the age of 33. Hemmings had taken the first all-ten for 13 years. The previous one had also taken place in September, usually a quiet month for records.

Not surprisingly the West Indies XI's 419 was the highest score in which a bowler had taken all-ten, beating the 360 that Kent scored while Jupp took ten for 127 in 1932.

Unfortunately rain had the final say and washed out the last day's play, possibly saving John Wright's side from defeat. The status of the match was initially unclear and for obvious reasons Hemmings was very pleased when he eventually learned later in 1983 that cricket statisticians had classified it as first-class.

Just over two years before, another off-spinner, Derick Parry, playing for Combined Leeward and Windward Islands, had taken nine for 76 against Jamaica, the first nine wicket haul at Sabina Park since first-class cricket began there in 1895. His record hadn't lasted long.

Hemmings' winter had other highlights. He played three Tests in the Bob Willis side that returned the Ashes to Australia. In the final one, at Sydney, he went in as nightwatchman on the fourth evening and resisted for nearly four hours, falling just five short of an improbable hundred and helping save England from probable defeat.

Hemmings was also an effective limited-overs performer: as well as playing in the 1987/88 World Cup Final against Australia he appeared in four Lord's finals for Nottinghamshire. In the 1989 Benson and Hedges Cup Final against Essex he faced the last ball of the match, bowled by John Lever, needing to hit it for four to bring the Cup to Trent Bridge for the first time. He did just that. His last match with Nottinghamshire was in 1992, but even then he wasn't finished. Three more seasons with Sussex saw him still playing in 1995 at the age of 46.

Capped by three counties, Hemmings took 1,515 first-class wickets, a total exceeded by only four cricketers who have made their debuts since 1966 (John Emburey, John Lever, Malcolm Marshall and Courtney Walsh). After county cricket he coached, ran a post office and then became groundsman at Caythorpe Cricket Club in Nottinghamshire. Sons James and Tom both played county Second Eleven cricket, whilst niece allrounder Beth Morgan played in seven Test matches and 72 ODIs for England Women.

Pradeep Sunderam

Rajasthan v Vidarbha, 1985/86
Ranji Trophy

Barkatullah Khan Stadium, Jodhpur on 17, 18, 19 November 1985 (3-day match)
Toss won by Rajasthan
Rajasthan won by nine runs. (Rajasthan were bowled out short of the winning target but when penalty runs for Vidarbha's slow over-rate were added they were declared winners)
Umpires: BR Keshavamurthy. R Mitra
Vidarbha 140 (P Sunderam 10-78) and 184 (P Sunderam 6-76); Rajasthan 218 (BB Thakre 5-44) and 115

Vidarbha first innings

+ PB Hingnikar	c and b Sunderam	1
*VS Telang	lbw b Sunderam	0
MT Kaore	not out	19
SG Hedaoo	c Ratan Singh b Sunderam	0
SP Takle	b Sunderam	0
PG Sahasrabudhe	b Sunderam	45
SJ Phadkar	b Sunderam	0
VS Gawate	c and b Sunderam	0
HR Wasu	b Sunderam	10
A Wankhede	c Asawa b Sunderam	15
BB Thakre	c Vyas b Sunderam	23
Extras	(b 4, nb 3)	7
Penalties		20
Total	(all out, 43 overs)	140

Fall of wickets 1-1, 2-5, 3-5, 4-5, 5-8, 6-8, 7-69, 8-78, 9-86, 10-120

Rajasthan bowling: P Sunderam 22-5-78-10, Yunus Ali 9-6-13-0, AV Mudkavi 2-1-2-0, Ratan Singh 7-1-16-0, SV Mudkavi 3-1-7-0

Rajasthan: SR Kaushik (wk), Parvinder Singh, PL Shastri, SV Mudkavi, AB Asawa, S Jain, AV Mudkavi, SM Vyas (capt), P Sunderam, Ratan Singh, Yunus Ali

In its first fifty years only two bowlers (Chatterjee and Gupte) had taken 15 wickets in a Ranji Trophy match. Medium pacer Pradeep Sunderam would become the third man to achieve the feat, and then for good measure go one better. Born in Jaipur, Rajasthan, northern India, in 1960, Sunderam made his first-class debut in 1982. His father Gundibail had played for India twice, opening the bowling against New Zealand in 1955/56.

He is another bowler whose all-ten probably came as a bit of a surprise. Although he had taken five wickets in an innings three times in his second season, in a 14-match career so far he had taken just 49 wickets at 37 apiece. He never played Test cricket, but after his success against Vidarbhar he might have hoped to be picked to go to England with the

Indian side in 1986, but wasn't. When Chetan Sharma was ruled out of the Second Test, India needed a replacement and called up the experienced Madan Lal from the Central Lancashire League. As he took three good wickets, in what proved to be his final Test, and India went two up in the three match series, it was a good choice. However Sunderam was also in the country playing league cricket in Surrey and given the chance would also no doubt have found the conditions conducive.

In 1985/86 the 27 teams competing in the Ranji Trophy were divided into five zonal leagues, with the first two teams from each league going forward into the knockout stage. Vidarbha and Rajasthan played in the five-team Central Zone. Neither side was particularly strong and there were no Test players on view, past or future. None of the Vidarbha side's batsmen would finish their careers with averages of 30, none of its bowlers with averages below 30. Failing to win any of their matches in the previous season the two sides had finished fourth and fifth respectively in the group, which was won by Uttar Pradesh. Both sides presumably therefore approached this their first match of the new season with some trepidation, especially Rajasthan who had four first-class debutants. Neither side had ever won the Trophy, although Rajasthan had reached the final a number of times in the 1960s, most recently against Karnataka in 1973/74 when Hanumant Singh's side failed to resist the wiles of India's spinners Prasanna and Chandrasekhar.

This was the first of only five first-class matches that have been played at the Barkatullah Khan Stadium, Jodhpur (although it has staged two one-day internationals). Rather curiously, the team batting last won by nine runs (of which more later!). Most matches in the Ranji Trophy were played on grass, but a few, including this one, were played on coir matting.

With the bespectacled Sunderam taking two wickets in his second over, and 5 for two quickly becoming 8 for six, the Rajasthan captain, Sanjay Vyas, must have been well pleased with his decision to ask the visitors to bat first. Having hit the stumps three times, to add to a leg-before and two caught and bowleds, Sunderam hadn't yet needed much help from the field.

At this stage several records were on the cards, including the best bowling figures in India (held by Chatterjee) and the lowest ever team score in India (21 by Muslims v Europeans, Poona 1915/16). The record for most ducks in a first-class innings was eight and as five Vidarbha batsmen had so far failed to score even this 'achievement' was looking vulnerable. However the visitors rallied and thanks to a dogged innings from Madan Kaore who had gone in first wicket down and remained undefeated, a hard-hit 45 from Prakash Sahasrabudhe and a tail that wagged to good effect, 8 for six, and then 69 for seven, became 140 all out. Bharat Thakre going in last made 23 on his first-class debut, a score he never came close to emulating in a 16-match career. Thirty-six-year-old Sahasrabudhe, the oldest player in the match, was in his last first-class season. He had made a century on debut 17 years before but in a 50-match career, all played for Vidarbha, only passed three figures once more.

Sunderam had bowled unchanged and easily improved on his previous best figures of five for 98. Although the other bowlers of course failed to strike, they supported him by conceding runs at less than two an over. Opening bowler Yunus Ali and slow left-armer Ratan Singh were both making their first-class debuts. Ali's career only amounted to four matches, but Singh would eventually take 94 wickets in 28 matches. Anju Mudkavi was a very occasional bowler but his older brother, off-spinner Sanju, had a quite successful career, finishing with 169 wickets from 75 matches. In the previous season he had taken eight for 60 against Railways (and 11 wickets in the match), with Sunderam picking up the other two wickets.

In 1983/84, as part of a new scoring system, penalty points for slow over-rates had been introduced for Ranji Trophy zonal matches and Vidarbha's 140 had benefited from the addition of an extra 20 runs courtesy of tardy Rajasthan bowlers. In fact 80 penalty runs, 20 in each innings, would be conceded in the match as the over-rate fell five short of the required number in each innings. Penalty runs would be replaced by fines in the early 1990s.

Medium pacer Thakre continued to enjoy himself when Rajasthan went in, taking the first four wickets and finishing with five for 44. The home side's final total score of 218 was much helped by the generosity of Vidarbha who conceded 23 byes, bowled 15 no-balls and also donated their opponents 20 penalty runs.

The Vidarbha openers, wicketkeeper Praveen Hingnikar and captain Vijay Telang, did no better the second time around, again scoring just one run between them as Sunderam once more struck early. Having failed to score in the first innings Vikas Gawate redeemed himself with an undefeated 50 and helped give his side a chance of victory. Taking six for 76 Sunderam finished with match figures of sixteen for 154 to become the third bowler after Frank Tarrant (England v India [12-a-side] in 1915/16) and Jack Meyer (Europeans v Muslims in 1927/28) to take 16 wickets in a match in India. He was of course the first Indian to do so.

Chasing 107 to win Rajasthan seemed to have little chance of victory when their ninth wicket fell at 62. With the exception of 20-year-old debutant Sohain Jain, whose 30 would be the highest score of his four-match career, none of the first nine batsman reached double figures. However a last wicket partnership of 33 edged them closer before the tenth wicket fell at 95. A narrow defeat? Well no, because when the penalty runs for Vidarbha's slow over-rate were added at the end of the innings Rajasthan's total jumped to 115, and a nine-run victory had been secured! Strange but true.

Having qualified for the knockout stages of the Trophy by finishing second in their group to Uttar Pradesh, Rajasthan advanced to the semi-final by virtue of a first innings lead in their quarter-final match against Andhra. Sunderam hadn't played in the quarter-final, and he only bowled four overs in the semi-final which Rajasthan lost to a formidable Delhi side in a match dominated by spinners. He retired five years later without playing in a Ranji Trophy final. In 40 first-class matches he took 145 wickets at an average of 28.78.

Rajasthan would eventually win the Ranji Trophy for the first time in 2010/11 and repeat their success again the following season. However, next season they finished second from bottom in their group and, in order to revive their fortunes, appointed Sunderam as their coach following his good work for over a decade in nurturing young talent at the Mumbai Cricket Academy. He was apparently not alone in thinking that bowlers should spend more time in the nets and less in the gym. Unfortunately his appointment did not lead to immediate improvement and Rajasthan have failed to qualify for the Trophy quarter-finals in any season since.

Stephen Jefferies

Western Province v Orange Free State, 1987/88
Currie Cup

Newlands, Cape Town on 26, 27, 28 December 1987 (3-day match)
Toss won by Western Province
Western Province won by an innings and 76 runs
Umpires: JW Peacock, W Richard
Orange Free State 134 (DB Rundle 5-33) and 113 (ST Jefferies 10-59); Western Province 323

Orange Free State second innings

PJR Steyn	c Cullinan b Jefferies	4
LJ Wilkinson	c Cullinan b Jefferies	12
AC Storie	c Ryall b Jefferies	13
AI Kallicharran	c Simons b Jefferies	6
BT Player	c Ryall b Jefferies	6
AJ Lamb	not out	30
*JJ Strydom	c Seeff b Jefferies	0
+RJ East	b Jefferies	1
ST Clarke	lbw b Jefferies	0
CJPG van Zyl	c Lazard b Jefferies	3
AA Donald	c Kuiper b Jefferies	25
Extras	(lb 7, nb 6)	13
Total	(all out, 47.5 overs)	113

Fall of wickets 1-17, 2-26, 3-44, 4-52, 5-58, 6-58, 7-60, 8-60, 9-64, 10-113

Western Province bowling: GS le Roux 15-7-29-0, ST Jefferies 23.5-7-59-10, EO Simons 4-1-6-0, DB Rundle 5-2-12-0

Western Province: TN Lazard, L Seeff, PN Kirsten, DJ Cullinan, JJE Hardy, AP Kuiper (capt), GS le Roux, EO Simons, ST Jefferies, DB Rundle, RJ Ryall (wk)

Born in Cape Town in 1959, Stephen Jefferies made his first-class debut, appropriately at Newlands, just before his 19th birthday. Most of his South African career was spent playing for his home province but he had two spells in English county cricket during the 1980s, in both of which his fast-medium left-arm bowling met with only limited success. Three years after his debut he was the second highest wicket-taker in South Africa in 1981/82, his 52 wickets beaten only by the 75 taken by Natal's exceptional Vintcent van der Bijl. For his performance the *South African Cricket Annual* made him one of its Cricketers of the Year. Three seasons at Lancashire followed and at first things looked promising. However his appearances were restricted by injury, and because of the regulations in force at the time he couldn't play when Clive Lloyd was available. Nevertheless his impressive bowling added much-needed penetration to the county attack. Unfortunately, although he batted usefully in the next two seasons, his bowling disappointed and the county released him. After a spell in the Lancashire League with the Blackburn-based club East Lancashire, Jefferies returned to county cricket again in 1988 on a two-year contract with Hampshire to cover for Malcolm Marshall.

Like many of his generation, Jefferies was denied the opportunity of playing Test cricket, but his form was good enough for him to be selected to play for his country against a variety of unofficial sides that came to South Africa during the 1980s. The South African sides of the period were a match for anyone: in his first match Jefferies' team-mates included Barry Richards, Graeme Pollock and Mike Procter. Jefferies held his own in this august company: in the eleven representative matches he played between 1982 and 1986 he took 39 wickets at 29.82.

The two teams that assembled for a Currie Cup match on Boxing Day 1987 at the beautiful Newlands ground included some fearsome quick bowlers. The home side fielded Garth le Roux, whilst the visitors opened with Sylvester Clarke and a promising 21-year-old named Allan Donald. However, it would be the slightly lesser pace of 28-year-old Steve Jefferies that would hit the headlines.

Under a new Currie Cup format there were now two sections of three teams, with the three playing the other two in the section home and away, and the teams in the other section once. The group winners would then go forward to the Final. Both teams had played one match. Orange Free State (OFS) had beaten Eastern Province in a match notable for Allan Lamb's career-best 294, whilst Western Province had the better of a draw with Natal, finishing on 71 for five chasing 79 to win. Western Province had a good Cup record having won it several times, most recently in 1985/86. OFS had never won it. They were heavily dependent on Lamb who, playing his first season back in his own country for six years, topped the national averages and was the season's highest run-scorer. While he averaged 87.80, no other OFS batsman averaged 30.

Put in to bat and making only 134 OFS didn't help themselves by losing their first two wickets to run-outs. Most of the damage was done by the off breaks of Dave Rundle. Jefferies only took one wicket but it was a useful one, West Indian Alvin Kallicharran, who was coming to the end of a long and successful career, bowled for one. Thanks to half-centuries from Terence Lazard (one of only seven batsmen to make a triple-century in South Africa), Lawrence Seeff and Peter Kirsten, Western Province passed OFS's score with only one wicket down. With their captain, big-hitting allrounder Adrian Kuiper, also making a fifty, Western Province achieved a substantial first-innings lead. Four years later Kuiper would make a solitary Test appearance in South Africa's inaugural post-apartheid return to the fold. Circumstances denied him the chance of a substantial Test career, although he did play in 25 one-day Internationals.

OFS's second innings was even more lamentable than their first and they never looked like making Western Province bat again. Jefferies opened the bowling with le Roux who was coming to the end of a career in which his pace-bowling had brought him 838 wickets, including 372 wickets for Western Province at the impressive average of 18.98. However it was the swing and movement of Jefferies that did the damage. Fifty for three at the close of the second day quickly became 64 for nine next morning as, in overcast conditions, Jefferies took six wickets in 20 deliveries. Captain Joubert Strydom, who had made a century against Eastern Province the week before, and Sylvester Clarke both failed to score. Clarke's duck completed a pair for the match and there were probably a few Western Province batsmen who were glad they didn't have to go in again and face retribution from the fiery Bajan.

OFS's 'recovery' to 113 all out was mainly due to Lamb who, having top scored in the first innings with 29, did so again, and Donald (25) who, having already been bowled by a Jefferies no-ball, eventually became his tenth victim, Kuiper taking a reflex catch at short leg. No bowler has had to endure a longer partnership for the last wicket before completing his all-ten. The in-form Lamb's resistance was not surprising, but in a 316-match first-class career Donald would pass fifty just once, and that feat would have to wait for another ten years. Jefferies had bowled unchanged. According to *Wisden* it was 'as fine an exhibition of seam bowling as one could wish to see'. He had been well supported in the field, particularly by 20-year-old Daryll Cullinan, who would soon be embarking on a successful Test career, and by Richard Ryall, still Western Province's most successful wicketkeeper with 388 victims.

It was over eighty years since Ernie Vogler had taken the previous all-ten in South Africa, although two bowlers had since come close by taking the first nine wickets before Tiger Lance and Graham Roope respectively spoiled things: Jackie Botten (nine for 23 for North Eastern Transvaal in 1958/59) and Keith McLaren (nine for 54 for Griqualand West in 1973/74). The previous best figures at Newlands were nine for 23 by Bill Howell for the Australians against Western Province in November 1902, just over three years after he had gone one wicket better against Surrey at The Oval.

Although their records were close to identical, Western Province were just pipped at the top of the Southern Section of the Currie Cup by OFS, the latter garnering a few more bonus points and going forward to the Final where they were beaten by Clive Rice's Transvaal. OFS would have to wait until 1992/93 before winning the cup (by then renamed the Castle Cup) for the first time.

Jefferies spent the next two English summers with Hampshire. His impact at the first-class level was limited. However, he hit the heights at Lord's in 1988 when he bowled Hampshire to victory in the Benson and Hedges Cup Final against Derbyshire. His inswinger going well, he took four for 1 in a spell of eight balls that decided the match in the first hour, and if a hard chance hadn't been missed at slip he would have had a hat-trick. His final figures were five for 13 and Hampshire, who were playing in their first Lord's final, the last first-class county to do so, cantered home by seven wickets against a Derbyshire attack led by Michael Holding and Devon Malcolm. For the second time in a year Jefferies had out-bowled illustrious and pacier opponents.

After playing all his domestic cricket with Western Province Jefferies had one last season with Boland in 1993/94 before retiring with a career total of 478 first-class wickets and a further 256 in one-day cricket.

Imran Adil

Bahawalpur v Faisalabad, 1989/90
BCCP Patron's Trophy

Iqbal Stadium, Faisalabad on 30, 31 October, 1, 2 November 1989 (4-day match)
Toss won by Bahawalpur
Faisalabad won by 31 runs
Umpires: Khalid Aziz, Saqib Irfan
Faisalabad 226 (Imran Adil 10-92) and 139 (Imran Adil 5-66); Bahawalpur 155 and 179

Faisalabad first innings

Aamer Nazir	b Imran Adil	0
Nadeem Arshad	c Shahid Anwar b Imran Adil	35
Mohammad Ashraf	c Imran Zia b Imran Adil	0
Saadat Gul	lbw b Imran Adil	0
+Bilal Ahmed	c Sohail Iqbal b Imran Adil	47
Tanvir Afzal	c Imran Zia b Imran Adil	57
Naseer Shaukat	c and b Imran Adil	13
*Wasim Haider	not out	62
Anwar Awais	c Mohammad Zahid b Imran Adil	7
Rashid Wali	b Imran Adil	1
Naved Nazir	c Imran Zia b Imran Adil	0
Extras	(lb 1, nb 1, w 2)	4
Total	(all out, 56.5 overs)	226

Fall of wickets 1-0, 2-0, 3-1, 4-86, 5-107, 6-180, 7-209, 8-225, 9-226, 10-226

Bahawalpur bowling: Imran Adil 22.5-3-92-10, Shahid Anwar 13-2-36-0, Tariq Ismail 2-0-12-0, Saleem Taj 1-0-8-0, Mohammad Zahid 6-0-21-0, Naeem Taj 9-0-44-0, Mohammad Shahid 3-0-12-0

Bahawalpur: Shahid Anwar, Tariq Ismail, Javed Rana, Imran Zia (wk), Saleem Taj, Mohammad Shahid, Aamer Sohail, Naeem Taj, Sohail Iqbal, Mohammad Zahid, Imran Adil (capt)

Three weeks short of his 19th birthday Imran Adil became the youngest bowler to take an all-ten, and the second teenager after Tony Pearson 28 years before. Unfortunately, unlike Pearson, his feat did not prevent him finishing on the losing side.

Born in Bahawalpur, Punjab, he made his first-class debut in November 1985 aged 14 years 358 days, which makes him younger than any debutant in Britain (beating Barney Gibson who was a month older when he played for Yorkshire in 2011) but way down the long list of (apparently) precocious Asian cricketers. Just over three years later the promise of Adil's fast-medium bowling earned him selection for the Second Under-19 Test between Pakistan and India, a 4-day non-first-class match. Numbered among a strong Pakistan side were three players who would go on to have a considerable impact at full Test level: Moin Khan, Inzamam-ul-Haq and Mushtaq Ahmed. In his only representative match Adil had the rather unimpressive figures of 11 overs, one for 69, although as Mushtaq, in a foretaste of the future, took 12 wickets, none of the other bowlers got much of a chance to shine.

Adil was another bowler whose all-ten probably came as a bit of a surprise. His first-class career had begun slowly: used sparingly his maiden wicket didn't come until his fourth match. Progress continued to be slow. Prior to becoming the second Pakistani to take all-ten in an innings he had played 15 first-class matches and only taken 24 wickets (only Moss (0) and Hinkly (9) had fewer wickets before taking an all-ten), and with best figures of four for 68 he had not yet even taken five in an innings. In his previous match he had taken two for 209 in 42 overs against Multan, at the wonderfully named Biscuit Factory Ground in Sahiwal.

Eight teams contested the BCCP Patron's Trophy in 1989/90, meeting each other once on a league basis before the top two played off in a final. Karachi fielded two sides, with their Blues eventually finishing top of the table above their Whites, but then losing to them in an exciting final by one wicket.

The Iqbal Stadium is named in honour of poet and philosopher Allama Iqbal. It has hosted 24 Test matches. England's record there is played four, drawn four, although the second of their visits might have achieved a result if it hadn't been for the infamous Shakoor Rana Mike Gatting 'disagreement'. Despite the effects of smog generated by the city's industries the ground was not unattractive. One side was open, and although there was concrete terracing on the other side, it was not quite as obtrusive as at some other subcontinent grounds. The slow pitch meant that bowlers had to work hard for their wickets (not least in the ground's second Test in March 1980 when Pakistan responded to Australia's 617 with 382 for two – match drawn!).

Both teams in BCCP Patron's Trophy match were very young, with nobody in their thirties, and only three having reached 25. In the absence of regular captain Abdur Rahim, Imran Adil, the team's third youngest member, led the Bahawalpur side. Nobody in the match would play Test cricket although Wasim Haider and Shahid Anwar would appear in one-day internationals. Faisalabad had finished above Bahawalpur in the Trophy the previous season, and probably had the greater strength in depth. However in long careers, Bahawalpur opener Shahid Anwar would score 26 centuries, a total which the whole of the Faisalabad line-up would fail to emulate, and left-arm spinner Mohammad Zahid would take 563 wickets, more than twice the total that would be achieved by any of the Faisalabad attack.

Adil made a good start by winning the toss. Reading the conditions well he put his opponents in. Having bowled 252 balls to get just two wickets in his previous match, he didn't hang about this time, quickly reducing Faisalabad to one for three. Aamer Nazir was his first victim, bowled without scoring, the first half of a pair that he would help him complete the following day. After such a good start Adil had to work harder for his wickets as solid contributions by a number of batsmen, led by captain

Wasim Haider and offspinner Tanvir Afzal, whose fifty would be the only one he would make in a 66-match career, saw a recovery to 226 all out about an hour and a half before the close. Adil's final wicket, caught behind, was slow left-armer Naved Nazir who had taken nine for 109 against Lahore City on the same ground the previous year, the first time this feat had been performed at the stadium since first-class cricket had begun there in 1966. His record hadn't lasted long. Perhaps surprisingly in a lowish score Adil used seven bowlers. His fellow opening bowler was Shahid Anwar who as opening batsman had a busy match. An occasional medium pacer he only once took more than three wickets in an innings, in November 1996 achieving the remarkable figures of six for 2 for National Bank of Pakistan against Pakistan Customs in a match in which he also scored a century. Anwar had bowled fairly steadily conceding less than three runs an over. The other five bowlers used had the unimpressive combined figures of 21-0-97-0.

Thirty-year-old umpire Saqib Irfan only stood in eight first-class matches, and this was his first and he had seen an all-ten on the first day. Quite a debut.

Bahawalpur's batsmen soon did their best to undermine Adil's efforts and the side was facing a large deficit before Saleem Taj (52 not out), at 29 the oldest participant in the match, and Mohammad Zahid (35) came together at 92 for eight and put on 60 for the ninth wicket to give the final score some respectability. Each first innings in the match was limited to 85 overs. Each side had finished about 30 overs short!

Adil took another five wickets in Faisalabad's second innings to finish with 15 for 158 in the match. The star of the innings was 21-year-old Imran Zia who became the second Pakistani wicketkeeper, after Wasim Bari, to take seven catches in an innings, and the first to take ten in a match. Imran Zia had a short, 26-match, career and played his last match just two seasons later. With Faisalabad's Bilal Ahmed picking up eight catches it was a good match for keepers.

Set 211 to win Bahawalpur never looked like getting close. Of their batsmen only opener Shahid Anwar (53) contributed and it was again left to Mohammad Zahid (33) to provide support from the tail. In a match largely dominated by the quicker bowlers he hadn't needed to do much bowling, but he was no doubt pleased to beat his own previous highest score of 26 twice in the match.

It was a curious season for Imran Adil. He didn't always bowl a great deal, and took 15 wickets in one match and seven in the other six. However he eventually had quite a long career, finishing his last match in 2002/03 with 186 first-class wickets at 27.52. It would be four years after his all-ten before he took five or more wickets in an innings again, but then he achieved the feat five times over two good seasons in which he took 64 wickets. Appropriately his last first-class victim was Wasim Haider, the one batsman who had eluded him 13 years before when he achieved his all-ten.

Pramodya Wickramasinghe

Sinhalese Sports Club v Kalutara Physical Culture Centre, 1991/92
Saravanamuttu Trophy

Sinhalese Sports Club Ground, Colombo on 15, 16, 17 November 1991
(3-day match)
Toss won by Sinhalese Sports Club
Sinhalese Sports Club won by five wickets
Umpires: MMT Bandara, SG Ponnadurai
Kalutara Physical Culture Centre 82 (GP Wickramasinghe 10-41) and 183;
Sinhalese Sports Club 108-3 dec and 160-5

Kalutara Physical Culture Centre first innings

T Silva	c Wickramaratne b Wickramasinghe	1
P Perera	c Gurusinha b Wickramasinghe	11
M Hemantha	c Wickramaratne b Wickramasinghe	0
TNS Warusamana	not out	36
M Wijesinghe	c Wickramaratne b Wickramasinghe	6
*L Karunaratne	b Wickramasinghe	0
K Mendis	c Ranatunga b Wickramasinghe	0
B David	c Wickramaratne b Wickramasinghe	0
+AR Silva	c WMCN Fernando b Wickramasinghe	10
TJ Fernando	c Jayawardene b Wickramasinghe	6
S Devapriya	b Wickramasinghe	4
Extras	(b 1, lb 1, nb 6)	8
Total	(all out, 39.4 overs)	82

Fall of wickets 1-1, 2-1, 3-28, 4-36, 5-36, 6-38, 7-43, 8-68, 9-76, 10-82

Sinhalese Sports Club bowling: FS Ahangama 3-0-6-0, GP Wickramasinghe
19.4-5-41-10, C Ranasinghe 3-2-6-0, AP Gurusinha 4-1-4-0, RS Jayawardene
9-2-21-0, A Ranatunga 1-0-2-0

Sinhalese Sports Club: AAW Gunawardene, WMCN Fernando, AP
Gurusinha, A Ranatunga, MS Atapattu, UNK Fernando, C Ranasinghe, RPAH
Wickramaratne (wk), RS Jayawardene, GP Wickramasinghe, FS Ahangama
(capt)

Pramodya Wickramasinghe was born in 1971 in the southern coastal city
of Matara just over two years after one of Sri Lanka's greatest, Sanath
Jayasuriya, also first saw the light of day there. He was another bowler
whose all-ten had been preceded by a modest career record so far: 39
wickets in 16 matches and best figures of four for 37. A reliable medium-
fast bowler relying on accuracy and movement in the air, he was still
only just 20 and recently out of Rahula College, Matara. However, he had
played for Sri Lanka Under-19s, been a member of a young Sri Lankan side
that had toured England in 1990, and on return had played in a one-day
international against Bangladesh.

Domestic matches in Sri Lanka had only been ruled as first-class by the Sri
Lankan Board three years previously. The Saravanamuttu Trophy was the
main domestic trophy in Sri Lanka, having existing in various guises since

1938. It was named in honour of Paramjoti Saravanamuttu, president of the Ceylon Cricket Association (1937-49), and the first president of its successor the Board of Control for Cricket in Sri Lanka. In 1991/92 it was contested by two groups of seven teams, with the group winners then playing off for the Trophy.

The Sinhalese Sports Club Ground was one of three grounds in Colombo to have staged Test cricket, to which a fourth would soon be added. It is the headquarters of Sri Lanka Cricket and has hosted more Tests than any other ground in the country. Built on an aerodrome which was used by Allied forces during the Second World War, it has a capacity of about 10,000, with the general public mainly accommodated on open grass banks.

Sinhalese Sports Club (SSC) had had considerable success in the competition's pre-first-class days and were current holders, but this year would just be pipped in the Final by Colts Cricket Club. They had a powerful batting line-up, with a middle order that included three Test stars: Asanka Gurusinha, Arjuna Ranatunga and Marvan Atapattu. The opposition was less well-endowed and, it has to be said, were their group's whipping boys, losing three matches and not even getting near a first-innings lead in the matches they drew. All of the side against SSC had made their first-class debuts in the season, and only two would go on to have first-class careers of any substance - 19-year-old allrounder Pathmanath Perera, 44 matches, and 17-year-old left-hand batsman Sanjeewa Warusamana, 52 matches. None of the rest would play more than ten times and, as Kalutura would not play first-class cricket for another 25 years, seven were playing in their only first-class season.

Without achieving spectacular returns Wickramasinghe had begun the season taking wickets steadily. The season's Trophy matches had been badly affected by rain, and with no play possible on the first day of the scheduled three-day match against Kalutara, the home captain Saliya Ahangama decided to hasten things along by putting the opposition in to bat. Wickramasinghe then did his bit by bowling unchanged and taking his all-ten in just 19 overs. He quickly reduced the visitors to one for two as both opener Silva and his replacement Mahesh Hemantha were caught by wicketkeeper Hemantha Wickramaratne, the latter for the first half of a pair. Mahesh Hemantha had a curious two-year career. He failed to score in one third of his 15 innings and only exceeded ten twice, scoring 30 and an unlikely 163. After Kalutara's disastrous start nobody stayed long apart from young Warusamana who went in when Hemantha left and remained undefeated with 36. (Wickramasinghe would dismiss him for a duck in Kalutara's second innings.) Ahangama was clearly keen to keep getting wickets because the 20 overs at the other end were shared among five bowlers. It would seem that if you didn't strike quickly somebody else had a go! Thirty-two-year-old Ahangama had applied this maxim to his own performance, opening the bowling, but for only three overs. Six years previously he had made his Test debut, taking 18 wickets in just three matches against a strong Indian batting line-up. These figures suggested that a successful career was in store. Unfortunately because of injuries and Sri Lanka's lack of Test cricket he had already played in his last Test.

Most of Wickramasinghe's victims were induced to give catches, with Wickramaratne picking up four of them behind the stumps on the way to a haul of eight catches in the match. He only needed to hit the stumps twice, cleaning up Kalutara's captain Lois Karunaratne for the first of three middle-order ducks in a row, and completing his full hand of victims by bowling last man Devapriya for 4, the highest score he would make in his six first-class innings. Later in the day Devapriya would take his only three first-class wickets.

Anxious to continue to make up for lost time Ahangama declared his side's first innings just 26 ahead and then got an early Kalutara wicket to leave them 8 for one at the close. Next morning Wickramasinghe soon dismissed Warusamana and the unfortunate Hemantha. Another collapse seemed to be in the offing, but this time Kalutara's batsmen showed more resilience and by the time they were finally dismissed (Wickramasinghe three for 46) SSC were left little time to chase the 158 they needed for victory. That they managed to achieve their target in only 18.3 overs was mainly due to Arjuna Ranatunga's 89 not out. Warusamana bowled for the only time in his 52-match career, five overs of medium pace yielding a rather pricey two for 61.

Having hosted the best ever bowling analysis in Sri Lanka, the SSC Ground would later host the highest ever partnership in first-class cricket when Kumar Sangakkara and Mahela Jayawardene put on 624 in a Test match against South Africa in July 2006.

Wickramasinghe's all-ten clearly impressed the selectors and a month later he was making his Test debut against Pakistan in Sialkot. After taking five wickets in an innings in the Third Test at Faisalabad, he became a fairly regular member of the Sri Lanka attack during the next decade, his steadiness often providing a useful foil to the more exotic skills of Muttiah Muralitharan. However, surgery on his shoulder in 2000 more or less ended his Test career. With 85 wickets from 40 matches he was then Sri Lanka's third highest wicket-taker behind the two men who are still well clear at the top, Muralitharan and Chaminda Vaas. He only played once against England, at The Oval in August 1998 when, as Sri Lanka's second most successful bowler (with two wickets!), he was part of an attack that provided a support act to the marvellous Murali who took 16 wickets and bowled his side to victory. In all first-class cricket he took 345 wickets; he also played in 134 one-day internationals, most notably on the winning side in the 1996 World Cup Final in Lahore, taking 109 wickets.

Having played his last match in 2002 Wickramasinghe remained in the game, later becoming both president of the Sri Lanka Cricketers' Association, and a national selector.

Richard Johnson

Middlesex v Derbyshire, 1994
County Championship

County Ground, Derby on 30 June, 1, 2, July 1994 (4-day match)
Toss won by Derbyshire
Middlesex won by an innings and 96 runs
Umpires: R Palmer, P Willey
Derbyshire 344 (KJ Barnett 148, MA Feltham 5-69) and 105 (RL Johnson 10-45); Middlesex 545 (MW Gatting 147, MR Ramprakash 131, JD Carr 108 not out)

Derbyshire second innings

*KJ Barnett	c Emburey b Johnson	4
MJ Vandrau	b Johnson	0
TJG O'Gorman	c Emburey b Johnson	18
CJ Adams	c Carr b Johnson	8
DG Cork	c Feltham b Johnson	4
+AS Rollins	c and b Johnson	2
CM Wells	b Johnson	32
AE Warner	c Brown b Johnson	2
SJ Base	lbw b Johnson	20
M Taylor	c Ramprakash b Johnson	5
DE Malcolm	not out	1
Extras	(b 2, lb 4, nb 2, w 1)	9
Total	(all out, 40.5 overs)	105

Fall of wickets 1-4, 2-9, 3-30, 4-34, 5-35, 6-36, 7-43, 8-93, 9-104, 10-105

Middlesex bowling: RL Johnson 18.5-6-45-10, KJ Shine 6-2-15-0, MA Feltham 12-4-37-0, PCR Tufnell 2-1-2-0, DL Haynes 2-2-0-0

Middlesex: DL Haynes, MA Roseberry, MW Gatting (capt), MR Ramprakash, JD Carr, KR Brown (wk), MA Feltham, RL Johnson, JE Emburey, KJ Shine, PCR Tufnell

When Derbyshire and Middlesex met in June 1994 four of the bowlers playing had, or would take, over 100 Test wickets: for the home side the pace pair Dominic Cork and Devon Malcolm; for the visitors spinners John Emburey and Phil Tufnell. However it was the fast-medium swing bowling of 19-year-old Richard Johnson, playing only his eleventh first-class match and with previous best figures of only four for 64, that hit the headlines.

The wide open spaces of the County Ground had had a varied and interesting history, having once been a racecourse, and the home of Derby County Football Club, but in well over a hundred years of county cricket they had never seen an all-ten. In fact, perhaps surprisingly given its reputation as a venue not usually welcoming to batsmen, Leicestershire's David Millns, three years before, was the only bowler to have taken nine wickets in an innings there in the 20th century (although Kent's Martin McCague would do so in the month following Johnson's big day).

Born in Chertsey, Surrey at the end of 1974, Johnson played his early club cricket for Sunbury. Not yet 18, he made his first-class debut at the end of 1992 season and established himself in the Middlesex side two years later. Well-built, six foot two inches tall, and with a high action, he was coming into a successful side. Champions in 1993, Middlesex would finish fourth in 1994 and runners-up the following year.

Neither Derbyshire nor Middlesex had started the season well and had had to wait until mid-June for their first Championship victories. Derbyshire had followed up theirs by beating the touring New Zealanders by an innings, and must have had hopes of success against a Middlesex side lacking opening bowlers Angus Fraser and Neil Williams. They started well, scoring 344 mainly due to captain Kim Barnett's 148 which took him past 20,000 first-class runs. Starting their innings early on the second day Middlesex achieved a hefty lead thanks to centuries from Mike Gatting, Mark Ramprakash and John Carr. Under TCCB playing conditions two extras were scored for every no-ball bowled whether scored off or not and so 27 no-balls made a significant contribution to a very useful 81 extras!

The County Ground would finish the season in equal second place in the TCCB Table of Merit for pitches (based on umpires' marks), and so in good batting conditions the high scoring so far was perhaps not unexpected. However things changed on Saturday when Johnson got his hands on the ball at the beginning of Derbyshire's second innings. Although his first-class career had so far been fairly modest, he already included Brian Lara among his victims, having dismissed him the previous month to end a run of five successive first-class centuries (and this a fortnight after bowling him in a Benson and Hedges Cup match). Johnson soon got going, dismissing both openers with only nine on the board, Barnett slashing a loosener to gully and Matthew Vandrau bowled through the gate. There was something of a recovery as the score reached 30 for two, but then Johnson got to work again to leave Derbyshire 43 for seven, his first nine overs bringing him figures of seven for 17. He was rested three overs later.

Writing later in the Middlesex 1994/95 Review, Johnson recalled how tired he had been feeling, and when he came back after tea for a second spell his first two and a half overs went for 18 runs. He eventually settled down however and was re-energised when he broke an eighth wicket partnership of 50 between Simon Base and Colin Wells (who had just moved to Derbyshire after a long career with Sussex), a yorker pinning Base in front of the stumps. Eleven runs later a full length ball hit Wells' off stump. Having taken nine wickets, most bowlers would be happy to see Devon Malcolm coming to the wicket (with due respect to a bowler who the following month would take nine for 57 against South Africa, figures only ever bettered for England by Jim Laker and George Lohmann). The problem of course was that Malcolm might get out to the bowler at the other end. With Middlesex miles ahead, another day left, and the weather set fair, captain Mike Gatting could afford to help Johnson get his final wicket (although Johnson later said he hadn't been too bothered) and so opening batsman Desmond Haynes was brought on to trundle, hopefully innocuously, at the other end. The plan worked, Ramprakash at third slip catching slow left-armer Matthew Taylor (playing the penultimate match of his four-match career) off Johnson but not before Malcolm had caused a fright by bottom edging one ball just past his stumps and nearly presenting Haynes with what would have been a ninth, and final, first-class wicket. Johnson recalled that Taylor got probably the best ball of the innings, a sharp lifter that took the top of the bat.

Derbyshire hadn't batted very well (*Wisden* called their batting 'reckless') but it was still an outstanding performance by Johnson on a pitch only doing a little bit off the seam. He had accomplished the first all-ten in Britain for 30 years, and only Imran Adil had done it at a younger age. Seven of his wickets had fallen to catches, five behind the wicket, Cork mis-hooking to fine leg, and Adrian Rollins lobbing a leading edge back to the bowler. Unfortunately, while the rest of the team celebrated in the dressing-room Johnson missed the excitement (and the champagne!) as he had to give several media interviews.

Johnson maintained his good form in his next match, taking four for 40 in the Sussex first innings at Arundel, but then the injury curse that was to blight his career struck, knee surgery meaning that he could not return to Championship cricket until September and one last game at a wet Trent Bridge. The selectors had seen enough however, and the following winter found him in the subcontinent as the youngest member of the England A team. Injuries restricted his appearances the next summer but, finishing the season near the top of the national averages, he was selected for the England tour of South Africa. Sadly back trouble forced his withdrawal and then, having recovered, he strained a shoulder and missed much of the beginning of the following season!

England recognition eventually came against Zimbabwe in June 2003 as Chester-le-Street staged its first Test match. With two wickets in his first over (a feat only achieved by one other Test cricketer: Graeme Swann, five years later), and first innings figures of six for 33, it was some debut as he outbowled fellow pacemen Jimmy Anderson and Steve Harmison, and achieved figures bettered by only six other England Test debutants. A substantial Test career seemed to beckon. However, with more injuries and competition from the likes of Anderson, Andrew Flintoff, Matthew Hoggard and Simon Jones it was over by the end of the year. Sixteen wickets at 17 apiece from three Tests was a good record, but with luck it might have been even better.

Out of contract at Middlesex, and to test himself on Taunton's pitches, Johnson had moved to Somerset in 2001 where, as well as giving good service with the ball, he hit two first-class centuries, the second of which against Durham in 2004 won the Walter Lawrence Trophy for the season's fastest as he bludgeoned 101 not out off 63 balls. He was back home again in 2007 as Middlesex tried to strengthen its attack. However it was not a successful return and he played only four matches before announcing his retirement at the end of the season having taken 528 first-class wickets at 29 apiece.

Fortunately Richard Johnson was not lost to cricket. In 2008 he was a member of the Berkshire team that won the Minor Counties Championship and later, as Middlesex bowling coach, together with England bowling coach Kevin Shine, his wicketless opening partner when he took his all-ten, he helped rehabilitate Steven Finn's career as an England cricketer.

Naeem Akhtar

Arbab Niaz Stadium, Peshawar on 2, 3, 4 December 1995 (4-day match)
Toss won by Peshawar
Rawalpindi B won by 121 runs
Umpires: Sajjad Asghar, Shakeel Khan
Rawalpindi B 230 and 132 (Sajid Shah 5-57); Peshawar 92 (Naeem Akhtar 10-28) and 149 (Sabih Azhar 5-50)

Peshawar first innings

Aamer Bashir	c Iqbal Saleem b Naeem Akhtar	9
Akhtar Sarfraz	c Asif Mahmood b Naeem Akhtar	6
Taimur Khan	b Naeem Akhtar	0
Jahangir Khan	c Asif Mahmood b Naeem Akhtar	2
Sher Ali	lbw b Naeem Akhtar	12
Hameed Gul	lbw b Naeem Akhtar	24
Shahid Hussain	lbw b Naeem Akhtar	12
+Rafiq Ahmed	b Naeem Akhtar	4
Sajid Shah	not out	2
*Arshad Khan	b Naeem Akhtar	0
Ijaz Elahi	b Naeem Akhtar	6
Extras	(b 5, lb 9, nb 1)	15
Total	(all out, 42.3 overs)	92

Fall of wickets 1-11, 2-11, 3-18, 4-21, 5-43, 6-73, 7-81, 8-84, 9-84, 10-92

Rawalpindi B bowling: Naeem Akhtar 21.3-10-28-10, Sabih Azhar 7-2-23-0, Javed Hayat 4-1-6-0, Alamgir Khan 4-0-10-0, Tauqeer Hussain 6-1-11-0

Rawalpindi B: Naved Ashraf, Arif Butt, Iqbal Saleem (wk), Tasawwar Hussain, Asif Mahmood, Javed Hayat, Arif Javed, Sabih Azhar (capt), Naeem Akhtar, Tauqeer Hussain, Alamgir Khan

1995/96 was a busy season for Pakistan cricket: three home Tests against Sri Lanka in September, three more in Australia, one in New Zealand, the usual plethora of one-day internationals, and the World Cup meant that Pakistan domestic cricket saw little of its stars. It was also a fractious season. Pakistan had optimistically hoped to retain the World Cup, but went out in the quarter-finals to arch-rivals India, leading to much recrimination. Completing an all-ten the day after he had celebrated his 28th birthday Naeem Akhtar however would at least remember the season with some satisfaction. Born in Lyallpur (now Faisalabad), Punjab in 1967, and having made his first-class debut in December 1990, his fast-medium bowling had progressed steadily and his first five-for (seven for 98 for Rawalpindi against Multan) came two years later.

Akhtar had started the 1995/96 season well with a first-innings six for 80 for Rawalpindi B against Rawalpindi A. He was also a useful batsman who would make two first-class centuries and he had preceded this performance by making 46, his side's top score, against a Rawalpindi A attack that included a fairly quick 20-year-old fast bowler named Shoaib Akhtar. By the beginning of December Peshawar had performed quite well in the trophy so far, winning two out of five matches. Rawalpindi B on the other hand had made a poor start to their season and were still awaiting a victory. In the event neither team would do well enough in the ten-team league upon which the trophy was now based to qualify for the semi-final stage. (In the final Karachi Blues beat Karachi Whites. However, the trophy might have finished differently. Lahore City had won it two years before and with five wins out of nine matches had done enough to qualify for the semi-finals. However, they conceded their match against Karachi Blues because they claimed that the Karachi players had changed the ball in the drinks interval of Lahore's second innings. The umpires and referee disagreed but captain Aamer Malik refused requests to continue. Lahore's punishment was to lose all their points for the season.)

Peshawar is situated close to the Afghanistan border, in the former North-West Frontier Province. First-class cricket had been played at the Arbab Niaz Stadium for ten years. It had taken over as Peshawar's main venue from the Peshawar Club Ground (where Mike Brearley had made, approximately, 312 not out for MCC Under-25s in 1966/67[1]). A round bowl with a capacity of some 20,000, the ground had hosted the first of its six Test matches three months earlier, and three years later Australian captain Mark Taylor would make a famous Bradman-equalling 334 not out there.

There were no current Test players in Rawalpindi's side, although opener Naved Ashraf who top scored in their first innings would later play twice for Pakistan. Peshawar similarly had one future Test cricketer in their side, captain Arshad Khan, who would play for his country nine times (to add to 58 one-day internationals). However, it was runs that would be Peshawar's downfall in this match, and Khan was an off-spinner. Their batting might have been strengthened by the inclusion of Wajahatullah Wasti who had been playing earlier in the season, although with limited success. Wasti would go on to have a brief Test career which included two centuries, both made in his second match, against Sri Lanka in 1999.

Winning the toss and asking Rawalpindi to bat first Arshad Khan was rewarded with an early wicket, but was then held up by Naved Ashraf's aggressive 76 and a more sedate 50 from wicketkeeper Iqbal Saleem. All out 230 was a middling sort of score, but it looked better by close of play when two early Akhtar wickets left Peshawar 18 for two. The first batsman to fall was Akhtar Sarfraz. Not yet 19, and playing in his fourth first-class match, his innings of 6 equalled his highest score so far. He would have a curious season. Batting nine times, he made 15 runs in seven of these innings, whilst in the other two, played successively, he made 134 not out, carrying his bat in an innings of 242, and 162 (out of 260). With 13 first-class centuries and four ODI appearances he would go on to have a reasonably successful career.

---

1   Brearley and Worcestershire's Alan Ormrod (61 not out) put on 234 for the fifth wicket against North Zone. However there have been suggestions that at some stage the scorers may have got the two batsmen mixed up.

Peshawar's batting had been erratic so far during the season with only two innings (out of nine) passing 200. Their most consistent batsman, with a century and two fifties, was Sher Ali. At nearly 26 Ali was the second oldest member of the Peshawar side after 28 year-old-wicketkeeper Rafiq Ahmed. However he only made 12, as on the second day Akhtar took out the middle order with a trio of leg-befores. Peshawar's top-scorer, Hameed Gul, showed considerable resolve in batting for an hour and a half, twice as long as anybody else. He was just a month past his eighteenth birthday and the youngest player in the side but would not go on to fulfil this early promise. He later played for Ilford CC in the Essex Premier League.

Having given the umpires plenty of work to do Akhtar then cleaned up the tail without help from anybody and finished with record bowling figures in Pakistan. Last man, opening bowler Ijaz Elahi, had bowled Akhtar (for a second ball duck) when Rawalpindi had batted and Akhtar was probably pleased to return the compliment in completing his all-ten. Ijaz might also have been feeling pleased to make what would be his highest score in his four-match season!

Eventually set an unlikely 271 to win Peshawar succumbed by 121 runs, Akhtar taking another three wickets, and the match, scheduled for four days, finished in three with Rawalpindi B completing their only win of the season.

Peshawar would finally win the Trophy for the first time just three years later with a side including only three of those who faced Akhtar, but Rawalpindi (by now fielding just one side) would have to wait until 2013/14 before finally breaking their duck.

Naeem Akhtar never played Test cricket, but his all-ten earned him selection for Pakistan A against Nasser Hussain's England A side in a 40-over match later in the month. A very effective limited-overs cricketer, both with bat and ball, he scored 28 not out going in at number six and, opening the bowling, took nought for 9 in five overs. Unfortunately this would be the extent of his representative career. Nevertheless he continued to perform consistently for a number of seasons, culminating in 51 wickets in 2001/02. He also played for Khan Research Laboratories and when his first-class career finished two years later he had taken 322 wickets at 21 runs apiece. He played all of his first-class cricket in Pakistan, although he appeared in 50-over matches in England both for Cornwall and for the Derbyshire Cricket Board.

Anil Kumble

India v Pakistan, 1998/99

Feroz Shah Kotla, Delhi on 4, 5, 6, 7 February 1999 (5-day match)
Toss won by India
India won by 212 runs
Umpires: SA Bucknor, AV Jayaprakash
India 252 (Saqlain Mushtaq 5-94) and 339 (Saqlain Mushtaq 5-122);
Pakistan 172 and 207 (A Kumble 10-74)

Pakistan second innings

Saeed Anwar	c Laxman b Kumble	69
Shahid Afridi	c Mongia b Kumble	41
Ijaz Ahmed	lbw b Kumble	0
Inzamam-ul-Haq	b Kumble	6
Yousuf Youhana	lbw b Kumble	0
+Moin Khan	c Ganguly b Kumble	3
Saleem Malik	b Kumble	15
*Wasim Akram	c Laxman b Kumble	37
Mushtaq Ahmed	c Dravid b Kumble	1
Saqlain Mushtaq	lbw b Kumble	0
Waqar Younis	not out	6
Extras	(b 15, lb 2 , nb 10, w 2)	29
Total	(all out, 60.3 overs)	207

Fall of wickets 1-101, 2-101, 3-115, 4-115, 5-127, 6-128, 7-186, 8-198, 9-198, 10-207

India bowling: J Srinath 12-2-50-0, BKV Prasad 4-1-15-0, A Kumble 26.3-9-74-10, Harbhajan Singh 18-5-51-0

India: S Ramesh, VVS Laxman, RS Dravid, SR Tendulkar, M Azharuddin (capt), SC Ganguly, NR Mongia (wk), A Kumble, J Srinath, BKV Prasad, Harbhajan Singh

Anil Kumble, India's leading Test wicket-taker, is a statistician's dream: all ten wickets in a Test innings, a maiden Test century aged nearly 37, and 100 wickets in an English first-class season (1995), this last a feat only achieved three times since. Conventionally described as a leg break and googly bowler, this simple description does not do justice to his singular style. Starting life as a medium pacer, at the age of 15 his elder brother suggested that he tried spin, and he developed into a purveyor of brisk top spin, making the ball turn a little both ways. His down-to-earth unassuming character belied the tenacity of his bowling. Tall, with powerful shoulders, his long, lively swing of the arm enabled him to make the ball bounce dangerously on hard pitches. Relentlessly accurate, he presented batsmen with difficult choices: play forward and that bounce might pop the ball into the hands of waiting close fielders; play back and risk your defence being breached by a fizzing top spinner.

Kumble was born in Bangalore, Karnataka, in 1970. From street to school to club cricket he progressed rapidly, his Test debut against England in

August 1990 coming only nine months after his first-class debut. It was the start of an exceptional 132-Test career.

By the time India met Pakistan at the beginning of 1999 Kumble had taken over 200 Test wickets. This was the first series between the quarrelsome neighbours for nine years. Previous attempts during the 1990s to organise Pakistani tours of India had failed because of threats of disruption but the two Tests largely went off without trouble, albeit that massive levels of security were provided. A little confusingly the bilateral series was immediately followed by another Test that was part of the Asian Test Championship but not of the preceding series.

As the previous 14 Tests before the hiatus had yielded one positive result, expectations for an exciting series were probably not high. Happily expectations were confounded, and it turned out to be an exciting, and diplomatically successful, spin-dominated series played in front of large crowds between two strong and well-matched sides. The First Test at Chennai was a nail-biter. Chasing 271 India slumped to 82 for five but then, mainly thanks to a Tendulkar century, reached 254 for six before a late collapse saw four wickets go for two runs. For Pakistan, off-spinner (and purveyor of the doosra) Saqlain Mushtaq took five wickets in each innings, a feat he would emulate in the next Test.

The Second Test was played at Delhi's Feroz Shah Kotla, a wide open, largely uncovered ground with relatively rudimentary facilities, on a pitch of variable bounce that still hadn't recovered from the effects of recent politically-inspired vandalism. Kumble's feat was performed on the fourth day as Pakistan chased a record-breaking 420 to win, India having scored 339 in their second innings to add to a useful first innings lead of 80. One record had already been set earlier in the match when Pakistan captain Wasim Akram took his 363rd Test wicket to pass his nation's previous record-holder Imran Khan.

Although the Pakistan side included eight Test centurions their chances of victory were slight. However at 101 without loss, and with Saeed Anwar and Shahid Afridi well settled, they would have had hopes of at least a draw and a series victory. Kumble had bowled an unpromising eight overs for 37 but by now had switched to the Pavilion End, and this soon did the trick. With the second ball of his ninth over, an astounded 19-year-old Afridi, playing in his third Test, was controversially given out caught behind by umpire Arani Jayaprakash, a former first-class cricketer standing in his second Test. Next ball Ijaz Ahmed was clearly plumb in front to a low full toss and, although he averted a hat-trick, Inzamam-ul-Haq played on soon after. Yousuf Youhana and Moin Khan didn't last long and when Anwar went at 128 for six, caught at short leg after resisting for two and a half hours (his 69 was the second highest score in the match), the end seemed close. Kumble, varying pace and spin, had taken six wickets in 44 balls.

Wasim Akram resisted for an hour and a half, but defeat was surely still inevitable. Kumble took the eighth and ninth wickets in his 26th over: Mushtaq Ahmed caught at gully off an awkward lifter, Saqlain Mushtaq leg-before. He now had a chance to go one better than Jasu Patel, Kapil

Dev and Fergie Gupte, the only bowlers who had previously taken nine in an innings for India.

Unfortunately for Kumble his last two successes had been with the last two balls of the over and Javagal Srinath now had a whole over at Waqar Younis. Fortunately for Kumble his captain, Mohammad Azharuddin, quietly suggested to Srinath that he bowl off the stumps. Perhaps he should also have spoken to Waqar since the great fast bowler proceeded to play a number of wild shots that might just have spoiled things. However he survived and Kumble got his chance. Wasim kept out Kumble's second hat-trick ball of the innings, and one more, and then propping forward was caught at short leg by V.V.S. Laxman. India had won by 212 runs.

The celebrations were a little more frenetic than those at Old Trafford just over 40 years previously as Kumble was chaired off and the 25,000 crowd, together with those watching from unofficial vantage points outside, went wild. After going for 37 runs in his first eight overs his next 19 had gone for the same number of runs and yielded all ten wickets. Five of Kumble's victims had been caught close in as the batsmen failed to cope with the variable bounce; the other wickets had needed no help from the fielders.

A remarkable feature of Laker's all-ten against Australia was Lock's failure to strike at the other end and we might also wonder that three bowlers who between them would finish with 749 Test wickets for India would similarly go wicketless whilst Kumble created history. Kumble's match figures of 14 for 149 had only been bettered twice by an Indian in Test cricket. (Two weeks later against a Pakistan team including eight of the same players he took one for 139!)

One of the spectators was Richard Stokes, an Englishman now living in Germany who was in New Delhi on business. Remarkably as a ten-year-old, taken there by his father, he had also been at Old Trafford in 1956 to see Jim Laker take all-ten against Australia. Thanks to the wonders of Youtube those of us who weren't at either match can at least compare and contrast the performances online.

Kumble's first-class career lasted another ten years. By now India's captain, fittingly his last match, the Third Test against Australia at the end of October 2008, was played at the scene of his all-ten. Unfortunately a nasty hand injury sustained during the match hastened his decision to retire. Again at the end of the match he was carried off the field by team-mates.

Kumble was a brave cricketer: his last Test wicket, the hard-hitting Mitchell Johnson caught and bowled, was taken whilst he bowled with 11 stitches in the little finger of his left hand. Six years earlier at St John's, Antigua, after having had his jaw broken by West Indies quickie Mervyn Dillon he had batted on for four overs and then, swathed in head bandages, bowled 14 overs the next day and dismissed Brian Lara before flying home for surgery.

Less obviously charismatic than Murali and Warne, Kumble was sometimes perhaps underrated as a bowler. His career figures and the longevity of his career are however the perfect rejoinder to any doubters. He was very much a modern cricketer, successfully embracing all forms of cricket and plying his trade around the world. He played for three English counties, including Northamptonshire where as a well-liked member of the side he took 105 Championship wickets in 1995, and had three Twenty20 seasons in the Indian Premier League, in 2009 achieving the remarkable figures of five for 5 for Royal Challengers Bangalore against Rajasthan Royals (in a match played at Newlands, Cape Town!). And he could bat a bit. His seven first-class centuries included famously a maiden Test century at The Oval in 2007 in his 118th Test, a record wait in terms of appearances. In a three-Test series he was the only one of a strong Indian batting line-up to reach three figures.

When Kumble retired he had taken 1,136 first-class wickets - among Indian bowlers only Bishan Bedi has taken more; 619 Test wickets - only contemporaries Muralitharan and Warne have taken more; and an Indian record 334 wickets in ODIs. According to *The Guardian* 'He was one of the good guys, and cricket is much the poorer for his departure'.

After retirement Kumble continued to be actively involved in the game, his appointments including president of the Karnataka Cricket Association, Head of the BCCI's Technical Committee, chairman of the ICC Cricket Committee and India's Head Coach.

Debasis Mohanty

East Zone v South Zone, 2000/01
Duleep Trophy

Maharaja Bir Bikram College Stadium, Agartala on 25, 26, 27 January 2001 (4-day match)
Toss won by South Zone
East Zone won by four wickets
Umpires: RY Deshmukh, SL Shastri
South Zone 113 (DS Mohanty 10-46) and 177 (Sukhvinder Singh 6-57); East Zone 124 (J Srinath 6-32) and 170-6

South Zone first innings

S Sriram	lbw b Mohanty	6
A Nand Kishore	lbw b Mohanty	8
VVS Laxman	b Mohanty	20
*RS Dravid	c Dasgupta b Mohanty	0
R Vijay Bharadwaj	c Dasgupta b Mohanty	0
+VST Naidu	lbw b Mohanty	5
SB Joshi	c Parida b Mohanty	32
AR Kapoor	lbw b Mohanty	12
J Srinath	b Mohanty	11
WD Balaji Rao	not out	8
BKV Prasad	b Mohanty	0
Extras	(b 2, lb 2, nb 6, w 1)	11
Total	(all out, 37 overs)	113

Fall of wickets 1-14, 2-16, 3-22, 4-22, 5-37, 6-49, 7-65, 8-102, 9-113, 10-113

East Zone bowling: DS Mohanty 19-5-46-10, Javed Zaman 15-4-47-0, P Jayachandra 3-0-16-0

East Zone: SS Das (capt), P Jayachandra, RR Parida, SS Raul, RS Gavaskar, SZ Zuffri, DB Dasgupta (wk), Sukhvinder Singh, US Chatterjee, DS Mohanty, Javed Zaman

A lanky medium-pace bowler who when conditions helped could achieve considerable movement both ways, Debasis Mohanty was the first cricketer from Orissa, one of India's weaker states, to be selected to play Test cricket. Mohanty made his first-class debut as a 20-year-old at the end of 1996. With nine wickets against Bengal, the eventual winners of the Ranji Trophy East Zone group, his impact was immediate. His prospects were exciting and his Test debut followed just nine months later at Colombo (against a Sri Lanka side that had declared at 952 for six in the previous Test a week before!). With first innings figures of four for 78, including three top order batsmen, he again made an immediate impression. He was less successful in the second innings taking 0 for 72 in 16 overs as Sanath Jayasuriya and P.A.de Silva both made centuries. Three months later he played his next Test. Match figures of 35 overs nought for 89 against Sri Lanka however did not endear him to the selectors, and his second Test appearance was his last. Although his figures had been mixed, arguably he should perhaps have been given more chances to prove himself.

Nevertheless he continued to take wickets steadily for the rest of his career but unfortunately his time coincided with that of a number of other very good opening bowlers (including Zaheer Khan, Javagal Srinath, Venkatesh Prasad, Asish Nehra and Ajit Agarkar) and even an all-ten couldn't get him back in the side. The selectors at least however showed faith in him in the shorter form of the game and he eventually played in 45 ODIs. He was a late choice for India's 1999 World Cup squad. (His fluid bowling action was used as the official graphical logo for the tournament.) India failed to reach the semi-finals but the English conditions suited him and for his side only Srinath bettered his ten wickets which included Alec Stewart and Graeme Hick in successive legal deliveries (separated by a wide) at Edgbaston.

The Duleep Trophy was first played in 1961/62 between teams representing the five geographical zones of India. It was named after the famous Test cricketer Kumar Shri Duleepsinhji who had died in 1959 aged only 54. In 2000/01 it was played on a league basis. Final positions would be heavily influenced by points garnered in drawn matches, leaving North Zone top of the table with East fourth and South last. Since its inauguration, North, South and West had shared the Trophy fairly equally. It would be over ten years before East Zone won it for the first time.

Orissa provided five of the East Zone side: the first four batsmen, including captain Shiv Sunder Das, plus Mohanty. Assam and Bengal supplied the rest of the side. Only three of the side would play Test cricket (finishing with a total of 33 Tests between them), a marked contrast to their opponents, South, whose seven Test players (419 caps) included two batsmen, V.V.S.Laxman and Rahul Dravid, who would make over 22,000 Test runs, and two bowlers, Srinath and Prasad, who would take 332 Test wickets. It should have been a relatively easy game for South. An attractive tree-lined ground in Agartala the capital of the state of Tripura in north-east India, the stadium had hosted first-class cricket for two years and has been a regular venue for Tripura's Ranji Trophy matches since. The South Zone attack was stronger than the previous year when, in the only other Duleep Trophy match that has been played on the ground, Virender Sehwag made 274 for North Zone, a ground record still to be beaten.

Mohanty had come into the match in good form having taken 25 wickets in his last three matches, and on a helpful green-top he continued in similar vein, soon trapping both South Zone openers leg-before. South Zone captain Dravid came in at 16 for two to join Laxman. His previous four innings had been 200 not out, 70 not out, 162 and 188. This time he would struggle for 20 minutes before edging an outswinger to wicketkeeper Deep Dasgupta, who would gain the first of his eight Test caps later in the year. Next man in was Vijay Bharadwaj. The previous season he had played the only three matches of an undistinguished Test career. He lasted just two balls, another Dasgupta victim. Meanwhile at the other end Laxman had been resisting solidly. He had reached a century (in some cases many more) in five of his previous seven innings, and later in the season would make a famous 281 against Australia. However, although he batted for nearly an hour and a half, on this occasion he never really mastered

Mohanty and could only manage 20 before he was bowled by a ball that angled in, pitched middle and leg, and moved away.

With six wickets down and the score only 49 a poor total looked likely. However East Zone effected a slight recovery, mainly thanks to Sunil Joshi, a left-arm spinner and left-hand batsman who had played in the last of his 15 Tests (one fifty, one five-for) a couple of months before, and who at least saw his side to three figures. When he eventually left, Mohanty had to watch while medium pacer Pinninti Jayachandra had an over at batsmen nine and ten. Srinath made four Test fifties, but leg-spinner Balaji Rao, playing in the penultimate match of a 33-match career, never got past 27 and Mohanty was probably a bit worried that the chance of an all-ten might be denied him. Fortunately Jayachandra managed not to strike and Mohanty had another over. He made no mistake, bowling Srinath with his third ball and last man Venkatesh Prasad with his sixth. Taking seven wickets without help from the field he had become the fifth Indian bowler to take an all-ten, with only Chatterjee performing the feat at lesser expense.

For a while the East Zone innings was remarkably similar to that of their opponent's: there was an early collapse, the first six wickets being taken by the same opening bowler (Srinath), before the later batsmen and tail righted things a little, taking the score from 33 for six to 124 all out just before the end of an eventful first day.

Next day Mohanty again dismissed both openers. However this time Laxman (40) and Dravid (66) both contributed, although nobody else did much in another low score. Mohanty finished with four wickets while slow left-armer Sukhvinder Singh took the other six. East Zone needed 167 to win. It was still touch and go. Two wickets went early, including the unfortunate Rashmi Parida, who was bowled by Srinath without scoring for the second time in the match. (He would find consolation later in the season with successive scores of 220 and 162 for Orissa.) With plenty of time left Das dug in for a three-hour 79. When he finally went 44 runs were still needed with only four wickets left, but Dasgupta (32 not out) atoned for his first innings duck and together with Singh (22 not out), who had top scored in the first innings with 31, the first of his three important contributions in the match, saw his side home.

Not surprisingly Mohanty performed at a more modest level for the rest of the season; however his final total of 58 wickets at only 16.27 each was surpassed only by Harbhajan Singh's 70. In a career that ended in 2010 Mohanty took 417 first-class wickets at 21.05 apiece and a further 160 in List A matches. He also spent three years playing for Colwyn Bay in the Liverpool and District Cricket Competition, and was later appointed coach of Orissa and of East Zone.

Ottis Gibson

Durham v Hampshire, 2007
County Championship

Riverside Ground, Chester-le-Street on 20, 21, 22, 23 July 2007 (4-day match)
Toss won by Durham
Match drawn
Umpires: B Dudleston, RA Kettleborough
Durham 252 (DM Benkenstein 114) and 221-5 dec; Hampshire 115 (OD Gibson 10-47) and 262-9 (MJ Brown 126 not out, PJ Wiseman 5-65)

Hampshire first innings

MA Carberry	c Harmison b Gibson	4
MJ Brown	not out	56
JP Crawley	c Mustard b Gibson	6
MJ Lumb	lbw b Gibson	16
CC Benham	b Gibson	2
+N Pothas	c and b Gibson	0
AD Mascarenhas	c Mustard b Gibson	8
*SK Warne	lbw b Gibson	1
SD Udal	c Mustard b Gibson	4
DA Griffiths	c Mustard b Gibson	2
JTA Bruce	b Gibson	0
Extras	(lb 4, nb 12)	16
Total	(all out, 35.3 overs)	115

Fall of wickets 1-13, 2-29, 3-65, 4-67, 5-67, 6-81, 7-85, 8-89, 9-115, 10-115

Durham bowling: G Onions 5-1-14-0, OD Gibson 17.3-1-47-10, SB Styris 7-1-24-0, DM Benkenstein 6-1-26-0

Durham: WR Smith, MD Stoneman, KJ Coetzer, SB Styris, DM Benkenstein (capt), P Mustard (wk), BW Harmison, OD Gibson, LE Plunkett, PJ Wiseman, G Onions

Born in Barbados in 1969 Ottis Gibson, itinerant fast bowler and hard-hitting late middle-order batsman, played for his home island, three different sides in South Africa, and for Durham, Glamorgan and Leicestershire in the County Championship. He waited a while to become the first West Indian to take all-ten. Having made his debut for Barbados in 1991, it came 16 years later, just two months before the end of a 177-match first-class career which yielded 659 wickets (to which should be added 310 List A victims).

2007 was quite a swansong. He took a Durham record 80 first-class wickets in a season and scored 578 runs. In the Friends Provident Trophy nobody exceeded his 22 wickets. No wonder his *Wisden* Cricketer of the Year citation referred to him as 'the greatest single force in county cricket', and he was named the Professional Cricketers' Association Player of the Year. Quite a comeback after having been dropped for Durham's third Championship match!

It wasn't his only record-breaking performance in his two years at Durham. At the end of the 2006 season Durham went to Leeds for their last match with a chance of being relegated. Yorkshire made 677 for seven declared (Darren Lehmann 339, Gibson one for 150) and when Gibson joined captain Dale Benkenstein with the score 191 for six things were looking bad. However when the next wicket fell (Benkenstein 151), the score had climbed to 506, and their 315-run partnership was the ninth highest in cricket history for the seventh wicket. Gibson made 155 (the second, and highest, first-class century of his career), the match was drawn, relegated Nottinghamshire lost to champions Sussex, and Durham were safe – by half a point! Remarkably ten years previously Gibson had also been involved in Glamorgan's seventh wicket record when he and Tony Cottey added 211 against Leicestershire at Swansea. (With the ball Gibson had match figures of nought for 209!)

With 23 wickets in eight Championship matches Gibson had had a quiet start to the 2007 season. Durham and Hampshire had met a month previously at The Rose Bowl, Hampshire winning by 50 runs. It hadn't been a particularly successful match for Gibson: one wicket in 36 overs, and although he made 33 not out in the first innings he made a duck, courtesy of Shane Warne, in the second. Batting first in the return Durham's 252 was mainly due to a captain's knock of 114 from Benkenstein. Gibson, who hit the only six of the innings, contributed a useful 28.

With rain about Hampshire couldn't start their first innings until the third day, but once they did Durham, or rather Gibson, made up for lost time and skittled them out in just under two and half hours. The unsettled weather worked to Gibson's advantage. Cutting down his pace and relying more on swing than seam he bowled unchanged but with the benefit of two breaks. Michael Carberry had made 192 not out in his previous innings as Hampshire successfully chased 331 to beat Warwickshire, and Durham would have been glad to see him restricted to just one scoring shot this time before he edged Gibson to slip. The prolific John Crawley (who had made 150 against Durham the previous season; Gibson two for 101 in 14 overs) was caught behind soon afterwards. Three more wickets fell before lunch which came with Gibson having taken five wickets for 31 in 12 overs, the fifth of which was the first of the two ducks that wicketkeeper Nic Pothas would make in the match.

Suitably refreshed, Gibson then took three more, including captain Shane Warne, in five overs after the break. At 89 for eight the innings might have been over quickly but opener Michael Brown was still there and together with Championship debutant David Griffiths he took the score to 115, the second highest stand of the innings. Gibson had bowled 17 overs and probably needed a break, and that fortunately is what he got, rain at 2.40 pm driving the players off until 4.30. Again suitably rested, Gibson finished off Hampshire in just three balls: Griffiths giving wicketkeeper Phil Mustard his fourth catch and James Bruce losing his off stump first ball. Durham had a very good bowling attack and England's Liam Plunkett and New Zealand off-spinner Paul Wiseman hadn't even been needed (they would get their chance in the second innings). Gibson told *The Guardian*,

'I've been around long enough to know that when it's your day you must make the most of it, but I got lucky today. Before I got Lumb I'd said to Benky it wasn't swinging any more, and then before the rain came I was going to come off. Even then I would have settled for eight, but Benky said at my age I wouldn't get another opportunity to get ten.'

Gibson's all-ten was only the third in the Championship in the previous fifty years. He was the first bowler to take an all-ten for Durham since they achieved first-class status in 1992, and in fact only the second to have taken as many as nine in an innings for them, Melvyn Betts being the first (although medium pacer Alf Morris took all-ten for 130 in a Minor Counties match against Yorkshire Seconds at Barnsley in 1910). Graham Onions and Chris Rushworth have since both taken nine for the county. In each case, taking the first eight wickets, they came tantalisingly close to a full house. Gibson is also only the sixth bowler to take an all-ten in his last first-class season. At the other end, Michael Brown became only the third batsman to carry his bat whilst his colleagues succumbed to an all-ten.

Conditions having eased when Durham batted a second time, a declaration left Hampshire 75 overs to make an unlikely 359. Gibson once more struck early, again picking up Michael Carberry and John Crawley cheaply. After that it was Wiseman who did the damage; when he took his fifth wicket 20 minutes were left to part last man Griffiths and the again undefeated Brown. The pair held out however, although Gibson almost had Brown caught at gully with three overs to go. Michael Brown (126 not out) had nearly become the eleventh batsman to bat through both completed innings of a first-class match. As Durham would eventually finish second in the Championship, 4.5 points behind Sussex, the ten extra points for a win would have been very useful!

Durham went one better with the white ball that season, winning their first-ever prize, the Friends Provident Trophy, beating Hampshire at a damp Lord's by 125 runs. Gibson again made Hampshire suffer. After hitting 15 from seven balls at the end of the Durham innings he dismissed Michael Lumb and Sean Ervine with the first two balls of the Hampshire innings: both left-handers were caught at second slip. As he pinned Kevin Pietersen in front soon afterwards it was no wonder he was made Man of the Match. He had been equally influential in a remarkably low-scoring semi-final against Essex, taking three good wickets and then, with the score 38 for seven chasing just 72, holding an end while Liam Plunkett (30 not out) saw Durham home. After Lord's Gibson took 32 Championship wickets in four matches. An impressive end to his season and career.

Gibson had already spent time as an ECB coach and when the opportunity arose to become England's bowling coach in the winter of 2007 he took it. At the beginning of 2010, after more than two years with England, he became coach to the West Indies, a side for whom he had played two Tests and 15 ODIs in the late 1990s. The highlight of his tenure was winning the World T20 in Sri Lanka in 2012. But there were also low points and the parting of the ways came in August 2014. However 'when one door closes...', and in 2015 he was back as England's bowling coach and now has a CV that includes 'Ashes winner'.

Mario Olivier

Warriors v Eagles, 2007/08
SuperSport Series

OUTsurance Oval, Bloemfontein on 29, 30 November, 1, 2 December 2007 (4-day match)
Toss won by Eagles
Eagles won by ten wickets
Umpires: GH Pienaar, DJ Smith
Warriors 108 and 215 (CJD de Villiers 5-65); Eagles 300 (HH Dippenaar 112, MW Olivier 10-65) and 24-0

Eagles first innings

D Elgar	lbw b Olivier	43
LE Bosman	b Olivier	46
JA Rudolph	lbw b Olivier	41
*HH Dippenaar	c Ackerman b Olivier	112
+MN van Wyk	c Ingram b Olivier	0
RT Bailey	c Ackerman b Olivier	2
D du Preez	lbw b Olivier	2
CJD de Villiers	lbw b Olivier	3
MS Tshabalala	lbw b Olivier	1
J Coetzee	not out	23
PV Mpitsang	c DJ Jacobs b Olivier	0
Extras	(lb 7, nb 10, w 10)	27
Total	(all out, 92.3 overs)	300

Fall of wickets 1-102, 2-115, 3-182, 4-182, 5-188, 6-204, 7-210, 8-224, 9-297, 10-300

Warriors bowling: LL Tsotsobe 16-2-62-0, MW Olivier 26.3-4-65-10, J Theron 20-3-59-0, Z de Bruyn 18-4-52-0, L Meyer 3-0-18-0, RJ Peterson 4-0-23-0, A Jacobs 5-0-14-0

Warriors: CA Ingram, CA Thyssen, Z de Bruyn (capt), A Jacobs, HD Ackerman, DJ Jacobs (wk), RJ Peterson, L Meyer, J Theron, MW Olivier, LL Tsotsobe

South African cricket used to be easy to understand with teams bearing obviously geographically-based names such as Natal and Transvaal playing for the Currie Cup. However, the franchise system has made understanding a little more difficult. It was adopted in 2004/05 for South Africa's primary domestic inter-provincial four-day competition (then named the SuperSport Series) in order to provide a stepping-stone between the domestic and international game. The six franchised sides played each other twice on a league basis. Warriors were the combined Eastern Province and Border team, whilst Free State won a sole franchise and named themselves Eagles.

Mario Olivier was born in Pretoria in 1982. He had a fairly short, but varied, first-class career, playing 59 matches in eight seasons. As well as 26 matches for Warriors, he played for Cape Cobras and Titans, and in the three-day first-class competition for Boland, Border, Northerns and Western Province. Before making his first-class debut he had played for Western Province Under-19s (in teams including future South African bowlers Rory Kleinveldt and Vernon Philander), Stellenbosch University and Stoneywood-Dyke, a team in the Scotland North Cricket League based in north-west Aberdeen, for whom he had played in 2004. He made his first-class debut the following season, playing two matches for Boland, and later in the year played the first of 26 matches for Warriors. Before he became the third South African to take an all-ten there had been no indication that a superlative statistical feat was in the offing, for in 27 matches his fast-medium bowling had brought him just 73 wickets, and five in an innings only once.

Olivier never played county cricket. However eight of the Warriors side did, in one or more forms, most notably Hylton (H.D.) Ackerman, who in five seasons with Leicestershire would average 47.50 in first-class cricket and make a county record 309 not out against Glamorgan at Cardiff in 2006, and Zander de Bruyn who would play for Somerset, Surrey and Worcestershire, averaging over 30 with the bat for each.

Eagles would eventually win the SuperSport Series in 2007/08. Before their meeting with Warriors they had won two and drawn two of their four matches, whilst Warriors had one win, two draws and a loss to show for their efforts. The match was played at the Eagles' home in Bloemfontein. Springbok Park takes its sponsor's name, hence in 2007 it was snappily called the OUTsurance Oval. It is a well-designed 20,000-seater stadium incorporating two large stands. Cricket is often played in a carnival atmosphere, in particular for day/night matches, when the ground's grassed banks attract large groups cooking barbecues, an innovation not yet embraced by Lord's.

When Warriors' opener Craig Thyssen left after nearly an hour's struggle with the score 18 for three Eagles' captain Boeta Dippenaar was no doubt feeling pleased that he had asked the opposition to bat first. Warriors continued to struggle, only Ackerman (21) and Robin Peterson (30 not out) getting past ten. Olivier wasn't expected to have much impact with the bat (although he has reached three figures at club level) but going in at 83 for eight his five runs at least contributed to a ninth wicket partnership of 20 with Peterson that enabled Warriors to limp into three figures.

Olivier opened Warriors' bowling together with left-armer Lonwabo Tsotsobe (later to play in five Tests for South Africa and briefly, and unsuccessfully, for Essex). Eagles nearly passed Warriors' meagre first innings score without losing a wicket but in the penultimate over of the first day Olivier dismissed Loots Bosman with the score 102. This was only the second three-figure opening partnership in an innings in which a bowler eventually achieved an all-ten, the 101 by Saeed Anwar and Shahid Afridi when Kumble took all-ten being the first.

Only 20 overs were possible next day, during which time Olivier dismissed Dean Elgar, bringing Dippenaar to the wicket to join Jacques Rudolph. Four years before, in Rudolph's first Test, the pair had put on an undefeated

429 for the third wicket against Bangladesh. Ominously for Warriors they were still there at the close with the score 177.

However Olivier struck two important blows in the first over next day, Rudolph going to the fourth ball followed two balls later by wicketkeeper Morne van Wyk. As van Wyk had made 200 not out against Warriors the previous year his team were probably happy with their morning's work so far. And Olivier continued to take wickets regularly in a spell of six wickets in eight overs that left Eagles 224 for eight and Warriors with some hope of restricting their opponents to a first innings lead of not much more than 100. But Dippenaar was still there and he found a resolute partner in Jandre Coetzee. Olivier had had to be rested, and with an all-ten a possibility he was honest enough to admit afterwards that during their 73-run ninth wicket partnership he had been hoping that none of the other bowlers would strike while he was waiting to be brought back.

When a refreshed Olivier eventually returned he soon ended the Eagles' captain's innings after four and a quarter hours' resistance. Olivier had one ball of the over left. The incoming batsman, Victor Mpitsang, would eventually play 103 first-class matches and take a creditable 245 wickets. However, with 417 runs and a highest score of 23, batting was obviously not his strong suit. Mpitsang survived the last ball, but an over later Olivier had another chance and he soon got his man, caught behind by wicketkeeper Davey Jacobs.

Olivier had given the umpires plenty of work: he was the first bowler taking an all-ten to dismiss five of his victims leg-before. He was obviously well pleased with his performance. Interviewed afterwards for television he said, 'I am in the clouds. I have just been looking at the scorecard and it is unbelievable. Everything came together today. I had good rhythm and the ball was moving a bit. I couldn't find good rhythm at the beginning of the season but I have been working hard in the nets and today it paid off.'

Thanks to 78 from Arno Jacobs (who had played a few matches for Leicestershire the previous summer) and useful knocks from the lower order, Warriors knocked off their first innings deficit, just. Olivier was the last wicket to fall, caught behind by Adrian McLaren who was playing as a full substitute for van Wyk who had been called up for international duty. It had been a good game for seam bowlers. Spinners on the other hand only bowled 14 overs, and didn't take any wickets.

When the two sides met the following month in the return match Warriors put up a much better show. Olivier again shone, but this time with the bat. After Warriors had batted first he had struck early when Eagles went in, but this was his only wicket in the match as the other bowlers shared the spoils. Going in for a second time Warriors were soon in trouble. De Bruyn followed a first-innings century with a duck and when Olivier went in at 120 for seven the lead was only 154. Olivier had only made 39 runs in his previous nine innings but with 51 (his only career fifty) in an hour and a half he ensured that Warriors had something to bowl at next day. Unfortunately bad weather prevented what might have been an interesting finish.

Without hitting the heights again after his famous feat Olivier continued to take wickets steadily for another four seasons, finishing his first-class career in 2012 with 168 wickets at 33 runs apiece. An accredited coach who has started his own bat repair business, he has remained in the game in a number of ways including returning to Britain to play club cricket for Carlton CC in Edinburgh.

Zulfiqar Babar

Multan v Islamabad, 2009/10
Quaid-e-Azam Trophy

Multan Cricket Stadium, Multan on 9, 10, 11, 12 December 2009 (4-day match)
Toss won by Islamabad
Match drawn
Umpires: Akram Raza, Ghaffar Kazmi
Multan 352 (Naved Yasin 131) and 332-5 dec (Rameez Alam 119 not out); Islamabad 418 (Ashar Zaidi 130 not out, Zulfiqar Babar 10-143) and 58-3

Islamabad first innings

Raheel Majeed	c Abdul Rehman Muzammil b Zulfiqar Babar	48
Umair Khan	c Gulraiz Sadaf b Zulfiqar Babar	63
Ali Sarfraz	c Rizwan Haider b Zulfiqar Babar	36
Ameer Khan	c Gulraiz Sadaf b Zulfiqar Babar	0
Ashar Zaidi	not out	130
Wasim Abbas	b Zulfiqar Babar	12
Imad Wasim	c Rameez Alam b Zulfiqar Babar	28
+Naeem Anjum	c Naved Yasin b Zulfiqar Babar	12
*Rauf Akbar	c Tahir Maqsood b Zulfiqar Babar	39
Fakhar Hussain	c Rameez Alam b Zulfiqar Babar	25
Nasrullah Khan	c Rameez Alam b Zulfiqar Babar	0
Extras	(b 7, lb 10 , nb 8)	25
Total	(all out, 103.4 overs)	418

Fall of wickets 1-86, 2-155, 3-155, 4-162, 5-206, 6-277, 7-302, 8-384, 9-418, 10-418

Multan bowling: Ansar Javed 14-1-67-0, Tahir Maqsood 19-5-66-0, Zulfiqar Babar 39.4-3-143-10, Mohammad Ali 1-0-5-0, Rizwan Haider 8-0-34-0, Abdul Rehman Muzammil 18-5-57-0, Shahid Abbasi 4-0-29-0

Multan: Abdul Rehman Muzammil, Gulraiz Sadaf (wk), Rameez Alam, Shahid Abbasi, Naved Yasin (capt), Mohammad Ali, Zafar Iqbal, Rizwan Haider, Ansar Javed, Zulfiqar Babar, Tahir Maqsood

Born in 1978, slow left-armer Zulfiqar Babar hails from the agricultural city of Okara 75 miles south west of Lahore. At the time of writing he is the only first-class cricketer still playing with an all-ten to his name. He was a bit of a late starter. He made his first-class debut for the Rest of Punjab against Islamabad in February 2002, but his next match, for Multan against Faisalabad, wasn't for another five and a half years, by which time he was nearly 29. This time there was no looking back and in 2009/10 he took 96 wickets, and became the fourth Pakistani to take an all-ten.

Wisden's reporting of the 2009/10 season in Pakistan makes depressing reading. Insecurity in the region meant that there was uncertainty in every part of society – including sport. With Pakistan forced to play all their international matches abroad, most of the national players were away so often that home supporters rarely got the chance to see them. There was an obvious decline in domestic cricket standards.

Multan and Islamabad were reasonably evenly matched; of the 22 players in the match only Babar would play Test cricket, although Islamabad's 21-year-old Swansea-born allrounder Imad Wasim would go on to play in ODIs and be a member of the Pakistan side that won the Champions Trophy at The Oval in 2017. The Quaid-e-Azam Trophy was organised this year into two groups of ten teams each playing the other once. When the two teams met at Multan in December each had two matches left. They would finish respectively fourth and fifth in their group, leaving leaders Karachi Blues to play, and beat, Habib Bank in the Final.

The Multan Cricket Stadium in the province of Punjab is a multi-use stadium hosting football as well as cricket. Seating around 30,000 spectators, the ground was a replacement for the earlier Qasim Bagh Stadium. Pakistan's Test match against Bangladesh in August 2001 was the maiden first-class match on the ground.

Put in to bat, Multan were 0 for two after the first over and Rameez Alam, who had made 222 not out in his previous innings, was back in the pavilion. Both wickets had fallen to the left-arm fast-medium of Nasrullah Khan who was in his debut season. Multan's eventual recovery was mainly due to opener and wicketkeeper Gulraiz Sadaf and to captain Naved Yasin who each batted for three hours, making 85 and 131 respectively. Twenty-two-year-old Yasin was one of only two batsmen to make 1,000 runs in the Trophy season.

Islamabad's innings began on the second day, 10 December, Babar's 31st birthday. Taking five wickets, he had quite a happy birthday. He had entered the attack first change and with a lively action following a diagonal seven pace run-up between umpire and stumps he would eventually bowl 39.4 overs. Islamabad batted steadily to reach 155 for one, at which point Babar took three quick wickets, including Ameer Khan caught behind first ball, and with another wicket falling just before the close the visitors finished the day 229 for five. Multan would have had hopes of a first-innings lead. However, left-hander Ashar Zaidi, fresh from scoring a double-century and a duck in his previous match, was still there, having just reached his fifty.

Next day, with considerable help from the lower order, Zaidi guided his side to a useful first-innings lead, remaining unbeaten having batted for just over four hours. When Babar took his eighth wicket, Islamabad captain Rauf Akbar, he had improved on his previous best figures (seven for 97 taken against Sialkot just six weeks before). The next batsman, Fakhar Hussain, kept Babar waiting by hitting a run-a-minute 25, but when he went Nasrullah Khan ended the wait by giving Rameez Alam his second catch in two balls.

Babar's all-ten was the most expensive ever in a competitive first-class match, and the second most expensive ever after Eddie Hemmings' ten for 175. He hit the stumps just once, the other nine wickets all falling to catches. Among bowlers taking all-ten, only Burton and Bannister had previously had so much help from their fielders. It had been hard work: of the 21 bowlers to take an all-ten outside England and Wales only

Hemmings (49.3) had bowled more overs.

Rameez Alam made up for his first-innings failure by making 119 not out in Multan's second innings. However, the home team's declaration left little time for either side to achieve victory. Babar, on a hat-trick, opened the bowling in Islamabad's second innings. He failed to get a three-in-three, but he did take two more wickets at a cost of 25 runs.

Babar went on to finish the season strongly. In his last two matches, playing for The Rest in the RBS Pentangular Cup, he took seven wickets in an innings against both Karachi Blues and Sui Northern Gas Pipelines Limited. His 96 wickets meant that he finished as the season's second-highest wicket-taker in the country, just one behind Karachi Blues' opening bowler Tanvir Ahmed, whilst only Rawalpindi's Mohammad Rameez (who took eight for 46 against Multan on the same ground a week after Babar's feat) equalled his tally of five wickets in an innings nine times, and ten in a match three times. Babar spent the following English summer playing for Little Hulton in the Bolton and District Cricket Association.

He continued to prosper but with Saeed Ajmal established as the side's leading spinner, supported by Abdur Rehman, it was difficult to break into the Pakistan team. There were suggestions that had he come from one of the larger cities he might have had greater support among the selectors. Three years later with 93 wickets he was the leading wicket-taker in Pakistan, and the following October he at last made a well-deserved Test debut, against South Africa at the Sheikh Zayed Stadium in Abu Dhabi. (He had actually made his international debut earlier in the year in a T20 match against the West Indies in which he had taken three key wickets, and then hit the last possible ball of the match for a winning six!)

Aged nearly 35, and with over 300 first-class wickets to his name, Babar was Pakistan's fourth–oldest Test debutant. With five wickets, including Hashim Amla, in a match that Pakistan won by seven wickets he did all right. But the next Test a week later was a different affair. First Pakistan were shot out for 99 with Babar, a useful tailend bat, going in at number nine and top scoring with 25 not out. He then took a humble one for 124 as South Africa piled up 517 and having been injured while bowling was unable to bat in Pakistan's second-innings. A year later, back in the UAE he found conditions to his liking, twice taking five wickets in an innings against Australia, and in November 2015, in his 13th Test, he took his 50th wicket when he dismissed England's James Taylor caught at slip by Younis Khan. Sadly none had been taken in Pakistan. He was a key figure in Pakistan's two-nil series victory. He played in all three Tests, and although his figures for the series (nine for 409) were statistically unimpressive, he suffered from several dropped catches. However despite bowling 189 overs in tiring conditions, making him easily the most hard-worked bowler on either side, he conceded just over two runs an over and his captain, Misbah-ul-Haq, later paid tribute to the importance of his role in providing a foil to the more exotic wrist-spinning skills of the attacking Yasir Shah.

Babar toured England and Ireland the following summer but was unable to break into the Test team and had to be content with one first-class match (and one wicket), although he returned to the side later in the year against the West Indies at the Sheikh Zayed Stadium.

Appendices

Chronological list of All-Tens

The dates are those on which the tenth wicket was taken.
* All ten taken on the same day
** All ten taken in a single session (where confirmed; the daily progress of some of the matches concerned is not known for certain)

E.Hinkly	10-??, Kent v England, Lord's	11 July 1848*
J.Wisden	10-??, North v South, Lord's	15 July 1850*
V.E.Walker	10-74, England v Surrey, Oval	22 July 1859
G.Wootton	10-54, All-England XI v Yorkshire, Sheffield	19 July 1865*
V.E.Walker	10-104, Middlesex v Lancashire, Manchester	22 July 1865
W.Hickton	10-46, Lancashire v Hampshire, Manchester	23 July 1870
S.E.Butler	10-38, Oxford University v Cambridge University, Lord's	26 June 1871*
J.Lillywhite	10-129, South v North, Canterbury	7 August 1872
A.Shaw	10-73, MCC v North, Lord's	1 June 1874*
E.D.Barratt	10-43, Players v Australians, Oval	2 September 1878*
G.Giffen	10-66, Australian XI v Combined XI, Sydney	18 February 1884
W.G.Grace	10-49, MCC v Oxford University, Oxford	22 June 1886*
G.Burton	10-59, Middlesex v Surrey, Oval	21 July 1888
A.E.Moss	10-28, Canterbury v Wellington, Christchurch	27 December 1889*
S.M.J.Woods	10-69, Cambridge University v C.I.Thornton's XI, Cambridge	13 May 1890
T.Richardson	10-45, Surrey v Essex, Oval	18 June 1894*
H.Pickett	10-32, Essex v Leicestershire, Leyton	3 June 1895*
E.J.Tyler	10-49, Somerset v Surrey, Taunton	23 August 1895
W.P.Howell	10-28, Australians v Surrey, Oval	15 May 1899*
C.H.G.Bland	10-48, Sussex v Kent, Tonbridge	7 June 1899*
J.Briggs	10-55, Lancashire v Worcestershire, Manchester	24 May 1900*
A.E.Trott	10-42, Middlesex v Somerset, Taunton	6 August 1900*
A.Fielder	10-90, Players v Gentlemen, Lord's	9 July 1906*
E.G.Dennett	10-40, Gloucestershire v Essex, Bristol	6 August 1906**
A.E.E.Vogler	10-26, Eastern Province v Griqualand West, Johannesburg	28 December 1906*
C.Blythe	10-30, Kent v Northamptonshire, Northampton	1 June 1907*
J.B.King	10-53, Gentlemen of Philadelphia v Gentlemen of Ireland, Haverford	17 September 1909*
A.Drake	10-35, Yorkshire v Somerset, Weston-super-Mare	28 August 1914*
F.A.Tarrant	10-90, Maharaja of Cooch-Behar's XI v Lord Willingdon's XI, Poona	12 August 1918
W.Bestwick	10-40, Derbyshire v Glamorgan, Cardiff	20 June 1921**
J.C.White	10-76, Somerset v Worcestershire, Worcester	20 June 1921
T.Rushby	10-43, Surrey v Somerset, Taunton	7 July 1921
C.W.L.Parker	10-79, Gloucestershire v Somerset, Bristol	30 July 1921*
A.A.Mailey	10-66, Australians v Gloucestershire, Cheltenham	23 August 1921
G.C.Collins	10-65, Kent v Nottinghamshire, Dover	18 August 1922

H.Howell	10-51, Warwickshire v Yorkshire, Birmingham	24 May 1923
A.S.Kennedy	10-37, Players v Gentlemen, Oval	8 July 1927*
G.O.B.Allen	10-40, Middlesex v Lancashire, Lord's	15 June 1929*
A.P.Freeman	10-131, Kent v Lancashire, Maidstone	24 July 1929*
G.Geary	10-18, Leicestershire v Glamorgan, Pontypridd	15 August 1929*
C.V.Grimmett	10-37, Australians v Yorkshire, Sheffield	10 May 1930*
A.P.Freeman	10-53, Kent v Essex, Southend	14 August 1930
H.Verity	10-36, Yorkshire v Warwickshire, Leeds	18 May 1931*
A.P.Freeman	10-79, Kent v Lancashire, Manchester	27 May 1931*
V.W.C.Jupp	10-127, Northamptonshire v Kent, Tunbridge Wells	6 July 1932*
H.Verity	10-10, Yorkshire v Nottinghamshire, Leeds	12 July 1932**
T.W.Wall	10-36, South Australia v New South Wales, Sydney	3 February 1933*
T.B.Mitchell	10-64, Derbyshire v Leicestershire, Leicester	17 June 1935
J.Mercer	10-51, Glamorgan v Worcestershire, Worcester	29 July 1936*
T.W.J.Goddard	10-113, Gloucestershire v Worcestershire, Cheltenham	9 August 1937*
T.F.Smailes	10-47, Yorkshire v Derbyshire, Sheffield	27 June 1939
E.A.Watts	10-67, Surrey v Warwickshire, Birmingham	22 August 1939
W.E.Hollies	10-49, Warwickshire v Nottinghamshire, Birmingham	24 July 1946*
J.M.Sims	10-90, East v West, Kingston-upon-Thames	10 September 1948*
J.K.R.Graveney	10-66, Gloucestershire v Derbyshire, Chesterfield	5 August 1949
T.E.Bailey	10-90, Essex v Lancashire, Clacton	24 August 1949*
R.Berry	10-102, Lancashire v Worcestershire, Blackpool	31 July 1953*
S.P.Gupte	10-78, Bombay v Pakistan Combined Services & Bahawalpur XI, Bombay	3 December 1954*
J.C.Laker	10-88, Surrey v Australians, Oval	16 May 1956*
K.Smales	10-66, Nottinghamshire v Gloucestershire, Stroud	11 June 1956
G.A.R.Lock	10-54, Surrey v Kent, Blackheath	10 July 1956
J.C.Laker	10-53, England v Australia, Manchester	31 July 1956
P.M.Chatterjee	10-20, Bengal v Assam, Jorhat	28 January 1957
J.D.Bannister	10-41, Warwickshire v Combined Services, Birmingham	28 May 1959
A.J.G.Pearson	10-78, Cambridge University v Leicestershire, Loughborough	7 July 1961
N.I.Thomson	10-49, Sussex v Warwickshire, Worthing	8 June 1964
P.J.Allan	10-61, Queensland v Victoria, Melbourne	8 January 1966
I.J.Brayshaw	10-44, Western Australia v Victoria, Perth	22 October 1967
Shahid Mahmood	10-58, Karachi Whites v Khairpur, Karachi	6 September 1969*
E.E.Hemmings	10-175, International XI v West Indies XI, Kingston	27 September 1982
P.Sunderam	10-78, Rajasthan v Vidarbha, Jodhpur	17 November 1985*
S.T.Jefferies	10-59, Western Province v Orange Free State, Cape Town	28 December 1987
Imran Adil	10-92, Bahawalpur v Faisalabad, Faisalabad	30 October 1989*
G.P.Wickramasinghe	10-41, Sinhalese Sports Club v Kalutara Physical Culture Centre, Colombo	16 November 1991*
R.L.Johnson	10-45, Middlesex v Derbyshire, Derby	2 July 1994*
Naeem Akhtar	10-28, Rawalpindi B v Peshawar, Peshawar	3 December 1995
A.Kumble	10-74, India v Pakistan, Delhi	7 February 1999*
D.S.Mohanty	10-46, East Zone v South Zone, Agartala	25 January 2001*
O.D.Gibson	10-47, Durham v Hampshire, Chester-le-Street	22 July 2007*
M.W.Olivier	10-65, Warriors v Eagles, Bloemfontein	1 December 2007
Zulfiqar Babar	10-143, Multan v Islamabad, Multan	11 December 2009

Some statistics about bowlers taking all ten wickets in an innings

Youngest: before the age of 20
Imran Adil 18 years 344 days, R.L.Johnson 19 years 185 days, A.J.G.Pearson 19 years 189 days

Oldest: over 45
W.Bestwick 46 years 116 days, J.M.Sims 45 years 120 days

Had never taken five wickets in an innings before
A.E.Moss, H.Pickett, A.J.G.Pearson, Imran Adil, G.P.Wickramasinghe, R.L.Johnson

Never took five wickets in an innings again
A.Drake, Shahid Mahmood

Took five wickets in an innings fewer than five times in career (including the all-ten)
2 A.E.Moss, 2 A.J.G.Pearson, 3 Shahid Mahmood, 4 H.Pickett

Played ten or fewer matches before taking all-ten
0 A.E.Moss, 3 E.Hinkly, 7 S.E.Butler, 10 A.J.G.Pearson, 10 R.L.Johnson

Had taken 30 or fewer wickets in career before taking all-ten
0 A.E.Moss, 9 E.Hinkly, 24 Imran Adil, 27 R.L.Johnson, 28 A.J.G.Pearson, 30 H.Pickett

Played fewer than five matches after taking all-ten
1 A.Drake, 2 Shahid Mahmood, 3 A.E.Moss, J.B.King

Fewest wickets taken in season in which all-ten taken: England and Wales
19th century: 22 V.E.Walker, 26 W.Hickton
20th century: 31 G.O.B.Allen, 40 R.L.Johnson

Fewest wickets taken in overseas season in which all-ten taken
Australia: 19th century - 17 G.Giffen; 20th century - 25 I.J.Brayshaw
South Africa: 32 M.W.Olivier
India: 14 S.P.Gupte (also took 55 wickets in Pakistan in the same season),
    18 P.M.Chatterjee
West Indies: 10 E.E.Hemmings (only played one match in the West Indies;
    also took 23 wickets in Australia)
Pakistan: 16 Shahid Mahmood
Sri Lanka: 38 G.P.Wickramasinghe (also took 11 wickets in Pakistan)
New Zealand: 26 A.E.Moss
USA: 25 J.B.King

Fewer than 150 wickets taken in career
26 A.E.Moss, 89 Shahid Mahmood, 106 S.E.Butler, 134 H.Pickett, 134 P.M.Chatterjee

All-ten in first season
A.E.Moss, A.J.G.Pearson

All-ten in last season
A.E.Moss, J.Briggs, A.Drake, T.Rushby, Shahid Mahmood

All-ten in fewest balls
53 A.Drake (he took the wickets in a spell of 42 balls)

All-ten in most balls
308 J.C.Laker (Fourth Test England v Australia 1956)

Least/most expensive all-tens in terms of runs per six balls
H.Verity 10-10 (0.51), J.C.Laker 10-53 (1.03), P.M.Chatterjee 10-20 (1.05)
J.M.Sims (10-90) 4.82, Imran Adil (10-92) 4.03, A.Drake (10-35) 3.96

Nine or ten wickets taken without help from the field
10: J.Wisden (10 b), W.E.Hollies (7 b, 3 lbw)
9: W.P.Howell (8 b, 1 c&b), A.E.Trott (6 b, 2 lbw, 1 c&b), A.E.E.Vogler (6 b, 1 lbw, 2 c&b), J.B.King (7 b, 2 lbw), P.M.Chatterjee (6 b, 3 lbw)

All-ten and scored a century in same match
V.E.Walker (1859), W.G.Grace, F.A.Tarrant

All-ten and top scored in both innings
V.W.C.Jupp

All-ten and a pair
E.D.Barratt (bowled Spofforth, bowled Spofforth)

Captain taking all-ten
V.E.Walker (1859), W.G.Grace, S.M.J.Woods, Imran Adil

Finished on losing side
Bowlers have taken an all-ten in 81 matches, finishing on the winning side in 53, the losing side in 18, with the remaining matches drawn. The bowlers who finished on the losing side were:

E.Hinkly, V.E.Walker (1865), J.Lillywhite, A.Shaw, E.D.Barratt, H.Pickett, A.Fielder, H.Howell, A.P.Freeman (1929), V.W.C.Jupp, T.W.Wall, W.E.Hollies, T.E.Bailey, K.Smales, N.I.Thomson, P.J.Allan, Imran Adil, M.W.Olivier.

Jupp and Lillwhite both played for sides defeated by an innings.

Bowlers conceding 100 runs during an all-ten
P.T.Mills 0-116 (C.W.L.Parker 10-79, Gloucestershire v Somerset 1921)
R.Smith 0-107 (T.E.Bailey 10-90, Essex v Lancashire 1949)
G.A.R.Lock 0-100 (J.C.Laker 10-88, Surrey v Australians 1956)

Six other bowlers used in the innings
J.Lillywhite, G.O.B.Allen, T.E.Bailey, Shahid Mahmood, Imran Adil, Zulfiqar Babar, M.W.Olivier

Bowlers who took an all-ten who also bowled in an innings in which another bowler took an all-ten
G.A.R.Lock (bowled when J.C.Laker [twice] and I.J.Brayshaw took all-tens), W.G.Grace (J.Lillywhite and A.Shaw), J.Lillywhite (E.D.Barratt), S.M.J.Woods (E.J.Tyler), A.Fielder (C.Blythe), E.G.Dennett (C.W.L.Parker), A.P.Freeman (G.C.Collins), T.W.Wall (C.V.Grimmett), C.V.Grimmett (T.W.Wall), T.W.J.Goddard (J.K.R.Graveney), T.E.Bailey (J.C.Laker)

All-ten against eventual national domestic competition winners
G.Burton, Middlesex v Surrey 1888[2]
E.J.Tyler, Somerset v Surrey 1895
W.P.Howell, Australians v Surrey 1899
H.Howell, Warwickshire v Yorkshire 1923
T.W.Wall, South Australia v New South Wales 1932/33
M.W.Olivier, Warriors v Eagles, 2007/08

There have been no instances in other countries

Players who both took an all-ten, and batted in a side against which an all-ten was taken
T.Richardson (batted in innings when E.J.Tyler and W.P.Howell took all-tens), J.C.White (T.Rushby and C.W.L.Parker), J.Wisden (E.Hinkly), J.Briggs (S.M.J.Woods), H.Pickett (T.Richardson), S.M.J.Woods (A.E.Trott), E.J.Tyler (Trott), C.W.L.Parker (A.A.Mailey), A.P.Freeman (V.W.C.Jupp), G.Geary (T.B.Mitchell), T.B.Mitchell (T.F.Smailes), W.E.Hollies (E.A.Watts), J.D.Bannister (N.I.Thomson)

2   The Championship was not formally organised until 1890. Before then Champions were 'proclaimed by the press'.

Batsmen who batted in most all-tens
4:   E. Robson (all-tens taken by A.E.Trott, A.Drake, T.Rushby, C.W.L.Parker)
3:   P.T.Eckersley, C.Hallows, J.L.Hopwood, J.Iddon, E.A.McDonald,
G.E.Tyldesley, R.K.Tyldesley, F.B.Watson (in each case while all-tens
were taken by G.O.B.Allen, and by A.P.Freeman [1929 and 1931]); R.Abel
(G.Burton, E.J.Tyler, W.P.Howell); J.Daniell (A.E.Trott, T.Rushby, C.W.L.Parker);
R.E.S.Wyatt (A.S.Kennedy, H.Verity [1931], E.A.Watts); R.Howorth (J.Mercer,
T.W.J.Goddard, J.M.Sims); R.T.D.Perks (J.Mercer, T.W.J.Goddard, R.Berry)

P.T.Eckersley (against Allen), R.K.Tyldesley (against Freeman
[1929]) and R.Howorth (against Sims) were not out

Batsmen scoring a century in an innings when a bowler took all-ten
149   L.E.G.Ames, Kent v Northamptonshire 1932 (V.W.C.Jupp)
130* Ashar Zaidi, Islamabad v Multan 2009/10 (Zulfiqar Babar)
126   F.B.Watson, Lancashire v Kent 1929 (A.P.Freeman)
112   H.H.Dippenaar, Eagles v Warriors 2007/08 (M.W.Olivier)
102   G.E.Tyldesley, Lancashire v Middlesex 1929 (G.O.B.Allen)

Batsman carrying bat through innings when a bowler took all-ten
56*   M.J.Brown, Hampshire v Durham 2007 (O.D.Gibson)
55*   A.Hearne, Kent v Sussex 1899 (C.H.G.Bland)
50*   G.A.Morrow, Gentlemen of Ireland v Gentlemen of Philadelphia 1909 (J.B.King)

Highest totals in which a bowler took all-ten
419   West Indies XI v International XI 1982/83 (E.E.Hemmings)
418   Multan v Islamabad 2009/10 (Zulfiqar Babar)
360   Northamptonshire v Kent 1932 (V.W.C.Jupp)

Lowest totals in which a bowler took all-ten
51   Griqualand West v Eastern Province 1906/07 (A.E.E.Vogler)
54   Assam v Bengal 1956/57 (P.M.Chatterjee)
60   Northamptonshire v Kent 1907 (C.Blythe)

Century opening partnership when all-ten taken
102 (out of 300 all out) D.Elgar and L.E.Bosman, Eagles v Warriors 2007/08 (M.W.Olivier)
101 (out of 207 all out) Saeed Anwar and Shahid Afridi, Pakistan v India 1998/99 (A.Kumble)

Highest last-wicket partnerships when all-ten taken
49 (out of 113) A.J.Lamb and A.A.Donald, Orange Free State v Western Province,
    1987/88 (S.T.Jefferies)
42 (out of 259) K.R.Miller and J.W.Wilson, Australians v Surrey, 1956 (J.C.Laker)
36 (out of 212) J.J.Bridges and R.C.Robertson-Glasgow, Somerset v Gloucestershire,
    1921 (C.W.L.Parker)
36 (out of 347) R.K.Tyldesley and E.A.McDonald, Lancashire v Kent, 1929 (A.P.Freeman)

Last wicket partnership accounting for half of innings total
34 (out of 60) G.A.T.Vials and L.T.Driffield, Northamptonshire v Kent 1907 (C.Blythe)

Umpires standing in most matches when all-ten was taken
A.Millward (3): Woods (1890), Drake (1914), Mailey (1921)
J.Moss (3): Trott (1900), Fielder (1906), White (1921)
J.Stone (3): Kennedy (1927), Allen (1929), Freeman (1929)
E.Cooke (3): Mercer (1936), Graveney (1949), Berry (1953)
K.McCanlis (3): Bailey (1949), Laker (1956, Surrey v Australians), Smales (1956)

Bowlers who took all-ten who later stood as an umpire while a bowler took all-ten
W.Bestwick: Freeman (1930), Verity (1931)
G.Wootton: Butler (1871)
J.Lillywhite: Richardson (1894)
C.W.L.Parker: Watts (1939)

Acknowledgements and selected bibliography

I would first like to thank Keith Walmsley for his meticulous editing of this book. Also Robby Wilton for reading the text at an early stage and making a number of very useful suggestions, and Kit Bartlett and Jenny Moulton for their thorough proof-reading of the final text (although of course any remaining errors or typos are my responsibility).

I am grateful to Tony Pearson and Richard Johnson for sharing with me their memories of taking an all-ten, and Frank McHugh for his memories of being on the receiving end of one.

Brian Heald very helpfully explained to me how the match in which Eddie Hemmings took his all-ten came to be classified as first-class.

For photographs I am indebted in particular to Roger Mann, Andrew Hignell (for providing a number of photographs from the Des Lee archive now maintained by the ACS), Richard Johnson for the photograph of his trophy on the front cover, New Zealand cricket historian Don Neely for permission to use the photograph of Albert Moss, and Middlesex CCC for permission to use a copy of the photograph of Richard Johnson.

For match scores and players' career details I have primarily used CricketArchive as my source.

Newspapers
Birmingham Post, Manchester Evening News, The Guardian, Hampshire Advertiser, Nottingham Evening Post, Rand Daily Mail, Sheffield Daily Telegraph, The Times, The Daily Telegraph, The Sunday Telegraph.

Regular publications
Cricket: A weekly record of the game, The Cricketer, The Cricket Statistician, Indian Cricket, Journal of the Cricket Society, Middlesex County Cricket Club Annual Review, South African Cricket Annual, West Indies Cricket Annual, Wisden Cricket Monthly, Wisden Cricketers' Almanack.

Websites
britishnewspaperarchive.co.uk, history.trentbridge.co.uk, bbc.co.uk birminghammail.co.uk, cricketarchive.com, cricketweb.net espncricinfo.com, haverford.edu/library, telegraph.co.uk telegraphindia.com, theguardian.com, thetimes.co.uk timesofindia.indiatimes.com

Books

Abid Ali Kazi, *First-class Cricket in Pakistan 1963-64 to 1969-70,* Pakistan Association of Cricket Statisticians and Scorers, 2001

Altham, H.S.; Arlott, John; Eagar, E.D.R. and Webber, Roy, *Hampshire County Cricket: The Official History*, Phoenix Sports Books, 1957.

Baloch, K.H., *Encyclopedia of Pakistan Cricket 1947-48 to 2004*, Dr K.H.Baloch, 2004

Bearshaw, Brian, *From the Stretford End: The Official History of Lancashire County Cricket Club*, Partridge Press, 1990

Bettesworth, Walter Ambrose, *The Walkers of Southgate*, Methuen, 1900.

Booth, Keith, and Booth, Jennifer, *Rebel with a Cause: The Life and Times of Jack Crawford*, Chequered Flag Publishing, 2016

Booth, Keith, *Tom Richardson: A Bowler Pure and Simple*, Association of Cricket Statisticians and Historians, 2012

Bose, Mihir, *A History of Indian Cricket*, Andre Deutsch, 2002.

Brodkin, Stuart, *Johnny Briggs: Poor Johnny*, Association of Cricket Statisticians and Historians, 2007

Brodribb, Gerald, *The Lost Art: A History of Under-arm Bowling*, Boundary Books,1997

Brooke, Robert, and Goodyear, David, *A Who's Who of Warwickshire County Cricket Club*, Robert Hale, 1989

Burns, Michael, *A Flick of the Fingers: The Chequered Life and Career of Jack Crawford*, Pitch Publishing, 2015

Chalke, Stephen, *Runs in the Memory. County Cricket in the 1950s*, Fairfield Books, 1997.

Chesterton, George, and Doggart, Hubert, *Oxford and Cambridge Cricket*, Willow Books Collins,1989

Coldham, J,D., *Northamptonshire Cricket: A History*, Heinemann, 1959.

Duckworth, Leslie, *The Story of Warwickshire Cricket*, Stanley Paul, 1974

Edwards, Alan, *Lionel Tennyson - Regency Buck: The Life and Times of a Cricketing Legend*, Robson Books, 2001

Foot, David, *A History of Somerset Cricket: Sunshine, Sixes and Cider*, David & Charles, 1986

Frith, David, *Silence of the Heart: Cricket Suicides*, Mainstream Publishing, 2001.

Frith, David, *The Fast Men: A 200-year cavalcade of speed bowlers*, Van Nostrand Reinhold, 1975

Frith, David, *The Slow Men*, Richard Smart Publishing, 1984.

Gover, Alf, *The Long Run*, Pelham Books, 1991.

Green, Benny, *The Lord's Companion*, Pavilion Books, 1987.

Green, David, *The History of Gloucestershire CCC*, Christopher Helm, 1990

Harragan, Bob, *Cricket Grounds of Essex*, Association of Cricket Statisticians and Historians, 2007

Hemmings, Eddie, *Coming of Age: A Cricketing Autobiography*, Stanley Paul, 1991

Hignell, Andrew, *Jack Mercer: A Bowler of Magical Spells*, Association of Cricket Statisticians and Historians, 2011

Hignell, Andrew, *The History of Glamorgan County Cricket Club*, Christopher Helm, 1988

Hill, Alan, *Jim Laker: A Biography*, Andre Deutsch, 1998.

Hill, Alan, *Hedley Verity: A Portrait of a Cricketer*, Kingswood Press, 1986.

Hollies, Eric, *I'll Spin You a Tale,* Museum Press, 1955

Jiggens, Clifford, *Sammy: The Sporting Life of SMJ Woods*, Sansom & Co, 1997

Jollands, Tim (Ed), *Test Match Grounds of the World*, Willow Books, 1990

Lemmon, David, *Essex County Cricket Club: The Official History*, The Kingswood Press, 1987.

Lemmon, David, *The History of Middlesex CCC*, Christopher Helm, 1988

Lemmon, David, *Tich Freeman and the Decline of the Leg-Break Bowler*, George Allen and Unwin, 1982

Lester, John Ashby, *A Century of Philadelphia Cricket*, University of Pennsylvania, 1951

Lock, Joan, *The Princess Alice Disaster*, Robert Hale, 2013

Luckin, M.W., *The History of South African Cricket*, W.E.Horton, 1915

Miller, Douglas, *Cricket Grounds of Gloucestershire*, Association of Cricket Statisticians and Historians, 2000

Mosey, Don, *Jim Laker: Portrait of a Legend*, Queen Anne Press, 1989

Pope, Mick, *Tragic White Roses*, Privately published, 1995

Powell, William, *Cricket Grounds of Middlesex*, Association of Cricket Statisticians, 1990

Rigby, Vic, *Laker's Match:19 Wickets and the Ashes*, J.W.McKenzie, 2006

Roebuck, Peter, *From Sammy to Jimmy: The Official History of Somerset County Cricket Club,* Partridge Press, 1991.

Rogers, Norman, *Eric Hollies "The Peter Pan of Cricket"*, Warwickshire Cricket Publishing, 2002

Shawcroft, John, *The History of Derbyshire County Cricket Club*, Christopher Helm, 1989

Sissons, Ric, *The Players: A Social History of the Professional Cricketer*, The Kingswood Press, 1988

Snow, E.E., *A History of Leicestershire Cricket*, Edgar Backus, 1949.

Stockwell, John, *1865 A Statistical Survey*, Association of Cricket Statisticians, 1985

Swanton, E.W., *Gubby Allen : Man of Cricket*, Hutchinson/Stanley Paul, 1985.

Thomas, Peter, *Yorkshire Cricketers, 1839-1939*, D.Hodgson, 1973.

Waters, Chris, *10 for 10: Hedley Verity and the Story of Cricket's Greatest Bowling Feat*, Bloomsbury, 2014

Webber, J.R., *The Chronicle of WG*, Association of Cricket Statisticians and Historians, 1998

Webster, Ray, *First Class Cricket in Australia Vol 1, 1850-51 to 1941-42,* The Compiler, 1991

Webster, Ray, *First Class Cricket in Australia Vol 2, 1945-46 to 1976-77*, The Compiler, 1997

Wilde, Simon, *Number One: The World's Best Batsmen and Bowlers*, Victor Gollancz, 1998.

Winch, Jonty, *Cricket in Southern Africa: Two Hundred Years of Achievements and Records*, Windsor Publishers, 1997

Winder, Robert, *The Little Wonder: The Remarkable History of Wisden*, Bloomsbury Publishing, 2013

Woodhouse, Anthony, *The History of Yorkshire County Cricket Club*, Christopher Helm, 1989

Wynne-Thomas, Peter, *The Complete History of Cricket Tours at Home and Abroad*, Guild Publishing, 1989

Wynne-Thomas, Peter, *The History of Nottinghamshire CCC*, Christopher Helm, 1992

Yardley, N.W.D., and Kilburn J.M., *Homes of Sport: Cricket*, Peter Garnett, 1952

Index of names

Page numbers in **bold** indicate the chapters dealing with bowlers who took an all-ten.
Asterisked names are players shown in the photographic insert.